THE RUMBLE IN THE JUNGLE

THE RUMBLE IN THE JUNGLE

Muhammad Ali and George Foreman on the Global Stage

LEWIS A. ERENBERG

The University of Chicago Press
Chicago and London

The University of Chicago Press, Chicago 60637
The University of Chicago Press, Ltd., London

Published 2019
Printed in the United States of America

28 27 26 25 24 23 22 21 20 19   1 2 3 4 5

ISBN-13: 978-0-226-05943-3 (cloth)
ISBN-13: 978-0-226-05957-0 (e-book)
DOI: https://doi.org/10.7208/chicago/9780226059570.001.0001

Library of Congress Cataloging-in-Publication Data
Names: Erenberg, Lewis A., 1944– author.
Title: The rumble in the jungle : Muhammad Ali and George Foreman on the global stage / Lewis A. Erenberg.
Description: Chicago ; London : The University of Chicago Press, 2019. | Includes bibliographical references and index.
Identifiers: LCCN 2018043830 | ISBN 9780226059433 (cloth : alk. paper) | ISBN 9780226059570 (ebook)
Subjects: LCSH: Ali, Muhammad, 1942–2016. | Foreman, George, 1949– | Boxing—Social aspects. | Boxing—Social aspects—United States. | African American boxers. | Boxing matches—Congo (Democratic Republic)—Kinshasa. | Boxing—United States—History—20th century.
Classification: LCC GV1136.8 .E75 2019 | DDC 796.83092/2 [B]—dc23
LC record available at https://lccn.loc.gov/2018043830

♾ This paper meets the requirements of ANSI/NISO Z39.48-1992 (Permanence of Paper).

This book is dedicated to the ones I love:

Marcelo López Erenberg
and Oriana López Erenberg

CONTENTS

ACKNOWLEDGMENTS

This project has developed over a number of years. Along the way I have benefited from the help and support of many different friends, colleagues, and scholars, in addition to several important institutions. When I was first beginning the research for this book, Loyola University Chicago awarded me a research leave, which provided me with time away from teaching and committee work. In addition, the Interlibrary Loan librarians at Loyola University, including Jane Currie, Avril deBat, and Victoria Lewis, made my task so much easier by quickly filling my orders for newspapers, periodicals, and books critical to this study. Equally important, the Joyce Sports Research Collection: Boxing, housed in the Rare Books and Special Collections of the Hesburgh Libraries of Notre Dame University had a full run of *The Ring*, the bible of boxing, which allowed me to follow Muhammad Ali and George Foreman, as well as their boxing contemporaries, across their careers. The Joyce Collection also holds a wide array of boxing publications from the United States and elsewhere that are devoted specifically to the Rumble in the Jungle. I owe a special thanks to George Rugg, curator of special collections and his staff for going out of their way to welcome me, making sure that I saw sources critical for my study, and copying materials from the Joyce Collection when it became clear that I would not be able to take notes on all their documents in the time I had allocated for research at Notre Dame. I would also like to thank Erika Doss, then chair of American studies at Notre Dame, and her husband, Geoffrey, for putting me up in their home while I conducted my research in South Bend. Early on, my former graduate student, Lindsay Hugé, provided some of the spark for this project when he gave me a VHS of *When We Were Kings*.

Because of health problems that made travel and research away from home difficult, I relied on research assistants for gathering materials at the National Archives in College Park, Maryland, and the Library of Congress in Washington, DC. I want to thank Elliot Gorn for putting me in touch with Mason Farr at George Mason University, who then found Lee A. Ghajar, for research at the National Archives, and Chris Elzey, who collected and digitized materials about the fight in the international, especially the African, press. I would also like to thank the staffs of the Library of Congress and Amy Reytar of the National Archives for their cooperation. The staff at the National Archives helped me find digitized communications between the American embassy in Zaire and the State Department. Once I had stories from the international press, I realized that my long-ago ability in French was not adequate to the task. To the rescue David Pankratz, a friend and director of the Language Learning Center at Loyola, put me in touch with Danielle Gould, who began the translation of the Francophone press. Along the way an old friend, Howard Sanchuck, chipped in, as did another friend, Malcolm Bush, for the Angolan press. Thomas Greene helped out as well. My greatest debt for the translations, however, I owe to Bernard Graham-Betend of Belles Lettres Global Communications, who undertook the bulk of the translations in a timely and affordable fashion. I would also like to give special mention to Tricia Gesner at AP Photos, who along with her researchers, Susan Boyle and Stephen Ciaschi, helped me find images suitable for this book at a reasonable price. Early on Kevin Gaines, of the University of Michigan, suggested useful sources, as did Patricia Ogedengbe, the librarian of Africana at the Melville J. Herskovits Library of African Studies at Northwestern University.

A number of other people deserve special mention. Steve Riess of Northeastern Illinois University and Gerald Gems of North Central College invited me to present an early version of the project at the Newberry Library Sports History Seminar in Chicago, where I received valuable comments. Steve and Gerald deserve thanks as well for serving on a panel with me at the North American Society for Sports History in Orlando, Florida, where the audience response was both helpful and very positive. Thanks also go to the *Journal of Sport History* 39, no. 1 (2012), for publishing an early version of this project, "'Rumble in the Jungle: Muhammad Ali vs. George Foreman in the Age of Global Spectacle," as well as Gerald Early, who invited me to publish a different piece, "Echoes from the Jungle: Muhammad Ali in the Early 70s," in the *Cambridge University Companion to Boxing* (forthcoming from Cambridge University Press).

Many friends and colleagues helped in a variety of ways. My dear friend Lary May read several drafts of an article that served as the genesis of this project. His insightful suggestions, especially regarding organization, helped strengthen this book. Another old friend, Clarke Halker, offered suggestions on selective parts of the manuscript. I would also like to acknowledge the anonymous readers of the manuscript for the University of Chicago Press, whose suggestions helped improve this book. Even more than in the past, Susan Hirsch has contributed mightily to the completion of this work. She went over several drafts of the manuscript with a fine-toothed comb, eliminating repetition, suggesting reorganizations, and pointing out problematic interpretations. In addition, she has continued to provide the love and support that has sustained me during the writing of this book and throughout the forty years of our married life. I could not have done it without her.

Early on my research assistants Dan Platt, Ebony Dejesus, and Basil Saleem dug up loads of material for me. A special thanks to them and an even bigger one to my son, Jesse Hirsch Erenberg, who took it upon himself to garner important sources in the various clipping files at the Schomburg Center for Research in Black Culture in New York City, as well as materials from their extensive collections of the African American press, most notably *Jet* magazine and *Muhammad Speaks*. It was a pleasure to work together. Thanks as well to the staff at the Schomburg for smoothing his way and making the job enjoyable. I would also like to thank the FBI for handling my Freedom of Information Act request with dispatch. Michael May of National Public Radio helped by sending along a transcript of interviews he conducted with George Foreman. Doug Mitchell at the University of Chicago Press deserves special thanks for early on recognizing the worth of this project and believing that I could overcome great odds to complete it. Kyle Wagner, his assistant at the press, as well as copy editor Katherine Faydash and the capable staff of proofreaders and designers kept this book moving smoothly from start to finish. I also want to thank those who agreed to be interviewed for this project: Bill Caplan, Jerry Izenberg, and Stewart Levine. Although I was unable to secure an interview with George Foreman, I want to thank him for answering my questions via email. I also benefited from discussions with Jonathan Eig and Michael Ezra as the manuscript neared completion. Needless to say, I am responsible for any errors.

Throughout the entire process of writing this book, I was sustained by the love and encouragement of my friends and family. At a time when my health seemed bleak and my spirits were low, Malcolm Bush, Mike Cabonce and Dave Yocum, Bucky and Toni Halker, Anne and Elliott Lefkovitz, Lary and Elaine May, Bernie and Joy Noven, Mary O'Connell, Harold Platt, Tom and Barbara Rosenwein, Carol Woodworth, John Faustmann, and Isaac and Adi Ohel provided encouragement and support. So, too, my brothers, Ira and Stan Erenberg. Above all, I want to thank Susan Hirsch and our son and daughter, Jesse and Joanna, as well as our son-in-law, Oscar López Flores, for their love and support. My two young grandchildren, Marcelo López Erenberg and Oriana López Erenberg, turned my attention toward the promise of the future. It is with love and gratitude that I dedicate this book to them.

Lewis A. Erenberg
Chicago/Oaxaca

INTRODUCTION

Zaire is going to be remembered for a long, long time for this fight.

JERRY IZENBERG, *SPORT*, SEPTEMBER 1974

Two great warriors will return to the heart of the Motherland. It is goin' home time. It is destiny.

DON KING

On October 30, 1974, heavyweight champion of the world George Foreman and former champion Muhammad Ali squared off against each other in the ring in Kinshasa, Zaire, at the improbable hour of 4 a.m. With great anticipation and excitement that had been building for months, an estimated sixty thousand Zaïroises looked on while millions more boxing fans in over 120 nations tuned in via home and theater television as well as radio. For Ali this was a desperate bid to reclaim the title from the current champion, the younger, more powerful, and seemingly invincible Foreman. Ten years earlier, a much younger Cassius Clay had won the title from another seemingly invincible champion, Sonny Liston, in Miami Beach, Florida, only to have his championship stripped from him in 1967 after he had joined the Nation of Islam, changed his name to Muhammad Ali, and refused to serve in the United States Armed Forces during the Vietnam War. Having endured exile from boxing for three and a half years while he appealed his conviction for draft evasion, he faced an uphill battle in perhaps his last shot to reclaim his title. The stakes were high for Foreman as well. He would need to defeat the best-known boxer of his generation in order to be considered the true champion.

Despite the long odds against him, however, Ali shook up the world, just as he had against Liston ten years earlier. Utilizing a strategy that came to be known as the "rope-a-dope," Ali surprised everyone by abandoning the fleet-footed, dancing style of speed and movement that had defined his career and electrified fight fans everywhere. Instead of floating like a butterfly and stinging like a bee, he lay on the ropes in a defensive posture and let Foreman pound away at him until Foreman punched himself out. In the eighth round Ali came off the ropes to knock out the champion with a series of lightning punches. It was a stunning upset, and one that solidified Ali's reputation as "the greatest" of all time, only the second heavyweight champion in history to reclaim his title.

Then and now the "Rumble in the Jungle," as it was indelicately dubbed by Ali much to the chagrin of Zaire's government, took on oversized importance as a global event that transcended boxing and sport itself. Not only was the fight broadcast around the globe via satellite to millions of boxing fans, including those in Africa and the Middle East who had previously shown little interest in American sports; the bout also earned extensive coverage in newspapers and magazines for months, especially across the African continent. As a sign of its importance, the match also drew the attention of major novelists, journalists, and filmmakers. Assigned by *Esquire* magazine to cover the bout, famed novelist Norman Mailer detailed the moment in his book *The Fight* in 1975. At Mailer's side, another proponent of the new journalism, George Plimpton, dispatched a series of articles in *Sports Illustrated*, followed by his longer assessment in *Shadow Box*, published in 1977. Novelist and boxing fan Budd Schulberg was there for *Newsday*; not to be outdone, *Rolling Stone* assigned journalist Hunter Thompson to deliver his countercultural take on the spectacle. We shall never know what he thought. As a result of his famed overindulgence in drugs and alcohol, he managed to miss the bout in its entirety. Later, the 1997 Oscar-winning documentary *When We Were Kings* reminded another generation of the importance of the Ali-Foreman confrontation.[1]

As historian Michael Ezra argues, much of the mythology of the bout as a major global sporting spectacle was rooted in Ali's personal redemption against his enemies after years of exile and vilification. Yet according to Ezra, this mythology places too much emphasis on Ali as "the transcendent conquering hero." While the personal fates of Ali—and, I would add, Foreman—were definitely at stake, one thing is certain: the fight attracted worldwide attention in part because it was one of the strangest events in boxing history. Not only was the $10 million dollar purse (almost $50 million dollars by 2017 standards) by far the most lucrative prize for a single title fight to that date, but to top it off, the match was also the first heavyweight title bout anywhere in Africa. Accompanied by a three-day music festival, Zaire 74, the Rumble in the Jungle proved to be the most spectacular global event in boxing history.[2]

While the match carried deep personal meanings for both combatants, the bout's symbolic importance transcended the mundane world of sport. More than a prizefight, the Rumble in the Jungle represented a turning point in

American culture, as the contentious forces at home and abroad came to a head in a global sporting event. With the US role in the Vietnam War just recently concluded and the civil rights movement in disarray, it was not just Ali who sought vindication in the eyes of the world. Rather, it was also the political forces at war with each other during the 1960s and 1970s and the contending models of the black athlete and black manhood. In this regard, Foreman and Ali stood in opposite corners. Foreman symbolized the liberal establishment and Cold War civil rights along with what Robert O. Self has called breadwinner liberalism, the set of government programs established under President Lyndon Johnson's Great Society to provide job skills, instill self-discipline for young men—large numbers of whom were black—and help them escape from poverty. Saved by the Great Society's Job Corps program from a life of grinding ghetto poverty and crime, Foreman remained grateful to an America that had helped him pursue the American dream of wealth, fame, and success. While other black athletes raised their fists in protest at the Mexico City Olympic Games in 1968, Foreman will always be remembered for waving a small American flag after he won a gold medal for the United States in the heavyweight boxing division. Ali, in contrast, continued to represent the rebellious spirit of the 1960s, which included athletes in revolt against racism and against the idea of sports as a color-blind arena. While he too welcomed the creation of strong black men, as a member of the Nation of Islam, Ali did not favor putting their fate in the hands of a white-dominated government.[3]

As figures of physical strength and athletic success, both boxers became masculine heroes in an era when, as William Van Deburg's *Black Camelot* posits, there was a proliferation of African American cultural icons unleashed by the African American struggle for freedom. Each fighter embodied different concepts of masculinity in an era when achieving full manhood was a major goal of the civil rights movement. Foreman was the hardworking, quiet young man grateful to American society, a juvenile delinquent who came in from the cold to express his gratitude to America for his rise. At the same time, Foreman's appeal lay in his imposing brawn, while Ali appeared to embody brains and, in his mind, religious enlightenment, along with the rebellious martyrdom of many 1960s heroes. Ali was more the angry jokester who rejected the notions that his country came before race and that he had to be modest and grateful, the demeanor of just about every other black heavyweight champion, including Foreman, since Jack Johnson. Instead, like many 1960s icons, Ali was outspoken and expressed the deep-seated anger of many African Americans toward white society's continuing efforts to keep black people down. To be a black man, he and many of his black fans asserted, was to stand up and be counted despite the risks. He rejected patriotic masculinity and sought his identity with the non-Christian, nonwhites in American society and across the globe.[4]

Black nationalism, civil rights, patriotism, and anticolonialism all had their sporting champions during the 1960s and early 1970s—not only in boxing but also in all fields of athletic endeavor. Ali's defiance of the boxing establishment, the American government, and a huge swath of the American public was perhaps the most notable instance of the heightened politicization of American sport, but hardly the only one. The attempt to boycott the 1968 Olympics, for instance, drew on the international movement to ban Rhodesia and South Africa from the Olympics because of apartheid. At the same time, many whites were wondering why African Americans were so upset, since so many aspects of American sports had been racially integrated. Would "they" never be satisfied? Why weren't "they" grateful for all America had done for them, as Foreman and other black champions before him were?[5]

The fusion of sport and politics in global media spectacles during the 1960s and 1970s resonated with millions of people worldwide, especially in the person of a Pan-African hero who embodied a form of black nationalism at home and anticolonialism abroad. The freedom movement and the Vietnam War transformed sport from an escapist playground to an arena in which divisive social, political, and racial issues battled for supremacy. In this environment, African American boxers like Ali and Foreman became cultural and political symbols as they stepped into the ring for their epic battle.

Satellite communications played an important role in the battle, transforming an event staged in an isolated locale far from the eyes of the world into a global confrontation that carried the hopes and fears of people across the planet. For most of the Cold War, American officials believed that as a counterweight to Soviet propaganda, their influence over world media allowed them to create a powerful narrative in which black athletes and entertainers served as patriotic examples of national progress in race relations. At the Olympics and in State Department–arranged tours to the "Third World," black athletes could be living examples of racial progress in the United States and powerful symbols of democracy in action. In a global media age, however, with the satellite no longer fully under government control, Ali's public defiance of American racism and its foreign policy could be broadcast everywhere.[6]

Satellite technology, however, was just one factor in the creation of a global spectacle. In fact, the success of the international closed-circuit theater phenomenon rested on Ali's international popularity. Whereas earlier championship bouts staged abroad featuring Foreman garnered money or attention, fans around the world flocked to the theaters in record numbers to see Ali in action. At home and abroad, Ali's adherence to Islam, defiance of white supremacy, and opposition to the Vietnam War made him a global anticolonial symbol. With Ali as a global attraction, promoters were able to stage title bouts anywhere in the world and reach fans worldwide.[7]

As happened every time he fought, Ali shaped the bout's drama, this time with international significance apropos the African locale. "This is going to be a holy war," he declared. "I'm the freedom fighter and Foreman will be fighting for the establishment." In fact, Ali claimed to represent "all the African people who are fighting for their freedom and independence." As a result, across Black Africa, the Rumble in the Jungle reincarnated the struggles of newly independent nations and those fighting for independence, with Foreman unhappily cast in the role of imperial oppressor. As a consequence, excitement was high in Africa, and local newspapers and magazines covered the event in great detail. Equally important, in the United States as in Africa and the Middle East, the fact that the match was taking place in a black African country, ruled by a black president, fought by two black fighters, supervised by a black referee, and promoted by a black promoter proved a source of great pride and a symbol of worldwide black power to those of African descent. Staging the championship fight in Africa, along with the three-day music festival featuring black musicians from Africa, the United States, and the Caribbean as part of the spectacle, enabled black Americans and people of color around the globe to vicariously experience the coming together of the black diaspora at a time when so many Africans and African Americans were searching for their roots and their power as part of a global majority.[8]

That boxing carried such strong political and cultural themes should not be surprising. Traditionally, in fact, in the early years of the twentieth century heavyweight prizefighting served as a testing ground for male aggression and masculinity played out in racial and ethnic terms. As Theresa Runstedtler demonstrates, the first black heavyweight champion, Jack Johnson, was one of a cohort of black boxers, musicians, and laborers who traveled the globe in search of greater freedom, better rewards, and unprejudiced judging. As the first officially recognized black heavyweight champion, Johnson challenged the notion of white physical and mental superiority. In addition, as the "strongest man in the world," he availed himself of the rewards of victory by taking a series of white lovers and wives, established and patronized racially mixed cabarets, and defied the political and cultural authorities that eventually forced him into exile. Johnson's physical prowess and his overt challenge to white fears of racial miscegenation excited the animus of white Americans who were creating and deepening the system of second-class citizenship for black Americans, symbolized by their persecution of Johnson and their barring of other black heavyweights from contending for the title. This practice was defended as necessary to prevent race riots, protect white women, and defend a national system of white supremacy. For the next twenty-two years, the heavyweight champion of the world was guaranteed to be white. On the run from federal officials after being convicted for violating the Mann Act in 1913, Johnson traveled the world during the 1910s as an early example of a global symbol of racial defiance. For this very reason he set off an even greater desire among European powers to create and maintain a global color line that would keep their "colored" imperial subjects from presuming to be equal or superior to their powerful masters.[9]

Twenty-two years later, in 1937, Joe Louis became the second black heavyweight boxing champion. Unlike Johnson, Louis emerged as a national symbol of American racial and ethnic pluralism in his two battles of international import against the German boxer Max Schmeling. With the rise of fascism in Europe, Louis and Schmeling tested whether fascist theories of racial supremacy or American pluralism would triumph. During World War II both men served in the armed forces and both were held up as symbols of national prowess and identity. Ironically, the African American Louis became an American hero despite American society's maintenance of segregation and white supremacy at that time. Unlike Johnson, Louis was expected to be a model athlete and a superior human being—a credit to his race—who accepted his place in America's racial order in exchange for the promise of eventual equal status of African Americans in American life. As part of this promise, black boxers were expected to be tigers in the ring but pussycats outside the ropes.[10]

During the Cold War, the American government sponsored international sports programs in which black and white athletes were to be examples of American physical and cultural progress against the Soviet Union and other communist states. The Olympics became a battleground for competing nations in a war for the allegiance of newly emergent Third World nations whose citizenry was made up of people of color. In addition, the State Department sent American black and white athletes and musicians on international tours as examples of the strength of American democracy. To counter Soviet propaganda aimed at American policies of racial segregation and white supremacy, black athletes especially were expected to follow in Joe Louis's example as living proof of eventual racial progress and inclusion. Olympic boxing champions from Floyd Patterson in 1952 to Cassius Clay in 1960, Joe Frazier in 1964, and George Foreman in 1968 all advertised the strength of the American ideal through their physical accomplishments and their presence on the American Olympic team itself.

Long forgotten, Jack Johnson enjoyed a revival of interest in the late 1960s and early 1970s as Muhammad Ali broke from the ideal of Cold War or patriotic civil rights to challenge white supremacy, American foreign policy, and the American government. Much as Johnson was, he was punished for his efforts. Unlike Johnson, however, Ali received a second chance to fight in the United States, raising the question of what had changed during the 1960s and 1970s that allowed him to go on to even greater heights as a global boxing celebrity. His comeback after years of persecution revived the importance of boxing as an international sport and of black boxers as important cultural figures across the globe. Perhaps these changes occurred as a result of challenges to American white supremacy, the global color line, and Western imperialism on every front. At home and abroad, a new racial and anti-imperial politics made it possible for Ali and Foreman to reenact the new global politics in an era when the global color line was in the process of crumbling.

Although many of the fight's themes were rooted in the 1960s, the fact that the match occurred in 1974 requires that we pay attention to the 1970s as a turning point in American culture. Indeed, the Rumble in the Jungle took place just as the nation's politics, economic life, and cultural attitudes stood on the cusp of a profound transformation. As Thomas Borstelmann argues in *The 1970s: A New Global History from Civil Rights to Economic Inequality*, the 1970s were notable for two major trends: the spread of egalitarianism between nations and among peoples, and the growing dominance of market values, both of which the Zaire match exemplified. Both black fighters were given due respect and commanded great sums of money, while an African nation seeking parity with countries of the West went out of its way to enter the arena of fight promotion. At the same time, the amount of money the fighters earned threatened to dwarf social and racial concerns and establish the dominance of market values above all others. As Walter LaFeber points out in *Michael Jordan and the New Global Capitalism*, moreover, it was the emergence in the 1970s of satellites and computers that would enable athletic stars like Michael Jordan and shoe companies like Nike to spread American capitalism around the globe. That satellites played a huge role in the success of the Ali-Foreman fight in 1974: the transcending of national boundaries and regulations underscores the truth of LaFeber's observation, but the political overtones of the bout suggest that the competing values of two different eras in sport and capitalism were still held in balance. By the late 1980s and early 1990s, the balance had shifted away from an overt politics of dissent to one where an apolitical, thoroughly business-oriented Jordan dominated sports and advertising. As one commentator put it in a 1999 headline, "Mr. Jordan, You're No Muhammad Ali."[11]

While the Rumble in the Jungle was the climactic meeting of these two complicated heavyweight champions, what do their subsequent fates reveal about American society and culture during the later years of the twentieth century? While it is clear Ali was a 1960s symbol, he was also champion again during the late 1970s. But after one disappointing, sluggish win after another, he seemed to embody the flagging of rebellious 1960s energy as he went for the big money in international bouts of little consequence, or at least with more hype than substance. No longer a sterling political or religious hero, he seemed to be just "staying alive," a survivor, as William Graebner put it, of one near disaster after another, in parallel to the dominant theme of late 1970s popular culture. Ali did enjoy a revival in the 1990s, however, as a pitchman for consumer goods and a broad humanism stripped of any overt politics. By the turn of the century, any antiwhite criticism of American politics and race relations by athletes had been whitewashed.[12]

In this shifting atmosphere, Foreman enjoyed one of the greatest reversals of fortune in American sport. After suffering a particularly dispiriting loss on the comeback trail in 1977, three years after his humiliating defeat in Zaire, Foreman retired from boxing and became a born-again Christian. Ten years later, overaged and paunchy, the mature former champion defied the experts by returning to boxing. In 1994, he reclaimed the title he lost to Ali, and at age forty-five he became the oldest heavyweight champion in history and a symbol for the baby-boom generation that one's dreams did not have to stop at forty. He too became a benevolent wealthy pitchman for Jesus, barbeque grills, and the American way of life.

The paths of Muhammad Ali and George Foreman thus intersected from the late 1960s through the turn of the twenty-first century, and both men will forever be linked. Ever since the Rumble in the Jungle, Foreman told BBC Sport, in an interview marking the thirty-year anniversary of the fight, the two men were bound together inextricably. "We're so tied in together you can't say rope-a-dope, you can't say 'The Greatest,' you can't say Muhammad Ali without saying George Foreman," Foreman declared. "Thirty years ago and I still hear about it. If I had known it was going to be such a big event I would have enjoyed myself a lot more, even in defeat." The event was a big deal and the two champions were so tied together because each represented different "spirits of the 1960s," different fates during the 1970s, and the trajectory of sports and American culture in recent decades.[13]

1

A REAL FREAK IN BOXING: MUHAMMAD ALI AND THE SPIRIT OF THE 1960S

> [Ali] is all the sixties were. It is as though he were created to represent them. In him is the trouble and the wildness and the hysterical gladness and the nonsense and the rebellion and the conflicts of race and the yearning for bizarre religions and the cult of the put-on and the changed values that altered the world and the feeling about Vietnam in the generation that ridicules what their parents cherish.
>
> **JIMMY CANNON, 1970**

> [Clay] is an American who doesn't wish to be an American, a fighter who doesn't wish to be a fighter for American patriotism. Now, if this man Clay isn't a genuine freak, one of the freakiest of all time despite his ideal physical proportions and ring skills, then we haven't had a real freak in boxing.
>
> **DAN DANIEL, *THE RING*, AUGUST 1966**

On their way to their epic battle in Kinshasa, Zaire, on October 30, 1974, heavyweight champion George Foreman and former titleholder Muhammad Ali had come to represent different poles in the raging debate over the role of black athletes in American sports and in the larger fields of race relations, politics, and culture. That the two champions were black raised questions about a Cold War narrative that emphasized progress in American race relations so that any talented young person, regardless of race, creed, or color, could achieve the American dream of success. Olympic athletes were expected to fulfill their patriotic duty and vanquish their Soviet and Eastern Bloc foes in symbolic reenactments of the Cold War. Once they achieved professional success, boxers were expected to serve as proper role models for American boys and young men, and this included a willingness to serve in the armed forces. Yet by 1968 the situation had changed dramatically, especially for black men and women in sports. The impact of the civil rights movement, the growing ascendancy of black nationalism, and the virulent anti–Vietnam War movement worked to challenge the assumptions about the role of black athletes in American life. At the center of this social ferment, Muhammad Ali joined the antiwhite Nation of Islam and refused to serve in the armed forces of the United States. Much to the chagrin of the boxing and political establishment, he rejected his role as an American patriotic symbol and assumed the identity of black and Third World hero. Conversely, his future opponent George Foreman seemed his exact opposite: a living example of the American dream. A beneficiary of the Job Corps, a key program in Lyndon Johnson's War on Poverty, Foreman symbolized a form of liberalism and patriotic civil rights that appeared to be increasingly old-fashioned as the 1960s flowed into the 1970s. In Kinshasa, the question was not just which individual boxer would win but also which set of opposing political and cultural values would triumph.[1]

No one meeting these two athletes as youngsters would have predicted that they would play such divergent political roles in the overall scheme of things or that boxing would emerge as a focal point for a national and international debate about such weighty matters. Under his original name, Cassius Marcellus Clay Jr., Muhammad Ali was the product of a relatively stable, two-parent, working-class family. He was born in the segregated black community of Louisville, Kentucky, on January 18, 1942. In the 1950s Louisville prided itself as a border city known for its moderation in race relations. Blacks had the vote and hence a measure of political power to temper some of the harshness of segregation. While schools, parks, neighborhoods, the downtown business district, and places of amusement were largely segregated, because of a strong interracial labor movement and the right to vote, African Americans found more economic opportunities and a better standard of living there than in most Southern cities. Black political power garnered a black park to offset the white one and a separate black college to rival the University of Louisville. In response to *Brown v. Board of Education*, the city fathers engineered the desegregation of the schools. Neighborhood segregation, however, remained strong. Growing up black in Louisville as the civil rights movement spread across the South, young Cassius could expect some limited economic opportunity, paternalistic white leadership, and a segregated public life to remind him of his second-class status.[2]

According to several family friends, the Clays were a proud family, descended from slaveholders—Henry Clay on his father's side and an Irish man named Grady on his mother's—as well as enslaved women. The family's apparent stability belied its tumultuous nature, however. As one of Cassius's early white backers noted: "There was a lot of trouble, bad trouble, between his father and mother . . . but Cassius would bite his tongue before he'd mention it. He had too much pride." Much of the family's explosiveness lay with his father, Cassius Clay Sr., a frustrated artist-turned-sign-painter whose artwork decorated many churches and small businesses in Louisville's segregated black neighborhood. Having witnessed his own aspirations shrink under the weight of discrimination, he took out his frustrations in violent arguments with his wife, the fair-skinned and gracious Odessa, who worked as a domestic for various white families. Cassius Sr.'s drinking and womanizing were sore points in the family. When he drank to excess, he would pick fights with his drinking buddies, his wife, and his sons, Cassius and the younger Rudy. Several times Odessa was forced to bring her husband to court for roughing her up. In one instance, young Cassius tried to protect his mother only to receive a stab wound in his thigh for his efforts. At other times the police picked up Cassius Sr. for reckless driving, disorderly conduct, assault, or battery, always when he was drinking. As an old friend put it, "The father isn't a criminal or even an evil man. He's just a frustrated little guy who can't drink." As a result, Cassius and his brother, Rudy, grew up in an atmosphere of impending explosion. At the same time, the young Cassius grew up hearing his father pour out his vitriol at a white society that had limited his hopes and dreams as well as those of most black people he knew. Cassius's father was a proto-black nationalist, though without any formal affiliation.[3]

Cassius Jr. found sanctuary in boxing, just as George Foreman would over a decade later. At twelve years old his cherished bicycle was stolen. He reported the theft to the nearest policeman, Joe Martin, who ran a boxing program in a nearby church basement. When Cassius threatened to thrash the thief, Martin urged him to learn to box first. From then on Cassius lived, breathed—and talked—boxing. He got up at 5 a.m. for roadwork, went to school, and at night spent hours in the gym. As a boxer he had "something to do every day. Go to the gym, put on my gloves and box." Although he hung out on the streets, and even belonged to a street gang for a while, he preferred the gym. Boxing became one of the key anchors of his identity.[4]

Hearing a Rocky Marciano title fight on the radio fed Clay's dreams of becoming a champion. The other kids made fun of his aspirations and his incessant bragging, but boxing made him "feel like somebody different." As his reputation as an amateur grew, "pretty soon I was the popularest [*sic*] kid in high school," he said. High school and college held no interest because people in his neighborhood who did well in school ended up frustrated and lost on the streets. Poor grades prevented him from graduating, but at the principal's behest he was awarded a certificate of attendance. Clay could fight but he could hardly read, the latter probably a result of undiagnosed dyslexia. Still, his intense ambition fueled a self-discipline that kept him away from smoking, drinking, and drugs. With the help of black trainer Fred Stoner, who worked on the youngster's style, and Martin's entrée with various amateur bodies and local television stations, Clay soon began appearing on Louisville television as he advanced through the amateur ranks on his way to becoming a local hero.[5]

His distinguished amateur career ultimately led him to the 1960 Rome Olympics, where the six-foot-three boxer won a gold medal as a light heavyweight by beating a Russian and a Pole. The garrulous and handsome Clay also made friends all over the Olympic Village. "With his frilly, hands-down, show boat style he affected as an amateur," noted Houston Horn in *Sports Illustrated*, "and the elaborate dance patterns he used to flit away from danger, he cha-chaed through three rounds with the Polish boy and reduced him to bloody defenselessness." His medal, Horn declared, made him "an international celebrity," and he spent the rest of his time in Rome making himself "one of the best-known, best-liked athletes in the Olympic Village."[6]

After winning his cherished medal, eighteen-year-old Clay followed a conventional Cold War script for American athletes. American and Russian officials understood that international sporting spectacles were perfect settings for their two nations to demonstrate their respective strengths and compete for the allegiance of recently independent Third World countries. In this setting, black and white athletes were expected to be vigorous symbols of an American way of life open to all, regardless of race, creed, or color. The Soviets would attempt to exploit American racial segregation and discrimination, but US athletes were advised to make clear that progress was being made and that racism's worst aspects were a thing of the past. Clay played his part perfectly, refusing to criticize American society, especially abroad. This made him acceptable in Louisville and across the nation as sit-ins and Freedom Rides raised the question of African American intentions and made many whites anxious about the future of segregation. As Clay recalled about the Olympics, "This Commie comes up [and asks], 'Now how do you feel, Mr. Clay, that even though you won a gold medal you still can't go back to the United States and eat with the white folks because you're a colored boy?'" Clay responded: "Tell your readers we've got qualified people working on that problem, and I'm not worried about the outcome. To me, the USA is still the best country in the world counting yours. It may be hard to get something to eat sometimes, but anyhow I ain't fighting alligators and living in a mud hut." When the Soviet reporter asked if he really meant it, he replied, "Man, of course I mean it. Who do you think I am? . . . Poor old Commie, he went dragging off without nothing to write the Russians."[7]

Clay's stance earned him praise in the local black weekly, a sign that moderate Negroes (the accepted term for people of African descent during the 1950s and mid-1960s) were also anxious about changes in the city's racial structure. The *Louisville Defender* called him "an ambassador of goodwill . . . with his stark honest interpretation of U.S. race conditions." Amid nationwide racial unrest, Clay's patriotism earned him praise and produced a sigh of relief from local officials. It also earned him a public reception and television interview with Louisville mayor Bruce Hoblitzell, as well as a celebration at Central High School arranged by Louisville's leaders. School officials lauded his achievements and his patriotism, and his father was invited to sing "The Star-Spangled Banner." The mayor also called upon Clay to meet with visiting foreign reporters and dignitaries, to whom he repeated that in the United States he did not have "to live in African mud huts." As Ali reflected years later, he felt proud to represent "America on a world stage." "To me," he said, "the Gold was more than a symbol of what I had achieved for myself and my country; there was something I expected the medal to achieve for me." Along with his poor school record and his ties to a white policeman, the young Olympic champion seemed like "a good Negro," one that Louisville and the nation could endorse.[8]

Just as George Foreman would discover in 1968, Clay found that there was gold in the gold medal for a "good Negro," acceptable to the larger white community. As a sign of the community's endorsement, a group of local wealthy white businessmen formed the Louisville Sponsoring Group (LSG) to help guide Clay's professional career. Initially, the group helped him preserve a safe image amid the racial turmoil of the early civil rights movement. Allied with the Louisville elite, Clay's first pro fight against white boxer Tunney Hunsacker was billed as a "good deed" benefit for the city's Kosair Crippled Children's Hospital. Needless to say, Clay wore trunks adorned with the words *US Olympic Team*.[9]

For his professional career, Clay might have chosen mob-connected managers and trainers, as had Sonny Liston, who parlayed his role as an enforcer for the St. Louis mob into a boxing career. During the 1950s and early 1960s the sport was under the control of the International Boxing Club (IBC), a creation of wealthy sportsman James Norris and mob kingpins Frankie Carbo and Frank "Blinky" Palermo. When he became champion, Liston's mob ties stained his crown, the sport of boxing, and, at the height of the Cold War, the reputation of the United States as a lawful country. Along with the television quiz-show scandals, juvenile delinquency, and mob-run unions, boxing was seen as part of the corruption of the American way of life.[10]

Clay might have chosen a black management team, as had Joe Louis and Sugar Ray Robinson, but black managers still had to rely on white promoters, like Madison Square Garden's Mike Jacobs. If Clay had to be dependent on white businessmen, a local white management group appeared to him the best choice for a hometown hero. To the public, it seemed that responsible members of the Louisville white elite were in charge. Under this arrangement, Clay became the first corporate athlete in sports, backed by young Louisville millionaires who controlled significant Kentucky industries such as newspapers, distilleries, horse racing, and tobacco. While they hoped to profit by investing in Clay's professional career, they paid his training expenses and also established a $50,000 trust fund for his future, a $10,000 signing bonus, a guarantee of $4,000 for the first two years, and $6,000 as a draw against future earnings for the following four years. As a result, the LSG came off as paternalistic white knights helping a talented colored boy in need of counsel and control in a sport that was still mob dominated. They wisely chose Archie Moore to train Clay full-time, but when that did not work out, they picked Angelo Dundee as his trainer but kept Clay away from promoter Chris Dundee, Angelo's brother, because of Chris's reputed mob ties. All in all, the LSG, composed of the city's "best" white people, seemed a beneficent influence good for Clay and for the image of the white community of Louisville.[11]

As Clay ascended the heavyweight ladder, his good cheer, clean-cut good looks, and reputable sponsors helped invigorate a sport dominated by the reclusive champion Floyd Patterson and his sinister challenger Sonny Liston, and reeling from the recent deaths in the ring of Benny "Kid" Paret and Davey Moore. In contrast to the sullen Liston and the desperately shy Patterson, Clay was handsome, open to the press, mob-free—and highly garrulous. Even so, it became clear early on that he was cast in a different mold from other heavyweight boxers, and black fighters in particular. A key symbol of the 1960s cultural explosion, even before he became champion, Clay revolutionized the norms of boxing just as others were challenging conventional wisdom in politics, race relations, and sexuality.

One of the things Clay brought to boxing was a different masculine image of the fighter at a time when young white and black men were beginning to revolt against the expectation that they conform to the rules of the corporation, racial hierarchy, and rigid gender definitions. Instead of slugging it out in the center of the ring as Jack Dempsey, Joe Louis, Rocky Marciano, or Sonny Liston did as emblems of tough, raw male power, Clay used his speed, guile, and improvisational skill to outthink and outmaneuver his opponents. As famed artist and boxing fan LeRoy Neiman put it in 1967, Ali "changed the heavyweight concept." He could not punch like the pile drivers, but he was constantly moving and racking up points: "The fact is that the Big Punch no longer is the major desideratum in heavyweight boxing. The game is counting points, resting heavily on combinations, and placing great reliance on a stiff, steady, punishing jab." Clay's punch would not knock a man out, as did Louis's, but it could cut a man to ribbons and so befuddle him that he never saw the more powerful right cross or left hook. This is what Clay's assistant Drew "Bundini" Brown meant when he urged him to "float like a butterfly, sting like a bee!"[12]

Although six foot three, the young boxer moved like a welterweight, dancing around the ring, peppering his opponents from every angle. Very few big men possessed his agility. This together with his phenomenal speed also allowed him to challenge other ring conventions by holding his left low and leaning his head away from punches. Writer and boxing enthusiast Budd Schulberg argued that this mobility was physically unnecessary, but it added a new psychological weapon: "hit and run, jab and dance, to befuddle, frustrate, and tire the enemy before zeroing in." Clay's speed also made him exceedingly difficult to hit. In fact, his willingness to withdraw from danger raised doubts about his toughness, and hence his masculinity, among boxing cognoscenti. Could a boxer who bragged about how pretty he was and how little he got hit get very far in a fistic milieu of bent noses and cauliflower ears? Was he willing to stand and trade punches or would he run at the first sign of trouble? To make the point explicit, Sonny Liston, annoyed by his young challenger's constant bragging, called him "a faggot," a lightweight who would fade at the first blow. Charges such as these were rife not only in boxing but in America at large. Along with breadwinning and soldiering, heterosexuality remained a key component of masculinity.[13]

According to trainer Angelo Dundee, Clay also "changed the way things work" in other ways. "In promoting boxing, he made the fighter the main guy." In the age of television, his good looks and outrageous manner made him a media star. A good deal had to do with his openness to the press. As Clay put it, "I'm the best friend a reporter ever had because I always give good quotes, changing them around so everybody gets a fresh one." Even more, he started accurately predicting the round in which his opponent would lose—this began with his two round KO of Lamar Clark, after which he proclaimed, "From now on they all must fall in the round I call." *Jet* hailed him as a prophet after he called thirteen out of fourteen predictions correctly in his first seventeen bouts. "I challenged the old system," he recalled, "in which managers, promoters and owners looked upon fighters as brutes without brains." In the past, boxers were "seen but not hardly heard on any issue or idea of public importance." As a result, noted Dundee, Clay became "an attraction, a celebrity. It was something he worked hard at becoming just as hard as he worked at becoming a better boxer and a champion." Clay proved highly adept at public relations, ever alert to new ways of attracting the attention of the media. Outside the ring, he abandoned the expectation that heavyweight fighters in general and black athletes in particular be modest and silent, letting white managers and promoters do the talking, as had been the style of Louis, Marciano, Patterson, and Liston. In and out of the ring, Clay's public presence demonstrated that he was not just a physical brute but also an intelligent and articulate human being.[14]

Three days before a match with Duke Sabong in Las Vegas in 1961, Clay met the outrageous wrestler "Gorgeous George" Wagner, with his dyed blond hair, flashy robes, and a habit of insulting opponents while touting his own good looks and wrestling skills. To Clay's surprise, the wrestler drew fans by the thousands who hoped for his defeat. A light went on. The more Clay bragged about himself, the more he sassed his opponents, the more outrageous his self-presentation, he realized, the more fans would come out to see him lose. He began touting his looks and his skills and denigrating those of his opponent: "I'd never been shy about talking, but if I talked even more, there was no telling how much money people would pay to see me." Lots of fighters boast, but Clay also took to ridiculing his opponents in rhyme, seemingly making up doggerel on the spot, using the black verbal art of the dozens. Boasting "I am the greatest," he took charge of his own identity in and out of the ring.[15]

Indeed, convinced that he knew more about boxing than anyone else, he refused to listen to his trainers, sparring partners, or ring veterans. Clay's egoistic insistence that he knew best started as soon as the LSG had him train with former light heavyweight champion Archie Moore. Bored with sweeping up and listening to the advice of one of the ring's wise men, Clay bolted. "I got my own style," Clay reportedly said. "Nobody tells me nothing." Or, as he put it on another occasion, "The one who made me is me!" That is how he ended up with Angelo Dundee, the ring veteran trainer who managed to refine his style but through indirection and applied psychology. "You can't handle him the way you do the usual fighter," Angelo noted. "You don't regiment him. He had enough of that. You just have to use indirection." For example, Dundee noted, at first Clay's left jab was not a powerful weapon: "A daily nicking at his pride did it. He'll be the last guy in the world to admit that anybody did it but him, but that doesn't bother me. He didn't have a left uppercut. He's got one now. He was throwing a left jab, but it was a slap. It had no authority." But, Dundee added, "you have to show him things slowly."[16]

With his verbal pyrotechnics rooted in African American oral tradition, his bragging, poetry, his use of black dialect, his acting out of white attitudes and black responses, Clay was more than a fighter—he had turned boxing into theater, with himself as the star. "The ring and the gym, they're his stage," noted Dundee. "He's like a guy going to the Academy Award dinner, only he's receiving the Academy Award every day! This is the thrill he gets. He's happy when he's performing for people. He's not just like any ordinary fellow." He was not just an ordinary black fighter either. Unlike Liston or Patterson—and later Frazier and Foreman—Clay was a hybrid black boxer, one not seen before. He was a fighter-poet, fighter-preacher, fighter-comic, fighter–public presence. And he fought like he talked: nonstop action, nonstop lip. He had, in other words, the energy of black and white youth breaking out of the old racial and cultural restrictions and a taste for the theatricality and self-expression of cultural politics that would become more prominent as the decade wore on. While Dundee caught Clay's new spirit, others were more skeptical. As late as 1966, ring veterans seemed to agree that Clay was one of the best champions, but he did not yet rank among the top fifteen heavyweights.[17]

In Cassius Clay boxing was witnessing the early 1960s youth rebellion and the development of the generation gap. In fact, in 1962, Clay appeared in the movie *Requiem for a Heavyweight* as a young boxer whose speed and power humiliate an aging pugilist. But the youth rebellion also infused the actual sport of boxing. The most revered name in boxing was Joe Louis, the idol of black—and white—fans during the Great Depression and World War II. Many black parents named their boys after Joe, and just as many hoped that their children would follow in his athletic footsteps. Cassius Clay Sr. was no exception. As Clay's father explained, his son "came into this world with a good body and a big head that was the image of Joe Louis. . . . That made me real proud. I loved Joe Louis." While Cassius grew up on tales of Louis, as soon as he turned professional there were signs of discord. Upon winning his first professional bout, he announced, "There's a lot of things I want to be in the fight game but I sure don't want to be a Joe Louis, that is I don't want to have the income tax troubles . . . Louis had." He would try to be more responsible and save his money, a pledge made easier by the financial oversight of the LSG. As Clay piled up victories and started proclaiming he was the greatest, the proud Louis showed signs of being miffed. Later, when Clay joined the Nation of Islam and refused to serve in the army, the rift between the two champions deepened.[18]

The full impact of the generation gap lay ahead, but noticeable signs emerged when Clay fought Archie Moore, former light heavyweight champ and one of the sport's grand "old men." "The Mongoose" was indeed old, but no one was sure if he was thirty-eight or fifty. As for other talented black fighters, it took him years to get a title fight. At an advanced age he finally won the light heavyweight crown and then, in 1955, went after the heavyweight title against Rocky Marciano but lost in a spectacular slugfest. When Moore fought Clay in 1962, he was at the stage of his career that saw him no longer a serious contender. Rather, Moore was reduced to being an opponent, but still a dangerous one. Moore's wry sense of humor made him a favorite among sports reporters and fans. Only Clay rivaled Moore's sense of humor and bravado. Their previous history together made the bout even more significant. Moore had been Clay's initial trainer as a pro, but the young boxer rebelled against Moore's regimented training camp.[19]

Jet dubbed their November 15, 1962, match in Los Angeles "Youth and Ability versus Age and Experience." For his first big test, Clay unleashed the new elements he had introduced into heavyweight boxing. His bragging, poetry, and predictions made him the fight's actual promoter. His outrageous verbosity made him the villain; nationally people flocked to closed-circuit theaters to see him get beat by old school Moore, a standard-bearer of humor and sportsmanship who promised he had a "lip buttoner punch." Young Clay retorted with a poetic prediction: "Archie has been living off the fat of the land / I'm here to give him his pension plan. / When you come to the fight don't block aisle or door / 'Cause y'all going home after round four." Young and sleek, Clay easily danced around the paunchy, gray-haired Moore, who fought at a snail's pace. In the fourth round Clay made his boast come true. He jabbed Moore silly, setting him up for an uppercut. Moore crumbled. As *Jet* proclaimed, "cocky Clay" beat an "antiquated Moore." The boxing establishment was forced to admit that Clay's ring skills just might match his self-promotion. His rankings jumped from seventh to fourth, and he became the hottest box-office attraction in years. Only twenty-one years old, Clay kept demanding a title shot as he cultivated a bad-boy image, though an apolitical and humorous one. When he failed to finish Doug Jones at Madison Square Garden in March 1963 in the predicted round and was forced to grind out a ten-round decision, fans threw peanuts into the ring as a sign of derision; Clay picked one up and ate it. As much as people loved to hate Clay's bad-boy verbosity and overweening ego, he was still tongue-in-cheek, clean-cut, and trouble-free.[20]

As he campaigned for a title match with Liston, Clay's fresh-faced challenge to boxing's accepted rules invigorated a dying sport. Floyd Patterson seemed a nice-enough fellow, but except for Liston, his manager Constantine "Cus" D'Amato kept him away from tough opponents, especially any with mob ties. In his battles with Liston, Patterson was "the good Negro," humble and modest, versus the surly, amoral black man from the ghetto, a Bigger Thomas with boxing gloves. The National Association for the Advancement of Colored People (NAACP) did not want Patterson to fight Liston, fearing the consequences of a black champion with criminal ties, but once the fight was announced, the civil rights organization, like President Kennedy, rooted for Patterson and was horrified when he was humiliated in 1962 and again in 1963 by the former mob enforcer. From the moment he won his Olympic gold medal in 1960, Cassius Clay stepped into this gloomy picture to help establish a new era in boxing. "Whether you like Clay or not," noted *Ring*'s Dan Daniel, "the fact remains that he performed for boxing a tremendous benefice similar to that which Babe Ruth achieved for baseball" after the Black Sox scandal had shaken public confidence in the sport. Clay knew how to capture the spotlight. He was "fresh, new, and filled with the liveliness of a new age," argued Angelo Dundee. "Put them all together and all of a sudden it was the Age of Cassius."[21]

Unlike the more sober heavyweights, black and white, Clay turned his title quest into pure theater, in the process taking on the image of a crazy man who would say or do anything unlike brutish Liston or his modest black predecessors. After cutting "Ol' Henry" Cooper to ribbons as predicted in the fifth round in London, where he wore a crown and royal robe into the ring, he taunted his opponent in the land of good sportsmanship and so earned Great Britain's ire. Afterward Clay turned toward Liston in earnest. He went "bear hunting," with taunts and tricks, poems and predictions, of what he would do to another "old man." After his devastating performances against Patterson, reporters considered Liston invincible. Clay replied, "I'm not afraid of Liston. He's an old man." For his twenty-second birthday, Clay had a cake with two figures atop: Clay standing over Liston in victory. Clay also predicted: "Liston will meet his fate in eight." He topped this with a nastier rhyme, adding a racial edge that would become more prominent after the bout: "Liston did not do as he should / He tried to move in a white neighborhood / If he don't like black / I know February 25 will find him on his back." To get Liston to agree to a fight, the young challenger chartered a bus and followed the champion everywhere, including a 3 a.m. surprise visit to Liston's Denver home. Liston was not amused. Many fans thought Clay was crazy to incite such a vicious man.[22]

Clay's rule breaking resonated with the cultural ferment of the 1960s. His underdog battle against Liston in their February 25, 1964, title fight was viewed as a youth rebellion against a ponderous relic of an older generation. Pandemonium erupted at the weigh-in, typically a dull affair during which the two fighters strip to their trunks and step on the scales. Not this time. While officials and the media looked on, Clay unleashed full-scale craziness. Together with his assistant "Bundini," he started yelling as soon as they entered the room, challenging the ugly bear, taunting Liston unmercifully, shouting "float like a butterfly sting like a bee—Rumble, young man, rumble," followed by Clay and Bundini roaring in unison. Then Clay lunged at Liston, forcing his handlers to hold him back. The doctor found Clay's blood pressure off the charts. Onlookers believed that fear had driven him crazy. Back in his hotel his blood pressure was perfectly normal. According to Dundee, it was all "pure theater" designed to rile Liston and show that he was not intimidated by the champ's prison-yard stare. Because of his "Academy Award rantings," noted *Jet*, experts were sure that the "cocky" Clay was "scared to death," but when the bell sounded, he was completely "cool." His detractors were left reaching for "salt and pepper to eat their words."[23]

Clay's victory over Liston ushered in a new day for the sport and for American culture. Fans and experts assumed that the challenger had no chance against Liston's experience and his vicious left hook: Liston was an 8 to 1 favorite. From the start, however, the younger man proved his mettle. As the referee gave his instructions, Clay stared straight at Liston rather than avoiding the fearsome look that had defeated Patterson before their bouts had even started. It was apparent that the challenger was actually taller at six foot three than Liston, who was six foot one, and lighter at 210.5 versus the champion's 218. Sonny did enjoy a reach advantage, however, which measured 80.5 inches to Clay's 78. When the opening bell rang, Clay came out dancing, jabbing, moving, and grooving. For four rounds he outjabbed and outmaneuvered Liston, nullifying Liston's long reach and making him look tired and older as the fight progressed. The fifth round provided real drama. Some of the ointment used on Liston got into Clay's eyes; he shouted that he could not see and wanted his gloves cut off. At that point, the experienced Dundee pushed his man toward the center of the ring and ordered him to dance. Dance he did, moving constantly away from the desperately lunging Liston, who saw his chance at last. By the round's end, however, Clay's eyes cleared and he reasserted his mastery of the tired champ. In the sixth round, Liston appeared hopeless, taking jabs, crosses, and hooks like never before. When the bell rang for the seventh round, Liston remained on his stool, looking too old and exhausted to fight on against a younger, determined whirlwind. Many fans concluded that he just quit and wondered whether the fight was fixed from the start.[24]

Clay's sixth round TKO of the invincible Liston "shook up the world" and established him as a different kind of black heavyweight champion. His press conference the next day, February 26, 1964, sparked major national controversy and revulsion. According to precedent, the new champion met with the media to usher in an era of good feelings, good write-ups, and future profits. Still sensitive toward boxing experts who had given him no chance, he ranted at the press. "Eat your words," he yelled, adding: "Look at me, I'm still pretty! I'm the only one who went bear huntin' bare handed and shook up the bear. . . . Look at me, the most beautiful champion in heavyweight history. I said I was going to shake up the world, and I did it."[25]

Stung by Clay's rants, plagued by rumors of his religious conversion, and prompted by Malcolm X's attendance at the fight, white sportswriters demanded to know whether Clay was a Black Muslim. "They don't call themselves that," he responded. "I believe in the oldest religion in the world [*sic*]—Islam, which means peace." His conversion from Christianity appeared to have racial overtones. "I ain't no Christian," he added, "and can't be as long as my people are beaten, kicked, bitten by dogs and bombed out of Christian churches." Besides, he said, "I'm the heavyweight champion of the world, but right now there are some neighborhoods right here that I can't move into." Then came words that marked him as a different sort of athlete: "I know where I'm going and I know the truth and I don't have to be what you want me to be. I'm free to be what I want." Confirming his friendship with Malcolm X, suspended minister of the Nation of Islam, admitting membership in a religion that terrified most whites and many blacks, and announcing that he was free of white expectations as to how he should conduct himself, Clay succeeded in frightening the boxing establishment, boxing fans, and a white America easily scared by racial change.[26]

Clay's conversion to the Nation of Islam and his close association with Malcolm X, the charismatic alternative to nonviolent integration stunned the nation. To the new champion, however, the NOI made psychological sense. According to Randy Roberts and Johnny Smith, Clay grew up living in fear of his father's drunken violence and explosive anger against the white world that he blamed for his disappointments. Clay also feared the violence of the white world outside the home. Repeatedly, he heard his father warn against leaving the neighborhood, shopping in white-owned stores, looking at white women, disobeying the police, and—scariest of all—getting arrested. His father repeatedly told stories about whites lynching and burning black men. In 1954, for instance, a black family bought a house in a white suburban Louisville neighborhood, only to have their white neighbors threaten them, burn crosses on their lawn, shoot at them, and ultimately dynamite the house. No one was tried for the crime, and the family was forced to move to the segregated West End, where the Clays and most blacks in Louisville lived, proving Clay Sr.'s warnings that contact with whites would inevitably result in violence. Clay was also seared by the lynching of Emmett Till and the Birmingham riots and church bombings, all of which were examples of white violence and hatred toward blacks, and proof that there was no justice for blacks in white America. In this atmosphere, Malcolm X's belief in the deep-seated racism of white America and the futility of racial integration was easy to follow. Moreover, in its emphasis on self-discipline, patriarchy, and black pride, the Nation also offered an answer to the anger, violence, and drunkenness that had roiled Clay's family life.[27]

Over the course of several years, Clay's experience as an athlete also accorded with Muslim teachings. It was a staple of NOI doctrine that black athletes and entertainers existed to entertain whites with their bodies rather than their minds and were tolerated as Americans as long as they did not question the country's racial hierarchy. In other words, like Joe Louis and Jackie Robinson, they were expected to be fierce competitors on the field or in the ring but quiet away from the fray. This claim resonated with Clay's experience after the 1960 Olympics. Proud to represent his country, he had expected the gold medal to bring him fame, fortune, and acceptance in white America. Honored by Louisville's mayor, he was trotted out to visiting dignitaries as a living symbol of improving American race relations. Deep down, however, he felt he was in danger of becoming a black "white hope," acceptable "as long as he believed what they believed, talked the way they talked and hated the people they hated." Despite wearing his medal, soon after meeting with the mayor, Clay was insulted by the owners of a local segregated restaurant who ordered him out of their establishment. Deeply humiliated, "whatever illusions I'd built up in Rome as the All-American boy were gone," he recalled. According to legend, he threw his medal away in disgust, although in fact he may have stopped wearing it and over the years misplaced it. Either way, "My holiday as a White Hope was over."[28]

Clay's renunciation of his "slave name" proved shocking, as did his announcement that henceforth he was Cassius X, the name given him by the Honorable Elijah Muhammad. Four weeks later, Elijah Muhammad, in a fierce war with Malcolm X for the allegiance of the champion who carried tremendous propaganda power, proclaimed his new acolyte "Muhammad Ali," which meant "worthy of praise" and "most high." This seemingly minor act became, as Gerald Early notes, one of "the most startling and contentious symbolic acts in American race relations in the nineteen-sixties." Many boxers and celebrities, including Joe Louis Barrow, Sugar Ray Robinson, and Jersey Joe Walcott had changed their names, but this sign of his conversion to a religion that preached the need for a separate black nation transformed Clay's image from "good colored boy" with rebellious tendencies to dangerous black menace. Older white sportswriters, reared on the doctrine that sports should be, and increasingly seemed, color blind, confronted a new champion eager to proclaim his racial pride independent of white and moderate black expectations. When he bragged that he was "pretty," he echoed nationalist beliefs that "black was beautiful." In fact, his conversion signaled the realization that black was no longer inferior, as he had been taught by American culture. "I used to think that black was bad," he declared, and white was good, but "then I found out that black wasn't bad." Rejecting the term *Negro*, Ali defined himself as a black man and insisted of his new name, "[It] freed me from the identity given to my family by slave masters." Ali's flamboyant politics of black style and black nationalism and his transformation of subsequent bouts into cultural performances of race brought the personal and the political together and made him an emblem of the antiestablishment counterculture of the 1960s.[29]

While his religious conversion shocked the nation, the new champion questioned what was wrong with loving his own people. Referring to Liston's having been prevented from moving into a white neighborhood in Florida, Ali said: "He's heavyweight champion and he's catching hell 'cause he wants to integrate. I want to be with my people and I'm catching more hell than he is." The absurdity was not lost on Ali: "This is real crazy, man, you're blown up and killed, you're bit by dogs and washed down the street by water if you want to integrate. And you're feared and criticized by whites if you don't want to integrate. What do they want? . . . Why is everybody so shook up by us wanting to get together to solve *our* problems?"[30]

Like other NOI followers, he grew critical of black athletes who did not follow his path. "Take those big niggers, Floyd Patterson and Sonny Liston. The whites make 'em rich and in return they brainwash the little Negroes walking around. Liston lives in a white neighborhood, Patterson lives in a white neighborhood . . . I can live . . . anywhere I want, but I live here [Miami] in a slum with my people." In accepting the Nation of Islam belief in racial separation, Ali challenged the idea that black athletes should succeed only as individuals and lose their identification with the black community. Following Elijah Muhammad's nationalist teachings, he hoped for "a peaceful, workable solution to the race problem. My goal is to see 22 million Negroes get freedom, justice, and equality."[31]

As a vocal member of the NOI especially tutored by Malcolm X, Ali no longer fit the accepted model of the modest, humble black athlete willing to let white managers and coaches speak for him. Speaking his mind in public, he represented a younger generation of black Americans who were no longer willing to placate whites. "I said things that black people thought, but were afraid to say." In return, the *New York Times* and many individual sportswriters refused to refer to him as Ali until the 1970s. Older sportswriters and the boxing establishment viewed the Muslims as worse for boxing than the mob was, and their criticism of Ali's religious beliefs reached fever pitch. Boxing had always been "the red light district of sports," wrote Jimmy Cannon, the dean of boxing commentators, "but this is the first time it has been turned into an instrument of mass hate. As one of Elijah Muhammad's missionaries, Clay is using it as a weapon of wickedness in an attack on the spirit. I pity Clay and abhor what he represents." His ties to the Muslims were "the dirtiest in sports since the Nazis were shilling for Max Schmeling as representative of their vile theories of blood." World Boxing Association commissioner Abe Greene demanded that Clay choose between being champion "or the fanatic leader of an extraneous force that has no place in the sports arena." In response, he declared: "I don't steal, abuse anyone or go around snatching pocket books, taking dope . . . but they are trying to take my title away. They are angry with me because I discarded the slave name, Cassius M. Clay for Muhammad Ali."[32]

Many older black sports fans, along with civil right workers of all ages, were dismayed by Ali's rejection of Christianity and integration just as the civil rights movement was achieving legislative victories. Having idolized Joe Louis, Sugar Ray Robinson, and Jackie Robinson, many black sportswriters viewed athletics as the one arena in American life where blacks enjoyed equal opportunity. Victories in the ring by model athletes would convince white Americans of black humanity and show that they had the qualities of self-discipline, good sportsmanship, and self-respect necessary for full inclusion in American society. As a result, many older African Americans were appalled by Ali's conversion. Charles P. Howard, columnist for *Muhammad Speaks*, the Nation of Islam newspaper, argued that the opposition went deeper. Ali, Howard claimed, was one of the "new Afro-Americans" who were "assertive, cocksure, determined, and of the don't-fence-me-in type." Equating the champion with Freedom Riders and sit-in participants, Howard asserted, "He shakes up the good white people as well as the 'correct' cullud people." Deep down, he continued, "They are frightened and shocked at Muhammad and his counterparts among young Afro-Americans for having the crust to break away from everything colored and embrace everything black." There were indeed some similarities between young civil rights workers and Ali, notably youth, Southern roots, and membership in a generation seared by white racial violence and the lynching of Emmett Till. But while many of them admired Ali's fighting ability, outspokenness, and racial pride, his defense of racial separation put them off. According to *Ebony*, many black people disagreed with "Cassius because they say his beliefs are a deterrent to the civil rights fight that is seeking full and equal citizenship for all Americans regardless of race, creed, or color." Still, just as many young African Americans were drawn to the new champion's outspoken challenge to white and black authority. Given this split, it would take Ali's opposition to the Vietnam War to make him a full-fledged civil rights hero.[33]

Just as puzzled as civil rights workers and many moderate African Americans, *Ebony* magazine defended Ali's religious freedom as an American constitutional right but was deeply critical of his rejection of integration. *Ebony* noted that most whites abhorred his religion "not because it preaches segregation of the races, but because it preaches the superiority of the black man."

While most blacks also rejected notions of black superiority, Ali's religious stance struck a chord with black nationalists who considered pride in all things black and rejection of a hopelessly white supremacist America necessary for black liberation. Still, while the black community supported his religious freedom, most African Americans felt "that he should not use his position as heavyweight champion to preach his beliefs." Heightening the growing generational split, the magazine asserted that "Joe Louis would have been no better nor any worse a fighter if he had been a Hindu rather than a Christian." As the Nation of Islam's most publicized convert, Ali was advised by *Ebony* to keep his religion to himself.[34]

Despite the hostility that greeted his conversion at home, Ali's open defense of his religion made him a Pan-African hero of the global black awakening. Immediately after winning the title, he accompanied Malcolm X to the United Nations, where he declared, "I'm champion of the whole world," and met with leaders of African and Islamic nations. Shortly thereafter he embarked on a tour of Africa and the Middle East to confer with various heads of state and "learn a little more about my people's background." He was supposed to travel with Malcolm X, who had tutored him in his responsibilities toward the "colored" world, but in the deadly split between Malcolm and Elijah Muhammad, Ali sided with the leader of his religion. Still, no American sports star had ever contemplated such autonomous action. Most who went abroad did so under the State Department aegis to promote the American way as open to all, regardless of race, creed, or color, and to demonstrate that American race relations were improving. Ali's travels were separate from this mission and instead placed him squarely in the Black Atlantic, which, argues historian Mike Marqusee, "shaped him and he helped to shape and ultimately to project into popular consciousness as never before."[35]

At the onset of the Cold War, mainstream black civil rights organizations had downplayed their links to African independence movements and lowered their attack on European colonialism as a crucial corollary of American racial oppression. In Ghana and Egypt, however, Ali reasserted the connection between racism at home and abroad, arriving as a hero critical of the United States and its role in perpetuating white supremacy around the globe. In fact, as Gerald Early asserts, Ali "was the biggest hero of the entire colored world in the post–World War II era" and the best-known Muslim on the planet. Together, "he combined protest and action and exhibited fierce racial pride and extraordinary egotism about his own powers." For colonial peoples "denigrated because of their color and their supposed 'inferiority' Ali's ego had no small meaning." In addition, Ali believed that being a Muslim black champion, his public role was a series of duties. Traveling to Africa and the Middle East was part of those duties, although he was criticized in boxing circles for putting them ahead of the obligations of his title.[36]

Eager to "see Africa and meet my brothers and sisters," he announced to huge crowds at the Accra airport, "I haven't been home for four hundred years." The Ghanaian press provided daily coverage of his visit, even depicting him in native dress, while thousands cheered the new champion, holding aloft signs that read YOU ARE WELCOME HOME KING OF THE WORLD and GHANA IS YOUR MOTHERLAND, CASSIUS CLAY. In a departure from his 1960 vision of Africa as a backward land of mud huts, Ali now told the crowd, "We are glad to be back home to see things for ourselves . . . and then go back to the States and tell our people that there are more things to be seen in Africa than lions, tigers and elephants." Ali also expressed his pride in modern black Ghanaian civilization, so unlike the United States, where "everything is white—Jesus, Moses and the angels." To top it off, President Kwame Nkrumah received the champion at a special reception, the first head of state to do so. Afterward Ali told the local press that he had humbled himself before Nkrumah: "I saw in him a dedicated man who is anxious to free Africa and bring about unity."[37]

Ali's reception in Egypt rivaled the one in Ghana, but there he was greeted by tumultuous crowds as a Muslim. "Every individual wants to express his love to this faithful believer champion," noted Cairo's *Republic*, a man "who asks for prayers from every Muslim in our country. Any such strong personality will do anything for the sake of principles." In return, Ali blamed the world's ignorance of Egypt's beauty on "the negative image created by imperialism," because, he said, "the imperialists know that Egypt is the cradle of Islam and that if its beauty is rightly portrayed it will give a positive image to other Islamic countries." These popular receptions helped create an image of Ali as a global icon, but they also earned the suspicions of the FBI and the CIA, as both Ghana and Egypt played central roles in the Non-Aligned Movement of Third World countries, which desired to remain independent of the United States and the Soviet Union. In defiance of American policy, the heavyweight champion consorted with leaders critical of the United States while making statements himself that challenged the official image of American life.[38]

Ali's trip and his membership in the NOI not only reinforced growing fears that the champion might prove dangerous to national security; it also helped transform Cassius Clay into his identity as Muhammad Ali. According to Osman Karriem, an NOI official who accompanied the champion while visiting a seemingly desolate part of rural Ghana, "there was a beating of drums" announcing their arrival and "then people showed up on the roads," chanting "Ali! Ali!" The champ was surprised and delighted that even in this isolated spot his name and deeds were the subject of veneration. "I saw the birth of a new human being," recalled Karriem. "It was like Cassius Clay came to an end and Muhammad Ali emerged." The incident confirmed his conviction that he was indeed the champion of the whole world, not just of the United States, and that he represented the hopes of oppressed peoples around the globe. Like other Pan-African cultural heroes, he saw himself not as a member of a minority but as part of a black majority. His African trip helped him fuse sports, black pride, and Pan-African popular culture.[39]

Upon his return to the United States, Ali's identification with the NOI began to infuse his matches with a religious and political tenor that he would have preferred to avoid. His rematch with Liston, for instance, ran into a buzz saw of bad publicity. Concerned about the influence of the Muslims, the World Boxing Association refused to sanction the rematch, while rumors circulated that followers of Malcolm X might kill Ali in revenge for the NOI's assassination of their leader. While Ali declared that he was not afraid, the promoters were. Delayed for months because Ali had a hernia, the fight got shuffled around before landing in a tiny gym in Lewiston, Maine. Before a small crowd, the champ came out of his corner, landed a short right hand, and Liston went down for the count. It happened so fast that many sportswriters and boxing fans dubbed it the "the phantom punch," which implied the match was fixed, although *The Ring* insisted it was a real knockout blow. The punch no one saw, the one-round knockout, the setting in Maine, and the rumors of Black Muslim violence worked to seriously damage Ali's reputation. The boxing establishment was not amused.[40]

Liston, though, did not attack the champion's religion. In pursuit of a title fight, on the other hand, ex-champion Floyd Patterson publicly criticized Ali's NOI membership. A soft-spoken Catholic convert with a white wife, Patterson supported the civil rights movement and opposed black separatism. Raised in worse circumstances than Ali, Patterson, a street kid who had been incarcerated at the Wiltshire School for Boys, posed as the antidote to Ali in *Sports Illustrated* and refused to use his new name. Patterson proposed to "reclaim the title for America" from a champion who, because of his segregationist views, "might just as well have joined the Ku Klux Klan" and had failed in his responsibility to be a fitting symbol of American life for the nation's youth. The ex-champ's continued use of "Clay" in particular irritated Ali. According to Dundee, "You called him Muhammad Ali or you lost a friend . . . it was not a topic for taunts or jokes." In response, Ali unleashed his own verbal onslaught, calling Patterson an Uncle Tom. "The only reason Patterson's decided to come out of his shell," he told *Playboy*, "is to try to make himself a big hero to the white man by saving the heavyweight title from being held by a Muslim." As punishment, Ali vowed to "put him flat on his back / So that he will start acting black."[41]

Their fight on November 22, 1965, became a holy war between Christianity and Islam. Fighting courageously despite a sore back, the much-shorter challenger was no match for the taller champion, who tattooed him endlessly with stinging lefts and rights. All the while Ali derided his helpless opponent for failing to use his "true" name and, rather than knock him out early, preferred to prolong Patterson's agony until the referee mercifully halted the slaughter in the eleventh round. Ali earned a victory for Allah, but his reputation suffered from what some sportswriters called his "cruelty." Instead of blaming Patterson for raising the religious issue and recognizing that Ali was unable to knock him out, they focused on Ali as the cruel representative of an ugly, violent black sect. While Ali continued to enliven a dying sport with his great physical and theatrical skills, he also cemented an image as a dangerous, politically naive black man who was doing great damage to himself, to boxing, and to civil rights. It was going to get worse.[42]

Ali's membership in the NOI also alienated him from the boxing establishment in very specific ways. In January 1966, at the behest of Ali's manager Herbert Muhammad (son of Elijah Muhammad), the NOI's national secretary John Ali, lawyer and promoter Bob Arum, closed-circuit television operator Mike Malitz, and former All-Pro football star Jim Brown, the already-controversial champion formed a new corporation, Main Bout Inc., to gain greater control over the ancillary promotional rights to his matches, including live and delayed broadcasts. Despite a cordial relationship with his Louisville sponsors, after six years Ali sought greater independence and the opportunity to help the Muslims. Key to the new company was the inclusion of Herbert Muhammad and John Ali. This was to begin with the multimillion-dollar bout against Ernie Terrell in Chicago in March 1966. The corporation was racially integrated but controlled by the NOI and its philosophy of economic nationalism. "I am vitally interested in the company," announced Ali, "and in seeing that it will be one in which Negroes are not used as fronts, but as stockholders, officers, and production and promotion agents." The entrée of a NOI-connected company alarmed the boxing establishment and led to fierce opposition to Ali.[43]

In essence, the new corporation attempted to do what black radicals in sports would try a year later—utilize their athletic prominence as a platform to demand greater economic power and profit in sport and address racial oppression in American society. By promoting Ali's fights, Main Bout also planned to hire more black people to provide related services. In effect, the new company threatened the balance of power in boxing. The white boxing establishment greeted the new promotional entity with hostility, fearing a Black Muslim takeover of boxing. Among peoples of color at home and abroad, the Main Bout episode led to the elevation of Ali's status as a race man and a race leader in the freedom struggle, and someone subject to the same discrimination as ordinary African Americans. When Ali announced his opposition to the Vietnam War in February 1966, the already-threatened boxing establishment worked to end his boxing career. Boycotts of his fights by veterans groups and politicians abounded, the Terrell match was canceled, and for a year Ali could fight only abroad. When Ali was convicted of draft evasion in 1967, however, Main Bout died an abrupt death, much to the joy of many whites in boxing.

Ali's religion was controversial, but his opposition to the Vietnam War made him an outcast at home and increased his worldwide popularity as a critic of American foreign policy. Despite being classified initially as 1-Y, or mentally unfit for service, in February 1966 he was reclassified 1-A in response to the expansion of the war and the need for more manpower. Instead of following Joe Louis's precedent during World War II and serving in the armed forces as a morale builder and symbol of loyalty, Ali astounded the nation by applying for conscientious objector status on the grounds that his religion forbade him from fighting in any wars but holy ones as defined by the Nation of Islam. Judge Lawrence Grauman ruled that Ali's appeal was grounded in religious doctrine and he recommended CO status. The Justice Department, however, urged the Kentucky Appeals Board to deny the claim, in part because of mounting public criticism of Ali. Of prime concern was the precedent for other Black Muslims to reject military service on religious grounds. L. Mendel Rivers, chairman of the House Armed Services Committee, told a Veterans of Foreign Wars audience: "If that great theologian of Black Muslim power . . . is deferred, you watch what happens in Washington. . . . What has happened to the leadership of our nation when a man . . . regardless of color, can . . . advise his listeners to tell the President when he is called to serve in the armed forces . . . 'I'm not going.'" Despite the avalanche of criticism, Ali held fast. "I'm a 1,000% religious man," he declared. "If I thought goin' to war would bring freedom, justice and equality to 22 million Negroes, they wouldn't have to draft me." The draft issue put him at war with the government and the majority of white America, but it made him a hero among the growing ranks of the antiwar young.[44]

Ali's antiwar stance challenged the belief that heavyweight champions represented the nation's fighting manhood and that as American champions they had a duty to put country before race. Indeed, his example raised questions about military service as a central tenet of modern masculinity. In February 1966, shortly before the planned Terrell match, Ali responded to the incessant telephone calls from reporters about whether he would serve if drafted: "Man, I ain't got no quarrel with them Viet Cong." Coming as the war had escalated into full-scale American commitment, the remark encapsulated the thoughts of many young men while also inflaming public opinion. Older sports columnists, already disturbed by the Muslim "invasion" of boxing via Main Bout, attacked Ali as an ungrateful, unpatriotic draft dodger, a symbol of everything wrong with modern youth. Red Smith, the dean of boxing writers, railed, "Squealing over the possibility that the military may call him up, Cassius makes himself as sorry a spectacle as those unwashed punks who picket and demonstrate against the war." With public outrage at fever pitch, Ali found himself the scapegoat for the growing youth revolt against the older generation, especially its devotion to duty, deference to authority, and obligation to serve the nation in the anticommunist cause.[45]

Outraged by Ali's remarks that "I am a member of the Muslims, and we don't go to no wars unless they are declared by Allah himself," as decreed by Elijah Muhammad, the *Chicago Tribune* labeled the champion a turncoat and condemned the March 1966 Ali-Terrell title fight, to be fought in Chicago. In response to the newspaper's patriotic tirade, Mayor Richard J. Daley and Governor Otto Kerner denounced Ali as a traitor, and the American Legion and the Veterans of Foreign Wars threatened a boycott. Former heavyweight champion Gene Tunney, "the Fighting Marine," fulminated via telegram that Ali had "DISGRACED THE AMERICAN FLAG, AND THE PRINCIPLES FOR WHICH IT STANDS. APOLOGIZE FOR YOUR UNPATRIOTIC REMARK OR YOU'LL BE BARRED FROM THE RING." With the bout in danger, the Illinois State Athletic Commission summoned the champion to Chicago to submit a formal apology for his "Viet Cong" remarks. After listening to a slew of condescending comments from the commissioners, and their refusal to call him by his new name, Ali defiantly refused to apologize. Those "denouncing me so bitterly," he later recalled, "had never said a single word against the injustices or oppression inflicted on my people in America. I felt they were saying they would accept me as the World Heavyweight Champion only on their terms. Only if I played the role of the dumb, brute who chimed in with whatever the Establishment thought at the moment even if it was against the best interest of my people or my country." Whites who disliked his religion, his braggadocio, and his cockiness now had "the one thing they could get together on: a holy, patriotic, crusade."[46]

Until he refused induction in April 1967, the champion was still allowed to fight outside the country. He found fans in Toronto, Britain, and Germany for his bouts versus George Chuvalo, Henry Cooper, Brian London, and Karl Mildenberger. In London, in fact, his presence helped invigorate a West Indian movement to organize Great Britain's "million colored immigrants into a political force." When Ali formally refused induction into the army in 1967, however, he was convicted of draft evasion and sentenced to five years in jail and a $10,000 dollar fine. In response, his enemies wasted no time in punishing him for his sins. The New York State Athletic Commission immediately stripped him of his boxing license, setting off a chain reaction in which every other state sanctioning body followed suit. In addition, the World Boxing Association removed his title and created an elimination tournament to name his successor. The State Department revoked his passport. Only *The Ring*, led by editor Nat Fleischer, a longtime proponent of boxing as a force for American inclusion, refused to recognize any other champion until Ali had either exhausted the appeals process or been beaten in the ring. The draft issue along with his "controversial" religion finally threatened to put Ali back in his place. He had managed to hit the trifecta, becoming a scapegoat for the three biggest issues roiling the nation—the growing mass disaffection with the war, the freedom movement and urban riots by black people angry about their deep-seated poverty and second-class citizenship, and the youth revolt against the authority of the older generation. By 1968 Ali was the quintessential loud mouth that Richard Nixon's "silent majority" hungered to silence.[47]

Not since the days of Jack Johnson had a heavyweight champion proved so unpopular. Unlike Johnson, however, the wrath of the American people was not over miscegenation, since Ali publicly opposed racial intermarriage. Rather, as Ali put it: "My religion is against the war and I am within my legal rights to claim exemption on the basis of being a conscientious objector. If I weren't the heavyweight champion, all the fuss in American newspapers wouldn't appear." Yet few people could accept that the heavyweight champion, a central emblem of American manhood, refused to go to war. Even though Nat Fleischer supported Ali's right to remain champion until the final court ruling, he could not accept Ali's refusal to serve: "If he announced his willingness to join the colors, as have thousands of his countrymen regardless of right or wrong attitudes on our war in Viet Nam, he would become a national hero." His refusal to do so, charged *Ring*'s Dan Daniel, made him "a freak." Despite his American birth, Ali renounced "American connections as a professed convert to Islam." Even more troubling, "here is a heavyweight champion of the world who announces that he has conscientious objections to fighting, a man of combat who wants nothing to do with more serious combat, a fighter who doesn't want to be enlisted with fighters." Along with his "talk, boasting, and out and out tomfoolery," Clay was "an American who doesn't wish to be an American, a fighter who doesn't wish to be a fighter for American patriotism. Now, if this man Clay isn't a genuine freak, one of the freakiest of all time despite his ideal physical proportions and ring skills, then we haven't had a real freak in boxing." In essence, Ali had become "a man without a country." Describing him listening to "The Star-Spangled Banner" before the Cooper bout in London, Daniel wondered, "Did Cassius Clay Muhammad Ali, Black Muslim and heavyweight champion of the world, give any thought to that flag as he awaited the summons to action?"[48]

Ali's antiwar stance deepened the 1960s generation gap to a chasm, symbolized by the overwhelming approval of Joe Louis as a model of sacrifice and patriotism during World War II. Louis had been hired in February 1966 to help Ali prepare for Terrell, but he quit abruptly. According to Dan Daniel, Joe "proceeded to give Muhammad Ali an artistic, logical and altogether unprejudiced going over." Pictured in uniform saluting the flag during World War II, Louis declared, "Any man fit enough to be champion of the world is fit enough for military service." The Brown Bomber continued: "Cassius is an American. . . . He earns his living here. . . . When your country is at war you don't have any place or time for personal regrets." Not only did Louis criticize "Clay," he embodied the World War II generation's belief that American citizenship and American masculinity required military service of all able-bodied males and that the heavyweight champion, as the acme of masculinity, was expected to sacrifice his career as a patriotic duty. Mainstream civil rights groups, moreover, argued that a black champion's display of patriotism would further African American freedom. In Ali's mind, however, these gains were limited, and one sacrificed first for religion and race. Ali and Louis thus symbolized two poles of American opinion divided by the generational conflict over the war. A pro-Ali GI put the matter succinctly: Ali "owes loyalty to himself, his race, and to any country that will not only accept him as a champion, but most important, accept him as a Negro." For many boxing fans, however, a heavyweight champion had to serve his country or incur the wrath of the nation. As Frank Allerdice urged in *The Ring*, "Drop anti-Americans in all classes. If an American called to the colors can't fight for Old Glory, boxing and *The Ring* should consign him to Hell." In refusing to name "Clay" Fighter of the Year for 1966, *The Ring* declared that "a boxer who defies the government of the USA to draft him into the Army emphatically" is not "a shining example to the Growing American Boy."[49]

While his appeals moved slowly through the courts, Ali worked as a minister for the Nation of Islam and lectured about his case, race, and Muslim philosophy at various universities, for which he received a decent speaker's fee. From all outward appearances, it looked like he would never fight again. As it was, he was forced to endure three and a half years away from boxing at the height of his career. At the same time, Ali's principled stance gave him "the martyr's role" and elevated his stature to heights no one could have imagined before his conviction. As he told *Sports Illustrated*: "I either have to obey the laws of man or the laws of Allah, God. I'd rather die a Muslim. Six hundred million Muslims are with me to see if I am punished in this land of religious freedom. . . . I have nothing to lose by standing up and following my own beliefs." To many African Americans his treatment at the hands of the government, the boxing establishment, and white America was no different from the treatment endured by the average black person. They might not agree with his religion, but they could see that his freedom of religion was being transgressed and that he was being punished for standing up and speaking out for his principles. That was something black men had been punished for throughout American history by violent lynch mobs.[50]

At a time when radical civil rights and antiwar activists were putting their bodies on the line, Ali did the same by his willingness to give up his boxing career, go to prison, and lose millions rather than give in to what he considered unjust authority. The reality that Ali refused to compromise and take the easy way out—serve in a noncombatant morale army unit, thereby retaining his title, as did Joe Louis in World War II—was convincing proof that he was no longer the embarrassing "Louisville Lip." Now *Jet* and other black publications portrayed him as the highest embodiment of black manhood. According to the radical black journal *Freedomways*: "In taking his stand as a matter of conscience, the world heavyweight champion may be giving up a small fortune, but he has undoubtedly gained the respect and admiration of a very large part of humanity. That, after all, is the measure of a Man." As Ali put it when the furor first arose, "One thing I ain't is a Uncle Tom. I'm a *warrior*. I'm a warrior on the Battleground of Freedom." He was becoming a key figure in the freedom movement alongside Martin Luther King Jr., Malcolm X, and Stokely Carmichael in redefining black manhood as a willingness to challenge the authority of white America.[51]

Because most mainstream civil rights organizations like the NAACP and the Urban League supported the war or like the Southern Christian Leadership Conference (SCLC) remained silent, and as both political parties were pro-war, Ali's opposition to Vietnam proved a major boon to the antiwar movement and raised his public stature as a man of principled conviction. As the world heavyweight champion in a tough and brutal sport, he could not easily be dismissed as "cowardly" or "unmanly," despite many charges to that effect. As a black American, moreover, he helped legitimate opposition to the war more widely by eroding the movement's lily-white image. In fact, Ali's actions may have contributed to Martin Luther King's decision to openly oppose the war. In a sermon delivered in response to Ali's stance, King praised him for "giving up fame. He is giving up millions of dollars in order to stand up for what his conscience tells him is right. No matter what you think of Muhammad Ali's religion, you have to admire his courage." While the NAACP and the Urban League remained hesitant, and Joe Louis continued to blast his lack of patriotism, other prominent African Americans began to express support for the champion. Former baseball star Jackie Robinson, for instance, wrote in his syndicated column "that there are many writers who like Negroes who 'stay in their place.' . . . Of course, by backing up his words with deeds, Clay or Ali has clearly demonstrated where his 'place' is." For the more radical members of the Student Nonviolent Coordinating Committee (SNCC) and the Congress of Racial Equality, Ali's antiwar stance now made him a hero of gigantic proportions because he was willing to defy the government and go to jail for his beliefs—as they also were. Black Power advocates had a defiant black masculine hero who merged nationalist ideas at home with anti-imperial impulses abroad.[52]

Among athletes Ali's status grew after he met with a group of black sports figures who sought to probe his sincerity. Jim Brown, All-Pro running back of the Cleveland Browns; Bill Russell, star center and coach of the Boston Celtics; UCLA basketball player Lew Alcindor; and members of the Green Bay, Cleveland, Kansas City, and Washington, DC, football teams, met with Ali at the behest of Herbert Muhammad to see if he would accept a compromise to his antiwar views and agree to serve in a noncombat morale unit, as Joe Louis did in World War II. By the end of the hours-long meeting, the champion refused to waver. In a glowing article for *Sports Illustrated*, Russell expressed admiration for Ali's sincerity. "I know what I must do," Russell quoted Ali. "My fate is in the hands of Allah, and Allah will take care of me." As "a Black Muslim and because he refuses to compromise his principles it will be difficult for him to get a fair trial," said Russell. Challenging the common view that the Black Muslims were manipulating a naive Ali, Russell concluded that Ali's position was sincerely rooted in his religion and that he was being hounded for his religious beliefs. "The hysterical and sometimes fanatical criticism of Ali is, it seems to me, a symptom of the deeper sickness of our times," Russell noted. He professed not to worry about Ali. "What I'm worried about is the rest of us."[53]

In his various speeches, Ali went farther than other mainstream civil rights leaders in linking the struggle for justice at home with his position against the war overseas. In this he challenged the Cold War civil rights bargain that promised progress against racial discrimination at home in exchange for loyalty to the United States in its global battle with the Russians. His linkage of the Vietnam War with domestic racism reinforced the Black Power view that racism was a form of domestic colonialism and that American peoples of color were the equivalent of the Vietnamese. When Martin Luther King's SCLC launched demonstrations against housing segregation in Louisville, Ali agreed to take part, despite his separatist views, since the civil rights action was taking place in his own hometown. Speaking to the demonstrators he made clear that his antiwar stance involved a broader racial picture of the world. It made no sense for American blacks to kill brown-skinned Vietnamese, he told the crowd, when black people in Louisville "are treated like dogs and denied simple human rights. No, I am not going ten thousand miles from home to help murder and burn another poor nation simply to continue the domination of white slave masters of the darker people the world over." Acknowledging that he would lose millions of dollars by refusing to serve in the armed forces, he argued in tones reminiscent of Malcolm X: "The real enemy of my people is right here. I will not disgrace my people and my religion, my people and myself by becoming a tool to enslave those who are fighting for their own justice, freedom and equality." Making his position crystal clear, the champion added: "I either have to obey the laws of the land or the laws of Allah. I have nothing to lose by standing up for my beliefs. We've been in jail for four hundred years."[54]

While his actions and his views gained him support among radical forces in the civil rights and antiwar movements, they also made Ali one of the most hated Americans of the late 1960s and early 1970s and the most divisive figure in American sports. The price of his actions was enormous. Stripped of his title and sentenced to five years in jail, he was forced to watch from the sidelines as new figures, such as Joe Frazier and George Foreman, emerged to take his place atop the heavyweight division. Yet even in exile his example helped spur an even-wider athletic revolt among black athletes. His return to boxing would once again bring the central political and cultural issues of the era into the ring.

2

1968: FISTS AND FLAGS

> [George Foreman] is proof that the American dream is just as real as it was 192 years ago.
>
> RONALD REAGAN

On October 7, 1968 *Sports Illustrated* profiled the US heavyweight boxing representative to the upcoming 1968 Olympic Games in Mexico City. Noting that the fortunes of American Olympic boxers had ebbed since they had won five gold medals in 1952, the article pointed out that the best prospect for gold at Mexico City was George Foreman, "The Fighting Corpsman," as was printed on the back of his robe. "A spiritual descendant of Ali," noted Gilbert Rogin, Foreman "is a poetaster with a proclivity for near rhymes and, like Ali, comes prepared to dwell on himself." Excited about the magazine's attention, Foreman recited poetry that bragged about his speed, his power, and his ambition. "George is nimble and George is quick / Watch me folks, 'cause I can really stick." The nineteen-year-old Job Corps product also shared Ali's lack of respect for his elders, including Ali himself. "Now everybody remembers old Cassius Clay," he rhymed: "You may say Ali is good / If you feel you should / But if he got me in the ring and asked my name / Why, that poor boy would die of shame." That they might meet in the ring seemed improbable at best given Ali's banishment from boxing and Foreman's youth and lack of ring experience. Yet six years later the fight was on.[1]

Over the course of the tumultuous 1968 Olympic Games, in fact, Foreman came to embody the very opposite of what Muhammad Ali stood for. As a proud graduate of the Job Corps, Foreman had become a symbol of the beneficence of American society in making it possible for poor young black men to develop the skills and self-discipline to succeed in life. As a potent political symbol Foreman was courted by both presidential candidates in the heated 1968 election campaign that was under way as he chased his gold medal. Much to his own amazement, he became a lightning rod for debates within the black community and the larger American society about the proper role of African American athletes in American life as well as the efficacy of the liberal policies of the Great Society versus a growing and insistent black nationalism. While Ali remained exiled from boxing and was prevented from traveling outside the United States after the State Department confiscated his passport once he was convicted for draft evasion on June 20, 1967, his defiant attitude toward the sports establishment played a key role in the movement to boycott the Mexico City Olympics and what came to be called the "Revolt of the Black Athlete." At the same time, while both men earned adulation during the late 1960s and early 1970s, they also inspired virulent dislike. The definition of a sports hero was no longer clear cut.[2]

Unlike Ali's youth in the North-South border city of Louisville, George Foreman's boyhood was like that of many black youth who were lost to the streets of large American cities. Yet like Ali, boxing proved his saving grace. Born January 10, 1949, seven years after Ali, George grew up in dire poverty in one of the nation's worst ghettos, Houston's so-called Bloody Fifth Ward, in the section known aptly as "the Bottom," where "anger and hunger shaped my youth." The fifth of seven children, George was raised by his mother, Nancy Ree Foreman, a single parent forced to work two jobs, seven days a week. The man he thought was his father, and the actual father of George's brothers and sisters, J. D. Foreman, was mostly absent, and before he was born, his mother had drifted into an affair with another man. The result was baby George. To avoid gossip in the small town of Marshall where she lived, and desperate to improve her economic opportunities, his mother moved the family to Houston shortly after George was born. When George was four years old, his parents separated, placing the entire burden of family support on his mother.[3]

The section of Houston that the family moved to, the Bloody Fifth Ward, was notorious as one of the most violent ghettos in the nation. In the shadow of modern downtown Houston, a dynamic city of the postwar "new" South overflowing with oil and petrochemical wealth, the ward still retained many of the features more reflective of the old South, including the small, dark two- and three-room shotgun shacks inhabited by rats and insects and situated on unpaved roads. When it rained for several days, the streets flooded. As with other city services, garbage pickup was poor. Crime was rampant, and policing, where present, was extremely brutal. It is no surprise that the neighborhood had one of the highest murder rates in the nation. Mrs. Foreman was lucky to find two jobs, one as a cook in a cafeteria, but the fact that the pay was scaled for black women's labor meant that the family lived only one or two steps ahead of the landlord in cramped circumstances where hunger was a constant problem. "I was a big boy, so I was *always* hungry," Foreman recalled. "It wasn't till years later, after I started boxing, that I could remember my stomach feeling full after a meal." For a large child like George there was never enough food, and what his mother managed to bring home from the cafeteria had to be divided among his siblings. Sometimes she brought home one hamburger from the cafeteria, cut eight ways: "It was such a luxury; I grew up believing that hamburgers were only for rich people."[4]

At home young George was often mean as well as hungry. Besides the hunger that fed his anger, his rage was also sparked by constant teasing from his siblings. A lot of that originated in the question of George's legitimacy, not that anyone mentioned this openly. Although he did not know he was illegitimate, the nonstop gibing by his siblings fed his belief that he had no solid place in his family or in the world. In response to the hostility, George fought with his siblings all the time. That rage at and distrust of the world and the people around him went a long way toward shaping the angry young man in every aspect of his life.

The rage that defined him was something his mother hoped to quell, because she knew what happened to angry young black men growing up in the South. In her experience, fiery boys in the Bloody Fifth who lacked fear and showed signs of rebellion against authority died early on, at the hands of either the police or other young black men. "The aim of the police was to tame you, to break your spirit," Foreman recalled. They took pride in beating tough guys savagely to show them who was boss. A big, strong woman herself, Mrs. Foreman tried to beat the anger out of her troublesome son. She preferred, she said, that George be "more afraid of what she would do to me if I disobeyed her than any of the trouble I might get into in the streets." Her efforts failed. With his mother constantly working—and for a year hospitalized with clinical depression—George lost whatever direction he had. He ran the streets with a rough crowd, getting into one scrape after another.[5]

His mother hoped that education might give him a more positive direction in life, but George took no interest in school. In fact, he managed to fail every subject in every grade. The object of his teachers' scorn and ashamed of his raggedy, hand-me-down clothes, he played hooky constantly, happier on the streets than in hot, stuffy classrooms. With the dime his mother gave him for school, he would shoot dice with his buddies, using his winnings for Marlboros and wine. He was passed from grade to grade even though he could not read or write. When he was in the sixth grade a teacher told him that he would never get past junior high school, and at the age of thirteen he abandoned any hope of learning.[6]

Only sports held his interest in junior high. He discovered football, a rough contact sport in which he could channel some of his anger. As a big, strong defensive lineman he could sack a quarterback gleefully, bring down a running back, or smash an offensive lineman to the ground without compunction, and in the process earn praise, rather than blame, for his violent tendencies. His bad habits, though, landed him in trouble. The coach caught him smoking and kicked him off the team. With no interest in academic subjects, he dropped out of E. O. Smith Junior High School in the ninth grade without a degree. Too young to get a job, Foreman ran the streets with his buddies, drank cheap wine on the corners, smoked marijuana, dabbled in minor criminal activities, and got into fights.

If school could not save him from the streets, his mother reasoned, perhaps religion could help. Although working seven days a week prevented her from attending services on a regular basis, she was a believing Baptist who relied on the Bible for guidance and hoped that George might do the same. He never followed through. His brothers and sisters not only read the Bible; they prayed seriously and attended services as often as they could. In those days, however, George despised the church as something designed exclusively for the weak. As he put it, religion was for "men who couldn't hit back anymore, women beaten by life—they bought religion. Nobody I looked up to." For this discontented, rebellious youngster, churches were a scam where mercenary ministers preached pie-in-the-sky sermons to bilk the poor and the ignorant out of their hard-earned pennies. He said, "I would have been ashamed if any of the guys I went around with thought I believed in Jesus; Jesus was a hoax."[7]

Trapped by race and poverty and lacking responsible male role models, an extremely alienated George Foreman, like many other young men raised in the nation's ghettos, turned to robbery, violence, and vandalism to express his deep-seated rage and take what was missing in his life. "By the time I was sixteen years of age, I was a vicious, savage teenager, picking fights in school or wherever I went," he recounted. Fueled by cheap wine and marijuana, he did not see robbery as a serious crime or the law as anything that applied to him: "For me, in those days, the law was the law of the jungle, where the end justified the means. Survival." By junior high school, he remembered, violence "had become second nature. Everyone knew my reputation, and they knew it was a reputation I cultivated." Growing up on the streets of Houston, "You had to learn to fight. That was my way of earning a reputation." His street gang turned to the six-foot-one, 185-pound George as their enforcer, because they knew he would not back down. To back down in this dog-eat-dog world was to lose his "manhood" and his "identity." Sometimes, he bragged, "[I] beat up two or three people a day. I was brutal, too. . . . Because my conscience was so encrusted with hate, it didn't bother me to see people bleeding or knocked out cold." Living in a world where survival seemed the only thing that mattered, young Foreman saw himself as "King of the Jungle," a man whose fists and size provided his only measure of identity.[8]

Running the streets meant constant run-ins with the police, although in George's mind that did not automatically make him a criminal. There did come a moment, however, when the realization finally hit him. After what looked like a successful mugging for him, the victim called the police. With dogs in tow, they descended on the neighborhood for a house-to-house search for the mugger. As police searchlights swept the area and the dogs began trying to pick up his scent, George desperately attempted to hide himself in the crawl space under one of the neighborhood's shotgun shacks. Lying in the dirt, damp from the filthy water dripping down on him from the house's pipes, he smeared himself with mud to ward off the approaching police dogs. At that crucial juncture, George came face-to-face with reality—he was a criminal barely existing at the margins of society. Fortunately for him, the police did not find him, but the harrowing experience convinced him to give up mugging at least and try to get a job and go straight. George's brother got him hired at the moving company where he was employed, but after George slept through an evening shift, the boss fired him, not without a lecture on his total irresponsibility.[9]

George may have wanted to go straight, but how? After all, in 1965 he was a sixteen-year-old black junior high school dropout with a penchant for crime and dissipation and a total lack of usable skills. The only thing going for him was his desire to make his clinically depressed mother proud of him. As if by way of miracle, it was the Job Corps, an antipoverty program that was part of Lyndon Johnson's Great Society, that helped young Foreman turn his life around and saved him from prison or an early grave. The answer to his dilemma arrived when his sister alerted him to an advertisement airing on television for the new antipoverty program that was seemingly designed for someone just like him. In the brief government-sponsored spot, all-time great football quarterback Johnny Unitas and legendary running back Jim Brown advised young men that they could overcome their impoverished backgrounds by learning a trade in the Job Corps. When George heard them endorse the program, he was determined to go. Mrs. Foreman was more than happy to sign the necessary papers to get her troubled son away from the bad elements that surrounded him. As far as the future champion was concerned, the experience changed his life.[10]

Foreman's decision to join the Job Corps placed him at the center of the Johnson administration's training plan, a key element in its desire to build a Great Society and eliminate poverty in the United States. Established in 1964, the Job Corps proposed to provide impoverished youth the skills, discipline, and character to lift them out of poverty. Much of the attention focused on young black men like George who came from broken homes, had dropped out of school, and were part of what *The Negro Family: The Case for National Action*—known as the Moynihan Report, for its author, then assistant secretary of labor Daniel Patrick Moynihan—would label "a tangle of pathology" rooted in a matriarchal culture. The focus was specifically on males who needed government assistance and training to attain the proper skills and character necessary to support their families. This mode of breadwinner liberalism had roots in conventional assumptions about the nuclear family and its emphasis on traditional male roles as breadwinners and females as mothers and wives in the home. What was different about the Job Corps was that it would extend government help to those young men who increasingly made up the ranks of the chronically unemployed. Unbeknownst to George, just as he volunteered for the Job Corps, the assumptions on which it was based would come under criticism by black nationalists like Malcolm X, Muhammad Ali, and Stokely Carmichael who supported the need to undergird black patriarchy but distrusted the paternalism of American government programs. Equally critical, but perhaps with longer-lasting effect, were the growing ranks of the feminist movement, which challenged breadwinner liberalism as biased toward men as workforce participants and women as restricted to the domestic sphere. Furthermore, after the urban riots and the Moynihan Report, many political conservatives and disappointed liberals criticized these government programs as useless. They were convinced that black males from the ghetto were too immersed in a culture of poverty and family dysfunction to be helped by government programs.[11]

For George, however, the Job Corps proved a major turning point. In 1965 the Corps sent him an airplane ticket to the Fort Vannoy Conservation Center in Grants Pass, Oregon, an idyllic natural setting far removed in geography and spirit from the Houston ghetto. Surrounded by forests and mountains, he realized for the first time that there was a whole different world outside the Fifth Ward, like the setting of a Roy Rogers television episode or a place where he could imagine Beaver and Wally, from the *Leave It to Beaver* television program, on a Boy Scout outing: "This was the place of my heroes and fantasies, and where I now lived." It was also a place where he learned construction, built roads and houses, and discovered that Job Corps personnel were "concerned with teachin' you something." The physicality of the labor appealed to him so much that he looked forward to getting up early in the morning and going back to work.[12]

Still, despite his newfound love for construction, George initially made few friends. In his case it proved easier to take the young man out of the ghetto than it was to take the ghetto out of the young man. Nearly full grown at six foot three and two hundred pounds, sixteen-year-old Foreman continued to use his strength to beat up his camp mates, many of whom were older than he was. Fighting was the only thing he knew, and if anyone did not give him full respect—and sometimes even if anyone did—George would smash him to the ground. In short order, he earned a reputation as the conservation center's bully. Worried about his suitability for the Job Corps, the counselors discussed sending him back to Houston.[13]

Finally George made a friend, Richard Kibble, a hippie from Tacoma, Washington, who introduced him to the new youth culture that was beginning to sweep the nation. On their first meeting Kibble asked him why he fought with everyone all the time and asserted that fighting was not important. Together they listened to Kibble's Bob Dylan records, which, according to Foreman, was when his real education began. Although he continued to fight with anyone and everyone, George discovered a love of learning. He learned grammar and vocabulary and for the first time in his life read a book. In fact, he began to devour books, especially the *Autobiography of Malcolm X*, which given its story of an alienated black young man who descends into crime and prison before being redeemed, must have spoken forcefully to him. It was through Kibble that he also made a few friends, most of whom he had beaten up at one time or another. While listening with them to the radio broadcast of the Muhammad Ali–Floyd Patterson bout on November 22, 1965, one of his new friends asked him why he did not take up boxing, since he liked beating up people so much. Excited by the challenge of the sport and the glamour of the heavyweight champion, six months later George transferred to the Camp Parks Job Corps Center run by Litton Industries near Pleasanton, California. Located about forty miles east of Oakland, the center would allow George to continue his education and make use of its excellent physical education facilities, including an already-established boxing program.[14]

The boxing program at Camp Parks was run by Nick "Doc" Broadus, one of the most important influences in George's life. More than boxing, the forty-eight-year-old former amateur and professional fighter strove to provide Foreman with discipline, direction, and a strong adult male role model. Only five foot five, Broadus had a boxing résumé and a background in martial arts that earned George's respect and made the coach fearless toward his towering young pupil with the hair-trigger temper: "You bigger than me, but I can handle you baby. Size don't mean nothin' to me." Broadus told him: "I been in that jungle, too, George. Whatever you did, I was doin' myself not long ago. But that's ol' history now, an' our job is to *make* history." As an amateur boxer Broadus had won one hundred straight bouts and twenty-four out of twenty-five as a professional. As soon as he lost, he turned coach, first in the air force, then in the Job Corps. Even with his vast experience, however, steering the angry Foreman proved challenging. When George threatened a counselor, he was nearly expelled from the Job Corps as an irredeemable hoodlum. "I was held responsible for him," Doc noted. "It was going to be his last opportunity."[15]

Foreman's last chance meant taking the boxing program seriously. Doc put him in charge of the gym and at night schooled him in the rudiments of the sport. George donned his first pair of boxing gloves in December 1966. In his first bout with middleweight Max Briggs, a camp boxing veteran, he was thoroughly embarrassed. His brute strength proved ineffective. Briggs made him look foolish by dancing him silly, peppering him with punches, and bloodying his nose. Worse, this occurred in front of many of the Job Corps mates he had bullied. Deeply ashamed, George skipped the camp's fight show without explanation, running off to Oakland rather than risk further embarrassment. When he returned, he blamed his disappearance on having boxing shoes too small to box in. Doc bought him a pair of tennis shoes. "After he found out there was somebody interested in him," Broadus recalled, "he worked real hard." The coach gave him more than shoes: "I gave him the basic fundamentals. Boxin' is slippin' an' slidin' an' blocking those punches. An', of course, conditioning. It's 90 percent conditioning." Even more, Doc taught character. "Somebody, somewhere down the line, gotta steer a guy like George, an' say, 'What you gonna do, gonna go this way, or revert back to where you come from?'" Motivated by a desire to make his mother proud of him, Foreman absorbed the lessons and began to devote himself to training.[16]

On January 26, 1967, shortly after his eighteenth birthday, the young unknown from Houston won his first amateur fight in the Camp Parks Diamond Belt Tournament with a first-round knockout. As he piled up a string of wins, George's boxing future looked promising since every one of his victories came by way of knockout, a pattern that would continue throughout his amateur and future professional career. Once again, however, he nearly derailed himself. One day he beat up a fellow corpsman outside the ring and the Job Corps wanted to expel him. "I said no," recalled Doc. "And I said George, if you wanna be a bully an' throw your chances down the drain, beautiful. And George went back to work." As Foreman trained and won, though, he realized that boxing helped channel his rage because he no longer needed to prove himself. Savoring his victories, he said, "it was now clear to me that my destiny would not be grim." The Job Corps and its boxing program taught him that he was "going to be somebody. And that's all I'd ever fought for."[17]

Through his dedication and the boxing victories he amassed, Foreman soon became a "poster boy for the Job Corps." As he noted, "I'd gone from being a junior high school dropout to a man who now devoured books; from an unemployable teenager to a skilled factory worker; from thug to humanitarian. Well, not quite humanitarian, but as I dedicated myself to the 'Sweet Science,' I discovered more compassion for others." After graduation from the Job Corps in May 1967 he returned to Houston rather than accept Broadus's offer to box full-time under the management of a collection of investors similar to the Louisville Sponsoring Group that had guided Ali's career after the Olympics. In Houston he passed his high school equivalency examination easily and hoped to find a job in which he could use his newfound skills. His hopes were not realized. In the first place, his draft status was 1-A and employers were reluctant to hire someone they might soon lose to the armed forces, a situation common to all young men of that era. In the second place, the Job Corps stressed training but did not guarantee employment in the private sector or provide specific job programs sponsored by the federal government. Despite his training, Foreman was subject to the usual problem faced by young black men—discrimination and lack of opportunities. He applied for job openings but was turned down every time, which led him to conclude that racial discrimination was at work. With little to do, Foreman went through a deeply frustrating period, and his deep-seated anger at the world around him returned in force. He hooked up with his old friends and hit the streets once more, looking for marijuana, pills, or anything else they might find. As his motivation waned, he became belligerent again or, in his words, "a monster." He began picking fights for no reason, was arrested for assaulting two men, and was forced to pay a fine. Things looked bleak.[18]

Once again, however, Doc Broadus came to his rescue. Doc had remained in contact with George and his mother, so he knew what Foreman was going through. At the urging of George's distraught mother, Broadus sent him a plane ticket to Oakland, paid for out of his own pocket, and hired him to mop up, wash dishes, and help coach boxers at the Pleasanton center for $465 a month. Doc also began to train him for the 1968 Olympics. It was unclear at first whether Foreman would aim for an Olympic berth in the upcoming games or turn professional immediately. If he turned professional, his coach advised, it would take a good deal of time to earn much money in the ring because of his lack of experience. When George asked him about the gold medal, he said: "I told him it means you the best amateur heavy weight champ in the world. An' he said, 'Okay, Doc, we'll go for the gold medal.'" Even more important, according to Foreman, Doc explained that Muhammad Ali's gold medal had led to fame and fortune and was likely to do the same for another promising former gold medalist, Joe Frazier. George now had a goal: "Boxing was my best opportunity to buy a decent living for my mother." One might add that boxing—and winning—had become the center of his identity.[19]

With a gold medal at the 1968 Mexico City Olympics as his goal, Foreman trained harder than ever. He also began to listen to his trainer rather than rely almost exclusively on his formidable strength. Amateur victories began to pile up. By this time, moreover, George had given up smoking, and after beating up a friend in a drunken rage, he quit drinking too. Except for a pair of losses to Clay Hodges, the reigning national Golden Gloves heavyweight champion, Foreman continued to win, including the national Amateur Athletic Union heavyweight crown, and earned a spot on the US Olympic team. In his final test in the Olympic trials at Albuquerque, New Mexico, on September 21, 1968, George won a unanimous decision against Otis Evans and became the US heavyweight representative on the team that would compete in Mexico City. With a record of sixteen victories and four losses after only nineteen months as an amateur, the nineteen-year-old Foreman was the least experienced boxer in American Olympic history, yet one, Broadus told the *Oakland Tribune*, who could "make the world forget Louis and Clay." While that remained to be seen, his performance at the Mexico City Olympics transformed his own life profoundly.[20]

While Foreman looked forward to his moment in the sun at Mexico City, the Olympic Games of 1968 capped the most turbulent year in American sports, and certainly one of the most tumultuous periods in American history. To a large extent, however, Foreman remained, as he put it, "cocooned" in the Olympic Village. He had no knowledge of the violent events that had just transpired as the Mexican army and the Mexico City police massacred more than two hundred students, workers, and administrators, and wounded many more in an attempt to repress antigovernment demonstrations designed to use the Olympic Games to capture the attention of the world regarding the repressive nature of the Mexican government. More than other athletes, the boxers were protected from protests in general by their coach, William Henry "Pappy" Gault, and were largely oblivious to the tense atmosphere as officials worried about even greater disruptions from within the ranks of the athletes. What would black Americans do to turn the international spotlight on American racism and oppression? As tensions mounted in Mexico City, both Muhammad Ali and George Foreman played key roles in the ensuing drama.[21]

Although he remained banned from boxing and faced a five-year jail sentence, Ali's outspoken attack on white supremacy and the Vietnam War during 1967 and 1968 had inspired many young black (and some white) athletes to challenge the sports establishment and the traditional view that victories on the field redounded to the benefit of the larger black population in the United States. Black sociologist Harry Edwards, a principal initiator of that revolt, declared that Ali "was the warrior saint in the revolt of the black athlete in America." The politicization of black athletes, Edwards further noted, was a response to the "disgust and dissatisfaction with the same racist germ" that produced the "Birmingham church bombing" and the "murders of Malcolm X, Martin Luther King, and Medgar Evers." Amid the assassinations of 1968, violent antiwar demonstrations, and urban racial rebellions going back to the Harlem riot of 1964 and the Watts riot of 1965, no aspect of American culture went unquestioned. The black athlete, he argued, had a responsibility to aid in his people's struggles. By standing up and putting his body on the line for a cause, "he is for the first time reacting in a human and masculine fashion to the disparities between the heady artificial world of newspaper clippings, photographers, and screaming spectators, and the real world of degradation, humiliation and horror that confronts the overwhelming majority of Afro-Americans." In other words, the modern black athlete had to confront the vast gulf between the artificial glory of sports and the fate of most African Americans, and the ways their individual accomplishments were turned into symbols of American racial progress for a Cold War world.[22]

Created in late 1967 by Edwards, the Olympic Project for Human Rights (OPHR) fed off the anger and militancy that had been building through 1967 and 1968 among black athletes in particular and black activists in general. The OPHR's chief tactic was a boycott of the Olympic Games of 1968. The project had strong roots in the experiences of black athletes at overwhelmingly white San Jose State University in California, such as discrimination in off-campus housing, lack of black coeds to date, and officials' distaste for interracial liaisons. Edwards, along with sprinters Tommie Smith, John Carlos, and Lee Evans conceived and supported the boycott in the face of intense resistance by older black athletes such as Jesse Owens and the Olympic establishment, led by Avery Brundage, head of the International Olympic Committee (IOC), and the US Olympic Committee (USOC). Although ultimately unsuccessful, Edwards's call for a boycott roiled the world of international sport. The OPHR's demands were global in their import. The issue that first provoked Edwards was Brundage's decision to lift the ban on South African and Rhodesian participation in the 1968 games despite blatant evidence that the countries' sports programs were as racist and as exclusionary as ever. The first demand, consequently, was the reimposition of the ban, which Brundage refused. Equally important, the OPHR demanded the return of Ali's title. The group considered its removal an unjust, racist act aimed at punishing an outspoken black man. Here was proof that black athletes were tolerated only if they obeyed white officials and kept their mouths shut outside the arena. The USOC refused to do anything about Ali, claiming rightly but with a tin ear that the Olympics had nothing to do with the decisions of professional boxing's sanctioning bodies. Other demands included Brundage's resignation as head of the IOC and the hiring of more black coaches. The latter demand emerged from the conflicts between black athletes and white coaches at largely white colleges and in the professional ranks, where black athletes felt that they were merely replaceable bodies for hire, not individuals respected for their mental skill and executive leadership ability.[23]

Despite months of agitation and a successful boycott of the annual track meet of the New York Athletic Club, an exclusive organization to which Brundage belonged but one that barred blacks and Jews from membership, the Olympic boycott itself failed for a number of reasons. Under increasing pressure, the IOC finally gave in and reimposed the ban on South Africa and Rhodesia. At the same time the US Olympic Committee pledged to hire more black coaches in the future. Many black athletes were relieved because the Olympics occurred only once every four years, and if the boycott were successful, they might never get a chance to compete at the Olympic level again. Still, the boycott's impact was enormous, even though it never came off. Protestors questioned whether sport provided an equal playing field regardless of race and whether black victories on the field would convince whites to end racial oppression in American society. Despite spectacular physical achievements, the higher echelons of sport and society remained off-limits to black athletes. Equally significant, the protests, and Ali's outspokenness on matters of race, religion, and war, led many other black athletes to question whether they were merely dumb beasts and whether, given their prominence, they had a special responsibility to speak out on questions of racism, poverty, and injustice. Was the banning of Ali apolitical, athletes might ask, or, as Edwards charged, was it not true that black athletes were prized because they helped the United States win a vicarious war against the Russians, the Cold War rival for prestige in the rapidly decolonizing new nations? Were not black athletes, especially in international competition, symbols of an integrated American society that did not exist? By challenging these hallowed beliefs at a global spectacle, the protestors transformed sports from an escapist playpen into a subject of serious debate. That they raised the issue of racism in sport and society at an international event made their actions even more dangerous for the sports establishment.[24]

Given his role in sparking the athletic rebellion, Ali verbally supported the boycott movement while Foreman remained removed from the controversial protest. "Giving up a chance at the Olympics and a gold medal is a big sacrifice," Ali declared when the boycott was first announced. "But anything they do that's designed to get freedom and equality for their people, I'm with 1,000 percent." Foreman first heard of the boycott movement when Edwards and some of his supporters came to the New Mexico Olympic training site to recruit athletes to their cause. They made speeches, but because there were no big-name boxing stars, they "passed us by the way a freight train would a hobo," Foreman recalled. "Not one of us high school dropouts [on the boxing team] were ever asked to be part of what they were doing. They never asked the poor people to join." Nor did they ask female Olympic athletes, because the radicals were focused on demonstrating their defiant black manhood. Foreman later asserted that the boycott worked best for UCLA basketball star Lew Alcindor and other college athletes who were accustomed to radical issues and protest movements on their campuses. "Whether the students' anger was righteous, I don't know," Foreman recalled. "I know only that their world wasn't the one I saw." He put it succinctly: "How could I protest the Establishment when it had created the Job Corps for guys like me?" Besides, Foreman rejected the black nationalist message that only white people were prejudiced. In Houston, he claimed that black teachers, some of his relatives, and members of the black community were prejudiced when they summarily labeled him a failure.[25]

While Foreman's class resentment against the boycott's organizers alienated him from their cause, it is also true that Olympic boxing coach Pappy Gault made sure his team ignored the protests. As the first black coach for the US team, Gault was older, forty-six, a World War II veteran, and, like many of his generation, more conservative in his views. Having fought with the marines at Iwo Jima, he ran the boxing squad as a quasi-military unit. Both he and assistant Ray Rogers, also an ex-marine, were addressed as "Sarge." Six of the team's eleven members represented a branch of the armed services. Since nine of the eleven boxers were black, Gault maintained: "My fighters believe in me. They do what I say." His major goal, in fact, was to make the notoriously individual sport of boxing "into a team sport. I don't want stars or individualists," he told *Sports Illustrated*. "I believe in unity. I think this will show a new side of the US. We are never individuals when we support the US." Victory surpassed racial protest. His boxers, he bragged, were not "involved in any of this demonstration stuff. . . . We're proud to be fighting for the United States. This is our country. We're all brothers aren't we?"[26]

Once it was decided that an Olympic boycott was impractical, athletes were left on their own at Mexico City to protest the injustices they felt existed in American sport and in American society. As "The Star-Spangled Banner" played and the American flag rose in victory, the gold- and bronze-medal winners in the two-hundred-meter sprint, Tommie Smith and John Carlos, engaged in a symbolic gesture that shook the Olympic establishment and the millions of American and international fans across the globe. Supported by the white Australian silver medalist Peter Norman, the two men on the medal podium bowed their heads respectfully and raised a fist adorned with a black glove. "My raised hand stood for the power in black America," Smith later explained in a television interview with Howard Cosell. "Carlos's raised left hand stood for the unity of black America. Together they formed an arch of unity and power. The black scarf around my neck stood for black pride. The black socks with no shoes stood for black poverty in racist America. The totality of our effort was the regaining of black dignity." For many young blacks and whites this symbolic gesture, seen globally, demonstrated tremendous black pride as well as a protest against American racial oppression.[27]

Not everyone reacted the same way. Their peaceful protest was decried by some as black Nazism, un-American, hate-filled Black Power, and an inappropriate politicization of the Olympics. The two track stars received thousands of hate letters, their families were threatened, and their living quarters vandalized in San Jose. Despite the fact that their protest was nonviolent, because of their introduction of "radical racial politics" into the officially apolitical Olympics, and their presumed disrespect for the American flag, the two young track stars were expelled from the games by the US Olympic Committee under the direct orders of Avery Brundage. Their careers never recovered.[28]

Under Pappy Gault's leadership the American boxing team remained apart from the controversy sparked by Smith and Carlos's raised fists. More immediately, the boxers were focused on winning medals in their events rather than what other Olympic contestants were doing. Foreman, for instance, had a rough set of matches in front of him, with what turned out to be his toughest test in his first elimination bout. His opponent was Lucjan Trela, a Polish left-hander who stood only five foot seven. Unlike most of George's matches, this bout went to a decision, largely because he had difficulty punching down at his shorter foe. The rest of his bouts went much more easily, and a lot more quickly. He knocked out the Romanian Ion Alexe, another Soviet bloc fighter, as well as Italy's Giorgio Bambini. After these victories the only one standing in the way of a gold medal was a Lithuanian representing the Soviet Union, the tough and experienced twenty-nine-year-old veteran Ionas Chepulis.[29]

With only his final match left, Foreman learned of the expulsion of Smith and Carlos and witnessed Carlos's shattered face as he was leaving the Olympic Village. Despite his distance from the boycott movement, the punishment of the two sprinters seemed unjust. He felt like "not fighting anymore," and he pondered whether to protest the actions of Olympic officials by forfeiting his gold-medal bout and going home. At this crucial juncture, however, someone—perhaps Doc Broadus—informed him that John Carlos was counting on the young American heavyweight to win a gold medal. The ruse worked. Foreman decided to go through with the bout and in spectacular fashion. Aware that Cold War loyalties often influenced the judges' decisions, he wanted to knock out the Lithuanian fighter to get the victory. George started out jabbing cautiously in the first round. After numerous left jabs, he threw a straight left that bloodied Chepulis's nose, all within the first minute of the fight. Unleashing the power that would characterize his entire career, Foreman staggered his opponent with a right cross, and a second blow buckled his knees. Ahead on points, he switched to a body attack in the second round. After a hard body shot again buckled Chepulis's knees, the referee gave "the Russian," as the American press referred to him, a standing eight count. One more powerful right and the referee stopped the bout, declaring George a winner by TKO in the second round. In storybook fashion, the desperately poor young black man from the Houston ghetto and the Great Society's Job Corps had pounded out a gold-medal victory in the heavyweight division, and over a Russian to boot. Foreman's future looked bright. His victory on that October 26, 1968, transformed him into a Cold War hero.[30]

If Foreman's patriotic victory was not enough, what he did next elevated him to iconic stature in the minds of many Americans. Elated by his triumph, he whipped out a small American flag from a pocket of his robe, kissed it, and waved it proudly around the ring. "Then it was," wrote George Girsch in *The Ring*, that "George Foreman won his way into the hearts of his countrymen." At the medal ceremony, moreover, he again waved a miniature American flag, a patriotic gesture that thrilled Americans in the stadium and millions back home watching on television. He described his gesture this way: "It was love of country, but I meant it in a way that was much bigger than ordinary patriotism. It was about identity. An American—that's who I was. I was waving the flag as much for myself as for my country. I was letting everyone know who I was at the same time saying I was proud to be an American."[31]

When asked by reporters why he had kissed the American flag before the final bell as well, he replied, "'Cause it's my flag." Foreman's symbolic gesture was not just seen in the Arena México, where the Olympic boxing contests took place, it was broadcast live and rebroadcast via delay on television stations around the globe. To everyone watching in the United States and across the world, here was a patriotic black man standing up for his flag and his country against enemies without—the Russians—and enemies within: black radicals at a perilous moment in the nation's history. George's actions created a sensation, providing a moment of pride and patriotism in the United States for millions of white sports fans dismayed by protests against the Olympics staged by black athletes as well as by the mass demonstrations against the Vietnam War that often involved the desecration of the American flag. Looking back from the vantage of 1971, *The Ring* offered a sense of the impact that George's gesture had in a cover story on his nascent professional career. Referring to his flag waving, the *Ring* declared, "This mark of confidence in the United States, in its forces in Viet Nam, in the American way of life, made a deep impression on interested Americans, and others." As the magazine asserted, "The benefits of this maneuver have stuck to Foreman, and will continue to stick to him as long as he is alive." In an age when a visible and vocal minority among black and white athletes threatened to follow Ali's example and refuse to be patriotic role models, Foreman stood out as an unalloyed black American hero. Like Jesse Owens and Joe Louis in the past, he would say little but defend American democracy with his deeds in the arena.[32]

Foreman's patriotic gesture did not go unheeded by Ali. Barred from attending the Olympics in person because his passport had been confiscated, the gold medalist at the 1960 Rome Olympics closely followed the televised events taking place in Mexico City. He was not impressed. "Look at that fool jumpin' around. Who's he tryin' to bullshit?" Ali demanded. "He can punch some. Might make some money with him." Many of Ali's politically aware fans were equally skeptical. They immediately interpreted Foreman's flag waving as a calculated response to the protests mounted on the victory stand by sprinters Tommie Smith and John Carlos. Whatever his motives then, Foreman asserted in recent interviews with sports columnist Dave Zirin that he would wave three flags today in honor of the Job Corps and all the program did for him. It was no accident that during the Olympics—and his early days as a professional—he proudly wore "George Foreman, The Fighting Corpsman" on the back of his robe.[33]

Despite Ali's derision, Foreman's patriotic display made him a prominent figure in one of the most contentious presidential contests in American history, fast reaching a climax as the Olympics came to a close. As the campaign reached its last weeks, both political parties solicited the support of a gold-medal winner whose exemplary victory and patriotism might sway voters to their cause. The Richard Nixon campaign valued Foreman for his simple patriotism in contrast to those vocal, un-American dissenters like Smith, Carlos, and Ali who disrespected the American flag or refused to defend it while the nation was at war. However, Foreman felt that Nixon's speech the day after he waved the flag misinterpreted his motives. At a rally at Madison Square Garden, the Republican presidential candidate mentioned "that young man at the Olympics who made us all so proud. He wasn't afraid to show his patriotism," just like the voters that Nixon hoped to attract. In fact, though, Nixon's representatives had been angling for Foreman's support as soon as he won the heavyweight spot. They wanted to align Nixon with a symbol of success. Even before the boxing team left for Mexico, a Nixon campaign representative told him: "You're a winner and we think we've got us a winner, too. We'd like you to come out to some of our events and campaign for Nixon."[34]

While the attention from the Republicans was flattering, Foreman decided instead to support the Democratic Party candidate, Lyndon Baines Johnson's vice president, Hubert Humphrey, who had helped start the Job Corps and was one of its most committed supporters. Foreman believed that if elected, Humphrey would continue this key program in the War on Poverty, whereas Nixon would eliminate it. As a result, immediately after returning from Mexico City, George took to the stump for Humphrey, along with a host of liberal sport and entertainment celebrities. It was in this context that Foreman appeared in *Jet* waving a small American flag as he campaigned for Humphrey. Over and over Humphrey praised Foreman as a sterling example of the Job Corps. In Peoria, Illinois, where the two campaigned together, for example, Humphrey declared, "I couldn't help but think of Mr. Nixon last Sunday as he condemned the Job Corps, which gave a chance to 200,000 kids that never had a chance." On that day, continued Humphrey, "a great American [Foreman] accepted the gold medal for you and for me and for his family and for the glory of this republic." Humphrey praised Foreman for acknowledging, "I got my chance in the Job Corps." Wearing his gold medal and waving the flag, George campaigned not for patriotism in the abstract but for a political party and a nation that had provided opportunities for poor young men like him. He was not just a flag waver, he was "George Foreman, The Fighting Corpsman," defending a key program of the Great Society. At that moment he represented breadwinner liberalism in all its glory against both conservative attempts to eliminate such programs and black nationalists who doubted that white America could do right for its black citizens.[35]

Soon after the election, the Fighting Corpsman received an invitation to the White House to meet President Johnson. Foreman took the occasion to deliver a plaque to the president "in appreciation for fathering the Job Corps Program which gave young Americans like me hope, dignity, and self-respect." In exchange, at the end of 1968, Foreman traveled to the headquarters of the Office of Economic Opportunity in Washington, DC, "to receive the Job Corps award of achievement."[36]

The significance of his actions and the controversy they generated did not begin to sink in until after Foreman returned to Houston to visit his family and read the thousands of letters of praise and condemnation that greeted him. Despite his support for the Great Society's Job Corps, which he would continually and actively defend, most white and black Americans saw him as a true patriot, a living rebuke to the antiwar movement and Black Power dissidents who burned and desecrated the American flag in a time of war. To a degree, his own actions set him up for this more conservative role, whether he wanted it or not. When he returned to California, for example, he gave a plaque, similar to the one he gave LBJ, to conservative Republican governor Ronald Reagan, who then declared, "[George] is proof that the American Dream is just as real as it was 192 years ago."[37]

Despite his defense of the Job Corps, conservative voices praised the black gold-medal winner for his American patriotism above all else. Delighted by Foreman's victory over the Russian and his patriotic gesture on national and international television, for example, embattled IOC president Avery Brundage underlined this simple conservative message when he met with Foreman and the US boxing team immediately after his victory "to erase the bad impression left by the Track and Field athletes," specifically Smith and Carlos. *Sports Illustrated* hailed Foreman's symbolism as "a fitting tribute to a surprising US Olympic team." Meanwhile, the *Chicago Tribune*, a bastion of American national pride, named the 1968 Olympic Games the sports story of the year without mentioning Smith or Carlos, but praising "Foreman's singing of the Star Spangled Banner and his waving the American flag." To top it off, the *Tribune* paired the story with a picture of his patriotic gesture.[38]

In fact, over the next several years—indeed, for the rest of his life—newspaper and magazine stories about Foreman in and out of the sporting press usually included a picture of him with the flag, not to mention the obligatory praise of his patriotic gesture. To publicize his first bout at Madison Square Garden in June 1969, for example, he was shown giving out flags on Flag Day to passersby in front of the arena, and in a cover story on his professional progress, *The Ring* published two photos, the top one with George and the flag at the Olympics. As sportswriter Wells Twombly declared, the act of waving the flag made him "a folk hero to the silent majority." As a result, George Foreman and the American flag were one in the hearts of many Americans, evidenced by the parade held in his honor in Oakland, California, when he returned to the Job Corps Center in Pleasanton, and by the two awards he received from the Freedom Foundation. Moreover, Vince Lombardi, the patriotic coach of the Green Bay Packers, publically called Foreman a good American and told him how proud he had made him at the Olympics.[39]

While the nascent "silent majority," many of them white and members of the Veterans of Foreign Wars and the American Legion, may have been delighted by George's patriotism, back in Houston it was clear that younger black people viewed his symbolic gesture with jaundiced eyes. For them, the symbolic protests of Smith and Carlos more accurately expressed how they felt. Proud of his accomplishment, Foreman wore his gold medal all around the Fifth Ward so that his friends and neighbors could share in his victory. Too many people, he soon discovered, did not see his actions as a victory, especially in the many homes where posters of Smith and Carlos with clenched fists in the air decorated the walls. As he noted, "It was pretty clear I didn't fit in." When he spoke at schools and community events, he ran into Black Panthers, whose faces said that "I'd betrayed the cause." Similarly, he met the Reverend Ray Martin, who put on amateur boxing bouts in the Bottom, at a local store that sold dashikis, fast becoming a fashion symbol of black pride in one's African roots. When Reverend Martin introduced the Olympic champion to the saleswoman, however, she "made some insulting remarks to him about the flag incident, more or less expressing the thinking of the black community at that time." Even old buddies questioned his flag waving. Wearing his medal, Foreman ran into an old friend who asked with a pained expression, "Man . . . how could you lift up the flag that way when the brothers were doing their thing?" As the words sank in, Foreman felt that his friend was saying what everyone thought: "It hit me like a hammer. It was true; I really didn't belong."[40]

"What a homecoming," Foreman remembered. "Imagine—the Olympic heavyweight Champion, an outcast." In an era of black pride and black nationalism some derided him and Doc Broadus as Uncle Toms. What stood out increasingly was that Foreman was a patriot who supported the white establishment over and against the antiestablishment figures of Ali, Smith, and Carlos. Rejection by the black community stuck with the sensitive Foreman for a long time. He had expected praise for his accomplishments, but there were no posters of Foreman on the walls of dormitory rooms and student apartments, only Smith and Carlos in their gloved-fist pose on the podium. In Oakland, California, the original home of the Black Panthers, not far from his Pleasanton base, posters of Smith and Carlos were displayed everywhere. The conflict between the two iconic gestures stood as a symbolic dividing point of the late 1960s and early 1970s. That such a great divide existed among blacks—and many young whites—struck even moderate Republican and civil rights champion Jackie Robinson. Watching the Olympics on television, Robinson viewed the nonviolent symbolic protest by Smith and Carlos as "the greatest demonstration of personal conviction and pride that I've really seen." But then, "you see a guy running around the ring waving a flag and you get sick inside. You know that's just what happened to me—I go[t] sick when I saw Foreman run out waving a flag."[41]

Despite the controversy, the Olympics propelled Foreman toward a professional boxing career and the heavyweight title, just as it did for Ali. At first, though, he was unsure what to do after his Olympic quest was over and the heated presidential election finally ended. In the 1960s a gold medal did not automatically guarantee millions of dollars in endorsements and promotions. He thought of going to junior college in Oakland on a football scholarship, but the lucrative boxing offers that he received after Mexico City were too tempting to ignore. Foreman might have been unsure about his future, but only boxing could provide the type of money he needed to live on, buy his mother a home in a better neighborhood, and help support his family. At Doc Broadus's invitation, Foreman returned to the Job Corps Center at Pleasanton, where he taught boxing. Broadus had signed him to a management contract for 50 percent of his professional boxing earnings, higher than the usual 30 to 40 percent, but in what would mark a temporary break between the two men, Foreman rejected the contract. He began hunting for a different manager, and with the counsel of Office of Economic Opportunity chief Sargent Shriver, a better deal. In 1969, when newly elected president Richard Nixon made good on his campaign pledge to cut back the Job Corps as a waste of federal funds, the Pleasanton site was eliminated, and the Job Corps' most conspicuous success story was out of a job. He decided to turn his full attention to professional boxing.[42]

Foreman eventually signed with Dick Sadler, Doc Broadus's good friend and the veteran manager of Archie Moore and Sonny Liston, during the last stages of his career. He moved into Sadler's house in Hayward, California, and started training at a local boys' club. Doc lived next door, and Moore, a former Sadler fighter and a churchgoing teetotaler, visited to offer advice based on his vast ring experience. Despite winning a gold medal at the Olympics, Foreman had fewer amateur bouts than any other Olympic heavyweight champion, and as a result he lacked basic ring skills. Given Foreman's relative inexperience, Sadler had a lot of work to do. "George was a diamond in the rough," Sadler declared, "and I do mean rough. He was what he was, crude, strong, with less amateur experience than anybody who had ever won the gold medal." Under Sadler's tutelage, Foreman made his professional debut at Madison Square

Garden on June 23, 1969, with a third-round knockout of Don Waldheim, but boxing experts continued to doubt his ability. In 1970, after Foreman outpointed Gregorio Peralta, a ranked heavyweight, *The Ring* noted Foreman's possibility as a title contender but urged that he be brought along slowly. But then, he easily whipped tough George Chuvalo, and "within six months, Foreman came charging out of virtually nowhere, into the list of the favored."[43]

As the manager of both Archie Moore and Sonny Liston, Sadler knew how to plan a professional career. He picked opponents carefully, varying them by size, weight, and style so Foreman could learn to adapt to all contingencies. Fighting about once a month against well-calibrated opponents, he began to learn the intricacies of the sport, gradually climbing the ranks with an awesome display of brute power. Sadler also kept him off television. Before he fought for the title in 1973, Foreman had only two televised fights, both of which ended very quickly. One reason for his lack of television exposure, according to *San Francisco Examiner* sports reporter Eddie Muller, was that George "was bad television." Foreman, Muller noted, was the most uninteresting contender around: "He was still learning. He looked clumsy. He'd just wade in there and dispatch the guy. He also made it look too easy." Fans refused to pay to see fights that ended in one or two rounds. "People want to see a struggle!" Foreman was just too strong. "He could just touch your shoulder with his glove, and you'd be off balance, ready for the right cross that'd end the fight," said Muller. Away from TV he could hone skills that needed work. When he fought Gregorio Peralta the first time at Madison Square Garden, he ran out of energy in the seventh round and nearly lost the fight. He also took heavy punches from routine fighters like Ron Stander and Terry Daniels. By his return match with Peralta in May 1971, however, Foreman had improved his defensive skills a good deal, he had developed greater stamina, and he had learned to cut off the ring on his opponent. As a result, he knocked out Peralta in the tenth round.[44]

Working with Sadler, Foreman also absorbed other boxing lessons. As he trained alongside Liston, who was in the midst of a comeback, the two boxers become close, and the experience led Foreman to identify with the former heavyweight champion. Liston was quiet and introspective while presenting a menacing face to a world that often scorned and disappointed him. As someone who felt equally sensitive to public rejection, Foreman took heed, and as his career progressed, he often appeared in public as an angry, sullen young man. The danger was that, just like Liston, he would be perceived as a thug. He also learned a variety of lessons from other highly competitive black athletes. When he met basketball stars Walt Frazier and his idol, football legend Jim Brown, both men dismissed him as a nonentity. As the heavyweight champion, he took them as his models, giving nothing away to the public, often treating fans as a bothersome nuisance. The new-fledged professional also learned about the sexual folklore of boxing when Joe Louis advised him to abstain from sex for a month before a bout because he believed intercourse weakened a fighter. This fit perfectly with Sadler's gospel: women were only after money and would disturb a boxer's concentration. As a result, he became an isolate; as Foreman put it, "boxing was my wife." Isolation, though, bred anger, which fueled his ferocious aggression in the ring. When Foreman married Adrienne Calhoun in December 1971, Sadler was irate. It turns out his manager had a point. The young boxer's marital troubles would soon disturb his concentration, but they kept his anger fully stoked.[45]

With a brutal display of power, Foreman worked his way into contention for the heavyweight title during the early 1970s. By the time he fought champion "Smokin'" Joe Frazier on January 22, 1973, in Kingston, Jamaica, he had ground through thirty-two victories in twenty-nine months and sixteen different cities. As boxing reporter Vic Ziegel put it, this was "a whirlwind pace by current boxing standards." Frazier, who replaced Ali at the top of the heavyweight ranks after the latter's conviction, and then beat him when he reentered boxing, thought the fight would be relatively easy. According to legendary trainer Eddie Futch, who went down to Kingston to supervise the last stages of Frazier's training, what he found was a party atmosphere with no one taking Foreman seriously. After all, Frazier thought, he was the powerful fighter who had ruined Ali's comeback from exile two years earlier. Despite having won thirty-seven straight bouts, thirty-four by KO, in Frazier's opinion George had fought "mostly tomato cans," with only Gregorio Peralta and the veteran George Chuvalo as quality opponents. Frazier, in contrast, had not only beaten the legendary Ali; he had also bested Oscar Bonavena, Eddie Machen, Jimmy Ellis, and Doug Jones. Rated an underdog with 3-to-1 odds against him, Foreman shocked the boxing world by knocking down Frazier six times in two rounds and pulling off what *The Ring* called "an all-time upset." Frazier planned to come out early, force the fight, wear down Foreman, and then knock him out. Unfortunately for Frazier, the much bigger Foreman (six foot three versus Frazier's five eleven and a half) "didn't follow the script." Foreman used his big guns, especially his left hooks, body shots, and a couple of uppercuts, to smash through Frazier's much-vaunted "perpetual motion machine." Frazier expected to take Foreman's best and then grind him down, as he did whenever he fought bigger men. Fighting "a near perfect battle," however, the challenger used his height and five-inch reach advantage to push the champ back, take charge, and hit Frazier with powerful lefts and rights as the determined champion kept coming forward.[46]

According to referee Arthur Mercante, "Foreman won the world championship with sheer power," especially the punch that produced the second knockdown in round one, an underhand right to the head. After five knockdowns through the second round, the champ "was a pathetic figure." He walked, almost stumbled, into a right that "lifted him off the floor and deposited him, leg bent grotesquely, like a bag of flour." After another knockdown, Mercante finally stopped the fight at 1:35 into the second round. "Frazier down six times? Impossible!" exclaimed *Ring*. As Mercante put it, "Joe Frazier, supposedly invincible, had turned out to be human, after all." According to *The Ring*, the win was no fluke: "George Foreman is one of the good ones. He will be around a long time."[47]

As the newly crowned heavyweight champion, Foreman inherited the goodwill he had built up from the 1968 Olympics. The public viewed him favorably as the Fighting Corpsman who had waved the flag in Mexico City and expressed his gratitude for all that his country had done for him. In fact, Foreman won the heavyweight title on the same day that ex-president Johnson died. Harold Sims, former chief of the Office of Economic Opportunity, noted the connection between the two events. "George Foreman would not have the heavyweight championship if Lyndon Johnson had not been President," Sims declared. After all, Foreman was "discovered in a vehicle created by Lyndon Johnson, the Job Corps Center, which was part of the OEO. The Job Corps financed his training, supplied him a coach, and got him involved in Olympic competition." Foreman's victory, said Sims, was "the finest statement of what Lyndon Johnson believed the Great Society was all about."[48]

For most Americans, Foreman remained the patriotic flag waver, and as such he found himself cast in an older mode of black heavyweights that predated Ali. The stark symbolic differences that separated the two men remained rooted in the nation's political divisions that lingered into the early 1970s. As George Girsch put it in *The Ring*'s biography of the new champ, "A fellow who waves a little American flag after winning the Olympic heavyweight Gold Medal can't be all bad." Despite his awesome power, Girsch saw Foreman as a "gentle giant" who "believes in God and the United States of America, not to mention Mom's apple pie." An earlier *Ring* profile noted that there would be "no Black Power gestures for George." Similarly, Shirley Norman noted, his devastating power was moderated by his out-of-the ring demeanor. In her view, Foreman was "a handsome, hulking, yet humble man whose feelings about his life and his title differ greatly from those of his predecessors." He "displays none of the arrogance of Ali." Rather, "He is, instead, in the cast of a

Joe Louis . . . soft-spoken . . . unassuming . . . and deeply grateful for the honor of being heavyweight champion of the world." In sum, Foreman was a true patriot who humbly appreciated what the United States of America had done for him. As he declared, "There's no place else in the world . . . where a poor black man like me can get to be heavyweight champion of the world." Not only was Foreman an American success story à la Horatio Alger, he was also a role model for kids—not an antihero like Ali but a genuine American paragon: "I feel that if I can overcome what I did . . . anybody else can."[49]

So much did Foreman's modesty, patriotism, and quiet retreat from the limelight make him seem a throwback to the pre-Ali Joe Louis era that Tim Tyler called him "the Great White Hope" in a *Sport* magazine special report on the new champion. According to Tyler, "In boxing, the search for a Great White Hope is constant—as much for financial reasons as racial. Now boxing has its man, even if he happens to be black." Other sportswriters agreed. Wells Twombly, for instance, noted that "there are occasions when George Foreman seems to be a man from another age." As Tyler noted, ever since the Mexico City Olympics at which he "waved an American flag, while other athletes were waving clenched fists, a lot of people have been calling George Foreman a 'credit to his country,'" a phrase "hauntingly redolent of the condescending 'credit to his race' that was bestowed on [Joe] Louis during the nineteen thirties." Very few called Ali that, noted Tyler, "except maybe some bearded radicals."[50]

According to Tyler, Foreman was most popular among middle-aged whites who hungered for an end to racial disruptions and antiwar turmoil. At an all-white Lions Club meeting in Vacaville, California, for example, a representative for California governor Ronald Reagan thanked the new champion for "raising sportsmanship to its highest ideals." Urging youngsters to stay in school, Foreman received a plaque for being "a great example for the young people of America." One guest in particular praised Foreman's character: "[He] has a clean mind. He doesn't wanna hurt anyone. He's a credit to his country." His rags-to-riches story was compelling, but it also appealed mainly to whites because it validated a social system that had been thrown in doubt during the preceding years. When he addressed black high school students in Berkeley, California, one girl asked him what he would do for black people now that he was champion. Foreman responded that he would eat well. Realizing that "he might be irrelevant" and "old-fashioned," he added that he would help black people by doing what he does best—boxing—and by being "the best person I could be." As a result of his remarks, he suffered by comparison to the committed, outspoken athlete Ali. Another student rated Foreman OK, but said, "[I] wished they'd get Ali here. He's a really good fighter."[51]

In his rise to the heavyweight crown, George Foreman's crushing power convinced many fans and boxing observers that he was invincible, a champion who would reign for as long as he liked. At the same time, Foreman's devastating knockout upset of Smokin' Joe Frazier served notice that the heavyweight boxing picture had changed dramatically in the early 1970s. Ali's exile from boxing for three and a half years made it possible for a new generation of fighters like Frazier, Foreman, Ken Norton, Jimmy Young, Earnie Shavers, Ron Lyle and Jerry Quarry to become credible contenders for the title. Yet once he returned to boxing and his conviction was overturned by the Supreme Court, Ali's name, his glamour, and his controversial beliefs overshadowed everyone in the fight game. To be considered the true champion, one had to beat "the People's Champion." For the Berkeley high school student, as for millions of fans, Ali was the real champion whose title had been stolen from him unjustly. In their eyes, Foreman—like Frazier before him—was merely an usurper, a tool of the white establishment. For many white fans, though, far more than Frazier even, a patriotic Foreman represented an ideal vision of an America which was open to all. Despite several setbacks, Ali was determined to reclaim "his" crown. George Foreman, the reigning heavyweight champion, was equally determined that his title was no fluke. Fists and flags would meet again on the road to Kinshasa.

3

THE ROADS TO KINSHASA

Under an aluminum canopy in an 80,000 seat soccer stadium, the gladiators will serve as the most expensive public relations men in the history of world government.

***NEW YORK TIMES*, 27 OCTOBER 1974**

Just days before George Foreman defended his title against Ken Norton in Caracas in March 1974, promoter Hank Schwartz surprised the boxing world with the announcement that Foreman's next defense would take place in Zaire, the former Belgian Congo, with a record $5 million prize for each combatant. His opponent would be the former champion Muhammad Ali, in what *Amsterdam News* reporter and columnist Elombe Brath called "the most historic meeting of two internationally renowned men in the heart of Africa since Henry M. Stanley uttered those still famous words, 'Dr. Livingstone, I presume.'" While fans of the sport had grown accustomed to championship bouts being staged in different parts of the world, few could understand why such a global spectacle would occur in a country unknown to the vast majority of Americans and on a continent so far away that for Americans to view the closed-circuit television broadcast in prime time, the bout had to be scheduled for the early-morning hours of the next day. The choice of Zaire seemed downright bizarre. Creating a global spectacle in Zaire would require the efforts of many people, some of whom were new to the sport, as well as new technologies that facilitated the portability of information and people, and new international political realities. First, however, Muhammad Ali had to return from exile.[1]

Ali's road to Kinshasa proved long and tortuous. While George Foreman's rapid ascent to the heavyweight title was certainly impressive, it was overshadowed by the return of Muhammad Ali from three and a half years of exile. His expressed desire to resume his boxing career because he needed money to pay his legal bills and support his family earned the censure of Elijah Muhammad, who suspended him from the Nation of Islam for a year. Ali had become a more sympathetic public figure as public opinion shifted against the Vietnam War, and his suspension from the black nationalist religious group made him even more acceptable to white fans. In the face of Richard Nixon's election and a powerful white backlash against black demands and government programs meant to address them, mainstream African American leaders and more moderate blacks began to reevaluate Ali as an example of enduring black strength and defiance toward American racism. His return to the ring was a sign that the public was in the process of reinterpreting his role in American culture. In addition, whereas he had been barred from boxing by every state commission, by 1970 those legal obstacles began to give way. Once more he stood as a major presence on the boxing scene.[2]

Ali's reappearance took on the quality of a second coming. As the Vietnam War dragged on, the defiant former champion framed his matches as highly symbolic battles against his political, religious, and racial foes. His first fight on October 26, 1970, against Jerry Quarry was greeted as the resurrection of a black folk hero who defied an oppressive government and American racism on behalf of all African Americans. Even before the Supreme Court ruled in his favor in his appeal in 1971, black politicians in Atlanta, where the fight would be held, mobilized their formidable power to pressure the city's Jewish mayor into breaking the ban on his fights and sanction the Quarry match. "This is goin' to be the biggest night in ring history," Ali declared. "Every eye in the world's gonna be on me to see if the government beat me." The bout became a battle between a white hope and a symbol of black pride. *Jet* saw it as a major civil rights victory, as it occurred in Georgia, where the KKK president lived, Lester Maddox was governor, Martin Luther King was buried, and Ali was "resurrected." Equated with King and Christ, Ali had become a monumental hero whose every fight carried political, racial, and religious import for his many black and white fans at home and across the globe.[3]

As fans filed into the arena, the event was transformed into a celebration of Ali's resurrection as well as a victory celebration by the black community, especially the Atlanta black political elite that staged the bout in the face of Governor Maddox's fierce opposition. As a sign of Ali's importance to the black community, the bout was attended by the black sporting, political, and entertainment elites, many of whom were led by Jesse Jackson in throwing up Black Power clenched-fist salutes before the match even began. Among the celebrities were entertainers Bill Cosby, Sidney Poitier, Diana Ross, the Supremes (Mary Wilson, Cindy Birdsong, and Jean Terrell), and Curtis Mayfield; Motown head Berry Gordy and comedian Stepin Fetchit; baseball great Hank Aaron; and boxers Ike Williams, José Torres, Jimmy Ellis, and Henry Armstrong. Black politicians were also prominent given Ali's role as a political symbol of black independence, as well as defiance against federal government suppression of black militants. In the crowd were SCLC's president Ralph Abernathy, Operation Breadbasket's Jesse Jackson, Georgia state representative Julian Bond, local alderman Q. V. Williamson, vice mayor Maynard Jackson, congressional representative Adam Clayton Powell, the Urban League's Whitney Young, Atlanta congressional candidate Andrew Young, former SNCC chairman John Lewis, and Chicago mortgage banker Dempsey Travis. In addition, the match was turned into a black happening celebration by a flamboyant array of black hustlers, pimps, players, and their ladies.[4]

The predominantly black crowd came to share in Ali's victory over America's racist justice system. As *Jet*'s Ronald Kisner put it, fans gaped as Ali "pranced to the center of the ring and simultaneously looked Jerry Quarry, the United States Army, other American cities, and Georgia Governor Lester Maddox squarely in their faces." Governor Maddox, "a historic impediment to Black liberation movements in the South," tried but failed to cancel the match, calling for "a Day of Mourning" and summoning "patriotic" Georgians to boycott the event. On the evening news the governor declared, "I don't see how this fight, with a man who disgraced this country's uniform by refusing to be drafted, could be held in this city—or any other city in this country." As a sign of his defeat, the governor was the sole prominent local politician absent from the fight. Atlanta's mayor Sam Massell, who had sanctioned the bout, had a prominent seat. Even the chief of police was there.[5]

As for the fight, Kisner noted that the audience watched "a man who may possibly be the greatest fighter to don a pair of gloves," slice up Quarry for a bloody third-round TKO. Apparently, Ali had defied Father Time and was as good as ever. "But," Kisner concluded, "viewers were also witness to an important victory for Atlanta and US blacks." That bomb threats were called into Ali's suburban Philadelphia home where his wife and three daughters waited out the match underscored the fact that violent white opposition remained a constant for Ali and the black community; their struggles were intertwined. As Ali declared, they were there to celebrate "one nigger the white man didn't get." In recognition of his symbolic importance, after his victory Coretta Scott King and SCLC president Ralph Abernathy awarded him the Martin Luther King Memorial Award "for his contributions to human dignity." Mrs. King proclaimed him "a champion of justice and peace and unity," while Abernathy called him "a living example of soul power, the March on Washington in two fists."[6]

The battle of the John Henry–like Ali versus boxing's white establishment continued apace six weeks later when the deposed champion stepped into the ring against Argentine contender Oscar Bonavena at Madison Square Garden. Ali's right to fight in Atlanta came about because of the lack of a Georgia state boxing commission and the power of black politicians in the city. Everywhere else, however, the right to a boxing license depended on state commissions, including the most important one, the New York State Athletic Commission. The latter was the first state commission to withdraw Ali's boxing license in 1967 immediately after he refused to be drafted into the armed forces. New York's action established the precedent for other state commissions. However, the right to fight against Bonavena in New York was made possible as a result of a successful yearlong suit by the NAACP Legal Defense Fund against the state commission, charging that, in denying him a license to box in the state despite granting licenses to more than ninety convicted felons (including Sonny Liston and Rocky Graziano), it had denied Ali his Fourteenth Amendment rights on political grounds. Veterans' groups protested the fight's being held on December 7, a date that lived in infamy for the Japanese surprise attack on Pearl Harbor in 1941, but the fight over the right to a boxing license in New York was over. The match itself, however, proved dull. Ali's jab lacked power, his legs deserted him, and it took a dramatic fifteenth-round KO to seal a victory. Nevertheless, historian Michael Ezra notes, Ali's victory "endeared him to the public, because it embodied the same kind of resolve, endurance, and determination that had fueled him throughout his exile."[7]

Almost four years after his banishment from boxing, Ali faced champion Joe Frazier in "the Fight of the Century" at Madison Square Garden in March 1971. For the first time two undefeated heavyweight champions fought each other for the right to be the true champion. A gold medalist at the 1964 Tokyo Olympic Games, Smokin' Joe won the heavyweight crown against Jimmy Ellis on February 16, 1970, and now stood as the major obstacle to Ali's recapturing "his" title. As a Supreme Court ruling on Ali's draft case was imminent, the fight reached deeply symbolic levels. While the Vietnam War and racial unrest continued to divide American society, the bout pitted a black nationalist antiwar hero against a pro-war proponent of law and order. The lingering resentments over race and the war transformed Frazier into a white man's hero. "What kind of man is this," asked Frazier, who enjoyed a draft deferment for being the sole financial support for his family, "who doesn't want to fight for his country? If he was in Russia, or someplace else, they'd put him up against the wall. He walks around like he's one kind of a big hero, but he's just a phony, a disgrace." A proud champion who had fled the segregated South Carolina Sea Islands for Philadelphia, Frazier resented Ali's charge that he was an Uncle Tom, and ugly besides, and he retaliated by always referring to Ali as "Clay." This went over well with many whites who were tired of Ali's black nationalist rants and his antiwar stance, and wanted him beaten—by whoever was Ali's opponent. As a more traditional masculine champion, sick of fighting in Clay's shadow, Frazier vowed to "do his talking in the ring" and shut Clay's mouth forever. As a resident of suburban Philadelphia, moreover, Frazier endorsed hard-line police commissioner Frank Rizzo, the law-and-order candidate for mayor. Many blacks "might even get mad and call me a 'Tom,' but I think Rizzo would make a good mayor."[8]

Conversely, many fans saw Ali as the first free black champion up against "the house nigger of the white chauvinist pigs." For black sports commentator Bryant Gumbel, Ali symbolized 1960s racial and political rebelliousness versus a more complacent black man. If Ali lost, "it was as if everything I believed in was wrong." To young antiestablishment blacks, "[Ali] was a heroic figure, plain and simple . . . the very symbol of black pride, parading black feelings about black heritage, speaking out against racial injustice." Frazier, however, "was more like your parents were. He just kind of went along. He did his job." No fan of the old order, "he didn't fight it either." Vietnam was the litmus test. Ali "was dead set against the war"; Frazier was supported by those who backed it. Public opinion had shifted in Ali's favor as opposition to the war grew, but he still faced massive disapproval among whites, particularly white Southerners and working-class white "ethnics." If Ali no longer held the title officially, he was considered "the people's champion," the antiwar "symbol of national dissent" who defied the government and the establishment by following his conscience and giving up millions of dollars in the process.[9]

Despite a valiant effort, however, Ali lost a fifteen-round decision in the fight. After a slow start, Frazier unleashed a brutal body attack with powerful left hooks in the middle rounds, nearly knocking Ali down in the eleventh and decking him with a powerful left hook to the jaw in the fifteenth. Ali proved his mettle by getting up, but Frazier won the decision and established himself as the official champion and the man who ruined Ali's comeback. Fans, however, were divided over who won, influenced as much by their views on the war as by the action in the ring. "I got my money's worth," declared one Vietnam veteran. "I saw the Muslim get a beating just short of a KO." Further, he had come "back alive with a fungus which is driving me nuts, and this guy Clay gets $2,500,000. . . . I despise Clay for what he is." Conversely, many fans expressed sympathy for Ali's position on the war. Another veteran wished he had "his money and strong arguments to stay out of the Army myself. I am . . . not a CO. Merely a draftee who has no desire to fight in Viet Nam."[10]

Legions of fans at home and abroad were devastated by the decision. In Ali's loss, Gumbel saw the promise of the 1960s turn sour. Others were equally disappointed. Several years after he got his passport back, Ali was in Tripoli, Libya, where President Muammar Gaddafi told him of the Muslim world's great disappointment over his loss, especially in Libya, where it had been a day of mourning. In fact, Ali claimed he heard the same thing across the Islamic world. A British black nationalist declared, "Tonight the black world weeps that their king has passed away." Whites, he lamented, "had willed that the king should die. But it took the might of the most powerful, most designing judicial system in the world to bring the king down." Frazier, he charged, "was the unreckoning tool of that design." Frazier resented that characterization to his dying day, but it emboldened Ali's fans to believe that it was not Frazier's left hooks that defeated Ali but his forced exile at the hands of the government. Ali had come back too soon and just needed more time to regain his old form.[11]

As a result, Ali survived to fight on as a symbol of the 1960s, helped enormously by the Supreme Court decision on June 28, 1971, that overturned his conviction on a technicality—the Justice Department had erred in failing to give a reason for rejecting Ali's initial claim to conscientious objector status—and enabled him to pursue the title without worries of going to jail. Bent on a return match with Frazier to reclaim "his" title, however, the "people's champion" found the crown ever elusive. Bitter over Ali's depiction of him as an Uncle Tom, Frazier put Ali off, preferring easier foes like Terry Daniels, Ron Stander, and George Foreman. Foreman's upset victory put off an Ali title fight even further. Even more discouraging for Ali, on March 31, 1973, he suffered a broken jaw and lost to unheralded Ken Norton, an ex-marine and a symbol of patriotism, in the conservative navy bastion San Diego, California. Most boxing observers assumed Ali was through.[12]

For the moment, Ali's two defeats rendered a title fight with Foreman in Zaire or anywhere on the planet highly unlikely. At the same time, any future match between the two heavyweights in Kinshasa required that Foreman subdue his demons and retain his crown. With Ali out of action while his jaw healed and Frazier licking his wounds, Foreman enjoyed a brief moment in the spotlight as the undefeated heavyweight champion of the world. Despite making his ascension to the championship look brutally easy and enjoying the public acclaim he received as a patriotic defender of the American way, however, Foreman increasingly isolated himself from friends and family, still warily anticipating negative reaction to his flag-waving episode. Once he won the heavyweight title from Joe Frazier in January 1973, he lost his moral direction, found himself immersed in contract disputes and legal battles, spent his money unwisely, and saw his marriage fall apart, in good measure because of repeated infidelities. By his own admission he became the "stereotypical heavyweight champion—surly and angry." His own mother was forced to go through an answering service when she wanted to speak to him. While he retained goodwill among black and white fans because of his admirable Job Corps stint and his demonstrated patriotism, Foreman often acted surly toward boxing fans and the press, withdrew from public life, and stoked his anger toward his opponents.[13]

Despite his personal problems, Foreman retained his title with brutal ease. In his first defense in Tokyo in September 1973, he knocked out the unknown Joe Roman in the first round, delivering the final blow while Roman was on the canvas. The awesome knockout made Foreman feel omnipotent: "All I could think about was my punching power. I'm the hardest puncher I've ever seen." The bout lost money for the promoters, however. According to Keiji Koyama, a member of the promotion team: "If George had been more cooperative we would have done better. He wouldn't give the interviews we asked for. George is very strange, don't you think? He has the cleverness of a lonesome man." Indeed, beneath Foreman's outer power old insecurities reappeared. After demolishing Frazier and obliterating Roman, he bristled at criticism of his skills and the lack of quality opponents. In fact, one observer called the Roman fight "a hoax."[14]

Comparisons to Ali only added to Foreman's angst. As in his Fifth Ward days, he yearned "to be king of the jungle" and convince every last doubter. As his next victim Foreman picked Ken Norton, who had just broken Ali's jaw in a twelfth-round victory, and lost a narrow decision in the rematch with Ali on September 10, 1973. The ex-marine was in for trouble. George trained hard and gave up sex for seventy-five days. Henry Clark, one of his sparring partners, told reporters he felt sorry for Norton: "Right now George is so mad about the divorce and the way a lot of his money's been going down the drain in those crazy contract deals, he's ready to drop somebody with one punch." Plus, "George is still trying to prove that he's champion," not Ali or Frazier. If he beat Norton, there was a good chance Foreman would next face Ali, who was sitting at ringside providing color commentary. "I want to send Muhammad Ali and his mouth into retirement." Many boxing fans applauded this sentiment.[15]

Foreman was at his meanest in March 1974 against Norton at Caracas, Venezuela, in South America's first world heavyweight title fight. As the two boxers awaited the referee's instructions, Foreman "stared at Norton with the intensity of that laser beam Goldfinger aimed at James Bond." When round one began, the champion stalked his opponent, "savoring the anticipation of the conquest." Norton tried two hooks and missed. Foreman hit him in the side with a solid shot. Another Norton miss was followed by a Foreman right to the head. "Down he went. As he fell against the ropes I swung and connected again," Foreman recalled. The referee issued a warning and the crowd booed. Norton barely survived the first round. In the second round, "I became a vicious thug, swinging wildly, connecting with almost every punch," said Foreman. After a second knockdown, the referee stopped it. He had leveled his senseless foe three times and won by TKO in the second round. Foreman's powerful showing recalled his destruction of Frazier. He seemed invincible.[16]

Ali's presence at the Norton-Foreman title fight in Caracas was no accident. By the time of Foreman's second title defense, Ali had won his case against the US government and had surprised most boxing observers, who had thought he was washed up after his bitter losses to Frazier and Norton. Showing his own brand of determination, Ali beat both men in tough rematches to work his way back to number-one contender, the logical opponent for Foreman and the only fighter capable of guaranteeing a large payday. Even before Foreman demolished Norton, a showdown loomed between the formidable champion and Ali. The stage was set for one of the greatest spectacles in boxing history. Surprisingly, the Ali-Foreman fight was announced in Caracas before the Norton-Foreman contest had even begun.

As soon as the fight was announced, Ali began demeaning his future opponent in his comments from ringside. Speaking to the assembled press and fight fans around the globe, Ali picked Norton because "Foreman don't hit hard." Claiming credit for having weakened Frazier in their first fight, Ali declared that Foreman "fights like a girl. George Foreman is a tramp. He's got no class, no skill. . . . I'm the resurrection, the prophet, the savior of boxing." At the same time, Ali framed the fight in grandiose political terms. Set for September 25, 1974, the fight would take place in the Congo, where "them Africans like me better than George Foreman" because "he gallop in the Olympics carrying that flag. He crazy to go to Africa. They'll cook him in a pot." Tired of Ali stealing the spotlight with his outrageous boasting, Foreman looked down from the ring after quickly dispatching Norton and declared, "I'm going to kill you." Many at ringside feared that this was more than likely.[17]

That the fight was announced in Caracas and would take place in Africa highlights the fact that heavyweight championship boxing went global during the 1970s. Several key factors made this internationalization of the sport possible, among them the emergence of new technologies that facilitated the spread of information and images from anywhere in the world as well as making it easier for people to move about the globe. Equally important were the new political and racial realities of the freedom movement at home and anticolonialism abroad that made it possible for new individuals and newly independent countries in Africa and the Third World to play significant roles in international sport. The declaration that Zaire's president Mobutu Sese Seko would host the first-ever heavyweight title match in Africa, for instance, transformed the fight into an international cultural and political spectacle that promoter Don King called "a symbolic black happening," one in which the world would learn "that there is more to Africa than beads, bones, and beating drums." A major part of the drama of the match lay in what King initially called "From the Slave Ship to the Championship." Although the Zaire government disapproved of the slogan and forced King to abandon its use, it suggested that black Americans who had left Africa in chains were now returning to the site of massive black enslavement in triumph and pride as well as in unity with their African past, a theme that resonated with the uprising of colonial peoples across the globe.[18]

The slogan also acknowledged that the global spectacles of the 1960s and 1970s could be staged anywhere—even remote Zaire—and broadcast across the globe via satellite technology. While professional sport had long attracted fighters from various countries around the world to major American and European capitals, the globalization of boxing in the 1970s represented a new egalitarianism that was sweeping the world as more and more former colonies achieved their independence. Instead of a tightly controlled New York–dominated boxing business centered on Madison Square Garden, in the United States prizefighting witnessed the rise of new centers for the sport that reflected the move to the Sun Belt: Miami, Houston, Las Vegas, and Los Angeles staged championship bouts with great success. Similarly, nations that had never hosted major sporting events were competing with US locations for the right to stage spectacles, just as Tokyo in 1964 and Mexico City in 1968 had competed successfully for the Olympics. In an attempt to confirm their stature as newly independent states, the leaders of "developing" countries realized that sports, especially boxing, with its universal appeal, was uniquely suited to their aspirations.[19]

The careers of both Foreman and Ali coincided with the spread of highly visible championship boxing matches around the globe. For the first time national governments competed with each other and with individual groups of investors to promote international title matches. Foreman won his crown in Jamaica and defended it in Tokyo and Caracas. Still, the emergence of boxing as a global spectacle drew on Ali's worldwide popularity as an anticolonial hero. His Islamic religion, defiance of white supremacy, and opposition to the Vietnam War coincided with the revolt against colonialism across the globe. Equally important, his sympathy for black and Muslim nations and his frequent travels to visit them gave bouts in developing countries a fighting chance to succeed and earn great profits. Governments in developing countries like Zaire were eager to promote their independence, showcase their stability, and attract tourism and international investment. To do so, they were willing to use national treasuries to guarantee huge paydays for the fighters. For the first time in sports history, Ali noted in his autobiography, "Fights supported by governments, as in Zaire, Malaysia and the Philippines, attracted bids from countries such as Egypt, Saudi Arabia, Iran, Santo Domingo and Haiti; and set up promotions and matches in Ireland, Switzerland, Japan, Indonesia and Canada." Ali credited manager Herbert Muhammad for this development, although others were definitely involved. Herbert had a poem for the new strategy: "Invite Muhammad Ali to fight / And your country will share the world spotlight."[20]

Still, there was more at work than Ali's individual story. The mythology of the Rumble in the Jungle as a global event was rooted in Ali's personal search for redemption against his enemies. Yet according to historian Michael Ezra, this puts too much emphasis on Ali as "the transcendent conquering hero." Although Ali—and Foreman—was at the center of a global event, the transformation of the heavyweight title match into a global spectacle of black liberation would not have happened without President Mobutu Sese Seko of Zaire and African American promoter Don King. More important initially were Barry Burnstein and Hank Schwartz, the closed-circuit television and communications impresarios and partners in the company Video Techniques who employed King and helped bring him to prominence. Schwartz also pioneered the communications systems that helped decentralize sports promotion. While these individuals were key players, they were part of the larger process of the globalization of boxing during the 1960s and 1970s. Because of satellite technology, major sporting events could be held anywhere in the world and broadcast to more than 120 nations. The expansion of closed-circuit television, moreover, made more lucrative prizes possible for the combatants, which in turn meant that only governments could afford to sponsor these matches. Yet technology and international promotion could not have produced such a spectacular event without a global media star like Ali, a pan-African hero who embodied black nationalism at home and anticolonialism abroad versus Foreman and his media image as a patriotic defender of the American way.[21]

New York's boxing power was being decentralized to regional centers and globalized with the spread of satellite communication systems. As *The Ring*'s Nat Loubet editorialized, "We find fight promotions originating in strange places," led by promoters less interested in the fights themselves, but "as sources of closed circuit television spurred by the vast possibilities of satellite assistance." In 1957 the US government had launched its initial military satellite, and by the early 1970s commercial satellites increased the speed at which communications could circle the globe. This is where Schwartz came in. Born in Brooklyn, Hank Schwartz served in the military during World War II, where he learned groundbreaking approaches to video communications. On the GI Bill after the war, he received a bachelor's degree in electrical engineering from Brooklyn Polytechnic, with a basic grasp of how TV signals were developed and transmitted. Eventually, he figured out how to use satellite and microwave technology to revolutionize how sports fans experienced major boxing matches in real time from all over the globe. By 1971, his firm, Video Techniques, was hired to transmit political and sports events, and it began to install new microwave systems to broadcast heavyweight championship fights to network TV and select theaters in the United States and other developed nations. Promoters had long recognized that they could make more money selling the rights to television stations or closed-circuit theaters via TV rather than ticket sales at actual arenas. Initially, Schwartz worked for Madison Square Garden to broadcast boxing matches to closed-circuit locations. By the time of Ali's comeback bouts against Quarry and Bonavena, Video Techniques led the industry in TV distribution technologies and pioneered in broadcasting international sporting events, including Ali's international fights.[22]

When Ali fought Mac Foster in Tokyo on April 1, 1972, for example, Japanese TV hired the company to provide television camera positions and advise on setting up exciting camera shots within the arena. The Japanese executives ignored Schwartz's advice, failed to make use of modern production techniques, and produced a dull event, but Schwartz learned from this experience how to improve television broadcasts. If he had the ring canvases painted blue instead of white, Ali's dancing feet would no longer be washed out. "If we could make it more 'real,' for the viewer" he reasoned, "the program was more saleable." He also realized that if he packaged "together all the technical services, including well-equipped television production, a communication infrastructure able to reach the newer satellites, and proper site selection, then I could change everything." As a result, he reinvented Video Techniques' business model to include the technological and communication infrastructures necessary for producing international sporting events rather than only ancillary services for other companies.[23]

Shortly thereafter, in the fall of 1972, agents of the Jamaican government contacted Schwartz about producing the Frazier-Foreman title match in January 1973. Similar to what would transpire in Zaire two years later, the Jamaican government wanted to use a major championship fight for its own purposes, in this case to build up its tourist industry. In 1972 Jamaica advertised itself as an island paradise, but bad publicity about its high murder rate and rampant street crime undermined tourism. Schwartz traveled to Kingston to meet with government officials, inspect the arena, install a ring, and decide where to put the TV cameras and light towers. He also had to figure out how to transmit the television signal up to Jamaica's satellite JAMINTEL, which he did by climbing the tower of JAMINTEL under the suspicious eyes of Jamaican military guards. Atop the tower he discovered that a microwave antenna installed at the tower's highest point could receive microwave signals from an antenna installed at the stadium's highest point. With this knowledge he convinced Prime Minister Michael Manley that Video Techniques deserved the contract to produce the high-profile event, distribute it worldwide, collect the revenues from outside Jamaica, and provide the public relations work necessary to promote the match and boost Jamaican tourism. As part of the company's new business model, moreover, he sold some of the TV theater rights abroad while contracting with the new cable entity HBO to show the fight on home subscriber TV.[24]

Just as the company adjusted after Tokyo, so too Schwartz realized that control over global communications potentially gave him greater power over international boxing events. One thing he did was to bring viewers closer to the action in the ring by having his top cameraman circle the ring with a new shoulder-mount camera to capture the fight from a variety of angles, ones not previously possible. A second decision proved even more important. "We needed to focus our efforts on getting contracts signed with the top fighters," he recalled. "We needed to be the promoter. No more middlemen! Work directly with the fighters." It was at this crucial juncture in international boxing that Don King entered the picture as a key Schwartz ally. On his return from Jamaica in February 1973, Schwartz kept getting calls from promoter Don

Elbaum urging him to hire King if he wanted to sign the top black fighters, because they would not sign contracts with a Jewish college graduate who did not speak their language. At their first meeting Schwartz noted that King's "quick change from the scholarly discourse to the cadence of the streets of Harlem . . . or Cleveland" made him a "valuable resource."[25]

One of the most remarkable figures involved in the promotion was Don King, then new to boxing. His road to Kinshasa took him from prison to international celebrity. Almost from the start, Americans viewed the outsized figure with his electrified hair, flamboyant attire, and verbal bombast as the major face of the event. As vice president of Video Techniques, King served as the company's contact with black fighters who dominated the heavier weight divisions in the 1960s and 1970s. An ex-numbers boss and tavern owner in Cleveland, King embodied his own variant of Black Power as a man who went from ghetto criminal to the heights of boxing promotion. With great intelligence and mob ties, a gargantuan gift of gab, and a hustler's will, he struck gold when Hank Schwartz hired him to help with the Norton-Foreman fight in Caracas and after that with the Ali and Foreman battle in Africa. As Schwartz recalled, the company needed a black front man like King. "Video Techniques had the capability of using the latest technology connecting into the developing satellite and microwave networks. I was confident we could deliver the best sporting event worldwide," Schwartz noted, "but I needed King's skill to pull it off. He could deliver the fighters." In an era when racial pride had become a rallying cry, and for many in government, entertainment, and sport a positive attribute, the top heavyweight boxers were black and aware of their subordination to the white boxing establishment. King appeared to be someone they would listen to. With King on board, Video Techniques could function as the promoter for an entire event rather than serving only as the contractor to someone else by providing the TV production, marketing, and distribution. Schwartz and King formed a strong, if ultimately fragile, partnership.[26]

Although often derided as an unscrupulous hustler, there is more to King. According to historian Jeffrey Sammons, his independence, race consciousness, and defiance of boxing's white power structure made him the Ali of boxing promoters. In fact, King maintained that *hustler* was "a mediocre word when applied to my talents. . . . I am a solitary black man up against the weapons of the white power structure, a bow and arrow against an atom bomb." Until King, blacks might have been accepted as superb athletes, but nowhere in the white-dominated offices of American sport were they believed to have the brains and organizational ability to work at executive and managerial levels. In its discussion of the newfound power of African Americans in the realms of sport and entertainment, *Black Enterprise* noted, "Until King, there had never been any Blacks who had major roles, behind the scenes, in the closed-door rooms where the deals are made and the power lies." According to *Sports Illustrated*'s Mark Kram, he snatched what could be the richest prize in sports "right out from under the smirks of those who never have anything taken from them—especially by a black man without a club in his hand."[27]

Although King's role in the event was initially minor, as soon as they learned of his participation in promoting the Rumble in the Jungle, black fans applauded King's pioneering role as a black promoter in a white-run business. No matter the outcome in Zaire, noted Howard Woods in the *Chicago Defender*, "the glamour of the two gladiators will be matched by the color of the man—a gregarious black man—who managed to put the whole thing together," and who portrayed the fight as an example of black unity and pride. Nation of Islam official Jeremiah Shabazz agreed: "[We] had a promoter we could be proud of, because Zaire was where Don King made his mark." Later, Shabazz realized King cared about only money, but in Zaire "I thought Don King was all right," as he represented the Nation of Islam's message of black empowerment and racial pride. King demonstrated to whites and blacks far beyond the ring world that black boxing entrepreneurs could negotiate complex business deals with the heads of banks, major corporations, and nation-states. King may have been in the game for the money, the power, and the action, but he also represented the kind of hustler-to-businessman success story that appealed to the black community at a time when many blacks were demanding Black Power.[28]

When King first appeared on the boxing scene in 1972, he had just been released from prison, where he had served a nearly four-year sentence for manslaughter. What landed him in jail was a particularly vicious crime. It was not his first brush with violence. Like Foreman he grew up in an impoverished urban ghetto, but in the Midwestern industrial city of Cleveland. Born on August 20, 1931, the first thing he recalled about where he grew up was "realizing I wanted to get the hell out. . . . It was a microcosm of the filth and despair that black people have had to live with all their lives." The only positive, he said, was, "It taught me how to survive. You'd have to fight for your life every minute because there was always someone wanting to take it." When King was twelve his father died in an explosion at the tool and die factory where he worked. His mother used the insurance money to move to Mount Pleasant, a bit nicer neighborhood, but "still a ghetto." Like other enterprising youth he graduated to the numbers racket, which brought him into the heart of the black nightlife district, with its share of gamblers, pimps, and hoods. Eventually he became Cleveland's numbers kingpin. Like other numbers racketeers, King saw himself a benefactor of the ghetto, not its enemy, since he helped finance the college and professional education of doctors, lawyers, and scientists, and also donated to many black charities. By the late 1950s, he was, noted his friend the R&B singer Lloyd Price, "a guy you had to know if you wanted to make it in that town. He could push you to the top or see to it you got nowhere."[29]

In the nightlife world, a gun was a necessity. On December 2, 1954, King had to use his weapon when three white criminals from Detroit tried to rob one of his gambling houses. In the fray King killed one of the robbers, but it was ruled self-defense and he escaped a jail term. He was not so lucky twelve years later. On April 20, 1966, King got into a violent argument with Sam Garrett at a bar over $600 that King believed his numbers runner was holding out on him. At six foot four and 240 pounds, King far outmatched the 134-pound Garrett. King beat his opponent while holding a gun on the unarmed man and then stomped him to death in full view of the bar's patrons. He claimed self-defense but was indicted for second-degree murder. According to reporter Jack Newfield, King attempted to bribe the police and threaten witnesses, four of whom changed their stories while another was run out of town. He was convicted of second-degree murder, but the judge suspended the life sentence pending a private hearing, attended only by the judge and King's lawyer. The beneficiary of an obvious fix, King was sentenced to three years and eleven months for manslaughter.[30]

Prison was the turning point of King's life. Jail gave him time to read and think about changing his life—with astounding results. "The experience was a soul cleanser," King declared. "I went in with a toothpick and came out with a nuclear bomb." Among the authors he read were Shakespeare, Maupassant, Machiavelli, and Frantz Fanon. He recalled: "When I left that fucking plantation with its straw bosses I was more dangerous than ever before. Now I've risen like the ashes of the Phoenix." Yet King was ever cognizant that he was black in a white man's world: "I'll be a number, a nigger, and an ex-convict until I die. I wanted to be a lawyer, but I knew that was white man's stuff. Look at me, this ain't no Horatio Alger story where you get to marry the boss's daughter. There ain't no boss's daughter for me, Jack."[31]

By the time King left the Marion, Ohio, prison at the age of forty on September 30, 1971, he had a firm understanding of the role that racism played in the black psyche. His views were similar to those of Ali and the Nation of Islam. "Our image as a people has a lot to be desired," King told the *Black Collegian* in 1980. "We have an inferiority complex. I think the greatest job our white counterparts done on us is the impairment of the Black psyche. He has made us feel so unworthy . . . to such a degree that when we look in the mirror and look at ourselves, we don't like ourselves." To overcome the sickness, black Americans needed a new, positive identity. "Black is more than beautiful," but saying it was not enough. Traditionally, black people looked to God, "but I recognize that God helps those who help themselves. Until we are able to deal with ourselves and to deal collectively for the betterment of the whole, we're always going to be on the short end of the stick." King's answer was economics, because "it's life itself." The road to success, he preached, required "self-help, self-determination, self-reliance."[32]

King certainly was determined when he left prison, but his quick rise to become boxing's first and most powerful black promoter in three short years could not have occurred without the help of others, not all of them black. After watching Frazier defeat Ali on the prison TV in March 1971, King vowed to go into boxing, an arena that promised huge paydays, exciting physical confrontations, and large numbers of black fighters and fans. Singer Lloyd Price had known King since 1959, when his band first played at King's New Corner Tavern. When King agreed to put on a boxing exhibition and music performance in 1972 to benefit Cleveland's Forest City Hospital, a financially troubled, predominantly black institution, Price put him in touch with Ali, who agreed to box for free. To help him put on such a production, King called on Don Elbaum, a local matchmaker and promoter in Pennsylvania and Ohio. Although he had never heard of King, Elbaum was mesmerized by his smooth-talking enthusiasm and agreed to serve as his mentor; he could see that King was a natural promoter. With help from Price, Elbaum, and Ali the benefit sold out. In a pattern that would renew itself often, King tried to stiff one of the black fighters, siphoned off most of the money, and eventually betrayed Elbaum too. Still, with his first boxing success and his connection with Ali, King realized that promotion provided a road to wealth and social legitimacy.[33]

King's path to becoming boxing's first successful black promoter was smoothed further by Elbaum, who recognized that "boxing needs a black promoter" who knew how to relate to black boxers. After a brief stab at managing fighters, King realized the money was in promotion. Among the many boxing figures to whom Elbaum introduced King, the most important was Hank Schwartz, executive vice president of Video Techniques, a rising company in satellite sports communications. Not long before King appeared on the scene, Schwartz was pioneering the transmission of world heavyweight boxing matches from all over the globe. He could play such a role because of the power vacuum in boxing in the early 1970s. Ali's exile had killed Main Bout promotions, and when he came back, there was no one promoter who enjoyed a monopoly on heavyweight champions. Madison Square Garden was still a player in boxing promotions, but its power had diminished with the rise of venues in Las Vegas, Miami, and Los Angeles. Except for Jerry Quarry, the top heavyweights were black, and the promoters, led by Bob Arum and his company, Top Rank, were white. The way was open for a black promoter to take over boxing.[34]

Despite his prison record, King seemed honest and focused, and Schwartz believed they could work well together. They especially proved good at brainstorming to come up with strategies for promotions beset by numerous competitors as well as financial and promotional obstacles. Schwartz made King a vice president. In Schwartz's eyes, this was the beginning of an exciting partnership. As for King, he initially said that Video Techniques "weren't the run-of-the-mill white guys who wanted to emasculate black guys." Later he amended that to "I was their token nigger. . . . A black face to deal with the blacks." As part of their deal, King kept his Don King Productions company, which he had established as the vehicle for his own promotion enterprise, alive as a business entity but would give Video Techniques 100 percent of his time. Schwartz offered to teach King broadcast technology in exchange for King teaching him how to negotiate with boxers. According to Schwartz, King replied, "You can teach me what you know about satellites and distribution, but you will never learn how to talk to these black fighters."[35]

With Schwartz's knowledge of satellites and King's ability to negotiate with black fighters, Video Techniques set about creating an Ali-Foreman heavyweight fight somewhere in the new wide world of global boxing. The Zaire bout started with a truly international cast of promoters: Americans Schwartz and King; Great Britain's John Daly; Telemedia de Panamá, a financial front organization later revealed to be controlled by Schwartz; and Risnelia, a little-known company based in Switzerland but incorporated in Panama. The world would eventually learn that Risnelia was actually controlled by the government of Zaire and its president Mobutu Sese Seko. The participation of a variety of international entities would require a level of international negotiations unseen before in boxing.[36]

One reason for going offshore to Zaire and other international locations was to avoid the heavy tax bite that New York State and the IRS demanded of championship fighters. In addition, Foreman was reluctant to fight in the United States because of his personal financial difficulties. While Schwartz focused on negotiating with the Venezuelan government for the Norton-Foreman match in Caracas, King dealt with signing the two fighters for the future championship match that would eventually end up in Zaire. In the process, King learned that Foreman was mired in divorce proceedings and a series of lawsuits against his manager, Dick Sadler, who had sold off more pieces of him than he possessed. As King told Schwartz, Foreman insisted on being paid outside the country "to keep the money outside the reach of these legal proceedings." To solve Foreman's problems, Schwartz set up Telemedia de Panamá for $1,000. "I can do the whole promotional deal off shore . . . in Brazil or . . ." in Venezuela, where the Norton-Foreman bout was to take place. "That way Foreman's money could be funneled through our Panamanian company. George can draw down the money he has earned where and when he wants to." This offshore arrangement convinced Foreman to fight Norton in Caracas. When Foreman demanded more money to sign with Video Techniques, King came up with $50,000 from his Cleveland "associates."[37]

Putting the Caracas fight between Foreman and Ken Norton together proved a dry run for Schwartz and King's strenuous efforts to promote the Rumble in the Jungle. After Ali defeated Joe Frazier in January 1974 at Madison Square Garden in a much-anticipated rematch, he became the logical and most lucrative challenger to face Foreman, the locale yet to be determined. The primary difficulty lay in signing both men. In this regard King proved invaluable. Schwartz thought he had an in with Foreman because they had worked together in Jamaica, so he went after Foreman and assigned King to sign Ali. This proved King's great opportunity and he went all out to land the richest fight in history and beat out the other promoters, such as New York's Bob Arum, Houston's Hofheinz family, and Jerry Perenchio and Jack Kent Cooke in Los Angeles, all eager to do the same thing. King was especially effective with Ali and his manager Herbert Muhammad, son of the leader of the Nation of Islam, by dangling in front of the fighter a prize of $5 million, which would be the biggest payday in boxing history up to that time. King also had to convince Ali and Herbert Muhammad not to go through with an Arum-run third match with Jerry Quarry. "The mere fact Arum tries to lead you down this path demonstrates his inability to relate to your blackness and the cause you've struggled for," King declared. "This isn't just another fight! Consider the monumental magnitude, the symbolic impact. Your regaining your title would do more for the cause of freedom and justice and equality than anything." If that were not enough, King used NOI rhetoric to remind Herbert: "You have to help the black man. This white man Arum is evil. He doesn't care for your man, even tried to set up matches finding a successor when they stripped him of his title. . . . This fight is the biggest, a chance for him to get that belt back. And it's being put together by me. A black man." The appeal to black pride worked. Ali turned down Quarry and agreed to fight Foreman if the promise of $5 million dollars was certain and Foreman could be signed.[38]

When it became evident that Schwartz was unable to sign Foreman, King went after the wary champion. Once it was clear that Foreman would receive his $5 million outside the United States, King brought in the big guns. At a time of heightened black consciousness, King persuaded Foreman that black promoters would "show all blacks around the world that we can succeed like no one has ever believed we could. I am black and this is my promotion. No white man gonna rip you off. My word is my soul." King stressed the greatness of the fight's "impact on black people and the whites," but the clincher proved to be King's assertion that "until you beat Muhammad Ali, the world will never recognize you as The Champion. As long as he's alive and fighting and you don't show the world who's the best, they'll look at Ali as the master." According to King, Foreman responded: "I never done this before but I'm giving you my word. You got the fight." Somehow King managed to get Foreman to sign three blank pieces of paper in lieu of a formal contract.[39]

King also proved invaluable immediately after Foreman demolished Norton in Caracas. Despite his spectacular victory, the champion was furious that the Venezuelan government prevented him from leaving the country until he paid a huge amount in taxes. He blamed Video Techniques. Instead of returning to New York from Caracas as planned, King accompanied Foreman to Houston, where he soothed the disgruntled champion, who by then had vowed that he would not fight Ali after all. Only by promising Foreman to get him whatever he desired did King manage to settle him down. What did Foreman want? A German shepherd that he named "Digo."[40]

Although King had managed to sign both fighters there was as yet no financing and no arena. King and Schwartz had promised letters of credit to both fighters by February 15 and the deadline was looming. This is where the real nature of global boxing is revealed and where Schwartz managed to put the complicated international deal together. Veteran British promoter Jack Solomons claimed he had the $10 million promised to the two fighters and invited Schwartz to London to finalize the deal. With only two days to go, Schwartz needed the money for the letters of credit and a financial backer of the fight so his offshore company, Telemedia de Panamá, could keep the contracts in place and so that Video Techniques would not lose all its ancillary rights and the right to promote and broadcast the very fight itself. At the last minute, Solomons's group pulled out; the fight and Video Techniques were on the line. At his wit's end, Schwartz wandered London trying to find a solution. By chance he passed the brownstone of Hemdale Leisure Corporation, headed by John

Daly, a promoter of small-time closed-circuit venues and the son of a former boxer. Daly saved the day, agreeing to provide the initial $100,000 for each fighter. However, a group that Daly assembled to come up with the $10 million in prize money tried to ace Video Techniques out of the picture. Schwartz turned them down. Once more he faced the collapse of the promotion and perhaps his company.[41]

At this point, a powerful international fixer, Bermuda-based Fred Weymar, called to say that a little-known Switzerland-based company, Risnelia, was interested in putting up the money for the fight, but only if it took place in Zaire. Weymar had the perfect credentials for boxing as it entered its age of government-financed multimillion-dollar promotions and hidden profits. He was a former German American supporter of the Nazi Bund who was banned from the United States, and a former investor implicated in the scandals of financiers Bernie Cornfeld and Robert Vesco, who were under investigation by the Securities and Exchange Commission. Most important, he was an agent for President Mobutu of Zaire and managed his Swiss bank accounts. According to Schwartz, Weymar told him that Mobutu "wants the world to consider him a major leader and an icon for all of Africa." For that to happen, he "wants to stage this championship as the world's most important sporting event and he wants it to happen in the stadium in his capital, Kinshasa." Since Weymar was barred from the United States, the meeting took place in Paris. Along with Schwartz, King, Daly, and Weymar, the meeting was attended by Mandungu Bula, another Mobutu financial adviser based in Brussels, who would eventually oversee the fight for Zaire. Rounding out the group was Geneva attorney Raymond Nicolet, who represented Risnelia Inc. Like Telemedia, Risnelia was a shell company chartered in Panama for Mobutu to transfer secretly Zaire's money for his own use and profit.[42]

Although Schwartz handled the financial negotiations, King played a crucial role. Over dinner, Mandungu asked how King could trust a Jew like Schwartz. King vouched for his boss. "You can trust this one," he replied. As a result of these negotiations, Risnelia agreed to put up two letters of credit for $4.8 million dollars for each of the fighters and Schwartz consented to hold the fight in Africa. Risnelia would get 42 percent of the profits, Hemdale 28 percent, and Telemedia, Schwartz's own offshore company, 10 percent. Video Techniques and Don King Enterprises would receive 20 percent, with the latter earning 4.33 percent, which King took in Video Techniques stock. Eventually, the TV personality David Frost, an Australian working in Great Britain and the United States, bought the promotion rights to Australia and New Zealand.[43]

Zaire's ground satellite station proved essential for the nation to stage the event for the rest of the world. Located twenty-six miles from Kinshasa, the station would transmit the signal up to Intelsat No. 4, which would then relay it to a ground station in Eaton, West Virginia. From there the signal went to the Telco Distribution Cable line in New York and throughout the United States. The broadcast to Europe and the United Kingdom would come direct from Kinshasa's ground station or be relayed from New York. The action in the ring would be transmitted instantaneously at 186,000 miles per second around the globe. Given the centrality of the satellite and closed-circuit television to the spectacle, one estimate projected that 75 percent of total revenue would come from live closed-circuit TV in up to 450 US venues. According to Hemdale's John Daly, the promoters expected to gross a minimum of $20 million, which would come to $8 million in profits, and a maximum take of $40 million. King was equally optimistic. "More people will see Foreman and Ali mix styles than any previous sporting event in history," he declared. A "total audience at more than a billion people is not a gross exaggeration."[44]

While Zaire's satellite station made it possible to stage a global spectacle, advances in airplane technology made it much easier to move people and sophisticated equipment around the world at incredible speed. Schwartz and King, for instance, were frequent flyers to and from Caracas to New York and Houston, and to and from New York and London and Paris, or to and from New York and Zaire. The modern jet airplane made it possible for Ali to train and fight in the United States and abroad and then interrupt his training to follow Foreman to Tokyo and Caracas to goad him into a fight. Similarly, as a symbol of his power and a sign of his modernity, plus evidence of his willingness to use the nation's money to enhance his prestige, President Mobutu of Zaire was the only black African leader to own a Boeing jumbo jet, which he used to travel the world for diplomacy and pleasure. Furthermore, for the Norton-Foreman match in Caracas, Video Techniques needed to move so much high-level TV equipment that Schwartz rented a Hercules C-103A transport plane from the US Air Force. High-speed jet travel was so integral to modern globalized boxing that as Schwartz and King discovered, jet lag had become a cost doing business.[45]

As soon as the boxing world learned that the fight would take place in Zaire, a country few Americans had even heard of, collective head scratching commenced. Why was such a bizarre locale chosen over American or European sites? Alan Hubbard, editor of Britain's *Sportsworld*, had a ready answer that spoke to the globalization of sport: "Is there any difference between holding the world heavyweight bout in Kinshasa and the Olympics in Mexico City?" As he put it, "the truth is promoting the 'richest prize in sport' is no longer the prerogative of America." As Hubbard concluded, distance no longer mattered; live satellite transmission obliterated issues of space and time. "The 'live' audience is relatively immaterial—with the bulk of the profits from closed-circuit television, an arena is required really as a studio," he said. In that case, "Kinshasa's 'Stadium of the 20th May' is as good as anywhere—if the communications work." Communications were indeed crucial, which explains Schwartz's decision to fly in US and European equipment and technicians to supplement local facilities. Eager to impress the world, the Zaire government wanted everything to come off as planned.[46]

What lay behind President Mobutu's decision to make sure that Kinshasa would be the place where all roads came together? Why did he decide to gamble his prestige on such a risky and expensive venture? An early account of the fight suggests that Mobutu conceived of hosting the match when he and Ali met by chance in Abu Dhabi in summer of 1973, or perhaps in Kuwait in February 1974. Mobutu's visit was part of a successful diplomatic effort to create rapprochement with Arab leaders. Ali, meanwhile, was in the Middle East to bolster his ties to Islamic nations and to support various causes in the Arab world. Their discussion in the Middle East of a possible title match underscores the rise of new nations across the globe and the entry of new players in boxing. "My ancestors lived in Zaire . . . I want to regain the title that was stolen from me," Ali told Mobutu. "This will be the greatest spectacle of modern times. I want to offer it to Africa." It is impossible to say what Mobutu replied to Ali at this juncture, but he, like leaders of other developing countries, viewed control of boxing as a sign of American power and prestige. Challenging the American monopoly over boxing offered Mobutu an opportunity to raise his nation's stature and shift power and assets to the Third World. When the opportunity arose six months later in February 1974, he ordered his agents to arrange for the spectacle to be held in Zaire.[47]

At the time of the Rumble in the Jungle, President Mobutu Sese Seko ruled Zaire with an iron hand. As part of a broader "authenticity" campaign, he wanted a grand international spectacle, a "Super Fight of the Century," to promote his country as a successful example of black liberation from European colonialism. Only fourteen years after independence, the fight would showcase an independent African state capable of rivaling the developed world with its own economic, social, and political progress. Mandungu Bula, the Zairian official in charge of the fight, put it succinctly: "The fight is the most suitable way to get our country known. The nature of the fighters is the reason. A man like Ali. I don't think you'll have the same type of fight for another 20 years." The *New York Times* concurred: "The gladiators will serve as the most expensive public relations men in the history of world government." Unlike

Jamaica's Manley, Mobutu was less interested in tourism and more concerned with attracting foreign investment in Zaire's vast mineral wealth of copper, diamonds, cobalt, and uranium. Mobutu also wanted to burnish his image as the independent enlightened leader of a modern nation, to cement his control over a far-flung, ethnically and linguistically diverse country, thus helping him outshine rivals for the leadership of Africa.[48]

In 1974, Zaire was at the height of its prosperity, just before the oil boycott and the dramatic decline in copper prices decimated the country's economy. As the *Chicago Tribune* put it in August 1974, under Mobutu "Zaire enjoys a stability and prosperity that would have surprised anyone who was there for the chaotic days following independence. The city of Kinshasa, for example, is noticeably wealthier than most other cities in West and Central Africa." Mandungu Bula concurred. "It is because of the peace and contentment in Zaire that the fight is possible for us." Not only would the fight provide an opportunity to showcase Mobutu's leadership; it would also present a portrait of a modern African nation far different from the common and racist view of the Congo as "the Heart of Darkness."[49]

Mobutu grew up in the Belgian Congo, one of the most brutal and backward European colonies in Africa. Born Joseph-Désiré Mobutu on October 14, 1930, he belonged to the Ngbandi tribe, one of the smallest of the Congo's more than two hundred ethnic groups. His humble roots and deep-seated resentment of his betters drove his ambition. His father died when he was eight, his mother had a dubious reputation, and an uncle in the administrative center of Coquilhatville sent him to a school run by white priests, where he was known as a good student but also a troublemaker. As punishment for running away to the capital of Léopoldville in 1949, the priests enrolled him in the country's military force, the Force Publique, for seven years. As the black army of the Belgian colonial power, the Force brutally helped its white colonial officers keep order and ensure that the valuable rubber and ivory supplies kept flowing.[50]

Just as prison turned King around and the Job Corps changed Foreman, the army transformed Mobutu's prospects. In the Force Publique he found a stern but caring mentor and a sense of self-discipline. He read widely, passed an accountancy course, and wrote for the local press. When his hitch ended, he took up journalism. In 1958 he traveled to the Universal Exhibition in Brussels, a tribute to Belgian colonialism, and stayed on for further journalism training. There he interacted with young Congolese intellectuals opposed to Belgian rule, among them Patrice Lumumba, who made Mobutu his secretary. A hard worker and a pragmatic restraint on his more impassioned friend, Mobutu was also courageous, staring down an army mutiny single-handed after independence. At the same time, the CIA was wooing Mobutu as a potential source of information and a future leader should the Congo exhibit "communist" sympathies.

Independence occurred abruptly in 1960, resulting in five years of chaos and political instability. Unlike the British, the Belgians had little interest in anything other than rubber and minerals. They failed to create an indigenous leadership class or bureaucracy; nor did they unify the Congo's disparate ethnic groups and vast territorial expanse into a coherent nation. Four separate governments vied for power, a Belgian-led invasion battled to retake diamond rich Katanga province, and UN peacekeepers struggled to maintain order. Spurned by the United States as a dangerous and mentally unstable revolutionary, Lumumba, leader of one of the competing governments, turned to the Soviet Union for aid, thereby further alienating the US. With Mobutu in charge of the army in 1961, and at the urging of the CIA, Lumumba was assassinated by political rivals, which Mobutu knew about in advance, and in all probability he was an active conspirator in Lumumba's murder. The next four years saw political turmoil, threats of armed secession, and Marxist rebellion. In 1965, again with the aid of the CIA, Mobutu led a coup that made him president and head of the army. He was welcomed as president by the US and European governments, which were desperate for a pro-Western leader, and he also received CIA support and remuneration. While the new regime repressed, exiled, and jailed the opposition, banning all political parties but Mobutu's, his authoritarian government did manage to restore a semblance of stability after five years of armed struggle.[51]

While repression did its work, Mobutu turned to the creation of an ideology to unify the fragmented nation and distinguish it from its colonial past. To remedy the continuing sway of psychological, cultural, and economic colonialism, many new black African states worked to develop a distinctive African sensibility, from Kwame Nkrumah's black consciousness in Ghana to Léopold Senghor's Negritude in Senegal, and Aimé Césaire of Martinique. Confident by the early 1970s of Zaire's independence and potential for prosperity, Mobutu launched his own "authenticity program," a vision of postcolonial Black Power that underlay his desire to host major sporting events and other regional and global spectacles. As with disparate concepts of Black Power flourishing in the United States, authenticity sought to recover a black African identity eviscerated by years of colonial rule. As Zaire modernized, Mobutu declared, it needed to do so with African spiritual values, not be ruled by western materialism. "Authenticity is the realization by the Zairian people that it must return to its origins, seek out the values of its ancestors, to discover those which contribute to its harmonious and natural development," he said in a speech to the United Nations. "It is the refusal to blindly embrace imported ideologies."[52]

In creating "authenticity," Mobutu and his advisers attempted to overcome a colonial discourse that deemed Africans—especially the Congolese—as backward primitives who lagged millennia behind a more powerful, enlightened West and needed white rule to evolve to civilized status. Henry M. Stanley, the famous white Congo explorer, articulated the central ideas of colonial discourse in *The Congo and the Founding of Its Free State*. "On August 14th 1879," he wrote, "I arrived at the mouth of this river to ascend it, with the novel mission of sowing along its banks civilized settlements, to peacefully conquer and subdue it, to remould it in harmony with modern ideas into National States, within whose limits the European merchants shall go hand in hand with the dark African trader, and justice and law and order shall prevail, and murder and lawlessness and the cruel barter of slaves shall forever cease." Whether it was Christianity or Reason, enlightened Western powers had a duty to define a geographic entity and raise prehistoric savages to civilized standards. It went without saying that to subdue a primitive people without history or traditions often required brutality on the part of "more highly evolved" white Europeans.[53]

When the Congo achieved its independence in 1960, white Americans viewed the political infighting through a Cold War lens deeply influenced by the colonial discourse. Molded by books and movies such as *Tarzan of the Apes* (1912), *King Solomon's Mines* (1950), *Watusi* (1959), *Something of Value* (1957), and *Congo Crossing* (1956), white—and many black—Americans continued to see black Africans as naked, illiterate, and emotional savages prone to irrational revolt. Indeed, US officials depicted Lumumba, who rejected the colonial discourse of white paternalistic leadership, as the devil and equated him with a history of black African savagery and chaos. Without a strong man friendly to the United States in charge, the Russians would have taken over. After all, Africans could not rule themselves.[54]

Assuming power in 1965, Mobutu moved to overcome Congo's colonial past. As part of authenticity he changed the country's name and the river that coursed through it, the Congo, to Zaire, and he ordered Christian names be replaced with "authentic" African ones, including his own—from Joseph-Désiré Mobutu to Mobutu Sese Seko Kuku Ngbendu Wa Za Banga. The government tore down colonial-era statues; renamed roads and squares after key independence struggles; and designated Léopoldville, named for the Belgian king responsible for the death of millions, as Kinshasa. Honorific titles and *madam* and *monsieur* were replaced by the more egalitarian-sounding *citoyen* and *citoyenne*. In addition, the national flag and the national anthem no longer reflected the Belgian past, and the twenty-one-gun salute for foreign heads of state was replaced by tribal drumming. The regime declared European dress inauthentic, ordering men to replace Western suits with the abacost, a Mao-style, high-collared coat of blue or brown wool, worn without a tie, also considered a colonial relic. More restrictive rules governed women's attire. Women could not wear miniskirts but had to dress in more dignified and traditional *pagnes*, or wraps. The government also penalized the use of lipstick and other cosmetics, and strongly discouraged wigs in favor of more natural hairstyles, which paralleled American black nationalist beliefs that skin lighteners and wigs were pathetic attempts to copy white forms of beauty.[55]

The emphasis on authentic African traditions might incite tribal loyalties, however, so the regime focused on inventing common traditions to unify the nation. Huge "animation" festivals of song, dance, and parades attempted to concretize invented traditions and consecrate a national spirit. However, the "words of traditional songs and chants [were changed]," according to political scientist Kenneth Adelman, "so as to praise the President and the national party, rather than the founding ancestors or the goodness of life." In his desire to make himself the undisputed leader of a fractured nation, Mobutu placed himself at the center of these rituals attired in an abacost, wearing a leopard-skin headdress, and carrying a staff like a traditional village chief, that is, as the complete embodiment of the nation. Because he believed himself fully in tune with the populace, he saw no need for opposition political parties or the chaos of democratic rule.[56]

Authenticity was also intended for international consumption. Much of the nationalist rhetoric was meant to alter Mobutu's reputation in the eyes of other African and developing nations, which saw him as a tool of the CIA and Western economic interests, and as a symbol of Western intervention in their independence struggles. To establish his credibility as an independent Third World leader, he expropriated the language and symbols of other Third World nationalisms and built a cult around the much-admired Lumumba. Zairianization, for example, was announced in 1974 as a radical economic plan to refurbish Mobutu's credibility in the developing world. Nationalization of the economy was borrowed from China, North Korea, and radical African countries, and from North Korea he adapted the concept of national pilgrimage points to which Zairians could travel and where they could pledge their allegiance to the country and its leader. Authenticity's debt to Senghor and Césaire's Negritude was obvious. He also drew on Western images of the Congo and transformed them into a Zairian national identity acceptable to the West. Most notably, he used the West's image of the autocratic village chief to justify his despotic rule, which passed US scrutiny, since most American leaders believed the Congo not ready for democracy. By the early 1970s, Mobutu had succeeded in raising the regime's international status. He received credit at home and abroad for elevating the Congo's economic prosperity and political stability.[57]

As a key element of his authenticity campaign, the Rumble in the Jungle was intended to bolster his popularity at home, strengthen his position in black Africa, and launch his nation onto the world stage. The Super Fight of the Century, to distinguish it from mere Fights of the Century, would take place on September 25, at the height of the authenticity campaign and was the most spectacular of many high-prestige events designed to raise the regime's stature at home and abroad. Equally satisfying to Mobutu, other nations took his campaign for authenticity seriously. Chad, Equatorial Guinea, Gabon, and Togo copied his ideas, and Dahomey, Burundi, and Togo adopted the abacost. Meanwhile, the presidents of Panama and Uruguay published Mobutu's speeches and ordered party officials to study them. As the Zairian newspaper *Taifa* put it, "The political sense of the Ali-Foreman fight is to give homage to President Mobutu." This explains why the original date of the match coincided with the Quinzaine de Mobutuisme, a two-week celebration of "Mobutu's thought," which encompassed public meetings, traditional dancing, and the opening of his political party's school. As late as the 1990s, many Congolese still expressed thanks to Mobutu for hosting the fight. Such a unique global event gave them a larger sense of national identity that transcended tribal and geographic particularities.[58]

Mobutu's willingness to spend more than $20 million to stage Africa's first heavyweight title fight revealed his desire to advertise Zaire and himself. Months before the fight, he seemed to have succeeded. Press coverage depicted Zaire as a stable, wealthy country under his benevolent autocracy. *Chicago Tribune* reporter Jim Mann, for example, argued that "journalists who will come here for the heavyweight championship fight will probably find this to be a pretty strange place," a nation poor by Western standards, "but which is quite wealthy by African standards" and "enjoys a stability and prosperity that would have surprised anyone who was there for the chaotic days following independence." Looking forward, the government wanted more corporate investment. Even more, noted the *Christian Science Monitor*, no matter who wins, President Mobutu has already won. The fight "has helped put this tremendous yet little-known country on the map, internationally speaking." According to one high foreign official, "It has made its impact overseas. And domestically it has caused a lot of excitement and activity too." The Super Fight had made Zaire and its proud president international household names.[59]

President Mobutu constructed an African setting for one of the century's great international spectacles, packed with huge symbolic baggage. As Mandungu Bula told American audiences: "Here is a country ruled by black men where there is no racial prejudice. We have no chauvinism. . . . We would like to show what a black nation can do. Especially a black nation that has been ruled by whites with aggression for so long. People who didn't believe we were human beings. There is no desire for revenge. There is a desire to work in peace."[60]

For their part, Schwartz and King ballyhooed the fight and its African setting as an international spectacle awash in the symbolic trappings of global Black Power. As the black American face of the production, King had a gift for providing narratives for major sporting events. In his hands, the bout became a way for black Americans to return symbolically to their homeland at a time when many of them were seeking their cultural roots in Africa. The return to Africa, "From the Slave Ship to the Championship," was a theme he enunciated repeatedly. This "symbolic black happening," he declared, would help transform the world's image of Africa.[61]

King was not alone in promoting the fight's African themes. At a press party on May 15 to formally announce the fight in the Rainbow Room at Rockefeller Center, Schwartz displayed African art he had collected in Zaire and pieces from New York's Tribal Art Gallery to define the theme of the fight. As a result, the Rainbow Room was adorned with "wooden statues, tribal masks, drums, and other African art. These had been arranged as a background display so that all the photographs included glimpses of the artifacts behind Ali at the microphone." While Schwartz emphasized the African setting and King stressed the symbolic return of former slaves to their ancestral homeland, with Mobutu's participation symbols of Black Power and anticolonialism were broadcast worldwide. As Griffin Booker declared in the *Amsterdam News*, the Mobutu regime saw the fight as the beginning of the new era of Pan-African brotherhood. "The pride of Black people the world over is at stake here and most Blacks have pledged an undying devotion to make this one a success."[62]

To emphasize his powerful black leadership, atop the stadium as the focal point that fans would see was a thirty- by fifteen-foot poster of a benevolent President Mobutu in leopard-skin hat and scarf. As representatives of the international media traveled from the airport to their downtown hotels, huge billboards hid from sight squalid squatters' shanties while proclaiming the regime's modernity and linking Africans and African Americans together against white supremacy. "BLACK POWER IS SOUGHT EVERYWHERE IN THE

WORLD," announced one sign, "BUT IT IS REALIZED HERE IN ZAIRE." Other signs amplified the message: "A FIGHT BETWEEN TWO BLACKS IN A BLACK NATION, ORGANIZED BY BLACKS AND SEEN BY THE WHOLE WORLD; THAT IS A VICTORY OF MOBUTUISM." Still another protested colonialism and proclaimed that Zaire should be the leader of liberation in Africa: "THE COUNTRY OF ZAIRE WHICH HAS BEEN BLED BECAUSE OF PILLAGE AND SYSTEMATIC EXPLOITATION," this billboard read, "MUST BECOME A FORTRESS AGAINST IMPERIALISM AND A SPEARHEAD FOR THE LIBERATION OF THE AFRICAN CONTINENT." Still another declared: "IT IS NOT ENOUGH FOR US TO CONDEMN COLONIALISM, IMPERIALISM AND RACISM, IT IS ALSO NECESSARY TO MEASURE OUR CAPACITY AND OUR WEAKNESS AND BE UNITED IN ORDER TO FACE THE CHALLENGE OF DEVELOPMENT."[63]

At the press conference at the Waldorf Astoria hotel in New York on September 9, 1974, the day Ali was to leave for Zaire, King announced another key component of the fight, a three-day music festival to showcase the musical culture of the African diaspora. Zaire 74 was scheduled to open for what King called "the greatest sporting event in the history of the world." When the microphone was turned over to Ali, he asked reporters who they picked to win. Most of them said Foreman. As a result, Ali would be the underdog for only the third time in his career. If he was considered an underdog, so too was the entire African fight promotion, including the music fest. Until the bout actually occurred, most observers remained skeptical it would ever come off, whether the music festival would take place, whether the events would attract any tourists, and whether there would be enough accommodations if they did come. Could a black African former colony pull off such a modern, sophisticated global event?[64]

In fact, massive problems abounded. In March 1974, only a month after the deal was finalized, Schwartz's inspection of Kinshasa's facilities left him severely depressed. Mobutu's claims of modernity fell far short of American standards. Schwartz discovered a Third World country lacking hotel rooms. Also lacking was the infrastructure needed to put on the fight, such as proper satellite technology, media facilities, and the people capable of mounting such a global spectacle. "The country," Schwartz recalled, "looked like a shithole." The route to Mai 20 Stadium was a dirt road, he recalled. "We approached a large vine-covered structure. I assumed it was an architectural ruin, perhaps a holy place" rather than the stadium for the fight. He told Jack Newfield: "I felt like I had made a terrible mistake. I went into a panic. It wasn't usable." Even more astonishing, Schwartz found crumbling seats and human feces on the floor of the stadium where local athletes changed their clothes. "There wasn't even a roof over the ring," he added. Most troubling, Schwartz discovered there was no microwave connection to the satellite earth station. “Physically sick,” he told Zaire officials that “the fight couldn’t go ahead with the contract.”[65]

Whatever Schwartz wanted built or fixed, they would do in time with money from the national treasury. But Zaire’s government insisted on using the stadium because of its symbolic import. Built in the 1930s under Belgian rule, the stadium was an example of colonial injustice. The stands for the whites were well appointed, but those for the indigenous lacked even latrines. It was after a soccer game here in 1959 that mass protests against Belgium erupted, and it was where Mobutu announced his authenticity programs. Indeed, the regime proved eager to renovate it so it would rank as the most modern stadium in Africa, a sign of the regime’s own modernity and independence from colonialism. The government “is virtually rebuilding its largest stadium for the fight,” noted the *New York Times*’ Thomas A. Johnson in July. The government built a new runway at the airport to handle the jumbo jets that would bring in performers, fighters, equipment, technical personnel, journalists, and however many brave fight fans would decide to attend. The government also invested in a four-lane highway from the airport to downtown hotels, built a bar for the world press, and hired French technical experts to put in a hundred telephones that would link up to the satellite station fifty miles away. In addition, the government refitted the microwave system to enable television signals to travel from the stadium to the uplink dish. According to Schwartz, Mobutu fulfilled his promises: “He converted a shithole into a first-class facility and he did it in six months.” In all this, though, little was said about the regime’s use of the stadium’s basement as a place where political opponents and criminals were tortured and killed.[66]

Still, doubts abounded. One skeptic was British promoter Jack Solomons, who had failed to come up with the money when Schwartz needed it most. He now planned to bring European tourists to Zaire, but his inspection trip to Kinshasa left him disappointed. “I stayed eight days,” he said, “and when I returned I had still not seen” the stadium or the relevant officials. “I had the presidential suite at the Inter-Continental Hotel in Kinshasa, and even then it took me ten minutes to get my key in the lobby. Imagine the turmoil on fight night.” Solomons also doubted that security would be sufficient: “I can see chaos there as the fight builds up and in the stadium on fight night. . . . Unless they get a real pro working with them all I can do is wish them the best of luck.” The *Daily Mail*’s John Edwards, who covered Kinshasa’s soccer team, also expressed doubts: “I just don’t see how they can do it. Corruption is rife and communications are impossible. The telephone, for all practical purposes, is non-existent.” With images of African chaos and the stereotypical view of

Africa as "the heart of darkness," it seemed like the entire promotion was as much an underdog as Ali was when the focus of the boxing world and a global public turned toward Africa on September 10, 1974.[67]

When Ali and his huge entourage deplaned at Kinshasa's airport on September 10, however, optimism and high spirits reigned as twenty-four women in colorful dress greeted them with traditional welcome dances performed to the beat of drummers. On the way to the terminal, where they were met by government officials, Ali's party walked between an honor guard of helmeted soldiers standing at attention. Upon exiting the airport, there were five thousand Zaïroises who had been waiting for hours to see their hero. Many had walked miles, arrived on bicycle, or in old jalopies. According to Schwartz, Ali was greeted not only as a sports icon but also as "a young, charismatic African American who represented them in the global landscape." As soon as they saw him the crowd began chanting his name.[68]

Standing on a bench with his arms raised to the sky, Ali shushed the crowd and announced that Foreman was "a white Belgian," adding that "I feel Foreman is a stranger coming to my home to fight me." This was part of his strategy to make independent Zaire his home turf and Foreman a foreign interloper on par with their former Belgian colonial rulers. This tactic was easy, noted Ferdie Pacheco, Ali's doctor, since there were "a lot more a lot more people in Kinshasa with the name Muhammad or Ali than George or Foreman." Nor was it hard to turn Ali into the hero and Foreman the villain—in Zaire and all of black Africa, Ali was the best-known American, and his fame rested on his courageous defiance of the American government and the racist nature of American society. Wherever he went in Zaire, Ali was greeted by the roar of massive crowds. He proclaimed himself an African and they accepted him totally, spontaneously cheering him on with the chant, "Ali, bomaye!" (Ali, kill him!).[69]

When a supremely confident George Foreman arrived two days later, he had no idea that Ali was already engaged in winning the hearts and minds of Zairians, and he played right into the latter's hands. Without a clue of what would follow, the champion deplaned to polite applause. Only Mandungu Bula and three government officials were there to meet him. The crowds that had turned out to cheer Ali were gone. To the reception committee's shock, Foreman led Digo, his German shepherd, down the steps. Little did Foreman know that this type of dog had been used by the Belgian police for crowd control and had become a symbol of police brutality and colonial oppression. After Belgian authorities departed the Congo, in fact, the newly independent

Congolese killed as many of the dogs as they could. Apparently, the champion took his dog everywhere, which gave Ali the opportunity to remind Zairians that the Belgian imperialists set such dogs on them. For example, during one of Ali's sparring sessions, noted reporter Jerry Izenberg, he would yell to the crowd, "Do you know that dog is white?" Everyone responded, "Oui." "Do you remember when the Belgians were here and they set their dogs on your people?" Ali asked again, and the excited crowd yelled back, "Oui." "Do you know that this dog is a citizen of Belgian [*sic*]?" Everyone was yelling and dancing, even urging Ali to kill the dog. By his actions, noted trainer Angelo Dundee, Foreman "hardly endeared himself to the local populace."[70]

"It was indeed Ali country," continued Dundee, "and he was playing the underdog card brilliantly." The extent that this was true can be seen in the different living quarters assigned to the two combatants. The fact that Ali and his entourage were housed in luxurious villas at the Presidential Palace at N'Sele, overlooking the mighty Zaire River, said it all. Foreman, conversely, found his quarters "less than deluxe," five kilometers from N'Sele on an old military base filled with rats, lizards, insects, and enclosed by cyclone fences and barbed wire. Rowdy soldiers armed with rifles and fueled by large quantities of beer patrolled the base. Bill Caplan, Foreman's publicist, told *Chicago Tribune* sports columnist Rick Talley that George's dog was the reason for being in a separate camp. "These people hate dogs," Caplan explained. "They were afraid Foreman's dog might cause an incident." As a result, the champion found himself up on a hill behind a fence isolated from everyone while the challenger awaited the fight in a riverside villa set aside for visiting dignitaries.[71]

As the fighters settled into their camps two weeks before the scheduled fight date of September 25, sportswriters began trickling into the country, and fans worldwide eagerly awaited the much-anticipated title match. Nine days before the fight, however, on September 16, a chance event jolted everyone's plans. Foreman was battering his sparring partner around the ring when the journeyman Bill McMurray threw up his arms to protect himself from the champion's savage blows. In doing so his elbow opened up a nasty cut a quarter inch deep and through two layers of skin above Foreman's right eye. According to Dundee: "Foreman was bleeding all over the place. The fight was off." Months of planning and hard work vanished. Foreman distrusted the local doctors and feared needles and stitches, and he had his trainer Dick Sadler temporarily close the cut with a butterfly bandage until he could fly to Belgium or Paris for proper medical attention. According to a Zairian doctor, "in one week's time, a moderate blow could reopen the cut." To the consternation of government authorities, Sadler immediately asked for a postponement: "And the promoters, trying to make chicken salad out of the chicken droppings they were suddenly left with, were seen scurrying around in an attempt to salvage the promotion."[72]

Fearing that Foreman would not return if he were allowed to leave the country for medical treatment, the Mobutu regime prohibited both fighters from departing Zaire. After all, the developing African nation had already invested nearly $10 million in purses for the fighters and another $12 million in infrastructure. Government officials may have been prompted by a plea Ali released to the press. Convinced that if Foreman left, he would not come back, Ali sent a message to Mobutu via the press: "I appeal to the President not to let anybody connected with the fight out of the country. . . . Be careful. George might sneak out at night. Watch the airports. Watch the train stations. Watch the elephant trails. Send boats to patrol the rivers. Do whatever you have to do, Mr. President, but don't let George leave the country. He'll never come back if you let him out. . . . Because he knows I can't lose!" To prevent the disastrous news from getting out, the Zairian authorities closed down all international telex and telephone communications to the United States, with the exception of John Vinocur of AP and the *New York Post*'s Larry Merchant, who had filed their stories before Zaire's officials realized the significance of the cut. "For several days it was unclear whether the fight would be postponed or canceled."[73]

In their initial attempts to avoid postponing the fight, Zairian officials ensured the enmity of the American press with their heavy-handed treatment. Mandungu Bula initially told the press: "You must not publicize" the cut. "It will be improperly understood in your country. This cut is nothing. I suggest you forget about this story. Go for a swim." To find out what was really happening and end the confusion and government obfuscation, several reporters and a US Information Agency officer traveled to Foreman's training camp at N'Sele to get the word from the champion and his manager. As they approached Sadler and Foreman, who appeared welcoming, security officers ordered them to get out: "You are bothering the champion." When the newsmen objected that this was untrue, the security men said, "You're bothering me." Suddenly soldiers armed with machine guns forced the visitors to retreat. This "general breakdown" of international communications led Dick Young, of the *New York Daily News*, to call Zaire a "police state." The American embassy concluded that it was fortunate for Zaire that only a handful of American reporters were in Kinshasa when the cut occurred.[74]

In an attempt to salvage the situation, a ninety-minute closed-door meeting was called on the afternoon of September 18 at the Inter-Continental Hotel. In a telex to the State Department, the American ambassador described the hard infighting that eventually resulted in an agreed-on postponement until October 30. Zaire's government representatives, Mandungu Bula, president of the Ali-Foreman Fight Commission, and his deputy, Tshimpumpu Kanyika, were made to realize that their desire for only a one-week postponement was unrealistic given the seriousness of the injury. Fearful of losing the fight to other countries, Zaire officials insisted that the match could not be canceled. It had to take place in Zaire. King also wanted the fight to remain in Zaire for financial reasons—and perhaps reasons of personal and black pride. After all, his reputation as a promoter was on the line, and he had emphasized the importance of a black-run spectacle in a black African nation. As a result, King helped Mandungu Bula ram through the date of October 22, although Sadler kept insisting that it was "premature" to set a fixed date. Mandungu reiterated that as far as Zaire's government was concerned, October 22 was the date. However, everyone soon agreed to October 30, as suggested by Schwartz, because it would more realistically give Foreman's cut a chance to heal. Still, both Foreman and Sadler left the impression that Foreman would fight only when he was ready. For more than a week, the vagueness drove the promoters crazy.[75]

The roads to Kinshasa proved bumpy, but there were still more obstacles to overcome before the fight would actually take place. Mobutu's officials became increasingly upset over foreign criticism of their handling of the fight, and the promoters scrambled to rearrange scheduling with closed-circuit television outlets across the globe and strove to whip up publicity all over again. For the fighters, an initial two-week stay in a foreign country had stretched to seven weeks. Boredom became a common enemy. Needless to say, doubts that Zaire could pull off a global spectacle of this magnitude increased, especially since the postponement pushed the event into monsoon season. Would torrential rains wash away the efforts of all the participants? Meanwhile, Zaire 74, the three-day music festival designed to precede the title match, would still take place on schedule, now five weeks before the fight.

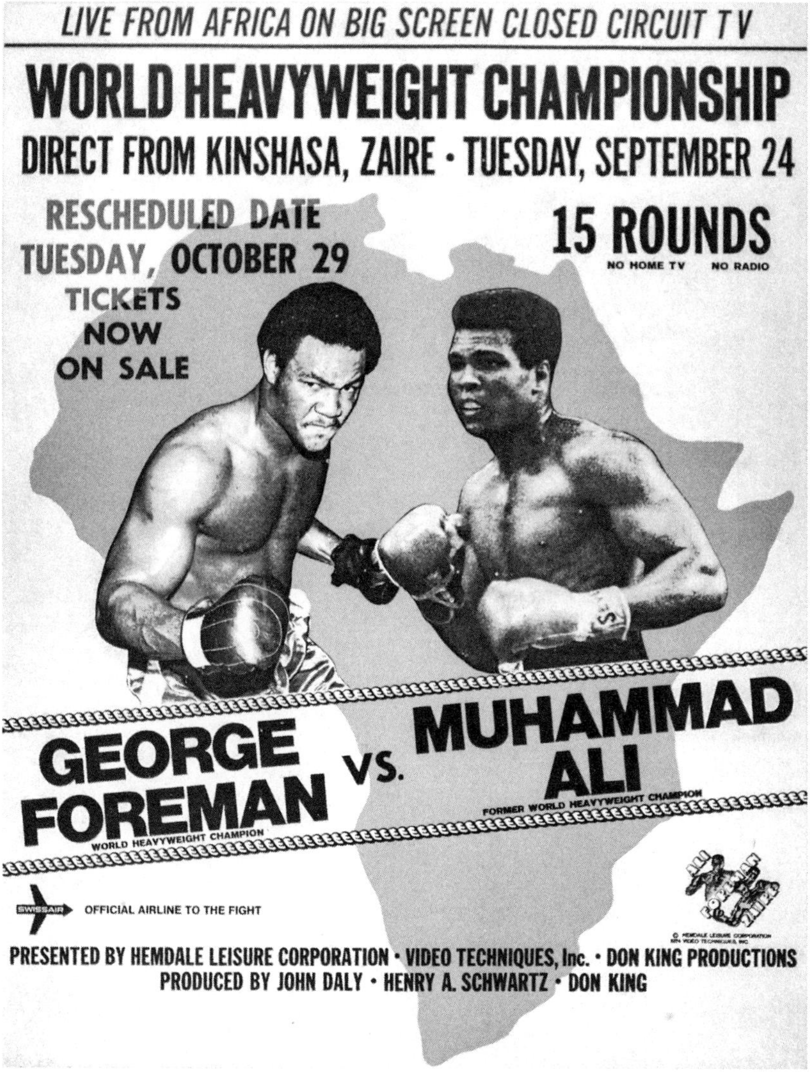

FIG. 1. The poster for the Ali-Foreman Title Fight with the original date September 24 replaced by the rescheduled date October 29 after Foreman's cut delayed the match. The dates are for the U.S. In Zaire the dates were September 25 and October 30.

FIG. 2. Cassius Clay, proud of his light heavyweight gold medal, Rome 1960 and left, Wilbert McClure of Toledo, Ohio light middleweight; right, middleweight Edward Crook of Fort Campbell, KY. Clay seen as a young, fresh-faced boxer loyal to the U.S. That image would soon change. (AP Photo).

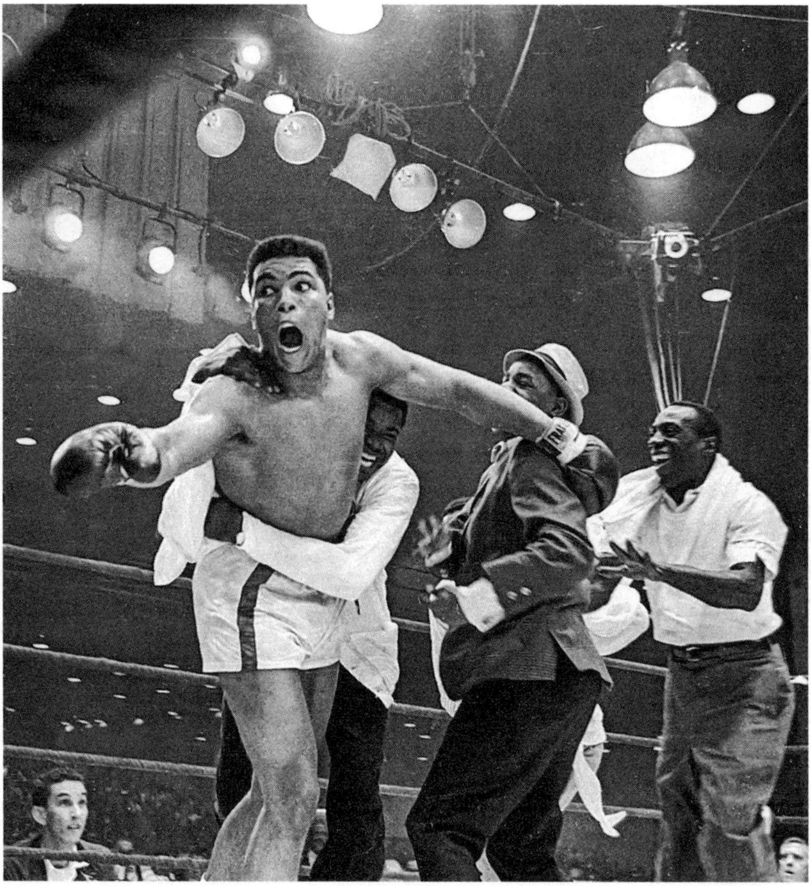

FIG. 3. Cassius Clay's handlers hold him back after he upset Sonny Liston to win the heavyweight title, Miami Beach, Florida February 25, 1964. The 'Louisville Lip' has his mouth open as he shouts his greatness and excoriates the press for doubting his boxing ability. (AP Photo).

FIG. 4. Champion Cassius Clay signs autographs in New York, NYC, March 1, 1964. Malcolm X, left, was a prominent member of the Nation of Islam and Clay's tutor in its precepts. Caught in the power struggle between Malcolm X and NOI leader Elijah Muhammad, Ali pledged his loyalty to Elijah who renamed him: Muhammad Ali. Becoming a "Black Muslim" and rejecting his "slave name" proved extremely controversial. (AP Photo).

FIG. 5. After visiting the UN, Ali pledged to be champion of the whole world and undertook an unprecedented, unofficially sanctioned tour of Ghana, Egypt, and Nigeria, where he was greeted by heads of state and huge crowds, as on June 1, 1964, in Lagos. Ali was extremely popular in Africa and the Middle East. (AP Photo).

FIG. 6. Ali confers with Dr. Martin Luther King March 29, 1967. Ali's refusal to serve in the army led to his conviction on draft evasion, a five-year jail sentence, and a $10,000 fine. He was stripped of his title and prevented from boxing. Shortly after conferring with Ali, King came out against the Vietnam War. Although reviled as a traitor and an ungrateful coward, once his stance was adopted by King and other civil rights leaders, Ali became an anti-war hero. (AP Photo).

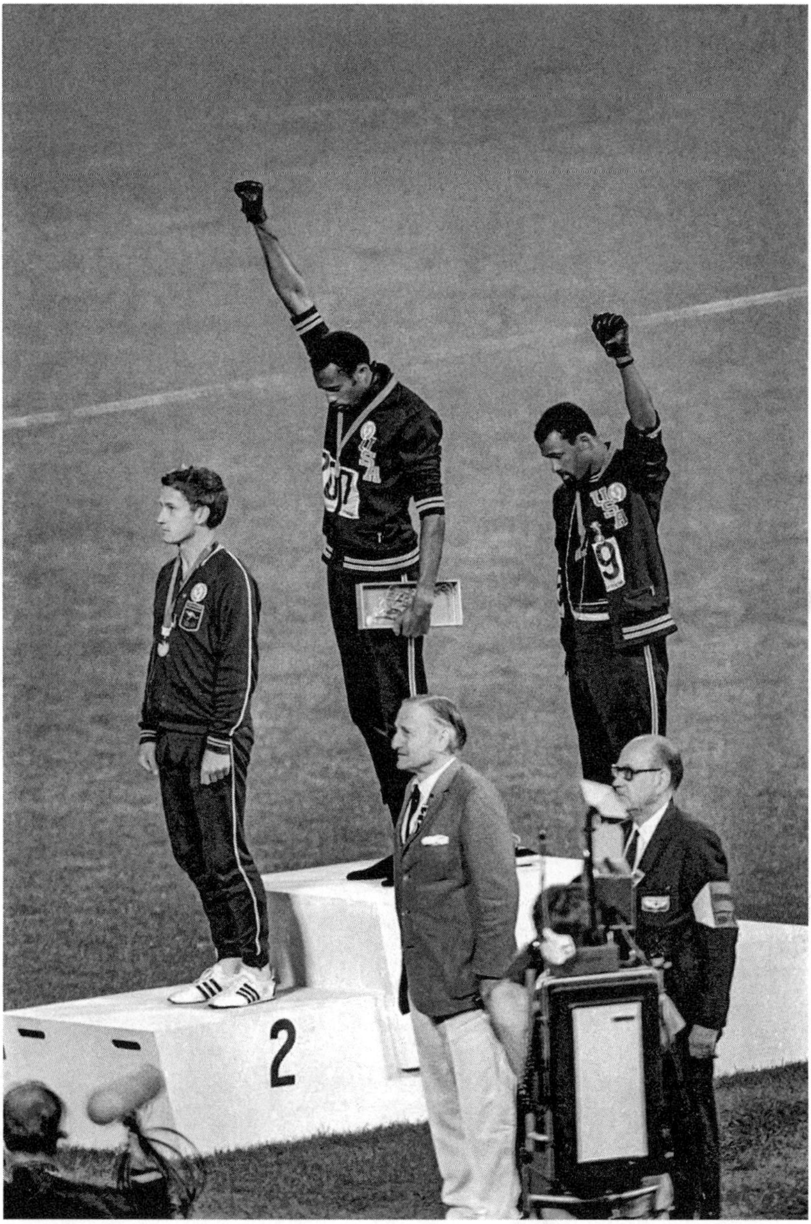

FIG. 7. Tommie Smith and John Carlos raise black-gloved fists during The National Anthem after Smith won gold in the 200 meters and John Carlos took bronze at the 1968 Mexico City Olympics. Silver medalist Australian Peter Norman, is at left. This "Black Power" demonstration climaxed a turbulent year in American sport and society. (AP Photo/File).

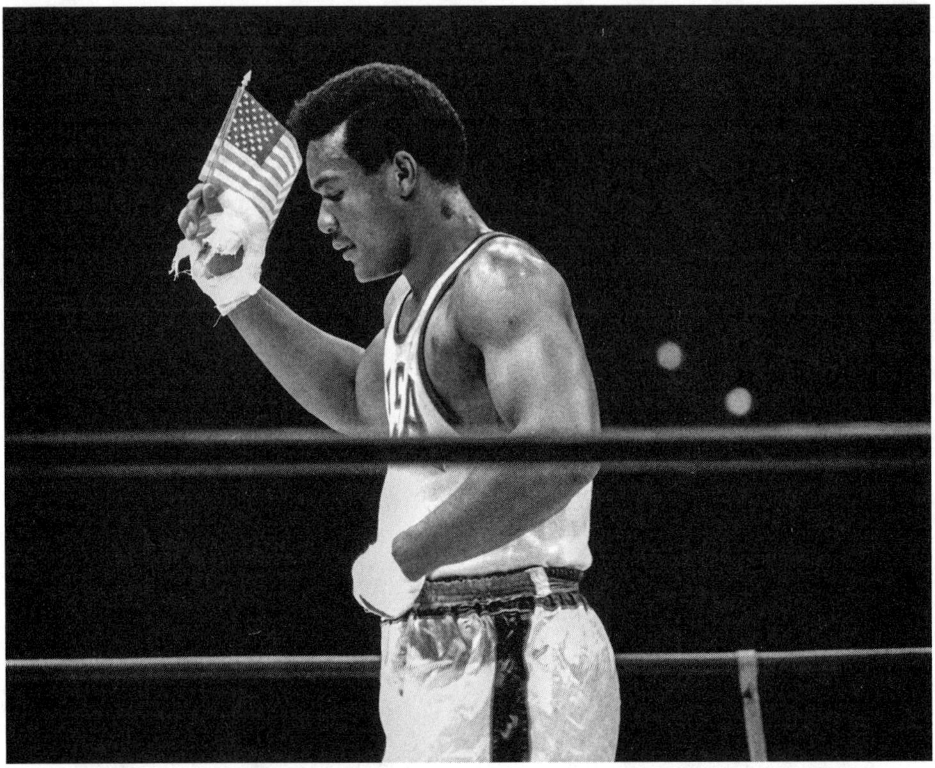

FIG. 8. George Foreman waves an American flag after winning the Olympic gold medal at the Mexico City games, October 27, 1968, by a second round TKO over Iones Chepulis of Russia. Foreman became a cold war hero by defeating the Soviet fighter and responding to black protesters at these games. His actions made him an anti-Ali. (AP Photo/Kurt Strumpf).

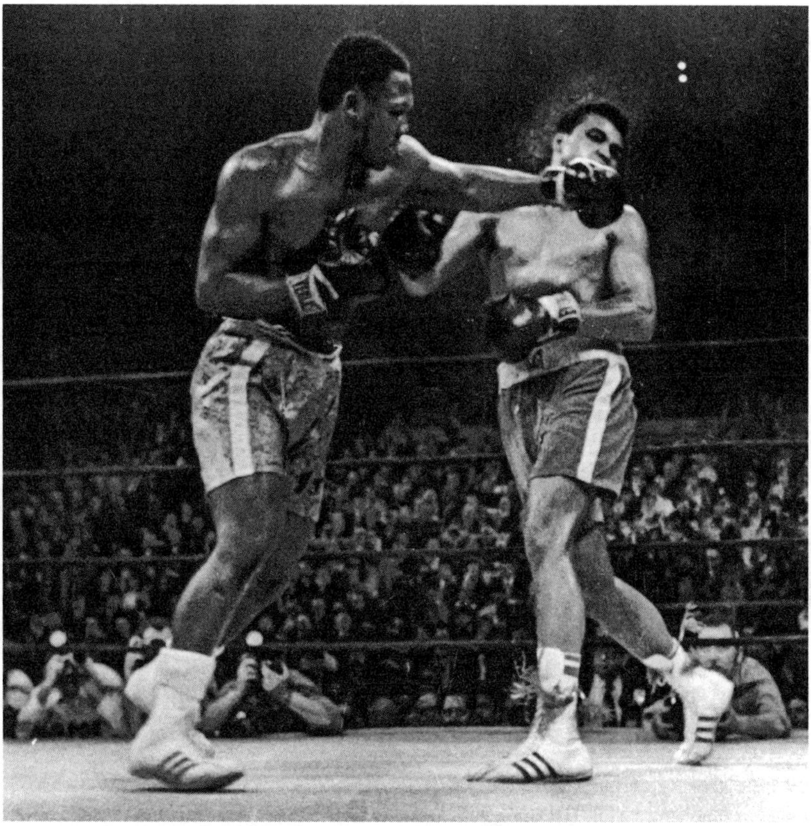

FIG. 9. In his comeback after 3½ years in exile from boxing Ali takes a left from champion Joe Frazier March 8, 1971, in 15th round of their heavyweight title bout at Madison Square Garden. Frazier won a unanimous decision, ruining Ali's return to the ring. The unprecedented match between two undefeated heavyweight champions was considered a battle between a defiant anti-war black radical and a defender of the Vietnam War. (AP Photo/File).

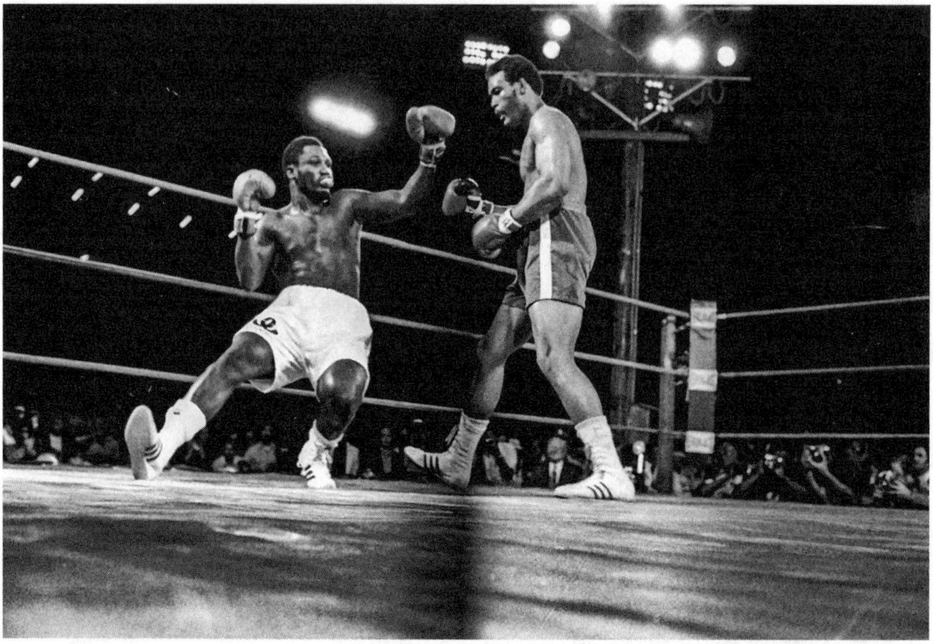

FIG. 10. Complicating the heavyweight picture, Foreman knocks down champion Joe Frazier in an awesome display of power to win the heavyweight title on January 22, 1973, in Kingston, Jamaica. (AP Photo/stf).

FIG. 11. Foreman at news conference, January 23, 1973, a day after winning the title. Right, Sergeant Shriver, former head of the Office of Economic Opportunity and Foreman's legal advisor. Foreman campaigned for Hubert Humphrey for president in 1968 and as "The Fighting Corpsman" publicized the Job Corps, which saved him from a life of poverty and crime. Left, Dick Sadler, Foreman's manager. (AP Photo).

FIG. 12. Champion Foreman at news conference in Republican Governor Ronald Reagan's office in Sacramento, Calif., February 7, 1973. While Foreman remained "The Fighting Corpsman," his flag-waving made him a hero to a vast majority of white boxing fans and older African Americans and an outcast to younger, more radical blacks and whites. (AP Photo/Walter Zeboski).

FIG. 13. Promoters of the Ali-Foreman title bout at a press conference in Caracas, VZ, March 27, 1974, just before Foreman knocked out Ken Norton in 2 rounds. The global matchmakers, from left: Foreman's Manager Dick Sadler, Henry Schwartz, Executive VP of Video Techniques, U.S., John Daly, Great Britain, and Mundungu Bula, Zaire President Mobutu Sese Seko's emissary. Absent is Don King, whose stature as a promoter would rise as he became the face of the promotion. (AP Photo/ML).

4

SAY IT LOUD, I'M BLACK AND I'M PROUD: ZAIRE 74

> The idea of the Negro's having "roots" and that they are a valuable possession rather than a source of ineradicable shame, is perhaps the profoundest change within the Negro consciousness since the early part of the century.
>
> LEROI JONES (AMIRI BARAKA), *BLUES PEOPLE*

George Foreman's cut not only placed the fight in jeopardy; it created severe problems for Zaire 74, the three-day music festival created to precede the Rumble in the Jungle. The fest would build on the global theme of the fight by bringing musicians from Africa together with those from the African diaspora in the United States and the Caribbean. For New World artists, the trip to Africa was a chance to find their roots in what many felt was an exile's return, parallel to the journey of Foreman and Ali. Yet on September 16 just as the musicians were about to board the plane to their African "home," Stewart Levine, chief organizer of the festival, learned of Foreman's cut and the fight's postponement. As a result, the concert and the fight would take place more than a month apart if they took place at all. Fearing that the musicians would consider the trip a fool's errand and refuse to take part in the concert. Levine, in a near panic, decided not to reveal the fight's postponement until the plane was in the air. The ruse worked because of the Jewish New Year; the musicians' Jewish business representatives were attending synagogue services and hence unavailable to protest the proceedings. Once the airplane, loaded with musicians, instruments, and recording equipment lifted off from Madrid on the second leg of the journey, however, the moment of truth arrived. Levine "announced on the plane that it was basically a fool's mission," all the while fearing open revolt by angry and disappointed musicians. To his great relief, however, they responded, "That's okay, man, we're singers." Everyone broke into song. "You couldn't write it."[1]

The world first learned of Zaire 74 when Don King, in an effort to make an epic global sporting event even more spectacular, announced that the Rumble in the Jungle would include a three-day music festival that would precede "the greatest sporting event in the history of the world," on September 20–22. As Ali declared, the Rumble in the Jungle was "much more than a sports event. It's a symbol of the Black American Awakening, with . . . all those beautiful black people goin' home to share their experiences with the black musicians who never left." Financed by the brother of President William Tolbert of Liberia and organized by Levine, Hugh Masekela, and R&B singer Lloyd Price, the festival featured the Americans James Brown, B. B. King, Bill Withers, the Spinners, the Jazz Crusaders, Sister Sledge, the Pointer Sisters, Etta James, and Price. Representing the Caribbean, where enslaved Africans had also deeply influenced the region's musical traditions, were Cuban, Puerto Rican, Dominican, and Mexican artists Johnny Pacheco, Celia Cruz, Ray Barretto, Jorge Santana, and Héctor Lavoe, among others, including the Caribbean music devotee Jewish pianist and bandleader Larry Harlow—the top names in salsa. Like the fight itself, Zaire 74 highlighted a global black consciousness that was an important element in the cultural politics of the era.[2]

The festival also sought to bring the music of Africa to the attention of the world. Among the major stars on the bill was transatlantic singer Miriam Makeba, the South African expatriate who had built an audience in the United States and Africa for her international repertoire of protest, popular, and native songs. In addition, Manu Dibango, the saxophone and keyboard dean of Paris-based African musicians, and the composer of "Soul Makossa," an Afrobeat hit that moved global dance floors, was also expected to perform. Zaïrois bands were scheduled too, including the Madjesi Trio, Franco and the TPOK Jazz Band, Abumba Masikini, the Pembe Dance Troupe, Abeti, and Afrisa with singer Tabu Ley.[3]

This unprecedented gathering of black performers highlighted the cultural ties among black people everywhere. For the Zaïrois commissioner in charge of culture and the arts, Citizen Takizala Luyanu, the festival featured the meeting of "Negro authenticities." African music, he noted in his speech marking the beginning of Zaire 74, was one of the cultural elements of diversified richness that had given birth to African American music such as blues, jazz, and spirituals. Lukundu Sampu, the Zaïrois organizer of the festival, took it a step farther, stressing that "music must be considered an authentic aspect of our culture," and that true black music is African in origin. Under colonialism, "our customs, our art, our civilization were judged only in reference to the colonists' civilization," he said. As a result, "our society was considered static," and to become men, "Zairians had to cease to be black and become white." American artists hit a similar note, stressing that they possessed an authentic culture rooted in Africa and that their African roots helped them survive slavery and racial oppression. African beats "kept us together," noted blues singer and guitarist B. B. King, the headliner on the second night, while Lloyd Price stressed the African roots of all modern black music. Ali, meanwhile, declared that blacks everywhere had created a distinct musical culture. Now, like the nation of Zaire, they "want to be independent."[4]

The organizers of this grandiose venture had high hopes for its success. Chief among them was record producer Stewart Levine, Hugh Masekela's partner in Chisa Records and his closest friend. "When the fight was announced, literally the day it was announced, I saw it was set for Zaire and something just went off in my head," Levine recalled. "We would use the fight as an excuse to give attention to Africa and African music," and show the world how they were integrally related. Some major stars proved reluctant, but for many others "the idea of going to Africa was very seductive." Like organizer Lloyd Price, they felt they were on a historic musical mission. The R&B singer Etta James, for example, "thought, dreamt, and wondered about Africa. Africa is the source, and I was curious to experience all I could." For many African Americans during the 1970s, finding one's roots was a way to overcome the sense of alienation from the US and the African past. This quest was a prime motivation for the interest in black history, the black arts, and African culture that characterized the era. Jazz and soul artists like Randy Weston, Dizzy Gillespie, Louis Armstrong, Duke Ellington, and James Brown had performed in Africa, but there had been nothing on the scale of Zaire 74, which would rival Woodstock in the number of artists and supersede it in its international character. Levine and Masekela contacted Price to see if he "would be interested in our helping him put such an event together." They also believed that "the film that could be made of the festival and Ali and Foreman preparing for the fight would be fantastic. The whole thing could be called 'Three Days of Music and Fighting,'" Levine joked, a reference to Woodstock.[5]

Masekela, a South African expatriate "in the twelfth year of exile from [his] ancestral home," had just completed a musical tour of Guinea, Nigeria, Liberia, and Zaire to discover new sounds and find a missing piece of his identity. Masekela knew the local musicians and would be responsible for contacting them. The first local artist he turned to, Franco, a giant in the world of Congolese rumba, agreed to arrange a lineup of local bands and singers. To Don King, Masekela was a key to the enterprise: "As black brothers armed with our different expertise in our chosen fields, we would capture the imagination of the entire world with our joint initiative. Billions of people will be watching this historical event." As to finances, King told Levine and Masekela: "You get the money to put on this festival and do a film of it. You give me ten percent of your budget and the profits, and you got yourself a deal." The two partners, along with Alan Pariser, an heir and musical entrepreneur, formed the Ace Company and through Masekela's connections managed to wangle $2 million from Steve Tolbert, the brother of Liberia's president, to stage the festival, produce a documentary film, and release record albums of this historic global event.[6]

It is not surprising that Levine was fascinated by the prospect of staging and filming a huge music festival. During the late 1960s and early 1970s music festivals proliferated; so too did their film documentation. Perhaps the most famous festivals were the Monterey Pop Festival in 1967 and Woodstock, which took place over three days in summer 1969 and then reappeared as a film documenting its three days of "Peace and Love," the following year. The spirit of celebration also had a profound impact on black music in the concert and film *Wattstax: The Living Word*, staged by Memphis's Stax Records label. The August 20, 1972, festival embodied Stax president Al Bell's desire, after Martin Luther King's assassination, to demonstrate a militant black identity, one that would also mark the Zaire event. Bell and Afrocentric promoter Larry Shaw saw the concert as a way to celebrate black culture as part of the Watts Summer Festival, staged annually after the Watts uprising of 1965 as a testament to the community's racial pride and cultural ferment. Shaw chose the Los Angeles Coliseum as the venue because of its proximity to Watts. To make it possible for poor blacks to attend, tickets cost a dollar, with the proceeds going to the Sickle Cell Anemia Foundation, the Martin Luther King Hospital in Watts, and future Watts Summer Festivals. More than one hundred thousand people attended, while many more watched the concert via simulcasts or listened over black radio stations. Only the March on Washington in 1963 had attracted a larger black gathering. The following year Bell and Shaw released *Wattstax*, with up-and-coming black comedian Richard Pryor discussing the black experience with poor residents of Watts in a manner that validated their plight in a racist society. Stax also released two double albums of the concert on its own label. The Wattstax concert, film, and albums along with the previous festivals and a filmed movie of a salsa concert, *Our Latin Thing* (*Nuestra Cosa*, 1972), served as forceful precedents for a music festival and a profitable film celebrating black musical culture as a global phenomenon.[7]

While Don King bragged about producing the great spectacle, it was Levine and Masekela who organized it. The two friends were well suited to arrange such a global black music fest. When young saxophonist Stewart Levine and South African trumpeter Hugh Masekela first met in 1960 as students at the Manhattan School of Music, Masekela considered Levine one of few Americans with any interest in or knowledge of Africa, and thus one of the few people with whom he could discuss the subject. Unlike the average white or black American, in Masekela's view Levine did not see Africans as savages, nor did he view the globe divided between a virtuous United States and a tyrannical Soviet Union. Raised in a liberal Bronx Jewish family, he was radicalized by his interest in black music, his sympathy for the civil rights movement, and his girlfriend Susan Carp, a Young People's Socialist League leader knowledgeable about independence movements across the globe. For his part, Levine's interest in black music not only helped cement a lifelong friendship with Masekela; it also expressed his discontent with the racial and political status quo. Together they formed an independent production company in 1965, Chisa Records, so Masekela could control his own musical destiny. Levine became a high-powered arranger of soul and R&B, and the two partners began producing records that were a hybrid of African township music and soul, R&B, and jazz. Levine also produced Masekela's global jazz hybrid hit "Grazing in the Grass," as well as albums by the Jazz Crusaders, B. B. King, and other musicians.[8]

As the other half of the partnership, Masekela had a deep interest in what today is called world music, a belief that black music fostered resistance, and a desire to reconnect his expatriate existence with his African heritage. Born in 1939 in the South African coal-mining town of Witbank, his experience revealed how interrelated American and African music had become. His grandmother ran an illegal shebeen, where she played big-band swing records. These American sounds profoundly influenced black South African bands like the Jazz Maniacs, the Harlem Swingsters, the Merry Makers, and the Merry Blackbirds, which played many American hits and dressed in hip American fashions of the time. There were also hybrid township versions of swing, such as *marabi*, *jit*, *mbhaqanga*, and *kwela*. Masekela's fascination with American music grew after hearing Harry James play the trumpet parts for Kirk Douglas in the film *Young Man with a Horn* (1950).[9]

After a stint in England, Masekela traveled to the United States with the help of fellow South African expatriate and his future wife Miriam Makeba and the American patron of world music, Harry Belafonte, who provided him with a scholarship to the Manhattan School of Music. When he arrived in New York in 1960 he immersed himself in the musical offerings at Harlem's Apollo Theater and took part in the jazz scene, where he befriended fellow trumpeters Dizzy Gillespie, Miles Davis, and his hero Clifford Brown. Belafonte was an important influence for Masekela, since his international folk songs underscored his interest in the downtrodden and paralleled his leftist political beliefs. Both Belafonte and Makeba encouraged Masekela to remain in touch with his roots.[10]

Since arriving in the United States in 1959, Makeba had enjoyed much success, performing at President Kennedy's birthday party, at the Hollywood Bowl, and at Carnegie Hall. When she appeared before African heads of state at the inauguration of the Organization of African Unity in Addis Ababa in 1963, she became well known across all of Africa. Paired with Belafonte, furthermore, she won a Grammy for the album *An Evening with Belafonte and Makeba*. Makeba's performances of black South African music and dance encouraged Masekela to use music to address the suffering of his people and rattle South African racists. To do that, he made up his mind, with the help of Levine, to incorporate other black expatriate South African artists in creating the jazz hybrid of "Grazing in the Grass." An eclectic mix of African diaspora music followed, and Masekela produced even more African-oriented work after 1973, when he and Levine toured Guinea, Liberia, Nigeria, and Zaire, where the music was exploding.[11]

Masekela and Levine were unable to land some of the biggest stars on their list, such as Stevie Wonder, Barry White, and Aretha Franklin. They also wanted Fela Kuti, but for political reasons the acclaimed Nigerian Afrobeat pioneer and political dissident was not allowed to travel outside his country. James Brown, though, was eager to return to Zaire, a country he had already visited. As a megastar he was crucial to the whole enterprise. "He was the most important guy because at that time although he was really popular in America, he was literally a king in Africa, much more than he realized," recalled Levine. "He was the make or break guy for us." First, however, they had to meet his many demands, including that he be first to board and deplane in Kinshasa, that his band occupy the first-class seats, and that he have a limousine, an audience with President Mobutu, and a luxury hotel suite with adjoining rooms for his valet and emcee. In addition, because the band was continuing on to Gabon after Zaire, Brown demanded that his revue's thirty thousand pounds of equipment travel on the plane. He also insisted on $100,000 for his performance. Although put out by Brown's terms, Levine, Masekela, and Price were forced to agree "because in Africa he was the most popular American performer."[12]

Similar to previous fests, the organizers planned to film the concert and the fight preparations. "Our purpose was to document the history of the beat," Price declared. To do so, the organizers chose documentary director Leon Gast. Gast had previously filmed a live salsa concert for *Our Latin Thing*, or *Nuestra Cosa* (1972), which interwove street scenes of Puerto Ricans and

Dominicans in New York with performances of the Fania All-Stars, who would appear at Zaire 74. In a nod toward the desires of African Americans to work behind the camera, Gast hired twelve black film crew members. To erect the stage at Mai 20 Stadium they contacted Chip Monk, who had overseen the job at Woodstock. Monk helped, but he insisted that the task was so big they also needed Bill McManus, the best stage director in American rock. Once in Kinshasa, the organizers envisioned music, dance, and drum ensembles performing in the streets, with special groups stationed at the airport and hotels to greet tourists in a festive manner.[13]

Meanwhile, as soon as everyone was settled in Zaire and the final preparations for the festival were under way, Levine and Masekela had Don King breathing down their necks. With so much at stake, tempers grew short. Frustrated by the postponement of the fight and its potential financial debacle and worried that the festival had grabbed all the media attention, the usually exuberant King became increasingly difficult. Not only did he call Levine a honky; at one of the all-night parties he called Masekela an Uncle Tom. "I'm really disappointed in you, Hugh Masekela," the trumpeter reported King saying: "You should be running the whole show, and instead you're letting that white boy Levine order you around." Masekela responded angrily that it was King who was doing the ordering and interfering with everything they were trying to do. "I don't know what the fuck you're talking about, Don," Masekela declared, "but you don't talk like that to me here in Africa, man. This is not fucking Cleveland! I will have you wasted, man!" According to Masekela, the two never spoke again. After their return to the United States, their relationship only worsened when King demanded another 10 percent for the film and recording rights.[14]

Despite the frustrations, once everyone settled in, Kinshasa came alive with music and dance; "the mood was electric," with lots of late-night parties fueled by the exuberance of the local musicians, as well as by alcohol and marijuana. When the festival began on September 22, the concert performances were joyful, usually going all night and ending at 4 a.m. On display were black American soul and funk music at the height of their creativity. As Levine put it: "This was . . . the apex of rhythm and blues music in America. . . . It never had a bigger moment than it did at that time. Shortly after that we had disco. Then we had rap." To everyone's surprise the festival actually took place, although the first two nights suffered because of poor attendance. Ticket prices were too high for local fans, there were few foreign tourists, and actual tickets were unavailable until the last minute. Those first two nights artists played to at most 5,000 people, in a stadium designed for 62,500. Hoping to avoid a complete debacle, Mobutu ordered that tickets be given away as a gift to his people for the third night, and the concert ended on an upbeat note with a full house. In total seventeen Zaïrois groups and fourteen from abroad performed. As Levine recalled, "This concert had a drama to it that led to great performances from everybody."[15]

Given her African roots and transnational musical and political appeal, Miriam Makeba, known as "Mama Africa," was chosen to greet the audience on the opening night, which she did in Lingala, the local dialect, as well as perform on the second evening. As the most famous African performer in the United States, Makeba highlighted the importance of African music and its crucial role in a musical culture that had traveled across the Atlantic with the many Africans who had left the continent in chains. As she demonstrated, African music featured many underlying similarities while also proving itself highly adaptable to new circumstances. On the second night of the festival, she topped off her set with her international hit "The Click Song," a reference to the sounds in her native Xhosa language. Makeba's performance reflected the dialogue between Africa and the world, with the West influencing Africa as much as the reverse. Her life expressed the theme of exile and return, displacement and the longing for home, and she turned this into a music of resistance against South African apartheid and Western colonialism. Makeba exemplified the fluidity of the musical culture that lay at the heart of the African diaspora and the ways it formed a mode of resistance.[16]

As her onstage remarks made clear, the theme of exile infused her life and her music. From her earliest interviews in the United States, Makeba stressed that although blacks in South Africa were treated as though they were worth nothing, "I still want to go home." Denied home, land, and family, she said, "I am in exile on the outside. We are in exile on the inside." Yet her music—like "The Click Song"—expressed the hope that justice would prevail and she would be allowed to return to a black-ruled South Africa. Early in life she had learned that music had the power to gladden the hearts of her listeners and give them hope: "Who can keep us down as long as we have our music?" She discovered music as a form of resistance when she joined a high school chorus that often performed songs written by South African composers in tribal languages. Some were seditious toward white rule, but they escaped scrutiny since whites remained ignorant of native languages. Sometimes the music was played on the radio, but when government officials discovered what it meant they would ban it. Through the worst of apartheid, young Makeba also took heart from black American music and culture, which provided a vision of an alternative, freer life. Every Sunday Makeba and her girlfriends gathered to play jazz records by Billie Holiday, Ella Fitzgerald, and the big swing bands. From them she learned to sing American songs, which she performed for her brother's friends.[17]

In the late 1950s after a string of hit recordings she appeared in a documentary about black South Africa, singing two songs in a nightclub scene. Because the authorities opposed the film, it had to be shot secretly at night. As a result of her performance, filmmaker Lionel Rogosin invited her to Europe to help promote the film *Come Back, Africa,* whose title was based on the anthem of the African National Congress. The film made her an international star, but because of its controversial nature South African officials withdrew her passport and prohibited her from returning to her daughter and family.[18]

Almost overnight, however, she became the first major black African star in the United States. Transfixed by her performance, Harry Belafonte became her sponsor, helping her to get a US visa, introducing her to influential music people, promoting her records, encouraging her to perform African music rather than jazz standards, and selecting her to open for his own shows. Moreover, the press and political groups took her up because African anticolonialism and American racial politics were heating up. She was repeatedly invited to the United Nations to speak on behalf of various black African movements, and she appeared with Belafonte at rallies sponsored by Martin Luther King. All of this made her "too dangerous" for South African authorities to allow her to return home.[19]

As a result of her growing prominence, various African leaders appealed to her for help. Tom Mboya, a leader of the Kenyan independence movement and head of the African Students Foundation, asked her to sing at benefits to raise money for Kenyan students to study in the United States, and then invited her to Kenya to help raise funds for Mau Mau orphans. Since she had no passport, Kenya permitted her to enter on special entry papers. That same year, 1962, Tanzania gained independence, and she was able to visit an independent black African nation for the first time. Knowing of her exile, President Julius Nyerere, a founding father of African nationalism, granted her a Tanzanian passport, a feat repeated by other newly independent black African countries. "For the first time," she recalled, "I feel that I am not only a South African native, but a native of all of Africa."[20]

Her role as a voice against colonial oppression grew during the 1960s, as did the animosity of the South African regime. Because of her consistent vocal opposition to apartheid and its brutality, the regime declared her a criminal and banned the sale of her records. That did not stop under-the-counter sales, however; nor did it lessen her importance as an anticolonial figure. In 1963 she was the only performer invited to Addis Ababa, Ethiopia, to mark the formation of the Organization of African Unity. Shortly thereafter, she was invited by President Jomo Kenyatta to celebrate Kenya's independence on December 12, 1963. From then on, whenever a black African nation declared its independence, she was invited to perform at the ceremony. No wonder Swiss documentary filmmakers pronounced her "Mama Africa," representing "the continent and its music to the Western world."[21]

By the time she appeared onstage at Zaire 74, however, Makeba was in exile once again, but this time from the United States. Despite hits with "Gumboots" in 1965 and "Pata Pata" in 1967, her popularity in the United States plummeted in 1968, when she married Black Power advocate Stokely Carmichael, whom many white Americans viewed as a revolutionary responsible for the urban riots. Tarred with the same brush, Makeba found herself described in the press as "soft-spoken" but "almost as angrily militant as her husband." Followed by the FBI, she encountered difficulty receiving US visas when returning from engagements abroad. More troubling, concerts were canceled "because you married a radical," lucrative nightclub and television bookings disappeared, and "this wonderful dream come true—the little African girl who becomes a big star in America—it's all over."[22]

Although she was a Pan-African symbol at Zaire 74, she could not return home to South Africa, nor was she willing to go back to the United States given its official hostility toward her. She could, however, return to Africa as a symbol of musical resistance and political solidarity with black Africans seeking their independence from their colonial masters. In songs praising Mobutu and calling for African unity, she represented a resilient Africa in the face of both colonial oppression and American fears. In her appearance, she also represented African womanhood: her dress, her inspired dancing, and her intricate African hairstyle expressed a black beauty and persona that had been defiled and denigrated under colonialism. During the 1960s Makeba was one of the first black women in the United States to wear her hair in a short natural style, but while living in Guinea in 1972, she fell in love with a Guinea hair tradition called *sahi ya maboho,* which involved more elaborate hair designs. In many ways, the exiled star had come home by blending tradition and modernity as she challenged the last vestiges of colonialism in Africa.[23]

While Miriam Makeba's return from exile expressed the resistance to colonialism and apartheid most explicitly, James Brown symbolized the racially assertive black pride that united all the performers at Zaire 74, including Motown acts like the Spinners, soul performers such as Sister Sledge, blues great B. B. King, and soul-funk jazz group the Jazz Crusaders. As the festival headliner and closing act on the opening night, Brown performed at the height of his powers despite a crowd of only five thousand people. Not only was Brown excited to perform for thousands of Africans; Zairians wanted to experience this black music titan who had so influenced African music. According to *Jet*, in Africa the "most-respected and asked-about Black American personalities are Brown and boxer Muhammad Ali." Brown's fame in Africa derived from a musical style rooted in extended dance jams and a willingness to tour Africa as the land of his racial and musical roots. After returning from a 1971 African tour, he declared: "We're all the same. Take the suit and collars off and everybody's the same, here and there. Over there, the brothers have the land and the potential; over here, we have the education and the experience. All of us can be free men as soon as we find a way to hook these things up." Because of these sentiments, *Jet* called Brown a "Pan-Africanist."[24]

Brown's fame at home and abroad lay in his ability to capture the militant mood among African Americans and Africans during the late 1960s and early 1970s. "He gives voice to the guys on the blocks," *Jet* asserted, "putting into words what they are only thinking." Not only was he flamboyant in dress and manner; he also expressed the pride in blackness and the defiance to oppression that was roiling black communities nationwide. While his politics were not militant, noted Ricky Vincent, his manhood was. He represented "the political black man, the successful black man, the sexual black man, the relentless black warrior that was 'Black and Proud.'" Like Ali, Brown was both the victim of racism and "a universal symbol of American black strength, pride, defiance and survival." The title of one of his most notable hit records, *Say It Loud, I'm Black and I'm Proud*, made this clear, but his artistry was even more epitomized by the grunts and shouts that characterized his music from the late 1960s on. "In these simple, primal utterances," noted historian Mel Watkins, "Brown comes nearer his poetic goal than in any of his more elaborate lyrics. For there, he is not singing about Black life—he is Black life."[25]

Like many black music stars, Brown grew up rough. He was born on May 3, 1933, in Toccoa, Georgia, a rural area north of Augusta. Abandoned by his mother at four years old, he lived with his father in a shack until he was taken in by an aunt who ran a brothel. The region's Ku Klux Klan activities frightened his father, who donned an acquiescent demeanor with whites but turned his bottled-up rage on his son. James vowed to be different—a fighter. This was reinforced by several searing racist incidents, including an attempt by a group of white men to electrocute him, which left him deeply distrustful of Southern white men.[26]

His love of music and dance was nurtured by the Augusta region's rich musical tradition. On radio, he heard the big bands and popular singers of the day. The region's gospel tradition proved an enormous influence, especially Bishop "Daddy" Grace and His House of Prayer. In the late 1940s and 1950s, Daddy Grace wore his hair long and curly, adorned himself with lavish clothes and glistening fingernails, and talked and sang his sermons to a drumbeat while engaging in call-and-response with his congregants, who were an essential part of the performance. From Grace and other gospel singers, James learned that that it was the emotional intensity of the singer rather than a cultivated voice that was important. A key element of that intensity was the scream, which expressed spiritual pain and ecstatic joy. As singer and congregation inspired each other to greater emotional heights, the cry of the oppressed became "a cry of liberation." Inspired by gospel music, at the age of twelve James formed his own gospel group, the Cremona Trio, to which he added jazz touches and the nascent rhythm and blues of Louis Jordan. He had quit school at ten, danced in the Augusta streets for money, and got in trouble for a series of crimes. He was sentenced to three and a half years in reform school, where he refined his skills as a gospel singer. Paroled at eighteen in 1952, he joined Byrd's Ever-Ready Gospel Singers just as they began experimenting with R&B. Like other soul performers, he blended the secular and the sacred, and the band became James Brown and the Famous Flames in the mid-1950s. As a soul singer he played largely to black audiences, developing his revue format, directing his band with an iron fist, and working constantly, earning the title of "Hardest Working Man in Show Business."[27]

When he started singing and dancing "on the one," the first beat in 4/4 time, Brown transformed himself from a soul singer into a cultural icon, and his music took on a more insistent, aggressive style. The origins of playing and singing on the one go back to 1965 and "Papa's Got a Brand New Bag," but it was during the late 1960s and 1970s, after the trauma of Martin Luther King's assassination, that the one characterized all of Brown's music and made him an embodiment of the freedom movement's insistence on liberation, self-ownership and soulful black pride. "Getting down with the 'One' is the whole key to understanding my music, where it came from, where it went," he declared. It connotes "force, leadership, and most important, self-pride." More than a musical change, Brown insisted the emphasis on the dominant beat expressed an aggressive desire for racial liberation. The blues were written on the two, the downbeat, and connoted black diffidence. "I was *born* to the downbeat, and I can tell you without question there is no pride in it," Brown claimed. By the late 1960s he helped articulate a more insistent message that resonated with the urgency of the civil rights movement and Black Power. He played benefit concerts for activists, applauded the actions of (some) militants, and by sacrificing his flamboyant pompadour for a natural hairdo, came to embody "black is beautiful."[28]

The notion of the one involved more than a new beat. The forceful rhythmic thrust fit perfectly with Brown's stage presentation and what fans expected from his revues: "I strut onto a stage at the start of my show, with my head held high, my feet taking wide strides, and a big smile on my face." According to Brown, the one emphasized the black masculine strength and forcefulness that characterized the era. When he shifted to the one, the music opened the floodgates for a rhythm-based extension of soul, renamed funk, that expressed the new forcefulness of black demands for equality and justice. Above all, he said, "Pride—that was the key. Pride and self-worth."[29]

By the time Brown released the song "Say It Loud, I'm Black and I'm Proud," funk had become Brown's major contribution to music. After the assassinations and upheavals of 1968, numerous other black performers preached messages of pride while attempting to "make it funky." Funk was a subtle shift—a belief that the "funk" in black life, which originally connoted negativity—was to be celebrated as a set of core values that were superior to the stale cultural values of the white majority. Whether it was black skin, nappy hair, flamboyant clothes, get-down music, or the communal warmth of the church, to quote Brown, "it's got to be funky." A 1975 *Ebony* editorial recognized the song's deeper importance: "Like James Brown, I can say, 'Say it loud. I'm Black and I'm proud.' He has helped us reach the point where there is no more apologizing. . . . The constant striving to measure oneself by white standards is out. The constant acceptance of 'white is right' is out. Black people are finding freedom that they never had before—the freedom to be themselves."[30]

Being funky also meant celebrating a forceful black masculine persona. Shifting to the one with a heavy bass beat underlined a refusal to repress the black body. Historically, whites' biggest fear was that strong, sexualized black men would steal or rape white women and hence needed to be controlled by the forces of order. In an era when the white counterculture was challenging conceptions of controlled manhood in favor of self-expression, and the freedom movement—especially its Black Power variant—posed new and more assertive models of black men and women, an opening occurred to question conceptions of masculinity and social order in general. Similar to the heroes of black-oriented films, Brown's sexuality was a prominent part of his act as he danced, sang, and strutted across the stage in revealing jumpsuits, open-necked shirts, and tight pants. As did his idol Ali, Brown put the black body on display in all its power, aggressiveness, and sexual potency.[31]

Brown had made his first trip to Africa in 1968, which had a "life-affirming and life-changing" effect on him. That trip helps explain why he was such an important part of the Zaire music festival. On the five-day 1968 tour, Brown often felt overwhelmed seeing children walking down the street clutching his albums, which were costly and could be played only on communal phonographs. "Here I was, in a land where Black meant something other than 'Hey, you' or 'You're not welcome here.'" In Africa, he said, he "found a new sense of who I was, where I had come from, and where I wanted to go." It was his affinity with black Africans, moreover, that proved a prime factor in his refusal to play Sun City, a separate state established by apartheid South Africa as an international tourist destination. He might have been tempted earlier in his life by the $3 million offer, "but I had become so aware of apartheid and all the troubles there that I simply said no." As he wrote, "I did not believe in working for blood money."[32]

For a black capitalist who believed in owning a piece of the American dream, Brown saw the solution to the nation's racial turmoil in making the game fair, not in revolution—and he believed in pushing for a seat at the table. Unlike Ali and the Nation of Islam, he was not willing to wait for the apocalyptic moment when whites would be punished and blacks would attain their national homeland. Despite his peaceful intentions, he felt that "Say It Loud, I'm Black and I'm Proud," the song that emerged during the tumultuous year of 1968 and the one most associated with him during the Black Power era, was misinterpreted as the sentiments of a militant revolutionary. In general, whites saw the song as a hostile, antiwhite statement meant to cause fear. White-owned radio stations refused to play what they saw as a call to further violence. It did not help when militant groups like the Student Nonviolent Coordinating Committee and the Black Panthers turned the song into their personal anthems, "all but obliterating its peaceful and positive message." Although it may have been a hit, the song cost him his crossover appeal, and he went back to entertaining black audiences almost exclusively in small clubs. Soon the Federal Communications Commission went after the Baltimore radio station he owned, he was involved in a payola scandal, his jet was repossessed, and white radio outlets refused to play his recordings.[33]

During the early 1970s, Brown continued to tour Europe and Africa to capacity crowds despite his economic and political problems. Driven back to performing for black audiences at home, however, Brown revamped his band and his soul revue to make the music aggressively funkier. With the addition of funk musicians bassist Bootsy Collins and his brother, guitarist Phelps "Catfish" Collins, along with trombonist Fred Wesley, and Afro-Latin jazz hand drummer Johnny Griggs, the new band, the J.B.'s, moved beyond the twelve-bar blues pattern to elongated, often improvised grooves designed for dancing. The new approach was rhythm based. "Unlike music derived from the Blues," notes Ricky Vincent, "it was not built around a melody or even an implied melody. This music came from the drums, bass and guitars and for the first time in America, this music spoke directly to Africa." In 1970 the band debuted with a megahit, "Sex Machine," followed by straight-talking tunes like "Get Up, Get into It, Get Involved," that was a seven-minute dance track counseling patience and doing right. Other funk hits of the early 1970s included "The Payback," "Hot Pants," "Get Up offa That Thing," "Papa Don't Take No Mess," "Stoned to the Bone," and "Funky President (People It's Bad)," all of which featured long instrumental jams, repetitive vocal riffs, references to soul food, ecstatic shouts and grunts—and a more explicit discussion of social issues that exuded confidence, strength, and group pride.[34]

With business falling off at home, his politics both respected and suspect, and his personal life in turmoil after the death of his son in a car crash, Brown was eager to travel to Zaire to headline the music festival. In Africa he was still king, and there he could bask in his racial roots far away from his troubles with the IRS and the loss of the radio stations he had accumulated on his road to success. With saxophonist Maceo Parker and trombonist Fred Wesley setting a funk groove for the J.B.'s, the Godfather of Soul hit the stage at Zaire 74, dancing furiously, doing splits, throwing the standing mic. Dressed in a sky-blue jumpsuit with an open-necked shirt revealing his muscular chest, Brown summoned all his energy to give one of the greatest performances of his life. Holding nothing in reserve, he poured out his soul to the African audience. They, in return, responded with ecstatic dancing of their own and tremendous applause. Opening with "The Payback," Brown ran through his soul and funk hits, moving from a frantic version of "Cold Sweat," to "I Can't Stand Myself," followed by the black anthem of that era, "Say It Loud, I'm Black and I'm Proud." He finished with the crowd-pleasing "Please, Please, Please." The band was the revamped funk version of the early 1970s, filled with rhythm and groove similar to the African bands of the Nigerian Fela Kuti or the Congolese rumba outfits like Franco and the TPOK Jazz and Tabu Ley and Afrisa. The concert proved that Brown's music had become global and it had returned home.

Brown received an enthusiastic welcome in Zaire surpassed only by the surprising response to Johnny Pacheco, Celia Cruz, and the Fania All-Stars. In fact, Cruz recalled that the other American performers could not believe how popular salsa was in Zaire. Fans met them at the airport screaming, "Pacheco! Pacheco! Pacheco!" in honor of Johnny Pacheco, the Dominican American flautist and leader of the Fania All-Stars. “I was amazed to see Pacheco received like a conquering king,” Cruz recalled. After all, “Zaire was so far from the Caribbean and the center of his fan base. Actually, I don't think they were treating James Brown or any of the other Americans the same way. It was Pacheco's show.” For Cruz the concert was a grand event: “A sea of black people dancing is a beautiful sight to see.” When she sang “Quimbara” and “Guantanamera,” the crowd went wild. “I was amazed that my version of that Cuban classic had made it all the way into the heart of Africa.” Actually, Afro-Caribbean music had influenced Congo rhythms enormously, and Congo rhythms had an enormous influence on Caribbean sounds. At Zaire 74 salsa had a chance to come home at its creative peak.[35]

Although a common African aesthetic underlay Caribbean and North American musical culture, Caribbean music retained many more overt “Africanisms.” In North America, white-majority society suppressed African instruments, dances, and religious forms. Yet in adapting to Protestant culture in the early nineteenth century, the enslaved transformed worship, European dance, and music into an Afro-American culture with a strong emphasis on call-and-response, improvisation, and dance as both spiritual and secular—but often within white religious forms and European dances. The result was a new cultural synthesis. In Cuba, by contrast, the Spanish came as conquerors, not settlers, and engaged in the cultivation of sugarcane, which required the continuous importation of large numbers of Africans until late in the nineteenth century. As a result, Cuba was dominated by black majorities whose numbers and closer African ties enabled them to retain their drums, their gods, and elements of their religious past which remained apart from Catholicism. Music and dance were part of religious ceremonies, musicians retained godlike status, and music itself combined religious and secular elements. Music influenced all of life, as it did in Africa, and dancing could be this-world sensuous and otherworld holy. Together the emergent Afro-Cuban musical culture served as a means to establish separate identities and helped the vast majority of Cubans liberate themselves from Spanish colonialism. Like African music, multiple rhythms, not melody, dominated the music, and individuals had greater freedom to contribute their own voices. Call-and-response between the sections of the band or between individual musicians—especially the drummers—and improvisation within a unified structure shaped the musical product.[36]

Zaire 74 offered citizens of the former Belgian Congo the opportunity to hear “their” music as it came back home. On Monday, September 23, sixty thousand Zaïroises witnessed the Fania All-Stars firing on all cylinders, the percussionists stomping out the beat, and the petite Cruz, attired in high heels, coiffed in a glorious wig, and sporting a flamboyant rumba dress that emphasized her curves, singing and dancing to the infectious rhythms. Meanwhile, Pacheco darted in and out on flute and maracas, all the while dancing joyously as he led the All-Stars to a rhythmic fury. The crowd responded in kind, dancing ecstatically as Ray Barretto, with his shirt opened to display his bare chest, pounded out the rhythm on his congas, Yomo Toro strummed the cuatro, Roberto Roena's bongos jumped, and trumpets and trombones pierced the air. On "Mi gente" (My people), singer Héctor Lavoe linked the Caribbean music to its African roots and the African audience as he sang "Mi gente Ustedes" (you are my people), added "how beautiful is Africa," and at the end proclaimed, "Viva África!"[37]

While Cruz's prominence exemplified the music's Cuban roots, in fact salsa had made New York City the new capital of Latin music through the influence of second-generation Puerto Ricans and other Caribbean migrants who had brought the insurgent spirit of the barrio to the music. Cuban music played by large orchestras had fueled New York's mambo craze and Latin jazz during the 1950s and early 1960s, but by the mid-1960s the popularity of these styles had ebbed. The Cuban Revolution and the US embargo on travel and commerce cut off the supply of new Cuban music and musicians. While Cuba stagnated, New York experienced an intense period of musical chaos and experimentation.[38]

The musical ferment in New York was led by second-generation musicians from Puerto Rico and the Caribbean who were influenced by the civil rights and Black Power movements to assert their own racial pride by exploring the gritty realities of barrio life and their Afro-Caribbean roots, especially the African-rooted rhythms of the *plena* and the *bomba*. Second-generation Puerto Rican, Dominican, Panamanian, Colombian, and Venezuelan artists renovated Cuban dance music to reflect urban barrio life in New York and the Caribbean's seething cities. They engaged in a "nonessential" musical strategy that adapted black sounds, the music of different islands, and a new cultural aggressiveness to express the conditions of urban life through music rooted in the transnational Spanish language. The resultant music was one of hybridity and cultural resistance that boomed in popularity as the Fania All-Stars made their triumphant appearance at Zaire 74. As historian George Lipsitz suggests, salsa opened its arms to young musicians of different backgrounds to create a pan-Caribbean culture that expressed the sense of displacement experienced in the barrios of New York and the Caribbean. According to trombonist Willie Colón, salsa was "a harmonic blend of all the Latin music of New York, expressed in a new way through a completely mestizo type of music." Johnny Pacheco, leader of the All-Stars and cofounder of Fania Records, emigrated as a child with his family from the Dominican Republic in 1946 and played music in New York with Cubans, Puerto Ricans, and Colombians. As a result, New York's musical influences "are very diverse, and that's why there's diversity in the rhythm and melody." Created in New York's melting pot, salsa was, argued Pacheco, "a Caribbean musical movement."[39]

The influential film documentary *Our Latin Thing* (*Nuestra Cosa*) shows salsa as rooted in the street life, bodegas, festivals, religious rituals, and tenements of Spanish Harlem and the South Bronx. So too younger Puerto Ricans were influenced by the antiwar movement and the racial ferment of the day to question governmental authority and the older generation. Emerging from the barrio, the new generation of the late 1960s and 1970s abandoned the tuxedos of the great mambo orchestras, welcomed more dark-skinned musicians into their bands, and assumed the personas of ordinary street guys. Their music reflected the barrio's anger and alienation caused by being part black in a "white" world, Spanish-speaking in an English-language society, and working class amid affluence. According to salsa-music commentator Alfredo Lopez, Puerto Rican youth "had always known we were Puerto Ricans, but we were never quite sure what that was." Then, he asserted, "heroes came onto the scene," young Puerto Rican kids like ourselves "who played a music that sounded right, touched a cultural nerve, was easy to dance to." Here was "Something of our own! Rhythms and structures centuries old—the passion and energy of our streets and of African slaves—the electronics of New York society and instruments and arrangements better than rock and roll."[40]

Salsa was rooted in Cuban music, especially the form known as son, but was reinterpreted by New York's Puerto Rican musicians less interested in cha-chas, mambos, and rumbas that were modified for white dancers. The son was a dance form that featured a solo singer or musician followed by a *montuno*, or improvised passage, in which the singer, vocal chorus, and musicians exchanged call-and-response riffs rooted in African music and allowing for individual and group improvisation. Learning from rock, jazz, and rhythm and blues, the *montuno* section featured spontaneity, improvisation, and a sense of freedom. The other influence from Cuba, the clave, set the 3/2 beat, anchored the different polyrhythms of the many other percussion instruments, and propelled the dancers.[41]

A critical factor in New York's dominance of salsa was the emergence of Fania Records, which tapped the Spanish-language music market across the Caribbean and the world. Founded in 1964 by Johnny Pacheco and his lawyer and business partner Jerry Masucci, Fania initially was a means to distribute Pacheco's music free of the royalty hassles and lax promotion he had experienced with other labels. Amid a burgeoning music scene and intense competition among Latin music companies, the partners signed other fed-up artists to a company "that would respect artists' rights and pay them their fair share." To promote their bands, Fania established the All-Stars, made up of their own orchestra leaders and stars from other labels. By the mid-1970s Fania controlled the top sixty salsa artists and promoted them heavily, which was unheard of among the small-budget Latin labels. Under Masucci, album covers rivaled those of the major labels and featured artwork, liner notes, and musician's credits. In addition, Masucci was the first impresario to advertise on non-Latin radio to reach English-speaking audiences, and his promotions were in English to reach younger audiences born on the mainland and more familiar with English than Spanish. As George Lipsitz points out, global music depends on modern transnational musical corporations that have the technology and distribution capabilities to sell their music globally as commodities. Yet those corporations need innovative musicians to create the musical product. In the beginning, Fania was willing to gamble on unknown musicians as well as established stars to produce commercial hits suitable for dancing without losing the music's creativity and freedom of expression. At its height, salsa combined spontaneous bouts of freedom with accessible music that could get airplay on radio and turn a profit on its recordings.[42]

In the midst of the early 1970s recording boom, Celia Cruz joined forces with the new music as one of the few female performers in the new firmament, earning the title "Queen of Salsa." A star of the 1950s with the formidable orchestra Sonora Matancera in Cuba and during the 1960s in exile in Mexico and the United States, during the 1970s Cruz recorded with Larry Harlow, Pacheco, and Willie Colón, and appeared as a soloist with the All-Stars. While many of her older contemporaries despised salsa music and its name, Cruz saw it as a lifeline for her fading career. As she noted, in the late 1960s and early 1970s Latino youth viewed Cuban music as a thing of the past, a music for exiles and older people that "just wasn't hip." Young people preferred dancing to English-language rock. Living in a world of Americanized youth alienated from their Spanish-speaking parents, in 1972, she said, "I began to seriously think that Cuban music was doomed." In her view, Pacheco and Fania records saved her career and provided youth with music that better reflected their roots. She became a star for a new generation, and by the early 1970s she and Pacheco were riding "the golden age of salsa." Her performances became celebrations of a modern "Latino identity" and "symbolized a sensibility that seemed under threat from the relentless homogenization of modern life."[43]

While Afro-American and Afro-Caribbean music received top billing, Levine and Masekela saw Zaire 74 as a means to introduce the United States to African music—especially from Zaire, which was producing some of the continent's most popular rhythms. Not surprisingly, American musicians and even the Fania All-Stars were unaware of how much Congolese music had influenced Afro-Cuban music and in turn how much Latin rhythms had influenced Congolese rumba. Just as African music and culture had followed the enslaved from Central and Western Africa to Cuba, so too did the music of the Caribbean cross the Atlantic to help shape the musical culture of Zaire. The centrality of this interaction explains the ecstatic reception that greeted Pacheco, Cruz, and the Fania All-Stars. Each evening Zaire's best musicians demonstrated the intermixture of Caribbean, North American, and African influences in the creation of Zaire's popular music. The featured African stars included veteran Zaire outfits such as Franco and TPOK Jazz, Tabu Ley and Afrisa, and Trio Madjesi, as well as relatively newer groups like Bella Bella, Zaiko Langa Langa, the Orchestre Stukas, the singer Abeti, and the Pembe Dance Troupe. This cultural circularity highlighted black music's powerful role in the global Black Atlantic.[44]

During slavery in Cuba, enslaved Cubans managed to retain much of their African heritage and traditional musical forms, which made it recognizable to Congo artists when they first heard Afro-Caribbean music. Introduced to the Belgian Congo by Cuban dance bands imported to entertain Belgian colonials, Cuban music grew in Zaire during and after the war to become, by the late 1950s, a highly recognizable Congolese dance music style. Léopoldville, like Brazzaville, its French counterpart across the Congo River, were major Congo River cities that drew migrants from smaller villages and foreigners with their different musical traditions. This process accelerated as a result of the mass mobilization of the population during World War II. Migrants from up and down the river, displaced from their traditional villages, moved to Léopoldville and Brazzaville. Like New Orleans in the United States, these river cities served as places where people, traditions, and music mixed as migrants looked for jobs in a new urban environment. The increase in urbanization and industrialization also led to greater discretionary income to spend on entertainment—records, radios, dance gardens, and nightclubs that sprang up in both cities to appeal to a new urban working class torn between traditional village ways and the demands and benefits of modern urban life.[45]

In this atmosphere music became a commodity and a profession that mixed traditional music and modern dance styles from up and down the river and from across the ocean. New record labels emerged to meet the demands for entertainment by working-class audiences, and by the 1950s dance bands formed that drew on the Cuban son formula. A riverboat mechanic Henri Bowane and guitarist Wendo performed on Congola Radio and on various new record labels in 1948 with the first major Congo music hit, "Marie-Louise." Like bands to follow, they transformed traditional communal music into a commodity, thereby making it possible for music to develop as a paid profession. While these musicians drew on the tensions between village and modern urban life, they themselves were part of modernization as they adapted to time limits on records, sought out the best-paying gigs, and incorporated instruments like the guitar and horns along with traditional instruments like the African thumb piano and a variety of percussion instruments. By the mid-1950s Joseph Kabasele, known as "Le Grand Kallé," served as a model for young players new to city life who aspired to professional musical careers. His Africa Jazz big band incorporated horns and electric guitars as they increasingly adapted music from the Caribbean, and to a lesser extent the United States, to more traditional rhythms.

The period just before and after independence witnessed intense competition among record labels and bands, especially between Kabasele's Africa Jazz and Franco's OK Jazz. In a period that saw three hundred music clubs in both river cities, bands formed quickly, drawing, as did Franco's OK Jazz, on American images of the Wild West (the OK corral), black American slang (*okay* and *KO*), and black American jazz, as well as Cuban rumba and son from the larger Black Atlantic. With Cuban maracas, congas, and bass, these new bands restyled older village traditions like call-and-response and falsetto singing to the newer rhythms of the rumba and son to portray the experiences of modern urban life. Like the *son muntuno*, the new dance music featured an introductory vocal setting the musical theme followed by the *sebene* section, in which the rhythms changed pace and instrumentalists spoke to each other in call-and-response in an increasingly intense and trancelike fashion that fueled the dance floor. In fusing tradition and modernity, the new bands created their own Congo sound. They sang in the pidgin language Lingala that had developed along the river as a fusion of the different ethnic languages and French. As a common argot, Lingala detribalized the music and became the voice of a generation of urban youth—especially young men—alienated from their past and from their colonial masters.[46]

Jesse Samba Wheeler notes that Congolese music was a sign of a radical new social consciousness that heralded independence in 1960. In borrowing from Cuban and US music, Congo musicians recognized familiar patterns with African roots. Sung in Lingala, the music transcended ethnic and tribal differences to create a new national consciousness. Congolese rumba, also known as rumba Lingala, was inclusive, referring to many different Latin musical and dance styles. Musicians also drew on other foreign influences that took them and their fans beyond their colonial identities. One of the longest-lasting and influential bands, Franco's OK Jazz, did not actually play jazz but adopted the term as a sign of hipness and modernity. Furthermore, the use of *jazz* in the name OK Jazz reflected an identification with American black musicians, who were viewed as living freer lives than Congolese colonial subjects. The use of *jazz* paralleled the adoption of the term *rumba*, whether a particular piece of music was strictly speaking a rumba or not. American jazz and Cuban rumba were produced by people suffering under racial oppression just like blacks in the Congo. Identifying with peoples across the Atlantic, Congo musicians were enlarging their own identities. This new hybridity of the Congo set the stage for independence and the hope of freedom in the rest of Africa.[47]

Some of this new consciousness entered explicit politics at independence in 1960. In fact, Kabasele was asked to form a group of musicians to entertain at the Brussels Conference in 1960 to decide the fate of the Belgian Congo. Seven musicians from his band and OK Jazz formed African Jazz to record the tune that marked the moment, "Independence Cha Cha," along with "Table Ronde." Vicky Longomba, of OK Jazz, contributed "Vive Lumumba Patrice." Independence and the subsequent chaos after 1960 saw greater elaboration of the music and greater freedom of expression, along with calls for unity by Kabasele and other musicians. Once Mobutu came to power in 1965 and imposed a semblance of order, bands enjoyed greater freedom and prosperity. Musicians formed and reformed into new orchestras. By the authenticity era, musicians such as Franco or Tabu Ley had to change their European names and also could speak to social or political criticism only through allusion. Still by 1974 many of the musicians had already gained favor throughout black Africa as emblems of independence and authenticity. Zaire 74 would introduce them to American fans and the American market.[48]

During the festival, African musicians took the stage with great confidence and enthusiasm. The Stuka Boys, with their electrifying singer Lita Bembo, showed some of the influences of the Americas. They began performing in the Kinshasa suburbs as a James Brown–style cover band, but by the time of Zaire 74 they had advanced to the capital's top clubs with a mixture of Congolese rumba and funk, along with harmony vocals. The Stukas were known for Samora Tediangaye's guitar playing, which he, like Jimi Hendrix, did with his teeth. Their major attraction, however, was singer Lita Bembo, who was famous for his wild stage dancing, dropping to his knees as if in a trance. His appearance at the music fest propelled him to be voted the most popular Congolese artist of the year. Equally powerful among the young bands, Zaiko Langa Langa was another big band famous for its James Brown funk rhythms, wild dance moves, and theatrical revue format as it incorporated rumba and rock. There were six singers, two lead electric guitars and two accompanying guitars, an American drum set and electric bass, along with Caribbean conga. Singer Evoloko stood out in his shades and hipster Zaire clothes as he demonstrated the *cavacha*, a new dance that had fired up Kinshasa in 1973. He claimed that he only modernized a dance from the Sakata people along the Kasai River. With their roots in rumba and funk, country and city, the newer bands appealed to a new generation of Zaire youth.[49]

The best-known musicians at the festival were TPOK Jazz, led by Franco, a guitarist, singer, and songwriter famous throughout Africa but virtually unknown in the United States. Born in 1938, François Luambo Makiadi was the son of a railway worker who moved his family from the small village of Bata to Léopoldville. He had been a street kid fascinated by the music and dances of migrants from the coast and up the Congo River, records imported from the United States and Europe, and the new music being invented in the city itself and sung in Lingala, the city's vernacular language. Known for his attacking guitar style, he was influenced by the singer Joseph Kabasele and his African Jazz band, which introduced the electric guitar and played Latin-influenced music. His OK Jazz Band debuted in 1956 at the OK Bar and gradually built an African following playing Latin sounds combined with local traditions. At Zaire 74 they employed a seven-piece brass section, several guitars, and singer Sam Mangwana.[50]

Franco and the members of his band embodied the new Congolese identity. They were hip urbanites, well-dressed professional entertainers who appealed to a generation that came of age in the city rather than the interior small towns and villages. They saw themselves as people of Léopoldville more than as traditional ethnic peoples. Furthermore, musicians like Franco projected a rebellious image. When he was jailed for reckless driving and speeding on his motor scooter, he cemented his rebel image. Yet his songs expressed empathy for a new generation of Congolese—for their love problems and economic woes. By independence he was seen as a hero because of the cultural image he expressed. Urbane yet still wild, he laughed at authority but remained cool. In sum, he expressed the hopes and dreams of a generation that looked forward to self-rule.

Independence brought new opportunities for musicians like Franco and OK Jazz. As civil war erupted in the fight for independence, most of the violence occurred away from Léopoldville, and the capital flourished. Restrictions on residence came to an end, which allowed people from the interior to flock to the city and take over areas formerly reserved for Europeans. Colonial-era racial curfews ended too. As a result, nightlife boomed all over the city, and bands and musicians flourished. OK Jazz followed other orchestras in playing upbeat and romantic dance tunes, but Franco also sang about the fears of this difficult period. "Bato ya mabe batondie mboka," for example, detailed the bad people and schemers taking advantage of independence. Avoiding explicit politics, he utilized the tradition of *mbwakela*, developed under the Belgian rule, to allude to and criticize current events sub rosa rather than openly discussing controversial subjects.

While initially critical of Mobutu for hanging five opposition politicians, by the early 1970s Franco promoted Mobutu's authenticity campaign and a call for national unity, as did many other Zairian musicians. Like other musicians, he was affected by the authenticity campaign in that he was forced to change his name from a European sounding François or Franco to Luambo Makiadi, while his rival, the singer and band leader Rochereau became Tabu Ley. Meanwhile the group Zaiko revised the story of its name. Instead of originating from a combination of Zaire and Kongo, the group claimed, it came from "Zaire ya bnakoko," or "Zaire of our ancestors." In addition, some songs dealt with authenticity. At the end of 1971, together with Camille Feruzi, Franco recorded "Recours à l'authenticité" (Recourse to authenticity), a mellow mix of acoustic guitar, accordion, and indigenous percussion. In 1972, Tabu Ley had a number-one hit with the old Bowane and Wendi hit "Mongali," on acoustic guitars, bass, and tam-tam, which explored the tale of a male spirit in the body of a younger man involved with an older woman. Shortly thereafter, Verckys topped the charts with "Nakomitunaka" (I ask myself), a response to the Catholic Church's criticism of authenticity. A bitter tune, "Nakomitunaka," challenged the church's veneration of a white god and white biblical figures like Adam and Eve and its portrayal of black as evil.[51]

When Franco and TPOK performed on the closing night at Zaire 74, they not only expressed the confidence of many Zairians in their leader; they also had benefited from the relationship with Mobutu. Franco owned Kinshasa's four most popular nightclubs, and he was given a parcel of land by the regime to establish his own music club, Une-Dois-Tres. The band often played at political rallies and wrote tunes praising the president and his policies; in turn, the president favored Franco. Indeed, Mobutu's support helped Franco become president of the national musicians' union and secured him a position with the nationalized record-pressing plant. In addition, Franco led the official royalty agency. In return, Franco's support of Mobutu helped establish the latter's legitimacy as a man of the people. This symbiotic relationship, however, would not last.[52]

Tabu Ley and Afrisa, Franco's main rival and the inventor of *soukous* (shake), which speeded up the *sebene* portion of the song and featured radical changes of pace, also appeared on the bill for the third and closing night of Zaire 74 and helped make it one to remember. In addition, the singer Abati and her guitar-playing brother Abumba, along with Sister Sledge, the Spinners, Lloyd Price, the latter accompanied by James Brown's band the J.B.'s, and the Kiamuangana Mateta orchestra added to the excitement. Finally, starting at 3:20 a.m. on the morning of September 25, the Fania All-Stars brought the festival to an ecstatic conclusion. The program ran so late that there were only ten minutes left for a clearly disappointed Etta James. Because of scheduling problems, Manu Dibango did not get to perform at all. Although the festival had a rocky start, by the third night the many skeptics had to admit that a black African nation had mounted a major international music festival that promoted the ideal of unity and common interests among American blacks, Latinos, and African peoples. Musicians with African origins the world over could hold their heads high as symbols of the promise and accomplishments of a global black culture. "Black and proud" was a theme that would resonate through the rest of the twentieth century and beyond as world music, rooted in a confident Pan-African ideal, became a genre that carried hopes of a freer Black Atlantic.[53]

Yet the hope that Zaire 74 would be a vehicle for showcasing to the world the power and beauty of black music, and especially African music, was not realized until years later. Once the fight was postponed, the prospect of tourists attending the concert disappeared. As a result, the initial idea of charging $10 per ticket to recoup Steve Tolbert's $2 million investment had to be abandoned. In fact, all hopes of profit faded when it became clear that even when ticket prices were reduced to $1, the cost was beyond what average Zaïroises could afford. After two nights of poor attendance (five thousand people at most), Mobutu decided to give tickets away for the third night to save face. Tolbert was furious since he stood to lose a fortune, and even angrier that he would have to wait to be paid until the concert film and record albums came out. To add insult to injury, by checkout time, the musicians had run up over $190,000 (nearly $2 million in 2017 terms) in expenses. Tolbert's business manager flipped out and had Mobutu place Stewart Levine, Hugh Masekela, and Alan Pariser under house arrest. The film was confiscated and sent to the president's office. Miriam Makeba helped get the three men released from custody and the film and audio returned since Mobutu respected her artistry and political commitment against apartheid. Tolbert died in a plane crash the following year and never recouped his investment. Nor was Lloyd Price ever paid. His contract stipulated that his salary would not be paid if the fight did not occur on the original date. The stars were paid in advance, but Price blamed Don King for not lifting a finger for his partner nor offering any of his own 4 percent cut. Nor was there an immediate payoff for Price from the film. Because of bitter legal disputes, with King at the center seeking more money, the film did not come out until 1996, as *When We Were Kings*. By then the focus of the documentary had shifted toward the fight, with the music getting little attention. That was only partially rectified in 2009 with the release of *Soul Power*, which focused on the music festival, but only on the American performers. It took until 2017 for Levine and Masekela to produce *Zaire 74: the African Artists*, a two-CD set of the African stars who helped make the festival so memorable.[54]

Moreover, the music, like heavyweight boxing, may have been at its apogee at Zaire 74, but it was not for long. As Levine noted, musical tastes were changing by 1974–1975 in profound ways. The political charge of the 1960s and early 1970s in Brown's music, though on full display in Zaire, waned as the political culture shifted, which "affected everyone, from the protester on the street to topflight entertainers." Like other top black leaders and prominent black entertainers, Brown was harassed by the FBI and the IRS, which worked to discredit him and his potential power. Soon after he returned home, a new apolitical sound appeared, disco, with drum machines, synthesizers, and repetitive dance rhythms. Although Brown had enjoyed hits on the charts continuously since 1956, his string came to an end in 1974, not to reappear again until 1986. His era of impassioned personal soul and funk was over.[55]

The year 1974 was one of change for salsa too. By then the boom was at its peak and Fania had taken control of the market with a formula composed of a clave beat and musical experimentation. However, the desire for mass audiences that had produced world tours to places like Zaire began by the late 1970s a retreat to tried-and-true conventions and little radical experimentation. Renewed attempts to capture an English-language market failed, however, and musicians like Eddie Palmieri, Ray Barretto, and singer Cheo Feliciano attempted to break free from the Fania monopoly and go off on their own. Still, new voices like Rubén Blades and old hands like Willie Colón succeeded at pushing a more politically conscious salsa, but that remained a minor note compared to the emphasis on repetitive dance numbers. Increasingly during the late 1970s, the salsa boom lost steam just as the underlying sense of political rebellion among New York Puerto Ricans faded, as it had among African Americans and antiwar youth.

Although Miriam Makeba continued as an icon of African independence and anticolonialism, her exile from the United States kept her from igniting new currents of rebellion there. Similarly, the vibrant Zairian music scene suffered as increasing oppression by President Mobutu and economic inflation drove many musicians into exile. Still, while the infighting over money undercut the stated theme of black unity, festival organizers, artists, and the Mobutu government did manage to stage a musical extravaganza in the heart of Africa. Could they do the same with the fight? Would the results be as ambiguous as Zaire 74?

5

A STITCH IN TIME

> This fight is the truth. It is our pride, prejudice, passion, and politics all boiling down to two giants fighting it out in the heart of darkest Africa to exorcise the devils of real-life hates and frustrations.
>
> DONN BRIDGY, LETTER TO *WORLD BOXING*, NOVEMBER 1974

On September 22, 1974, President Mobutu Sese Seko officially welcomed Muhammad Ali and George Foreman to Zaire at the dedication of Mai 20 Stadium. In a huge rally attended by one hundred thousand people, the "Guide," as the president was often called, presented the newly refurbished arena to the Department of Sports and Youth and to the nation as a whole. It took three and a half months "of intense work" beginning in April by five hundred workers toiling day and night to bring this "jewel-gift" to the nation on time for the global boxing spectacle and Zaire 74. The workers poured tons of concrete, redid the bleachers, added classrooms and parking, built showers and changing rooms for the athletes, and most important, installed bathrooms for people in the cheaper seats. Throughout the negotiations, before and after Foreman's injury, Mobutu's representatives insisted that the fight had to take place in this stadium because of its symbolic import. Like authenticity, its renovation would be a signal of a nation independent from its colonial past.

As Mobutu addressed the rally, attended by many members of his Popular Movement of the Revolution (MPR) party, Muhammad Ali and George Foreman learned that the stadium had always played a central role in the nation's political and cultural life. Built in the 1930s under Belgian colonial rule, the stadium in its original form represented colonialism's flagrant injustices. Mobutu took the opportunity of the fight and the music festival to correct the situation. Hence, the stadium was far more than a physical plant; it was "a social achievement dedicated to sport." It was also a key element in the authenticity campaign.[1]

The plan must have seemed perfect to Mobutu and his representatives. The music festival and the fight would coincide with the dedication of the stadium and the sparkling reality of authenticity would shine for his people, his guests—the fighters and the musicians—and the world. Unfortunately, the cut that George Foreman suffered put a hitch in everyone's plans. The music festival became divorced from the fight, resulting in the festival's financial failure, and while the dedication of the stadium went off as planned, the world press was not there to see it. Zaire 74's three days of music may not have been particularly successful financially, but they did demonstrate the common threads—as well as the differences—of African diaspora culture in the music of Africa, the United States, and the Caribbean. On a more mundane level, the presence of so many musicians and their entourages, plus the technicians, the music, and the general air of festivity that prevailed in Kinshasa, provided a welcome distraction for the fighters as they waited out the aftermath of George Foreman's cut. Similarly, the dedication of the stadium and the welcoming of the fighters at a mass authenticity rally was a highlight for Ali and Foreman that would not be repeated until days before the actual match.

Once the official welcome was over and the festival ended, the musicians and their entourages soon departed for home or their other bookings. Foreman and Ali, however, were forced by the government to remain in Zaire. Uncertainty and boredom settled over the camps of the two fighters as they were forced to endure five weeks of delay as virtual prisoners of the government. In this environment, the usual excitement and anticipation that attended a heavyweight championship fight were hard to find. For those trapped in Zaire, the bizarre location for the fight seemed to get stranger and stranger.

As soon as Foreman's cut was reported, it became apparent that the fight would need to be postponed, but initially no one knew for how long. Foreman's camp worried that the almost five-week postponement that eventually resulted would not be long enough for the champion to heal properly and restart the training cycle again. With only a butterfly bandage to cover the wound, rather than stitches, the doctors prohibited him from sweating for a minimum of ten days, which meant no roadwork and no sparring. A man of few resources in those days, all Foreman could do was wait until he healed, bored out of his mind and seething about his fate. Although the cut was the first sign of vulnerability during his professional career and something he had to worry about given Ali's deadly accurate jabs, Foreman remained supremely confident—at least on the surface. As he put it, "I convinced myself that I didn't need sparring and road work anyway; knocking out Muhammad Ali was a mere formality." Despite Ali's continuing bragging, Foreman noted, "I still believe he was afraid."[2]

When Ali first learned that Foreman had suffered a cut severe enough to warrant a postponement, he "just about went crazy," recalled Howard Bingham, Ali's friend and personal photographer, who was in the room with Angelo Dundee and Bundini Brown when Ali got the news. "He wasn't happy about it. He'd worked harder to get himself in shape for that fight than anytime before in his life," noted Bingham. In fact, he had begun training at Fighter's Heaven, his specially built Deer Lake, Pennsylvania, camp a full six weeks before official training started. When Budd Schulberg visited Ali at N'Sele he found him "a restless tiger. He had honed himself physically and psychologically to a fine edge, pointing his entire year toward the night of September 25. Now he would have to ease off, put on weight so he could carve it off again, timing himself to the bell." That might not be easy, given that Foreman had the advantage of deciding when he was ready. Truth be told, Bingham recalled, Ali was already sick of Zaire, despite his public comments praising the country. When they were alone, Ali complained: "I'd give anything to be training in the United States. They got ice cream there, and pretty girls and miniskirts." According to Bingham, "He was upset. He was tired of worrying about the food and drinking only bottled water." After a couple of bad hours, however, "he was back to his old self again." Schulberg even reported that Ali was beginning to turn the cut into a positive. "Poor George is goin' to come into that ring knowin' he's no superman, knowin' if a sparrin' partner c'n cut him, I c'n jab-jab. . . . Well, I'll just wait him out."[3]

Perhaps the biggest enemy the fighters now faced was not each other but the boredom that ensued from waiting almost six weeks for the bout to take place. As Ali told Schulberg: "I don't know what I'll do with myself, outside of trainin'. Wish I knew French. I don't understan' what they're sayin' on television. I wish they'd show some Westerns like we have back home." He was reported saying he felt like he was in prison. Needless to say, the sparring partners, lacking Ali's incentive, imagination, and patience "were going up the wall. Another month in this God-forsaken splendor? Nothin' to do but stare at them weeds in the water." Even ever-patient Angelo Dundee wondered "out loud how he'd get through another month of splendid isolation in equatorial heat," especially after his wife returned to the United States over fears of civil unrest. It was up at dawn, down to the gym, then back to the encampment. The villas were nice, but as Angelo discovered, they were filled with bugs and lizards. As a result, Dundee worried that "everybody's going to get stir crazy around this Mission Impossible compound for another six weeks." The wait seemed interminable.[4]

By his own admission, Foreman was miserable in Zaire, "not least because of the food." His cook Tyree Lyons, who had worked at the Pleasanton, California, Job Corps site, searched all over Kinshasa for food that George would eat, but he found little that pleased his employer. No one in either camp developed a fondness for monkey meat. Lyons did, however, develop a mysterious ailment that swelled his hands and eyes, which must have been a further deterrence to Foreman's mixing with the local populace. Rats, insects, and lizards infested his quarters in an old army base, up the hill from Ali's more luxurious digs. Rowdy, beer-sodden soldiers patrolled the base fully armed and cyclone fencing and barbed wire turned Foreman's camp into a prison. Except for daily press conferences "we're restricted," noted the champ's publicist Bill Caplan. "Nobody is allowed in the Foreman camp. Government orders." Seeking relief from this claustrophobic environment, the champion demanded a suite at the Inter-Continental Hotel. Even there, however, Foreman worried that someone might break in and mess with him and his things. As a deterrent, he hired guards to watch his room twenty-four hours a day. Never much of a social being, he would have to live surrounded by so many people who favored Ali.[5]

Even the distractions and excitement provided by a garrulous sporting press took another month to develop. Those boxing writers who had arrived before Foreman's injury were described by George Plimpton as "especially forlorn . . . overcome by the sort of wan melancholy that besets journalists unable to think what to write about." It is not surprising that after the music festival, most of the boxing writers were forced to return home. Those traveling to Kinshasa by plane, like Jerry Izenberg of the Newark *Star-Ledger*, Dick Schaap of *Sport*, Jim Murray of the *Los Angeles Times*, Vic Ziegel of the *New York Post*, and Milt Richman of UPI, all of whom were among a plane load of a hundred or so fellow journalists, learned of the cut while en route. Hearing that the fight had been postponed for at least a month, only a dozen reporters decided to continue the trip from Europe to Zaire. The rest immediately reversed course. Nobody could say with certainty that the fight would ever take place. "And so," recalled Izenberg, "we were back at Kennedy Airport 24 hours later."[6]

While the delay severely inconvenienced the news media, the promoters were beside themselves with anxiety. In New York, Hank Schwartz learned of the cut the evening of September 16, when sports writer Dick Young of the *New York Daily News* called him from Kinshasa in a desperate bid to have Schwartz file his story about the cut because he could not get through to his newspaper. Soon after, Howard Cosell phoned during a break in his *Monday Night Football* broadcast to demand that Schwartz come to the studio and deny that the fight had been canceled. After anxious calls to Dick Sadler and

Gene Kilroy, an Ali adviser, Schwartz could tell Cosell on national television that the fight was rescheduled to October 30, although given the negotiations under way in Kinshasa, that date was actually far from certain. While his staff worked to turn the newspaper group around from Europe, Schwartz found himself in a race against time: "If we delayed the fight, the media would assume it was canceled."[7]

Turning into "Crazy Henry" by this unexpected development, he had his staff call Video Technique's production crew to prevent them from taking off and immediately arranged to fly back to Zaire to make sure the Mobutu government would agree to a delay or a shift in venue outside of Zaire or a smaller indoor arena. Mobutu agreed to a delay but not to a shift in venue. Zaire's president had invested too much money in refurbishing the highly symbolic Mai 20 Stadium to move the fight, but Schwartz did get him to agree to build a canopy over the ring and the surrounding seats in case of rain. Once back in New York he began the arduous task of renegotiating theater and television contracts, reconfiguring conflicts with other scheduled events, such as the World Series, rearranging promotional interviews and press conferences, and reprinting the tickets. It was clear to both Schwartz and Don King that the delay meant abandoning any hope of foreign tourists arriving for the fight in massive numbers. Once the bout came off, the fighters' purses were guaranteed. For Hank Schwartz, Don King, and John Daly, the whole enterprise stood on the brink of failure with no chance of profit at all. Adding to their worries, the new date of October 30 was "smack-dab at the start of the rainy season." In fact, "the first guaranteed rainless date would not be until next May." While Schwartz returned to New York to handle the enormous logistical problems, King remained in Zaire to hold things together and keep Ali and Foreman happy. As a result, King became the face of the promotion in Africa.[8]

Meanwhile, what Ali began calling "the $10 million cut," served only to raise further doubts about the entire spectacle. Most of the boxing establishment—promoters, licensing boards, managers, trainers—had expressed their skepticism as soon as the fight was announced. The boxing press was just as skeptical. As Dick Schaap noted, as soon as the newspapermen traveling to Zaire heard of the cut, they immediately began discussing the great frauds in boxing history. Obviously, they were worried that the fix was in. Writing on September 17, the day after Foreman's cut, Norman Unger, the *Chicago Defender*'s sports editor, maintained that the delay of anywhere from "six to 45 days" only reaffirmed his earlier prediction that the fight "would receive a KO before either Ali or Foreman." He speculated that the promoters were worried that the bout was "out of touch with the people." The price of one week in Zaire and a ringside seat was originally set at $2,700. A month later, after "adverse publicity," the promoters dropped the cost to $2,175. This proved beyond the reach of what American fight fans could pay. Instead of five thousand Americans rushing to the "motherland," fewer than two hundred had fully paid. Unger also suggested that the closed-circuit audience would stay away because of the high prices of $20 to $30, much higher than those of the Ali-Frazier fight in 1971, which sold out theaters across the country at prices ranging from $5 to 15. Adding to the suspense clouding the entire promotion, nobody could be certain what would happen when the bandages came off Foreman's eye, which would be determined sometime in late September. "If there's evidence of infection," noted the *Chicago Tribune*'s Rick Talley, "Foreman may decide to postpone the fight indefinitely . . . or set a date far enough in the future, and then take his dog and go home."[9]

While Ali initially received the news of the cut and the postponement with dismay, he settled down to running through the countryside, interacting with the locals, and solidifying his position as a Third World hero in a black African nation. In fact, Dundee believed that the delay swung the pendulum back in Ali's favor because they could go back to the gym and fine-tune their strategy, whereas Foreman was unable to resume training for fear that sweat would reopen the cut. Others, like *Ring*'s Dan Daniel, speculated that the delay in fact gave Foreman more time to lose weight and get in better shape. While Foreman sequestered himself in his room, harboring the anger that he focused on his opponent, Ali continued to prepare. The challenger certainly saw the cut to his advantage and quickly used it in his prefight poem "Shaving in the Morning," with the line "So, George Foreman, do yourself a favor. Stay away from my left, it cuts like a razor." Ali's positive mood also drew on an unexpected source. The long delay gave him the opportunity to start a romance with nineteen-year-old Veronica Porche, one of the beautiful young women hired by the promoters to ballyhoo the fight at home and abroad. Despite the continuing tension that the affair posed for his marriage to his second wife, Belinda (also known as Khalilah), the excitement of new love in an exotic setting made the delay more than bearable for the challenger.[10]

Already surly, the champion Foreman, meanwhile, became intractable, refusing to talk to the press, biding his time until he could get back to training. Only the move from his isolated quarters in N'sele to the Inter-Continental Hotel improved his mood. Even headquartered in downtown Kinshasa, however, he treated any interaction with the public as an intrusion. In fact, according to his publicist Bill Caplan, he would agree to interviews only on Tuesdays and Thursdays, which severely handicapped Caplan's ability to do his job. Instead of courting the locals or the press, Foreman spent a good deal of his time playing ping-pong with his publicist, who, angered by the champion's withdrawal from public view, refused to let him win even one game in their interminable series of matches. In this vacuum Ali had a field day baiting George and courting the locals, the overwhelming majority of whom were already his fervent supporters. While George's surliness and isolation offended Zairians, Ali devoted himself to befriending everyone he met, especially children.[11]

While Foreman's cut sidelined the fighters and Zairian officials detained them, the global media had another six weeks to contrast the two combatants, a relatively easy task since the two men represented such starkly different boxing styles, personalities, and eras. At the same time, the delay gave Ali more time to psyche his opponent and create a narrative of the bout more favorable to his chances. On the most basic boxing level, the match was portrayed as "truly the classic confrontation between Super Puncher versus Super Boxer," between strength and finesse. To most boxing observers, George Foreman appeared unbeatable. After all, he was twenty-five years old, rippling with muscles, with an unblemished record of 40–0, with thirty-seven knockouts. To date his knockout percentage of .923 (before his KO of Ken Norton) ranked highest among heavyweights, including Rocky Marciano, who stood second at .878. Some might say that despite this fantastic record, the champ was far from a polished boxer. "Nevertheless," wrote *The Ring*'s George Girsch, "statistic-wise or not, Foreman hits like the kick of a mule." As he awaited his defense in Zaire against Ali, only three men had gone the distance with him. "Power, especially among heavyweights," concluded Girsch, "is the name of the game. Nowadays it's spelled F-O-R-E-M-A-N."[12]

In Jack Welsh's opinion, "only Joe Louis was comparable in the manner with which he dispatched his victims." Foreman himself maintained that his power put him in charge. "I believe that a man," he said, "once he gets in the ring, he does what I *let* him do. How would I stop Ali from running? By knocking him out, that's how." The champion's trainer and sometime manager Dick Sadler agreed. "I have created a monster," he said, a combination of Jack Johnson, Joe Louis, Bob Fitzsimmons, Archie Moore, and Rocky Marciano's "tear-in-and-kill-'em qualities." Every contender for the title would now have to fear the champion. That was the opinion of Dan Shocket in *International Boxing*, based on Foreman's destruction of Norton. Foreman had the power, he asserted, to be the first man to knock out Ali. He was too strong to be held like Ali held Frazier in their second fight. Based on his size and punching ability, Foreman would control the fight and would not have to work too hard to win.

No one could challenge the champion's physical superiority. "His strength is superhuman and it has taken him to the top." Shocket predicted he would be champion for a long time.[13]

For most observers, Foreman's punching power was just too strong for an aging Ali. In this, heavyweight contender Jerry Quarry's views were typical. "George Foreman will knock out Muhammad Ali in at least the fourth round, if not earlier," confidently predicted the fighter who had been stopped twice by Ali. By the second round, the champion will "be pushing him to the ropes. It'll look like he's fighting like an amateur because he'll start throwing those heavy, roundhouse punches." The fact that Ali had been laying on the ropes in his recent fights worked to Foreman's advantage. Quarry noted that some boxing experts believed that Ali did this as a challenge to his opponents, but Quarry was having none of it. Ali did it, according to Quarry, because he had to: "If he does this again he will get hurt and hurt early, and probably knocked out. Ali has already proven he can take a good shot. But I don't think he can take a continued assault of hard punches from Foreman. And that's what he's going to start taking by the end of the second round." Ali's best strategy was to keep running and jabbing, but "Foreman will win it because he's too strong, punches too hard, and is too big for Ali."[14]

Quarry's assessment came before the original September 25 fight date. Judging by what former light heavyweight champion Archie Moore said shortly before October 30, little had changed. As an adviser to Foreman, Moore's views were necessarily biased. Yet they were consistent with most assessments of the bout. Befitting Moore's public image as "a character," his remarks were steeped in African American folklore and included a poem that rivaled anything that Ali might produce. In "When Foreman Connects Goodbye Jaw," published in *Sports Illustrated*, Moore compared Ali to the fable of "The Top Dog. Ali had skill, the swiftest feet in his sport and a thinking man's brain. The dog in the fable had everything, too. Then he looked down in the water and saw a bigger dog with a bigger bone. He dropped his own bone and leapt into the water. For Ali, the bigger dog isn't just a reflection. It's George Foreman." This leap would not just cripple his future; it would cripple his ego. Foreman's total concentration would beat Ali, predicted Moore, not just the "TNT in his mitts," but "*nuclearology* as well." Moore called Foreman "the most improved heavyweight since Joe Louis" up against a "loquacious Ali" whose act was "as thin as a Baltimore pimp's patent leather shoes." Moore was blunt: "Ali, George will half kill you." Archie's poem made the same point. After detailing how Frazier and Norton ended up, the poem declares: "Foreman's left will make you dance Turkey in the Straw/ When his right connects with your lower mandible: / Goodby, jaw."[15]

Like most other prognosticators, Moore assumed that Ali could not survive the powerful onslaught of the much-younger, much-stronger heavyweight champion and that he would be severely injured in the process. As Moore put it, "I don't want your blood on my hands." This was another common theme: youth versus age. A younger, indestructible, twenty-five-year-old Foreman was on the rise, while the older, slower Ali appeared to be in decline, with almost no chance to survive, let alone win. At thirty-two, Ali had slowed down from the pre-exile years when his feet danced opponents silly and his fists flashed like lightning. Ever since his return to the ring, Ali was not just fighting opponents; he was facing the inevitable depredations of Father Time. At thirty-two, he no longer had the speed and agility to withstand the power of a younger man. Once the fleet-footed marvel, he was now too often on the defensive, lying on the ropes or clinching and holding to save his strength. "If this fight had been held three years ago," noted Robert Markus in the *Chicago Tribune*, "Ali would have chopped up Foreman like a chef mincing onions." In 1964 he had been the younger man against Sonny Liston. Now the roles were reversed. To many observers, this fight would end in the apocalypse of defeat. Could he even survive the beating that was in store for him?[16]

Despite all the dire predictions, however, Ali appeared confident that speed would trump power, that the hare would beat the tortoise, and that age was no obstacle to victory. Because of Foreman's lumbering pace, Ali dubbed him "a big Mummy" and vowed to be "the Mummy's curse." Days before the match, he berated the assembled press for being "impressed with Foreman because he looks like a big Black man and he hits a bag so hard." He let the press in on a little secret: "Colored folks scare more white folks than they scare colored folks. I am not afraid of Foreman." To many Ali rooters, however, he was fated to lose.[17]

Faced with the long shadow of Ali that had fallen over the entire world of boxing for at least a decade, Foreman had to beat Ali to be considered a credible champion and a boxer of the first tier. That was a lot to consider, but he had youth, punching power, and a sterling record to give him confidence. Ali, in contrast, faced the grinding effects of age, the skepticism of the boxing experts, and, not to be taken lightly, boxing history. As boxing publications constantly reiterated, former heavyweight champions who had lost their crowns "never come back" to reclaim the title. As Jack Welsh put it in *Boxing Illustrated*: "John L. Sullivan couldn't do it . . . *Jack* Dempsey couldn't do it . . . Joe Louis couldn't do it. And Tunney and Marciano wisely didn't try once they bid adieu." At the time only Floyd Patterson had managed to achieve this feat. After losing his crown to Swedish boxer Ingemar Johansson in 1959, Patterson managed to win it back the following year. Could Ali really be expected to defeat historical precedent? Against such a formidable foe as George Foreman, it appeared that history would win. "There is no turning back the clock," noted Welsh, "the time is now," and to achieve the near impossible, "Ali's performance must be of epic proportions." He would have to "reach down in that deep reservoir of stamina and guile and in that final moment of truth, produce an inning in which myths are born."[18]

Yet the fight was a major cultural and political spectacle in which the participants assumed highly symbolic, contrasting roles. Ali's mystique may have been running a bit thin, but his verbal antics reached new heights in Zaire while Foreman withdrew even farther into himself. For boxing writers, Ali remained "the Louisville Lip," a public man who came alive in any crowd—especially in front of television and the press. His fans viewed him as garrulous and verbally inventive, a 1960s man and a model African American whose wit and rhyme sparkled as they cut his opponent to ribbons. Deriding Foreman as a mummy out of his own horror movie favorites, claiming the champ was Belgian, or with his dog at least a tool of the Belgians, rhyming dire threats of razor cuts, charming the Zaïroises with magic tricks, warning of cannibals and Mau Maus—Ali found no match in the stoic Foreman. The champion was "an emotional iceberg" who seemed a throwback to earlier boxing champions who had little to say verbally but relied on their fists to do the talking—just like Joe Louis of old. Ironically, initially Foreman had tried to model himself on Ali with rhymes, verbal wit, and nimble feet. This phase did not last long. His treatment as a hero and a villain after he waved the flag at the 1968 Mexico City Olympics and the constant press probing into his divorce proceedings and his financial difficulties rendered him a recluse.[19]

Foreman's cut only exacerbated this pattern as he withdrew to his quarters and avoided the press and Zaire's public. At a time when the promoters needed all the help they could get to keep the fight in the public eye, Foreman remained truculent and isolated, leaving the field open for Ali to do and say whatever he wanted. Psychologically the challenger had gained an enormous advantage. To boost sales of the fight and pump up distribution, Hank Schwartz arranged for a press conference with Foreman and Ali to be broadcast live from Kinshasa shortly before October 30. This would answer questions of whether satellite transmission of the match would work. Setting up a small television studio took two days. As Schwartz remembered, "Ali and his group were there but, once again, Foreman didn't show." Instead, Henry Clark, his sparring partner, appeared in his place, but only to explain Foreman's absence. Clark said that Foreman did not want to come into the studio with Ali only to have Ali verbally hurling insults at him. If that happened, the fight would break out right on camera. Once the cameras were rolling,

Schwartz and his team "were relieved to see that we were broadcasting Ali's voice and fine crisp image all the way to New York City." As a result of this example of Foreman's isolation and lack of cooperation, it was Ali who stood out even though he was the challenger and the underdog.[20]

Fans were divided, because for them, the Rumble in the Jungle was more than a "run-of-the-mill title fight." As one of the most highly symbolic cultural spectacles of its day, it transcended sport. In a letter to *World Boxing* Donn Bridgy, of La Puente, California, asked: "What shall we call it? The Battle of Zaire? Armageddon? How about Last Tango in Africa?" Whatever its title, noted Bridgy, "this Event transcends reality and enters the realm of pure allegory and fantasy." The dramatic aura surrounding "this epic duel is obvious, because this fight symbolically reflects the mass hysteria of our times." In this highly charged universe, Ali was "the true revolutionary, the shining idol of a million ghettos, who defies white power when he says, 'I don't have to be what you want me to be!'" And in the other corner, stood Foreman, "the metaphorical white man's hero who wraps himself in the stars and stripes and proclaims, 'Don't knock the American system to me!'" With battle lines drawn and the whole world watching, "this fight is the truth. It is our pride, prejudice, passion, and politics all boiling down to two giants fighting it out in the heart of darkest Africa to exorcise the devils of real-life hates and frustrations." Fittingly, Bridgy picked Ali to win because "Allah has brought things around full circle from triumph, exile, purgatory to final redeeming triumph," to teach the world a lesson. Ali would find redemption for his suffering ("rising from the cocoon of a broken heart and a broken jaw") and the suffering of his fellow Americans and would emerge triumphant.[21]

On the other side, Steve Heger, of Honolulu, wrote that he was "tired of hearing the man talk about how he isn't treated fairly. He always expects people to kiss his feet and worship him for what he has done for boxing. He says when he goes to Africa he is loved by his black brothers." Here was a black boxer who was never satisfied. "Well, if he loves Africa so much why doesn't he live there? Why doesn't he just move there and stop his bellyaching about this country?" For Foreman, like Frazier and Norton, "who are thankful to boxing and are satisfied with what they get," Heger had great respect. "But people like Ali who bellyache and whine over every great detail, full of excuses and ungrateful, turn me right off." There were many who agreed with Heger and wanted Foreman to shut the mouth of a man clearly dissatisfied with the evils of American society.[22]

As these fan letters suggest, the hyperbolic symbolism of the match enacted the clash of American cultural and political values of the 1960s and placed them on the world stage. For many, the outcome of the fight would determine who had actually won the deep and virulent clashes of that turbulent decade, an era that in fact came to fruition in the early 1970s. Although diminished once the draft ended and American troops came home from Vietnam, the battles were not over. Ali made the link explicit: "If you think the world was amazed when Nixon resigned," he told reporters, "wait 'til I beat George Foreman's behind." At the height of the Watergate affair and the impeachment and resignation of Richard Nixon, many Americans and people around the world rooted for Ali because of the way the government had nearly ruined his life, stolen his youth, and in effect made him the underdog in this match. While many whites rooted for Foreman, who had been silent on the Vietnam War, as a national hero of "the silent majority," many black people and younger whites openly hoped for his defeat as a sign that they no longer fully believed in the beneficence of American society.[23]

The stark political and cultural differences earned Foreman a good deal of support from whites who had little interest in boxing but sensed that the champion represented more patriotic impulses and a healthy love of America that harkened back to a more conservative era. From the start what appealed to them was that Foreman seemed so different from Ali. Greeted skeptically in African American circles, Foreman "made hearts jump to the tune of 'The Star Spangled Banner' in American Legion posts all over the Middle West," according to sports columnist Wells Twombly. In the many stories about the champion that appeared in the boxing and more general press, it was inevitable that his flag waving at the 1968 Olympics assumed iconic status as an antidote to the Olympic boycotters, the glove-fisted protesters, and Ali himself, who was portrayed as the inspiration for the critical attacks by black athletes. Black reporter Elombe Brath made this contrast explicit in his article "Ali-Foreman Fight Shaping Up as Battle of Armageddon." On one side, wrote Brath, stood Ali, the former champion who "lost his title at a time when "the reality of Vietnam and the fears of the cries of 'Black Power' were hitting home hard." Unjustly stripped of his title because of his religion and his politics, "he is still 'The People's Champion' because of his identification with the problems of the 'wretched of the earth.'" Although Brath considered Foreman far from an Uncle Tom or a black white hope, "it was not Ali who suggested that George parade around the ring" in Mexico City, "waving a small flag in his hand, a fact that was not too well taken by many spectators" sympathetic to John Carlos and Tommie Smith and their "black-gloved clenched fists."[24]

Foreman's personality made him a perfect foil for Ali and earned him white support as a figure of revenge against an ungrateful agitator and symbol of cultural disorder and disruption. The champion's public image was as the "guileless good guy facing the wily, witty operator." For the most part, he left the prefight hype to his challenger, coming off as a strong silent type, a representative of an old-fashioned masculinity who refused to brag. While Ali talked about serving his people, "Foreman isn't out to save the world nor lead his race to salvation." He might let his public figure be used for good, "but causes are not his realm." Whereas "in prose or doggerel," Ali was always "the Mouth," Foreman was "reticent, talking slowly in a monotone with just the hint of a lisp." His modesty and his reluctance to shoot off his mouth was what made him so appealing to Ali's white enemies, who expected black men to retreat to silence outside of the ring and mitigate their presence and strength in the public arena. "All I am is a fighter," George declared. "I learned that three years ago. Remember, I'm not the greatest. I'm nothing special. I'm just a basic guy who exercises a lot." This caused Dan Shocket to comment: "Just a basic guy who plans to remain heavyweight champion for a long time. And he'll remain in that exalted position not by telling the world how he'll do it but by doing it to the best of his ability. He'll let his fists do the talking, a means of communication he has depended on all his life."[25]

The contrast carried over to religion. *Time* argued that Ali loudly preached the teachings of the Black Muslims, continuously vowing to retire if he won and become an itinerant minister for Islam. Foreman, meanwhile, quietly practiced Christianity. "I ain't got no denomination," the magazine quoted him as saying. "I just go to church regularly." As a result, compared to Ali's rhymes, witticisms, magic tricks, and boasts, "Foreman's verbal acrobatics seem hopelessly square." He would ask someone if they knew the Pledge of Allegiance or test a visitor to recite the Lord's Prayer. What appealed to white boxing fans and those who followed the sport just enough to see Ali defeated, was Foreman's squareness, his seeming uprightness, his public reticence, and his roots in American Christianity. Yet there was more to Foreman's appeal. Like Joe Frazier he was an anti Ali. Unlike Frazier, though, Foreman defended liberal government programs, such as the Job Corps, against those who would tear down American society. An unabashed patriot, he appeared to be defending the American way of life and the ethic of success at a time when those beliefs were perceived to be under attack.[26]

From the moment the fight was first announced, Ali shaped the bout's drama, as he presented himself as the champion of worldwide black nationalism, Islam, and anticolonialism while painting Foreman as the white oppressor. At the New York Boxing Writers Association dinner at the Waldorf Astoria hotel in June 1974 to present Foreman with the "Fighter of the Year Award" and his WBA championship belt, Ali disrupted the proceedings to contrast himself with Foreman. While Ali bragged about his prowess and what he would do to Foreman in the upcoming match, Foreman attempted to turn the tables on his challenger and began to needle him—he ultimately ended up ripping his expensive coat. Playful scuffling turned rough as Ali "went berserk." As the two men grappled, Ali denounced the champion as "white America, Christianity, the Flag, the White Man, Pork Chops." Bystanders had to pull the two apart while Ali continued shouting: "I'm going to beat your Christian tail . . . you flag-waver." In fact, Ali's camp continued to deride the champion as a white hope. Until they got a look at the dark-skinned Foreman when he stepped off the plane, most Zairians and other Africans assumed Foreman was indeed white. This was a prejudice that Foreman was never able to fully overcome. Once it was clear that the champion was a black man, many Africans looked upon him as a black tool of the white man, which may have been worse for him.[27]

The African setting of the fight worked to Ali's great advantage. In fact, veteran manager and trainer Gil Clancy noted early on that if Ali "had an ace in the hole at all (and I doubt that there is), then the key is Zaire. It is his kind of place. He will turn the entire arena against the other guy. He will keep terrific emotional pressure on him." From the start that is exactly what Ali strove to accomplish. The delay occasioned by Foreman's cut gave him more time to work his mind games and transform Zaire and all of Africa into Ali country, while Foreman's withdrawal into his own private space made the task fairly easy. Publicly, Ali continually proclaimed his pride "being in a country operated by black people. . . . I wish all black people in America could see this. In America, we've been led to believe that we can't do without the white man, and all we know about Africa is jungles." Nowhere in America did blacks know about African television stations, and how "everything here is black. The soldiers, the president, the faces on the money." On the way to positioning himself as a freedom fighter, Ali linked anticolonialism to the plight of American blacks "who have no future, black people who are wine heads and dope addicts. I am a politician for Allah." Outwardly confident, the Foreman camp realized they barely stood a chance of gaining any fan support in a black African nation where this type of bombastic propaganda was spreading like wildfire.[28]

As he hid from the press and the Zaïrois people, Foreman was forced to admit early on that this was Ali country and that worldwide most people wanted Ali "to win back the title as much as he did. As far as he was concerned, he said, George Foreman held the championship taken from him for refusing to register for the military draft." Compared to Ali and all he represented: "Who was I? The goof who'd waved the American flag." All in all Foreman could not win no matter what happened in the ring. If he knocked Ali out, at most he would receive "grudging respect for vanquishing a legend. If I lost, there'd be a big crowd at the station, jeering me back to Palookaville."[29]

Given that this match was the first heavyweight championship fight on the African continent, black Africans took an especial interest in what was billed as "the Super Fight of the Century." Unlike in the United States, in Africa Ali was favored to win. After all he was the best-known black American in all of Africa, and his religious and political beliefs had earned him an enormous following going back to his trip to Ghana, Egypt, and Nigeria after he first won the title in 1964. The Zairian press, for example, posed the fight as one between the official champion and "the People's Champion," with the latter as the most popular boxer on the planet. Faced with a young "bulldozer," the challenger would need to use all his scientific boxing skills plus his speed to achieve a victory. Power versus speed and finesse, youth versus age—these were key elements to the upcoming battle, along with Ali's commitment to Islam. Equally important, the two foes stood on the opposite side of a political divide, just as in American depictions of what was at stake. In various portraits of the two men just before the bout, Ali was described as a revolutionary who joined the Black Muslims because he was denied service at a segregated Louisville restaurant when he went there to celebrate his Olympic medal. He refused to accept the draft into the armed forces: "I have no valid reason to kill Vietnamese. These people have done nothing to me." As a result of his stance on the Vietnam War, "this apostle of the noble art" was forced from the ring by the institutions of American justice. This was his last chance to capture the title, and what he sought was redemption for the injustice he had suffered. Foreman, however, was propelled to the title by his victory at the Mexico City Olympics, and he was perceived in the United States as "a good black" as he embraced the American flag during the Vietnam era as opposed to those rebellious athletes who raised their fists for Black Power.[30]

If the coverage in other African newspapers is to be believed, Ali's appeal as a hero of black independence throughout the world reached its height as the fight neared. Articles in the *Ghanaian Times*, for instance, noted that Ali was a "symbol of independence and freedom from white domination for millions of blacks in the United States and also in the world," and as a result, he was "the people's choice in Kinshasa," despite the facts suggesting that Foreman would win. The latter possessed the advantages of strength and youth, and he "was at the peak of his career." Still, the proud and sensitive Foreman, who felt the injustice of not being universally accepted as champion, had grown "withdrawn, snappy and uncommunicative." In large part this was due to Ali's mind games: "Ali's main tactic has political undertones portraying himself as the representative of blackness and Foreman as a stooge of whites." In Zaire, noted the Ghanaian newspaper, "a bastion of black authenticity where nearly all reminders of the colonial past have been obliterated, Ali's black militancy has great appeal."[31]

While the two combatants wiled away their time as best they could during the long delay in Zaire, it still remained unclear whether the fight would actually take place. Once the bandages came off Foreman's eye and he began sparring around October 15 for the first time in twenty-nine days, the fighters, promoters, fans, and the government of Zaire breathed a collective sigh of relief. Whatever problems remained—and there were many—it looked like the Rumble in the Jungle would actually take place on October 30. For the news-starved press, the event at the Salle du Congrès in the presidential compound in N'Sele took on the significance of a major turning point. While outside Muhammad Ali delighted the camp cook, some of the security guards, gardeners, and chauffeurs with magic tricks to reinforce the idea that, as he said, "I'm magic," inside the hall a relaxed champion worked his two rounds and afterward seemed more outgoing than he had any time since arriving in Zaire. "I was worried about that cut," he said, "but now I'm extremely cured physically and mentally." Time, which had hung heavy on his mind, had come to seem to Foreman only a minor obstacle on his road to victory. Don King seemed mentally upbeat as well, free from the worries that had plagued the promotion ever since Foreman suffered his cut. "It remains but for the fighters to step into the ring. The little intricacies, the little bitty problems are all gone by. I feel very colorful," noted King. Ali, however, topped everyone in his confidence and volubility. "In two years' time," he predicted, "when of course I will still be champion of the world, 10 million people will be watching me meet the new White Hope from Mississippi—with Governor Wallace in his corner." Claiming he alone would dance and punch, Ali predicted the fight would be "the biggest upset in sporting history."[32]

Before the two combatants could begin to settle their differences in the ring, they first had to endure a suddenly heated-up atmosphere several days before the match, which marked a sharp departure after the long delay. In the last few days before the fight, Ali ratcheted up his psychological attack on the champion. After one of his last workouts on Friday, October 25, Ali continued to attack Foreman as the villain in their fast-approaching battle. "I'm dedicatin' this fight to all the African people who are fighting for their freedom and independence," he said. "I'm looking at this man as a Belgian, he is the oppressor of all Black nations." "The fight was "a Holy War," he declared, and "therefore all the powers of the heavens are against him. I predict I will have no problem.

The same powers that got me the victory over the draft, the same powers that got me past Ken Norton and Joe Frazier will get me past George Foreman. I leave you by saying, 'War.'" Aligning himself with Africa proved a tactical victory. With a red, green, and yellow sash around his waist, Ali had been declared the "champion d'Afrique" by several members of the African Boxing Federation on Monday, October 28. "George is not the champion over here," said Ali. Noting its oversight, the federation announced that Foreman would receive a similar sash the next day, October 29. While most Zairians favored Ali, many expected Foreman to win. "Ali, bomaye," one fight fan announced, but "Foreman, boom."[33]

Ali tried to keep up his psychological and political barrage at the weigh-in on Saturday night, October 26, but he was in for an unexpected surprise. One of the most unusual preliminary events of its kind ever held, the weigh-in was scheduled to take place shortly before midnight to accommodate American television viewers. Free and open to the public, as a spectacle it was rivaled perhaps only by the chaos of the Miami weigh-in for the fight with Sonny Liston in 1964, when Ali first won the title. According to Hank Schwartz, however, the weigh-in ceremony—much like the fight itself—almost did not take place. On the morning of the weigh-in the promoters learned that Foreman was telling people he wanted an additional $500,000 or he would pull out of the fight. Schwartz was desperate; he needed Foreman at the weigh-in to reassure a skeptical worldwide public that the fight would take place as scheduled. As a result, Schwartz and John Daly had the champion's bagman go to Hemdale's London offices and wait for the payment while Foreman appeared at the televised weigh-in. Once the ABC televised event came off, George could not back out of the fight. Once this happened, the promoters could and did stiff the champion's emissary. If this was not problem enough, on his way down to the ring, someone in the audience kicked Foreman's dog and he ran off. Until the dog was found, George refused to get into the ring to be weighed. Fortunately for all concerned, the prized German shepherd returned to his master.[34]

With this latest series of problems laid to rest, there was one more major hassle waiting. Just as ABC was about to televise the ceremony, the screen went blank. Schwartz raced off to the communications center to discover that a technician in Zaire had turned off the crucial switch. The thoroughly rattled head of Video Techniques switched it on, and the one-hour ceremony could finally take place in Mai 20 Stadium in front of ten thousand (some estimates said fifteen thousand) ecstatic fans and an audience of millions watching via satellite television on ABC's *Wide World of Sports*. While brass and drums hammered out Congo rumbas and hard rock music, at least seventy people—

and Foreman's dog—occupied the ring to watch the two fighters step on the scales. Their weights—Foreman at 220, Ali at 216.5—were announced to a crowd of Zairians who did not appear to care. According to *New York Times* columnist Dave Anderson: "They were there to enjoy a spectacle, probably not realizing that they, not the gladiators, had created the spectacle. They cheered for the champion but they chanted for the challenger." Ali was clad in a flaming African shirt called a *bubu* and pale blue slacks, and he carried a delicately carved ivory cane. At first, he used the cane to imitate a tired old man wandering around the ring, clearly intended to play on the dominant belief that he was too old to win the title. "Then he whirled and raised his cane. And instantly the Zaïrois throng shattered the steaming night with their new favorite chant, 'Ali boom ye Ali boom ye,' which as Foreman knows well, is translated 'Ali, kill him.'" At the fight, Anderson rightly predicted, "'Ali, bomaye' will be the shout heard around the world." Ali certainly heard the chants at the weigh-in because he was hoarse from constantly leading them during the preceding days, "inciting them almost." He was hoarse from hollering, he said, "from making too much noise. That takes a lot of energy. Wears out your throat." Ali hoped that the psychology of a crowd that clearly favored him would wear down the champion. "Around the third," he said, "I'll back off, wave my arms and get 'em chantin'. Somethin' like that can bother a man."[35]

For his part Foreman, clad in a brilliantly colored African robe that he shed to display a sculpted, awesomely muscled body, seemed unaffected by the crowd. "I'm absolutely confident," he declared when he stepped off the scales. "I'm in 100 percent physical shape." He certainly looked it. Coming into the ring "sleek and menacing," Foreman had the advantage since Ali's constant talking and chanting deprived him of his voice, "his most vital piece of armor." For the first time, moreover, Foreman stole the show. He appeared to hold a psychological edge, as Ali was unable to do more than gesture since his throat was so sore. Foreman, however, took the stage as an emperor with both heavily muscled arms in the air. Foreman gained points with the overwhelmingly pro-Ali crowd when he threw up a Black Power salute and displayed the quiet dignity on the stand befitting a true champion. To the cheers of the crowd, the champion took a victory lap around the inside of the stadium. Ali could only perform his own lap, seemingly copying the champion. Whether Foreman's one-day advantage would last to fight time remained unclear. Still, his physical edge and his confidence awed the crowd.[36]

With the press and the media in full attendance, on the evening before the title fight President Mobutu met separately with both Ali and Foreman to give his blessing and to take full credit for the spectacle as "a gift to his people" and the world. The president met with the two fighters to claim ownership of the event and thereby raise his status as one of the most powerful leaders in Africa. To fulfill this goal, Mobutu invited both Ali and Foreman, and their entourages, to the Presidential palace gardens on the hilltop overlooking the Zaire River and the city of Brazzaville across the water. To achieve maximum publicity, more than a hundred newsmen from around the globe ambled behind the president and the two fighters as they walked and talked along the garden path. The president gave the two men equal but separate time, and told each of them, "May the best man win."[37]

Foreman arrived first, dressed in a colorful African robe, a *nzambala*. Recognizing Foreman's love of animals, Mobutu promised to send him a lion cub for his daughter. He also explained the meanings of his elaborately carved walking stick, which he described as the symbol of his office. The woman on the stick represented reproduction and the growth of the nation, and the snake symbolized war. Two doves symbolized the peace that "all leaders must seek after." After this explanation of the power of the presidency, Foreman's trainer, Dick Sadler, injected a note of American democratic culture by doing something no Zairian citizen would ever do—he slapped Mobutu on the back with a hearty "See you later, Mr. President." The security guards winced.[38]

When Ali and his entourage arrived, American informality once again broke the rules of sacred presidential etiquette. Dressed in a conservative brown abacost, the official attire of the Zairian authenticity campaign, Ali reached out, embraced President Mobutu, and kissed him on both cheeks. Despite instructions that no ordinary person was supposed to touch the president, neither Ali nor Sadler could resist. Once more utilizing any forum to deliver his message that this was Ali country and that he represented black Africa, Ali declared how good it felt to be in Zaire, which he regarded as his true home. According to the *Pretoria News*, Ali used the occasion as a platform for his black militancy and his attack on the champion for a lack of commitment to the black freedom struggle. The president replied that Zaire was "Africa for the Africans." Then the two men exchanged pins, an Ali one for an MPR button. Drew "Bundini" Brown, a key member of the Ali entourage, expressed some of the awe that the other members of the Ali party must have felt on having been received by the black president of a black African nation—and its contrast to the whiteness of political power in the United States. "All my life, I have been hearing about the White House," Bundini reflected out loud to reporters. "Today I visited the Black House."[39]

Although President Mobutu wanted to take ownership of the Super Fight and portray it as his gift to the people of Zaire, at the last minute he decided not to attend the fight for fear of assassination and his belief that as president he was a sacred personage who stood removed from the people. Instead of watching from the stadium he would instead observe from the presidential palace through a separate television feed. He was not entirely absent, however. Hanging over the inside of the stadium was a huge banner portraying Mobutu's face, replete with his zebra hat. On the one hand, it looked like he was watching the fight; on the other, he appeared to be watching his subjects.

While the fighters were going through the official events leading up to their meeting in the ring, another sort of drama was taking place backstage. One of Angelo Dundee's tasks involved going in early on the Tuesday afternoon before the match to check on the state of the brand-new ring. He was especially concerned that the heat might have softened the padding of the specially imported canvas, making it hard for Ali to backpedal, which was part of his plan to utilize his speed and his dancing ability to stay away from Foreman while peppering him with his flicking jab. He also wanted to make sure that the ring was a boxing ring, not a wrestling one, which had occurred in Lewiston, Maine, during the second Liston match. Assisted by Bobby Goodman, a publicist with Video Techniques, Dundee discovered that the ring was in worse shape than the one used in Lewiston. It was "so slanted it looked like a miniature ski slope with droopy ropes that hung from the ring posts like wet wash, which is almost what they were, having sagged from the brutal humidity." He tried to get some workmen to help him, but they ignored his pleas. Ever since the fight, he has been accused of loosening the ropes, but Dundee swore that "nothing could be further from the truth." In fact, he tightened the ropes because they were so loose he feared that Ali could be driven over them by one of Foreman's powerful blows. Using a razor, he worked for hours to cut and refit the ropes so that they were taut enough to bear the weight of both boxers. Then he used some wooden blocks to level the ring from underneath. According to Goodman, Dundee specifically told the ring chief that he should tighten the ropes again before the first preliminary bout and then again before the main event. "They just didn't do it, so by the time Ali got in the ring, the ropes were slack; but there was nothing underhanded in what Angelo did." In fact, Goodman added, Dick Sadler and Archie Moore saw us that afternoon "sweating our butts off," but because of the heat they refused to help out.[40]

As the early morning of October 30 approached, it looked like only the start of the overdue rainy season could delay one of the greatest sport spectacles of all time. As little spits of rain occasionally and intermittently began to fall that morning, would Muhammad Ali's magic hold or would the heavens open up and prevent the fight from taking place or disrupt the proceedings once the fight had already begun? At a deeper level, as fans filed into the stadium, they must have wondered whether Ali would be able to defy boxing history, recapture the magic, and overcome the skeptics, or whether it inevitable that the younger, more powerful, and invincible champion George Foreman would knock Ali out and essentially end his career and his quest to reclaim the title. Whatever the outcome, the match carried an enormous political and cultural charge as "two fine representatives of the Establishment and the Dissident step into the ring."[41]

6

ROPE-A-DOPE

They call it rope a dope, I was the dope.

GEORGE FOREMAN, "TOTAL FAILURE: HOW GEORGE FOREMAN'S LOSSES SHOWED HIM THE LIGHT," NATIONAL PUBLIC RADIO, MAY 24, 2017

After the agonizing thirty-five-day delay filled with boredom and uncertainty, the official heavyweight champion of the world finally entered the ring against the "people's champion" at Mai 20 Stadium on October 30 at 4 a.m. Before a crowd estimated between sixty thousand and seventy thousand—nearly all Zaïroises—the two formidable warriors prepared themselves to fight for the title under rain-threatening clouds on an early, hot tropical morning, with the temperature hovering at a sultry eighty-six degrees and humidity at 90 percent. Beamed by satellite all over the world to an audience of hundreds of millions in more than seventy-five countries watching via closed-circuit theater, free television, or tape delay, with more than five hundred journalists using typewriters with English, French, and German keyboards, the bout had become "the ultimate universal spectacle" that transcended sport. As Jack Welsh declared in *Boxing Illustrated*, "Now a fistic epic is at hand belying logic, defying sanity and stunningly boggling the imagination of even the ultra-extrovert, proving irrevocably for all time that man can reach for the stars and maybe get Mars."[1]

In the overheated atmosphere of the Kinshasa night, could Ali achieve the impossible and redeem himself and his fans against impossible odds? Having cast himself into the mold of a classic hero, could the aging ex-champion—reconfigured as a defiant man of principle—come back from the effects of exile and adversity to triumph once again over a much-younger opponent? Only a small minority of the boxing community believed he would win. His trainer Angelo Dundee predicted a knockout, although he was clearly biased. Less so was sports columnist Jerry Izenberg. In a visit to Deer Lake to observe Ali's fight preparations, Izenberg noticed that for the first time in years the challenger was hitting the heavy bag with power and authority, which he interpreted as a sign that Ali's hands were in good shape and capable of powerful right hand punches, something which was not possible since his comeback. Still, most of Ali's fans were pessimistic that their aging hero would come out of the fight without serious—even fatal—injuries. In this apocalyptic moment, the question remained whether he could survive the onslaught of a behemoth Foreman who was bent on his destruction.[2]

As the fighters and their entourages gathered in their dressing rooms beneath the massive stadium in the early morning of Wednesday, October 30, the mood remained one of supreme confidence among Foreman's camp and deep gloom in Ali's. Showing no ill effects from the cut that had nearly scuttled the bout, Foreman was a 3 to 1 favorite. "Foreman might be the heaviest puncher in the history of the heavyweight division," noted Dave Anderson of the *New York Times*. Ali, in contrast, had not demolished an opponent since he was champion seven years earlier. His chance for an upset, noted Anderson, would "depend on his flamboyant mystique rather than his speed, which has deteriorated." According to Anderson, Ali had no punch to keep Foreman off of him. Sooner or later, he predicted, the champion "will walk through Ali's weak jab and demolish him as soon as he hits him with his best punch. That could happen in the first round."[3]

The overwhelming belief among experts that Foreman could not lose seemed to have invaded Ali's camp as well, despite the crowds that had cheered his bus as it made its way from N'Sele to the stadium in the darkness of a new day. In marked contrast to the uproar that generally prevailed backstage before his fights, according to Norman Mailer, who was in attendance, no one had much to say. Wali Muhammad, the third man in the corner along with Angelo Dundee and Bundini Brown, later recalled: "George had been built up to be such a great fighter. People thought he'd kill Ali." "Everyone's teeth were chattering," said Ali's old friend Bernie Yuman. "We were shaking like leaves on a tree." The only "cheerful presence" in the dressing room aside from sparring partner Roy Williams appeared to be Ali himself, noted Mailer, who told the challenger that he was afraid for him. "Nothing to be scared about," responded Ali. "It's just another day in the dramatic life of Muhammad Ali. Just one more workout in the gym for me." Addressing George Plimpton, he said horror films and thunderstorms scared him, and jet planes shook him up: "But there is no need to be afraid of anything you can control with your skill." That is why, he declared, Allah "is the only One who terrifies me." This fight was nothing: "Getting into the ring with Liston the first time beats anything

George Foreman ever had to do, or I have had to do again. Except for living with threats against my life after the death of Malcolm X. Real death threats. No, I have no fear of tonight."[4]

Perhaps Ali was buoyed by the cards and telegrams he received from all over Africa hailing his victory even before he stepped into the ring and thanking him and his manager Herbert Muhammad for supporting Black Africa against South Africa by refusing to break the ban on sporting events in that apartheid state until freedom existed for the black majority. Despite Ali's exuberance, however, the room remained glum. Even the usually ebullient Bundini Brown, the man who most vocally claimed that Foreman's flag-waving past rendered him a white hope, seemed morose. His downbeat mood darkened even further when Ali decided not to wear the robe that Bundini had designed especially for the occasion. When his deeply disappointed comrade-in-arms glared at him, Ali slapped him hard once and then once again. As Ali called out, "Bundini, we gonna dance?" Bundini remained silent. "You know I can't dance without you," Ali tried again, but the disconsolate Bundini could only say, "You turned down my robe." The challenger shrugged, claiming that he had to make some decisions on his own. Finally Gene Kilroy responded that "We're going to dance and dance," and Bundini, buoyed by Ali's reciting of verses he had a hand in devising ("Float like a Butterfly" and "Let's Rumble in the Jungle") joined in: "All night long." The challenger's fight plan seemed firm: he would keep Foreman away by dancing and jabbing until the champion tired. No one expected anything different, including Foreman's camp.[5]

When Foreman's representative Doc Broadus came in to check the hand wraps, Ali brought some smiles to his entourage by telling Broadus, "Tell your man to be ready for the dance." When Broadus replied, "He don't dance," the entourage finally regained some of the high spirits usually associated with Ali's dressing rooms, but the atmosphere remained fretful. There was no downing Ali, however. He received a short message from Elijah Muhammad that said Ali was fighting for his people and if he did his best "Allah would be with [him]." After a short prayer, it was on to the ring. Despite the overwhelming odds against their man and their own dire fears, as Ali's personal "fight doctor" Ferdie Pacheco put it, "We had the official champion, Foreman, up against our man Ali, who was still the champion in our book, no matter what the official commission had declared. This fight would settle things." To other Ali supporters, however, defeat and possible injury seemed more than likely. Not only did victory seemed far fetched, but as a *Chicago Tribune* headline declared, "ALI NEEDS A MIRACLE TO SURVIVE." As Mailer recalled, "defeat was in the air."[6]

Across the hall, Foreman's camp looked forward to an easy victory. At 4 a.m. Foreman recalled, "I awaited my fate in the locker room. Later I would read that Muhammad Ali's arrival in the ring was greeted by tribal drumbeats and a crowd roaring" his name. "But," the champion recalled, "I was aware of none of that. My thoughts were elsewhere. I wanted to end the fight, collect my money, and get home." While Ali was shadow boxing in a jock strap, the champion did not even bother to warm up. Dick Sadler was equally confident. "When George hits a guy he lifts him off their feet," he said. "To win, Ali must have some sort of a break, a fluke. There's too much against him—me, Sandy Sadler and Archie Moore—that's two Hall of Famers and over 300 knockouts between us. And then George Foreman . . . no, no, that's too many things." Foreman did not even seem bothered by Ali's promise to whisper something to deflate him once the two were in the ring together. "I guess he'll just have to say it," Foreman declared. "I never get a chance to talk much. By the time you get to know a man, it's all over." To all outward appearances the champion felt that there was nothing special about this match at all. Foreman's camp was so convinced of their man's ability to deliver an early and overwhelming knockout that as Foreman and his circle held hands in their prefight prayer, Archie Moore prayed silently that George would not kill the challenger. Still, they were not beyond attempting to mess with Ali's head. When Ferdie Pacheco attempted to check Foreman's hand wraps, he was initially refused admittance. This was nothing compared to letting Ali wait in the ring alone for almost ten minutes before George deigned to appear in order to make him nervous and edgy. "But" noted Angelo Dundee, "like everything George had touched, this, too, would work to his disadvantage."[7]

Dundee was right. The long delay gave Ali "an edge I know how to take advantage of," he said. As Ali entered the ring, he was buoyed by the huge response. The crowd erupted with applause and the "Ali, bomaye!" chant as he danced around the ring, tested the ropes, and got a feel for the ring, the overhead lights, and the distance from the center to the corners. While sports reporters assumed this was all showmanship, Ali claimed that in fact it gave him a chance to get to know the crowd, the atmosphere, and the psychic feel of the arena. Just as he had used his time in Zaire to cement his stature as an African hero, he used the nearly ten-minute delay to take command of the spectacle and turn the stadium into his home turf. According to *The Ring*, while Foreman had his supporters, Ali's partisans were "much louder in voice and number, over-powering to the point where one's hair began to prickle." Wearing a white satin robe that Ali described "as African and everyone can look at it and tell it's African," he greeted singers Lloyd Price, Miriam Makeba, and Bill Withers, football great Jim Brown who was acting as a ring commentator, and some of the press, and then he began leading the crowd in the "Ali, bomaye" chant, spurring them on with a wave of the glove, his fist in the air as a sign of black liberation. In the time Foreman made him wait, Ali whipped up the crowd and transformed a heavily pro-Ali crowd that he had nurtured during his fifty-one-day stay in Zaire into screaming partisans of "the People's Champion." As Ferdie Pacheco recalled: "I've heard crowds respond to Ali throughout the world, and I thought I would never feel the electricity of the first Frazier fight again, but here, in the middle of Africa, I felt a completely unique surge of love and excitement come pouring over the ring. People were chanting the Ali chant and singing, laughing, and some crying."[8]

Foreman finally entered the ring, dressed in a red velvet robe with a blue sash over red velvet trunks with a white stripe and a blue waistband. It appeared to Norman Mailer at least that "the colors of the American flag girdled his middle." Little noted, however, his robe carried the inscription "The Fighting Corpsman," a nod to his continuing gratitude toward the program that had changed his life. Compared to Ali's reception, the champion received only scattered boos and polite applause "that seemed even more sparse in contrast." According to Dundee, the champ ran down the aisle, with his entourage struggling to keep up "like he was in a hurry to get this thing over with." Once in the ring he barely moved around. "No testing of the ropes, no feeling of the canvas, nothing. He just sat there" awaiting referee Zack Clayton's instructions. Foreman looked over at his opponent clowning around in his corner. "When he wouldn't return my stare, I knew he was afraid of me," he recalled. Still, throughout the playing of the national anthems of both countries, "The Star Spangled Banner" and the "Le Zaïroise," Ali began to mock Foreman. Later, when Foreman sat on his stool having his gloves tied, Ali swooped near him and taunted him with a look that delighted the crowd. However, when Foreman removed his robe and stood across from Ali for the referee's instructions, Foreman's huge muscles appeared to dwarf Ali's, awing the crowd. Even Dundee and Bundini, who were manning Ali's corner, were taken aback by Foreman's formidable size and power. The closer they got to him, "the bigger he looked. He had NFL-thick arms and legs and even his muscles had muscles. I thought the only thing he was missing was a necklace around his neck strung with his opponents' teeth."[9]

As referee Zack Clayton gave the champion and his challenger their instructions, "our eyes are locked like gunfighters' in a Wild West movie," recalled Ali in his autobiography. Foreman stared with disdain as Ali whispered, "Chump . . . You're gonna get yourself beat tonight in front of all these Africans." The insults continued, despite Clayton's entreaties that Ali stop, but to no avail: "You been hearing about how bad I am since you were a little kid with mess in your pants! Tonight . . . I'm gonna whip you till you cry like a baby." Through this verbal assault, however, Foreman remained impassive, convinced that Ali's talk was nothing more than a cover for his fears. "My only thought was to knock him out early."[10]

In a fight that *The Ring* described as "a slugfest, a real pier six bangaroo and one of the better heavyweight title fights from the standpoint of action," Ali came out as the opening bell sounded as fast as a rabbit, dancing and jabbing as everyone in the entire world, including Foreman, knew he would. "He'd flick a jab at me and run," Foreman recalled. "Me, I rushed him like a tiger, throwing hard shot after hard shot, going for that early shower." Unexpectedly, however, Ali rushed to ring center and threw a hard lead right to Foreman's forehead; fifteen seconds later he landed another right-hand lead, followed by a straight left and right. The pace was fast and the challenger aggressive, but soon the champion unleashed his own punches, a right-hand uppercut that missed, followed by another right uppercut that got in. "But he was one tough rabbit to catch, even for a tiger," George recalled. As promised by his trainers, Foreman proved adept at cutting off the ring, forcing Ali to the ropes, "with me whaling away and him covering up. I'd jab, jab, jab, then throw several knockout punches that couldn't find their mark." Several times Ali was forced to tie up the champion and wrestle him to the center of the ring.[11]

To the surprise of Ali's corner and everyone watching live or via satellite, however, after thirty seconds Ali could be found either in a corner or on the ropes, the last place he needed to be against such a powerful puncher as the champion. In unison, Ali's corner stood up in alarm, screaming for their man to stay out of the corners and off the ropes and dance. Indeed, this was exactly where Foreman's camp wanted Ali to be, sure their man would destroy Ali once he was forced to the ropes. As the champ's corner man and trainer Archie Moore recalled: "At first, that seemed like a fine strategy. Everything we'd planned and designed to get Ali on the ropes, where George could hit him. But once George got him there, and when Ali stayed there, George didn't know what to do." Yet Ali let Foreman pound away, while he worked at blocking the champion's punches to the body and his head. While his corner yelled for him to get off the ropes and dance, Ali seemed content to lean back and block punches, although this left him perilously close to Foreman's power.[12]

At the time, this move looked so perilous that to George Plimpton at ringside "for one sickening moment it looked as if a fix were on, that since the challenger was to succumb in the first round it would be best if he went quickly and mutely to a corner so the champion could go to work on him." Afterward, however, it seemed totally different. Like a black trickster on the order of Br'er Rabbit, Ali seemed, according to Plimpton, to be leading Foreman to destruction "as surely as the big cartoon wolf, licking his chops, is tricked into some extravagantly ghastly trap laid by a sly mouse." Initially, however, that was far from a sure thing. As things got tough, Foreman threw heavy punches, both lefts and rights, from down around the hips, but he telegraphed the massive shots so that Ali was able to slip and block many of them. When the action got too fierce, Ali tied Foreman up, pushed his head down, and bulled him to the center of the ring, but that did not last long. After a Foreman hook to the body, Ali was backed into a corner again, yet he continued to work off the ropes with jabs and right crosses that kept finding their mark. Foreman figured out that Ali was using his famous flicking jab "to open the cut over my eye. But I wasn't worried. Any minute, I knew, he was going down, just as every other opponent of mine had." Just before the bell to end round one, however, Ali again came off the ropes with a series of quick shots to Foreman's face that knocked the sweat flying around his head. The crowd roared, and Angelo noticed that George's face was already beginning to swell. After such a furious beginning, both fighters faced the question of who could keep it up the longest and who would succumb to the heat and the humidity.[13]

When Ali returned to his corner, his handlers pleaded with him to stay off the ropes, to dance as they had planned or else be killed by any one of Foreman's mighty blows. Seemingly calm and collected amid the storm, Ali told everyone, "Shut up! All of you. I know what I am doing. Don't tell me nothing! I don't want to hear another word. Shut up." Then, according to Ferdie Pacheco, he explained: "The champ has nothing. He has nothing. He can't hurt me. I'm going to let this sucker punch himself out." All during training Ali had planned on using his speed to dance away from the champ's power and tire him out by rounds eight to ten. Gregorio Peralta had gone the distance with Foreman earlier in the champ's career, but in that case it was fighting off the ropes. Having watched tapes of the Foreman-Peralta match, Ali's camp planned to test Foreman's stamina, but not by laying on the ropes right in front of the champion. Rather, the challenger would dance around the ring and tire Foreman out. Echoing the feelings of the entire camp, Dundee recalled that "when he went to the ropes, I felt sick. I thought Ali would win but not that way." The goal was to dance for five or six rounds and against a stand-up fighter who didn't move his head much, Ali could jab him silly. Then when Foreman tired, Ali would knock him out in the late rounds. "But," Dundee recalled, "everything we planned was built around not getting hit."[14]

But Ali realized something in rounds one and two—George was very effective in cutting off the ring on him quickly and at that feverish pace, with Ali taking six steps to George's three, Ali feared that he would run out of gas. It would be he who tired early, just as he had done in his first disappointing loss to Joe Frazier back in 1971. Asked later by *Playboy* whether he had planned what came to be known as the rope-a-dope, Ali replied, "Well, I didn't really *plan* it," but after the first round, "I felt myself getting too tired for the pace of that fight." George would not get tired, Ali reasoned, "'cause he was just cutting the ring off on me. I stayed out of the way, but I figured that after seven or eight rounds of dancing like that, I'd be really tired." At that point should he go to the ropes to conserve his energy, "my resistance would be low and George would get one through to me. So while I was still fresh, I decided to go to the ropes and try to get George tired." Hence, with necessity as the mother of invention, Ali improvised and the "rope-a-dope" strategy was born: Ali would work with his back against the corners and the ropes, blocking and slipping, feinting with his eyes and his head, to invite the champ's power, and then he would counterpunch in quick spurts whenever George left an opening. Given that George was throwing such wide roundhouse shots, there were a lot of openings. That Ali kept taunting him ensured that an enraged Foreman would try even harder to knock him out. Still, this was a very dangerous strategy against someone who could take out an opponent with one monster blow. To every eye in the place, it looked initially like Foreman was in the process of crushing Ali, just as so many experts had predicted. How could he survive such punishment?[15]

With his corner continuing without success to yell for him to dance and move, rounds two and three followed the pattern of round one, but at a bit slower pace and with Ali doing even more of his work from the ropes or the corners. In the second round, Ali retreated to the corner almost immediately, a hard place to fight from because there was little room to slip and slide. Foreman continued throwing wild lefts and rights, but he was unable to land anything clean. Before the champion could gain his rhythm, Ali wrestled Foreman to center ring, where the champion stung him with a hard right and then another, which forced Ali to hold on with both hands and convinced him he could not continue to wrestle with George and keep up his energy. Better to box him off the ropes. After Ali again retreated to the corner, Foreman unleashed a good right to the body followed by a right and left hook that also tattooed Ali's midsection. Nobody watching could figure out what was going on. According to *Time*: "In the second round, the bee unexpectedly threw away the tactics of his entire career. Off his toes and seemingly off his rocker," Ali continued to lay on the ropes. The champ pounded Ali's middle, but missed upstairs as Ali continued to keep his head back, but "it seemed to be only a matter of time before Ali's belly would turn to pulp." Plimpton called the developing pattern "the hugely terrifying and unique process of seeing a man slowly drained of his energy and resources by an opponent swaying on the ropes, giving him . . . 'lot of nothing.'" All the time Ali kept talking to Foreman, enraging him with "You can't hurt me!" "You punch like a sissy!" and "Is that all you got?" From the middle of the second round he lay back on the ropes, and from that position he fought "at an angle of ten and twenty degrees from the vertical and sometimes even further, a cramped near-tortured angle from which to box." At the end of the round, though, Ali once again came off the ropes to sting Foreman with hard rights and lefts; the champ's right eye began to look puffy.[16]

The first two rounds proved hard to score. Foreman appeared the aggressor as he whaled away at Ali's body while Ali seemed content to cover up—although he was effective with left jabs off the ropes. Nat Loubet, editor of *The Ring*, had "Foreman eking out a narrow advantage" after two rounds. Once again Ali's corner pleaded with him to dance and move, but to no avail. Dundee appeared particularly upset by Ali's tactics. Ali's fans and members of his extended entourage could not believe what they were seeing. To nearly everyone but Ali, it looked like he was taking a tremendous pounding on the ropes and that he could not survive much longer. Anyone watching the fight, declared Ferdie Pacheco, "could have been forgiven for thinking sooner or later the referee would be forced to step in to save his life." Typical was the reaction of Lana Shabazz, Ali's longtime cook. "I wasn't worried during that fight," she put it ironically. "I just died three or four times. Oh, my goodness; I flat out died. I couldn't look. I just covered my face with my hands, and every now and then I'd ask, 'Is he still alive?' Never mind winning or losing; I feared for his life." Apparently the only one who wasn't worried was Ali—and he had every right to be.[17]

As far as Foreman was concerned, for the first two rounds, he said, "I unleashed a torrent of punches, none of which really found its mark." Not until the third round did he feel he landed a punishing blow. After pounding Ali with lefts and rights to the body, Foreman was forced back by Ali's punches that landed right on the jaw, followed by lots of fast lefts. Yet Ali once again retreated to the ropes, and Foreman caught him with a vicious right hand that landed under the heart. "Blows like that can drive the wind—and the will—out of a man," Foreman recalled, and he figured Ali would respond by finally standing toe to toe with him, "his pride getting the better of his intelligence." When Foreman charged him, however, "his intelligence prevailed. He backed into the ropes and began covering up to avoid another barrage of heavy shots." Still, Foreman unleashed a merciless pounding, landing four tremendous body shots and an uppercut that seemed "to blow my jaw off." As Ali recalled, "it's the longest round I've ever fought in my life," but sensing that this was the round that the Foreman camp planned for his doom, he struggled to remain on his feet and take the champion farther in a fight than he had been in years. In fact, while the fans in the stadium chanted "Ali, Bomaye!" in the last thirty seconds, Ali's head appeared to clear and he landed a powerful right, left, right combination to Foreman's face to take something out of the champion. "I know this round will go down on the judges' scorecards as belonging to George, but there's something in it that belongs to me," Ali recalled in his autobiography. Indeed, the ferocious pace seemed to be telling on Foreman. As Foreman returned to his corner after the bell, he appeared wobbly, his legs weak, and he appeared to stumble just a bit.[18]

With constant pressure on him, noted Plimpton, Ali unloaded some "concussive shots," staggering Foreman, "and suddenly everybody except Foreman seemed to understand not only the plan but that it was working almost inevitably." While still concerned, Ali's corner "looked at him as if they were a trio of Professor Higginses looking at their Eliza for the first time." After that third round Ali told Dundee that the plan to make George punch himself out appeared to be working, that Foreman's punches were "not that bad," and that he was going to continue to let Foreman punch at him. "I wanted to make him shoot his best shots," Ali said later. The crowd had come alive, chanting for Ali as they saw him take "the worst shelling I've had in my life, and they still believe I can take the fight. It's like a charge of electricity." While Foreman slumped on his stool, Ali kibitzed with Jim Brown at ringside, telling him he would lose the sure-thing money that the ex–football star and motion-picture actor had bet on the champion. In Foreman's corner, Dick Sadler and Archie Moore insisted that he keep up the pounding. "But," Foreman recalled: "I was already nearly exhausted. I couldn't understand why. I'd fought only three rounds, yet felt that I'd gone fifteen." As Dundee looked across the ring, he "couldn't believe what he was seeing." By the end of the third it was evident that George's parachute "was beginning to close. What I couldn't understand for the life of me was why George's corner kept telling him to 'Go out and mash him' after every round instead of telling him to pace himself, to change his tactics instead of just continuing on the attack, round after round, wearing himself out."[19]

As the bell sounded for round four, Dundee told Ali to go after the tiring Foreman. Ali, however, had other ideas. He took the rope-a-dope even farther, laying on the ropes as comfortable as can be, as if inviting Foreman in for a chat, and taunting George to unleash his best shots to tire the champion even more. "You done run out of gas; now I'm going to kick your ass." "Is that the best you can do?" he demanded after a hard shot to the body by Foreman. "You can't punch. Show me something. That's a sissy punch." Each taunt was aimed at egging Foreman on while he measured the waning strength of George's punches. Then he declared, "Now it's my turn." Meanwhile the crowd cheered every punch by Ali, no matter how slight, observed Dundee, but the bombs that Foreman landed elicited complete silence. "And make no mistake about it," Dundee noted, "had the bombs landed, the effect of those punches would be like someone getting hit with a railroad tie."[20]

While Ali continued working from the ropes and corners, he was helped by the loose top strand which allowed him to lean beyond the champion's reach. No one in his camp, Foreman recalled, had bothered to check the ropes. "Why bother? For years now, my fight plan had been to take off my robe, get a quick knockout, put the robe back on, and return to the dressing room. Who worried about the tautness or slackness of the ropes? Now Muhammad was the beneficiary of that lack of attention to detail." Even more worrisome was the crowd reaction in favor of Ali that dispirited Foreman. "The sad part was that my blows, which numbered at least five to one over his, were met by the crowd with silence," while Muhammad's "little jabs brought tumultuous cries. I was winning these rounds, but Muhammad Ali owned their hearts and minds more completely with every punch he absorbed." For the fans, it was a morality play. Ali was "good and I was evil," Foreman said. As Ali taunted Foreman and snapped his head back with stinging jabs and right crosses, the champion finally managed "to land a thundering right on the back of his neck" during the fourth round. It weakened Ali and Foreman cocked his right for what he deemed would be the knockout blow. He pulled back, however, when he saw something that stayed with him long after the match had ended. Just as he was about to unload, he saw the face of a "friend" at ringside, waving his arms and screaming that the punch was a foul. It felt like the whole stadium seemed to have turned on him: "A man I'd considered family was rooting against me. In a state of shock, I couldn't deliver the punch that probably would have ended the fight right there." Prodded by the crowd's hostile reaction and Ali's constant taunts, Foreman's spirit and his stamina began to wane. Back in his corner, he was so tired that he "could barely get off the stool."[21]

The rest of the fight was similar, with Foreman pressing, driving Ali to the ropes, and hitting him with body shots that grew slower and weaker and wider with every punch. Increasingly the challenger unleashed a series of accurate left jabs and right crosses to the head and face that staggered the champion. The difference was that from the fifth round on Ali fought with renewed confidence and the conviction that he could not lose, while Foreman was shocked that he could not knock his man out despite all the firepower he had mustered. As Ali rested between the fourth and fifth rounds, he told Dundee: "He's mine . . . He's got nothing left. I can knock him out now." Dundee urged him not to wait, but Ali responded: "Not yet . . . He had his turn, now I'm gonna play with him." Rising from the stool, he raised his fist in the air and led the stadium in another "Ali, bomaye" chant. The crowd was alive with anticipation. In rounds five through seven, Ali played with Foreman, lulling him into a false sense of invulnerability as Ali lay on the ropes letting Foreman whale away. Still, Ali was absorbing punishment. To many observers he was behind on points. All through, though, he took control of the fight, punishing the ever-rushing Foreman with harder and harder left and right shots to the head. Ali proved adaptable, but Foreman refused to change tactics; following his corner's instructions, he single-mindedly pounded away like "the mummies of Ali's beloved horror films." As Foreman's punches weakened, Ali came off the ropes in the last thirty seconds to throw twenty hard, on-the-button blows that revved up the crowd to near ecstasy. By the sixth and seventh rounds, the champion was so arm weary he could hardly punch. By then, Ali was so confident that in the seventh he took his eyes off George to lead the crowd in another chant and to yell at Archie Moore to "be quiet, old man, it's all over." Concerned that Foreman might have just enough left for a knockout and upset about the needless and dangerous grandstanding, Dundee screamed at Ali: "Don't play with that sucker. Don't play." Ali listened for once and retreated to the ropes.[22]

Going into the eighth round, *Ring* editor Nat Loubet had Foreman ahead by four rounds to three; Egypt's *El Ahram* newspaper scored it five for Ali and only two for Foreman. The judges at ringside also had Ali way ahead. Clearly Ali had come on strong after the first two rounds to take control of the fight and take George into the later rounds, a distance the champion had not gone in years, and rarely in his entire career. Although he seemed to be fading, Foreman still possessed powerful weapons and he could be considered the aggressor by the judges and anyone watching the fight. During the pause, Foreman's team tried to ready him for the round. He stood up heavy and weak but determined to land the big KO shot. Ali's corner had other ideas. Between rounds Ali's manager Herbert Muhammad relayed the message from his father for Ali not to play around as he had done with Frazier. As the bell sounded, Angelo reinforced the sentiment. "He's out of gas," he yelled, "Take him out of there . . . He's ready to go!" This time Ali and Dundee were on the same page. He felt uneasy because the pace that was killing Foreman was "also taking a heavy toll on me." It was time to go for the kill before an exhausted champion found his second wind and managed to deliver that one knockout blow.[23]

Foreman came out for the bell a bit unsteady, but he immediately began winging punches as Ali secured himself along the ropes or in the corners, where he effectively blocked the telegraphed blows that the tired champion struggled to land. Ali managed a few lefts and rights of his own while Foreman's roundhouse blows continued to land far off the mark. With one of these desperate punches, the champion nearly propelled himself through the ropes. Untangling himself, he looked tired and a bit sheepish; Ali taunted: "You missed by a mile! You look bad, chump!" The round looked like the previous seven, only slower. The two fighters appeared exhausted, though Ali continued to fight from the ropes as if he were sitting in a big, comfortable easy chair in his own living room punching carefully and looking for openings. Toward the end of the round, Foreman attempted to pummel Ali along the ropes. "I was tired, but I still didn't respect his punching power, so I was chasing him with my hands down," George recalled, trying to entice Ali to come to him, "to step into my web; there was no way he could hurt me." Foreman then "missed with a right hand, turned around with my hands down, and he [Ali] moved with speed that he wasn't supposed to have at that point in the fight after taking all those blows." Slightly off balance, Foreman was open for a brief second. Seeing his chance, Ali threw a right and then a left-right combination. George found himself even more off balance, and taking advantage and using the tremendous hand speed he had scored with all night, Ali landed a more powerful combination, followed by a hard right that caught Foreman flush on the right side of the jaw. As the punches landed Foreman recalled thinking: "*Boy, I'm going down*. Muhammad, I'm sure, was as surprised as I was." It certainly appeared that way. As Foreman began a slow, lazy pirouette to the canvas, Ali looked on in wonderment at his own handiwork, his right fist cocked in reserve should another shot be necessary. No need. For the first time in his career, Foreman lay on the canvas, confused but still alert, believing in the depths of his soul that he would finally get a chance to mix it up with Ali once he bounced back up. Looking to his corner for the signal to rise, Foreman heard Zack Clayton count to eight. As Dick Sadler motioned for him to get up, Foreman struggled to rise, but Clayton counted him out before he could do so.[24]

As Clayton's count reached ten, several hundred people in the crowd, overwhelmed with joy at the surprising conclusion of the match, surged into the ring, yelling Ali's name, and chanting "Ali, bomaye!" with even greater enthusiasm than they had all during the fight. In the confusion, Ali appeared to faint to the canvas in exhaustion, but he was quickly back on his feet to bask in the glow of the crowd and in the glow of his great upset victory—not just in defeating Foreman against all odds but also in defeating the boxing experts who had predicted his defeat, defeating boxing history to become only the second heavyweight champion to reclaim his title, and defeating the ravages of time. Not only had he beaten the odds; he had triumphed when so many worried about his health and safety. "Muhammad Ali has done it," proclaimed David Frost, one of the television announcers: "The great man has done it. This is the most joyous scene ever seen in the history of boxing. . . . The place is going wild."[25]

While the festive crowd celebration continued in the ring and in the stands of the stadium, George Foreman took the long, lonely walk to his dressing room, moving haltingly as if in a daze through a crowd that appeared to ignore him as if he weren't even there. "My God, it was over," he recalled. "It was really over. I felt disappointed, less for losing than for not getting the chance to mix it up. Then the magnitude of the loss began to hit me. I would be sorting it out for a long time." The mood of his dressing room was funereal. George Plimpton found Foreman lying on the rubbing table in "his red-walled dressing room, gold lame towels draped over his shoulders, ice packs applied to his face." Thoroughly exhausted, the now ex-champion had to take impertinent questions that reporters would not have asked twenty-four hours earlier. "Now these guys believed they could get away with anything," Foreman realized. "*So that's how it is*?" he asked himself. "*You're either on top, or you're nowhere*." Foreman's answers suggested confusion. When Plimpton asked him if he had been knocked out cold, Foreman replied "he won the fight . . . but I cannot admit that he beat me. It's never been said that I have been knocked out." Slowly he added: "There is never a loser. No fighter should be a winner. Both should be applauded." The reporters present took all this for a self-serving attempt at consolation by a very confused and disappointed young man. Eventually, they figured, he would realize he had indeed lost and had indeed been knocked out.[26]

It did not take long for the reality of his ignominious and humiliating defeat to sink in. Days after the fight, the by-then ex-champion Foreman seemed to take responsibility for the loss, but even so he quickly placed the blame on Ali for not fighting him toe-to-toe in the center of the ring. "The tactics were mine," he told the press. "Every time I fought someone he eventually got it. Regardless of where he went or what he did in the ring, eventually he got it." Throughout the match with Ali, Foreman kept thinking that one of his big punches would get him. But it did not happen this time "because this guy never really fought. He was like someone in a canoe. He rolled along with the tide, waiting for it to turn. He was clever." What Foreman took as weakness, however, Ali and his fans took as strength. The new champion had proved how great he was by fooling the unwary and stupid young man who was way out of his depth.[27]

Soon a depressed and devastated Foreman found that losing was a bitter pill to swallow for a twenty-five-year-old who had enjoyed the world's adoration and all the privileges that went with being the strongest man in the world. "I felt empty, totally empty," he recalled. "I hadn't just lost the title. I'd lost what defined me as a man." His whole identity had been constructed around being the "King of the Jungle," the biggest and baddest man around, capable of using his brute strength to impose his will on all other men. Unfortunately, the loss exposed the fact that he had little else to go on. Even the Bible that he had brought with him to Zaire had failed to guarantee a victory, and he set it aside as a sign of weakness and ruined hopes. Running from himself and his sense of emptiness, an angry and depressed Foreman spent months in a futile attempt to escape with a string of different women in Paris, Los Angeles, and Hawaii. Losing had completely thrown him. He had cars, money, houses, and women, but he hungered to become again the man who had not been knocked out in Zaire.[28]

Ali's entourage, in contrast, was triumphant. Against all odds and in dramatic fashion, Ali had reclaimed his title after seven long years of frustration. After the ecstatic outpouring of joy in the ring, Ali faced reporters and the millions in the satellite television audience as he asked ring commentator David Frost, "Am I the greatest of all time?" To which Frost responded, "You've proved it." Remarkably, although his right eye was bloodshot, there were no other marks on a face better known across the globe than any other sport, entertainment, or political celebrity. The newly crowned champion was exultant as he spoke into the microphone. Just as he had in 1964 after defeating Sonny Liston, Ali castigated the press for making him an underdog. Claiming he was "the scholar of boxing," he derided the experts for betting against him. As to what had allowed him to achieve such a monumental upset, Ali announced that his victory came from "all these people" yelling "Ali, bomaye" for him. Even more, he laid his victory to something bigger than himself and his earthly following. "I learned a special prayer of Allah," he said. "What you saw was the power of Allah in helping me win. That must have been Allah in there because I can't punch." Indeed, the power of his religion must have made his hands strong, he argued, because his hands were sore for Frazier and Norton, "but they were good this time. I'm not known for being a hitter. Can you picture me making George Foreman helpless?" To add to this victory for Allah, Ali greeted all Muslims with "As-salaam-alaikum," and advised his black followers to read *Muhammad Speaks*, the newspaper of the Nation of Islam, and attend services at the Nation's mosques.[29]

The outcome of the fight was perhaps the most satisfying of Ali's career. In ten years he had come full circle to reclaim the title he had first won against Sonny Liston in 1964. The boxing establishment was astounded by the outcome. Former champion Joe Louis, for instance, expressed complete surprise: "I couldn't believe it. I just couldn't believe it. I couldn't see Foreman losing like that." After taking a slew of powerful punches—more than he ever had to take from Liston—Ali was back on top, the king of the world. As Dave Anderson put it: "Muhammad Ali has been looked upon as a buffoon. He has been defiled and defrocked of his title for defying the military draft because of his Black Muslim beliefs. He has been castigated for his cruelty. But he has proved he is a gladiator. He just might be 'the greatest,' as he has always proclaimed." After seven long years since his banishment from boxing he could finally enjoy the exile's return. Looking over the Zaire River, an unusually subdued Ali told reporters: "You'll never know how long I've waited for this. You'll never know what it means to me."[30]

Almost immediately, the dramatic turn of events prompted George Foreman and many boxing experts and fans to question how such an upset could have occurred. For the now ex-champion, finding explanations for his humiliating defeat began to plague him just as soon as he left the ring. He especially resented that Ali immediately began bragging about his great rope-a-dope strategy, which translated in Ali's estimation into George being "the dope." According to Foreman, Ali's only strategy was survival: "When I cut off the ring from him, he had nowhere to go but the ropes, and nothing to do but cover up." Rather than a brilliant strategy on Ali's part, Foreman wrote in his autobiography, was the fact that, he said, "I fought a foolish fight by not letting him come to me more, especially when I was tired and far ahead on points." He failed to do that, he argued, because he did not want the world to think he was afraid of Ali and because he followed his trainers' advice and went all out for the knockout. That he fought a foolish fight certainly rings true, especially since the tapes of the match show continued scenes of futile effort on his part with little variance or even consideration that his fight plan was not working after the third round. As Ali assessed the situation, Foreman lost because he thought he was "*supreme*. He believed what the press said—that he was unbeatable and that he'd whup me easy." He thought he was "a big indestructible lion—but George found out the facts of life when we had our rumble in the jungle."[31]

More bizarre, perhaps, was the suggestion that he had been doped, that someone had put a chemical agent into his water that worked to tire him out. Perhaps, Foreman implied, there was real dope in the rope-a-dope. How else, he reasoned, could he explain the medicinal taste when he drank his water just before the start of the fight? What else might explain how tired he felt? The implication he leaves the reader with in his autobiography is that his trainer, Dick Sadler, might have been the responsible party. There is no proof of doping, and like his other charges, this led to Foreman's being labeled by Ali "a sore loser." To top it off, Foreman felt that he received a quick count by referee Zack Clayton. Foreman recalled hearing the count of eight, looking over at Dick Sadler in the corner, and on his instructions standing up. "I stood at once, but Clayton waved me off with a quick count—nine and ten became one word to me."[32]

The shocking upset and Foreman's suspicions, noted Dan Daniel in *Ring* magazine, left behind "more questions, more queries unanswered, more puzzlements than any other heavyweight title fight in the book." In his role as "the Ring Detective," the longtime boxing commentator investigated Foreman's charges and those circulating among boxing fans. To Foreman's charge that the loose ropes worked to Ali's advantage, Daniel retorted that the ropes "were just as loose or just as tight for Foreman." Still, Ali's use of the ropes was a splendid strategy, and "Foreman was outwitted in this matter as he was outwitted in general." As we have seen, long after the fight, there were suspicions that Angelo Dundee loosened the ropes. The evidence, however, suggests that he worked tirelessly before the bout to tighten them and urged the ring attendants to make sure that the ropes were tightened before and after the preliminary bouts, which they never did. It is true that when he saw various ring officials attempting to tighten the ropes between the fifth and sixth rounds, he yelled furiously at them to stop messing about because he was worried that they were loosening the ropes even more. As to the loose canvas, the Ring Detective decreed that it had no effect on the fight, but might have hurt Ali had he tried his old tactic of moving about, pirouetting, and dancing. Daniel also denied that Foreman received a quick count by referee Clayton, having checked with viewers at ringside and the tape of the fight itself. In his account of the bout, Norman Mailer explained that viewers watching in theaters did not realize that Clayton had actually started the count two seconds before the ring announcer began counting.[33]

Puzzled and disturbed about Foreman's charge of a quick count, Clayton responded: "There was no quick count. And there was no loosening of the ropes. It sounds to me," declared the referee, "like George Foreman is just looking for an out." Hoping to put an end to the growing controversy paralleled in boxing history only by the Gene Tunney–Jack Dempsey long-count bout of 1927, Clayton explained that "the count begins the second his knee touches the canvas." As soon as Foreman went down, he said, "I turned around to direct Ali to a neutral corner. He doesn't have to be standing exactly in the corner for the count to begin." After whirling around, Clayton said he "picked up the count just before the tick of three. He was laying on his back at five. When I said six he started to stir. No way in the world a person exhausted and hurt could make an attempt to clear the deck when he's still on his back at six. I even shouted the count right in his ear to wake him up. Sometimes you can do that." Foreman rolled over, but as he was in the center of the ring he had no ropes to help pull himself up. "He had nothing to reach for and he was in no condition to jump up. I was still shouting the numbers at him but he was turning over slowly. When I reached nine he was on his knees. When I reached 10 he still had one hand or one knee, I forget which, on the canvas. Either way, he wasn't standing."[34]

It is interesting that Daniel said nothing about Foreman's charge that he had been doped, and ever since the fight Foreman retained suspicions that he was doped. What made Foreman so tired and sluggish? Was there something to the medicinal taste? Did it have to do with a fix? No one knows for sure. But we do know that Sadler's policy was to toughen up his fighters by limiting the amount of water they could drink until just before the match. In an email to me Foreman confirmed that he and Sadler agreed to abstain from water from the day before the fight to the beginning of the bout. Since Sadler had trained other champions, Foreman assumed his trainer knew what he was doing. The feeling of near dehydration, was intended by Sadler to make his fighters angry and aggressive. When the bell rang, Sadler would send them across the ring with curses to destroy his enemy. Although this training regimen had worked superbly in forty wins, in the heat and humidity of that Kinshasa night, it proved a terrible strategy. Even at 4 a.m. the air was hot and muggy, and Ali did not cooperate by falling in the first three rounds. The pace was intense and the already-dehydrated Foreman, not used to going past two rounds, found himself running out of gas by the end of the third round. Foreman's lack of energy was heightened by the fact that he had trouble getting into shape and by ring time had to lose thirty pounds, dropping from 250 pounds at the beginning of training to 220 pounds at the weigh-in. Indeed, according to Dan Daniel, "Foreman may lay most of the blame for his defeat on his failure to keep in shape and his inability to get himself down to 220 pounds in a normal way." By contrast, Ali was in superb condition, perhaps the best since before his layoff, and there was a major difference.[35]

Whatever the causes of Foreman's defeat, they did little to restore his reputation or his pride after such a humiliating performance. Indeed, Ali's dramatic victory destroyed the myth of George Foreman's invincibility. One fight fan put it succinctly. Ali, the Chicagoan Seeley Hagan wrote *The Ring* magazine, "is the only interesting fighter in the business. He made a monkey out of the greatest hitter in years. George knows about as much about boxing as he know[s] about flying to Russia. How did he ever stop Joe Frazier?" Promoter Don Fraser was equally adamant. "George Foreman turned out to be the ghost of Sonny Liston." At the hands of Ali, "within a few minutes, Foreman's portrait went from invincible, unbeatable powerhouse to pathetic chump." Indeed, asked Foreman's supporters, where was the Foreman "who had smashed Joe Frazier down six times to win the championship and destroyed Ken Norton in defense of it." How could it be that a Foreman who had "mastered those two with contemptuous ease, was a stumbling amateur against their victim." The answer according to *Chicago Tribune* sports columnist Rick Talley was this: Ali "did it the simplest way. He just sat back and hit him in the face." Instead of dancing, he lay back on the ropes and counter punched against Foreman's head, a target that was always right in front of him.[36]

In destroying Foreman and his myth of invincibility, just as he had done to Liston ten years earlier, Ali sealed his legend as the greatest heavyweight boxing champion of all time. "Can the world bear it?" asked *Los Angeles Times* boxing columnist John Hall. "If not a legend before, the strutting, swaggering, shouting Ali most certainly is now. Instantly, the promoters rush back to beat upon his door." The shock of the upset and the seeming magic of Ali's accomplishment brought the skeptics to their knees. No matter what other fighters thought, and "never mind what the critics say," Hall continued, "Ali is king. He's magic. He's magnificent. He's a hypnotist. He casts a spell over himself as well as his people, all the people." Speaking for his former critics, Hall admitted that "we bow and scrape at the Ali shrine." Even more, boxing experts had to take responsibility for building up Foreman into a myth of invincibility. "It was the ghost of Liston," he wrote, "another swift disintegration of a myth we all helped to create."[37]

As a classic hero, moreover, Ali's victory was an uphill struggle over the privations and tests that seemed to thwart him at every turn: his bitter loss to Joe Frazier in 1971 and his broken-jaw defeat against Ken Norton in 1973. As he saw it, his comeback victory made him even greater than Patterson. "I'm greater than Patterson was," Ali told the press. "He fought a white fella, that Ingemar Johansson, and won it back the next year. I fought a strong good, black scientific boxer [Liston]), who beat Patterson twice, whipped him at 22, and 10 years later I fought another black fighter. Black fighters are better than white fighters. That's really getting the title back. Wise people listened to me but a few fools bet on him." Coming full circle, Ali transformed himself into the man who had not only challenged "the man"—he had beaten him. He was now a full-fledged folk hero who defied the power of an oppressive society, a John Henry who had defeated the captain.[38]

That sense of fulfillment and liberation was felt all over Kinshasa. It was dawn when Ali left the stadium, and at every village and crossing crowds were leaping and yelling as he passed, many holding up babies so that they could see the victor who had set their hearts aflame. Hundreds of fans remained in the stands and in the ring itself, mimicking the dramatic manner in which Foreman was knocked out. While Foreman lay awake in his hotel room tortured by his inconceivable loss at the hands of a seemingly washed-up former champion, Ali and his wife Belinda sat in the back seat of their Citroen as they were driven back to N'Sele. As Ali told George Plimpton, he and Belinda were struck by how odd it seemed to be leaving the arena in the light of day. They just could not stop talking about how unusual it seemed. Normally, they knew, prizefighters arrive at the arena during the daylight hours and when the fight is over they exit while it is dark. "It seemed so symbolically appropriate that on this occasion he should be coming out of darkness into light." After seven years of battling the government, the boxing establishment, and the ravages of Father Time, the newly crowned champion indeed felt that he had survived the dark days of struggle and doubt and emerged into a lighter, more optimistic future.[39]

Equally symbolic, reporters covering the fight remarked that the drenching monsoon rains that were expected any time after late September began to fall only after the fight had taken place and Ali had triumphed. In fact, according to Hank Schwartz, he felt the first drops of rain begin to fall at 5:15 a.m. as fans crowded into the ring and the wild celebrations began. It seemed that the Ali magic not only brought victory in the ring; that very same magic had the power to control the heavens. The monsoon downpour that began immediately after the victory in fact knocked out the satellite sending facilities in the basement of the stadium. All of Video Techniques' equipment was under two feet of water and had to be moved to higher ground. Had that occurred before or during the fight, millions of viewers around the globe would have missed the fight. The Ali magic had held. Not only did he win against great odds, but the fight in Zaire that so many had doubted would come off actually managed to defy nature and take place.[40]

That sense of triumph and rebirth suffused the buses filled with the Ali entourage that followed Ali and Belinda through the African dawn. As their cavalcade rolled through the early morning light and the rain that had begun to fall, it was clear that Ali's victory carried meanings that went far beyond his personal victory and Foreman's terrible loss. Out the window of the buses, Ali's supporters witnessed hundreds of natives lining the road. "Arms upraised," recalled Ferdie Pacheco, "they chanted Ali, Ali, Ali, Ali and held up small children to see him." Sitting in the back of the bus, writers Budd Schulberg and George Plimpton, along with fight doctor Pacheco, smiled to one another as they compared the scene "to the liberation of Paris. We who had shared the second coming of Ali in that glorious night of black awakening in Atlanta, and shared the bitter hospital scene after the first Frazier fight, and the tough night in San Diego when we sweated out the broken jaw operation, rode numb with pleasure and fulfillment and virtually unable to speak." In its uniqueness and dramatic finish, noted Pacheco, "it had to be the greatest fight scene I had ever been involved in."[41]

FIG. 14. Workers busy with preparations on August 12, 1974, at main entrance of 20 Mai Stadium. President Mobutu invested millions in refurbishing the stadium, the highways, phone lines, and a satellite receiving station in his bid to put Zaire and his regime on the map. (AP Photo).

FIG. 15. At the dedication of the refurbished stadium, Mobutu raises the arms of Foreman, left, and Ali, right on September 22, 1974. Note the bandage over Foreman's eye, which was cut in training and required postponing the fight five weeks. Mobutu wanted the fight to cap the two-week celebration of his authenticity campaign. (AP Photo/Horst Faas).

FIG. 16. Singer and bandleader James Brown in concert February 12, 1974. Brown and his band were the headliners of Zaire 74, the 3-day music festival to accompany the fight. The festival featured an unprecedented international cast of musicians across the African diaspora. Foreman's cut delayed the bout and killed any chance of a profit. (AP/Photo).

FIG. 17. Foreman and promoter Don King in traditional African dress. During the delay King became the face of the promotion. Foreman's German Shepherd Digo accompanied him everywhere in Zaire, reminding the Zarois of dog's role as a vicious tool of the Belgian Colonial Regime, making it easy for Ali to depict the champion as a Belgian oppressor and himself as their liberator. (AP Photo/Horst Faas).

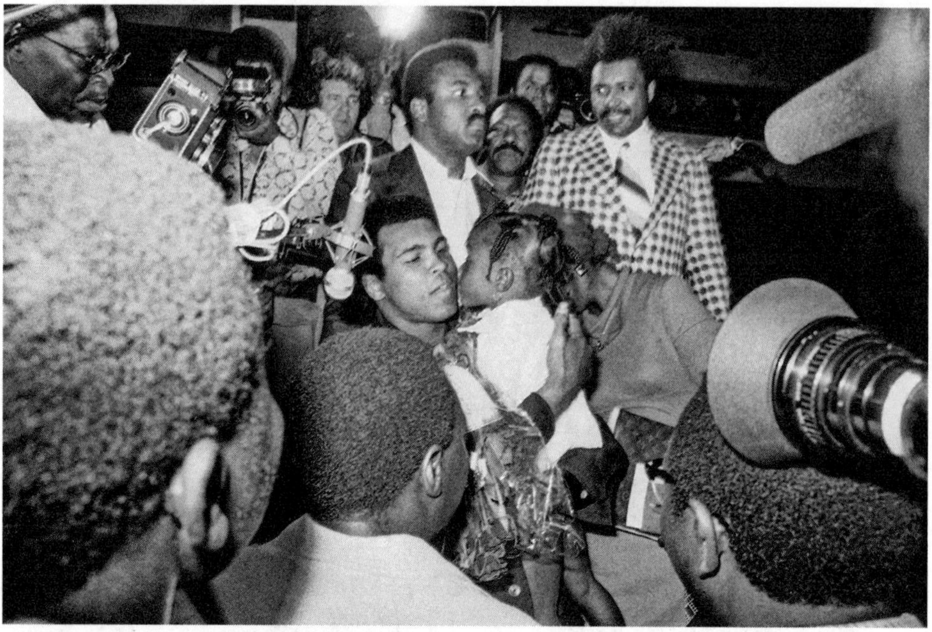

FIG. 18. While Foreman and Digo stood apart from the Zarois, Ali cultivated them as soon as he deplaned in Kinshasa, September 10, 1974. Here he is seen kissing a Zarois child. Children flocked to Ali whenever he appeared in public. The woman is Ali's second wife, Belinda. (AP Photo/ Horst Faas).

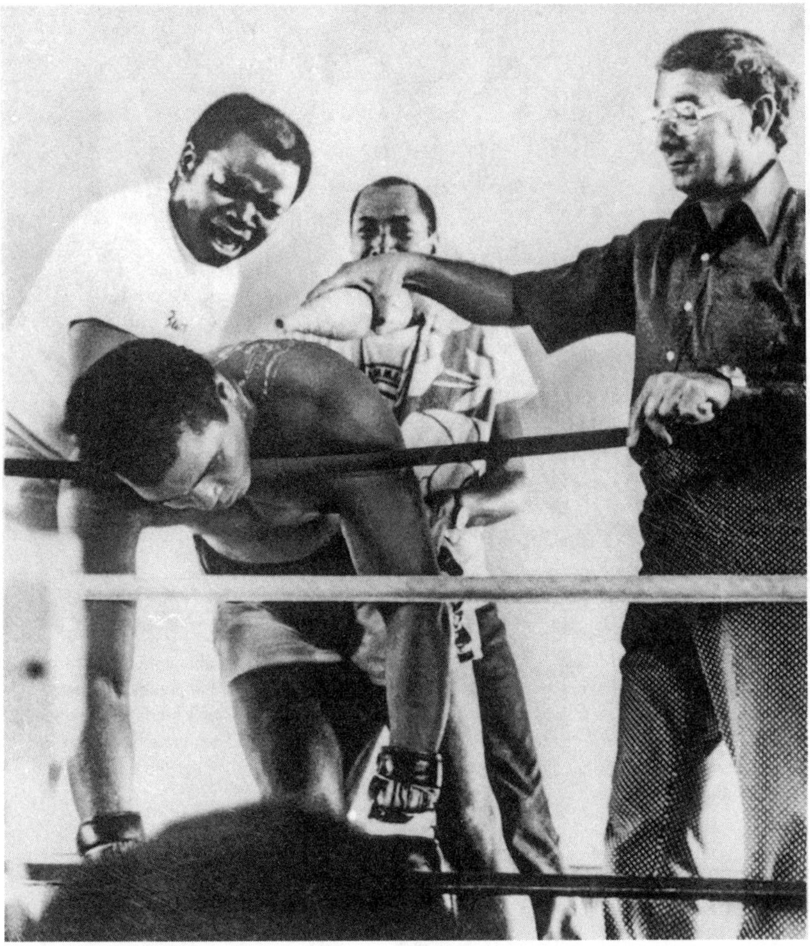

FIG. 19. Ali cultivated the Zarois during his training sessions at N'Sele, where he recited poetry and harangued Foreman as a Belgian oppressor. Ali enjoyed entertaining his fans. Here he mimicks exhaustion after sparring, mocking predictions that he was too old to win. His cornerman "Bundini" is at left and his long-time trainer Angelo Dundee is at right. Man, center, unidentified. October 1974 (AP Photo).

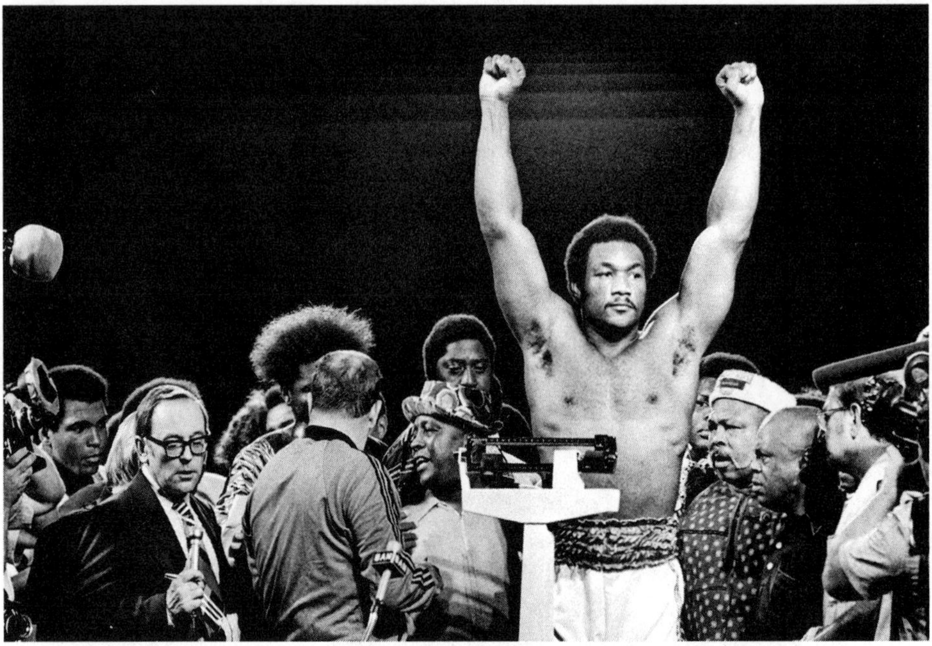

FIG. 20. At the weigh-in on October 26 in 20 Mai Stadium, a healed and confident champion responds to cheers of the crowd, finally steals some of Ali's thunder, and impresses the world with his awesome muscles. Could Ali beat such a goliath? At left, Foreman's manager Dick Sadler, in hat, talks with Don King, identified by his electric hair. Right, in white hat is Archie Moore, Foreman's trainer and former light heavyweight champion. Next to Foreman is Job Corps trainer Doc Broadus. (AP Photo).

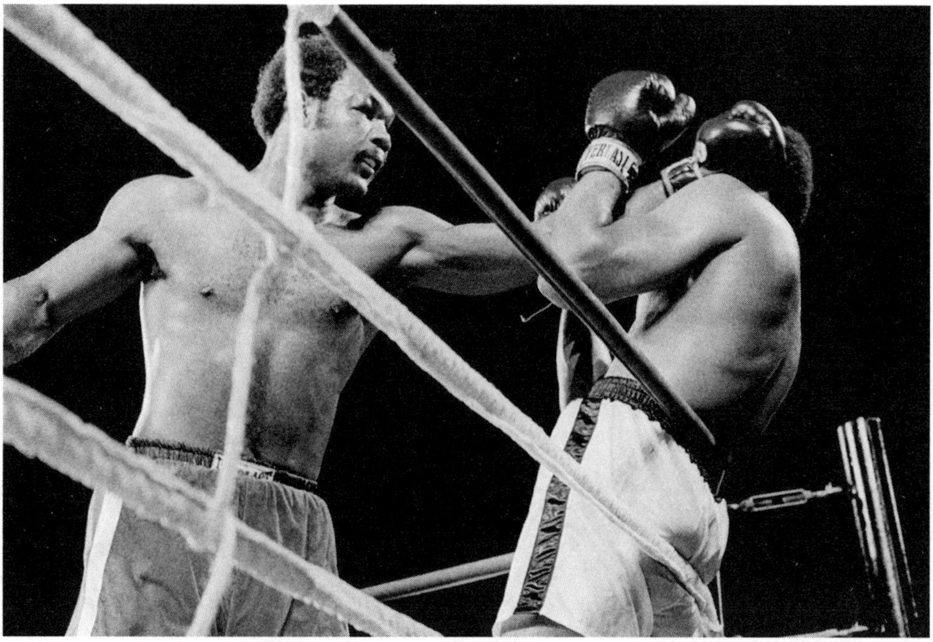

FIG. 21. Foreman, left, has Ali on the ropes in the first round. As Ali retreated to the ropes in what became known as his rope-a-dope strategy, it appeared that the champion was too powerful for the aging challenger, on October 30, 1974. (AP Photo).

FIG. 22. Ali watches Foreman pirouette to the canvas in the 8th round. This was the first time Foreman had been knocked down, let alone knocked out. The loss of his title in such a humiliating upset threw the former champion into a depression. Given little chance to win, Ali proved his greatness. The victory vindicated him and a generation of black and white radicals who identified with his defiance of the American Government, the U. S. Military, and a racist white America. At right, open-mouthed are George Plimpton and Norman Mailer dumbfounded by the KO. (AP Photo).

FIG. 23. Newly-crowned heavyweight champion Muhammad Ali meets with President Gerald Ford at The White House, December 10, 1974. In 1967 Ali, the most conspicuous draft resister of the Vietnam War, was now accepted by many politicians and government officials who had previously scorned him. At left is Ali's brother, Rahman Ali. (AP Photo).

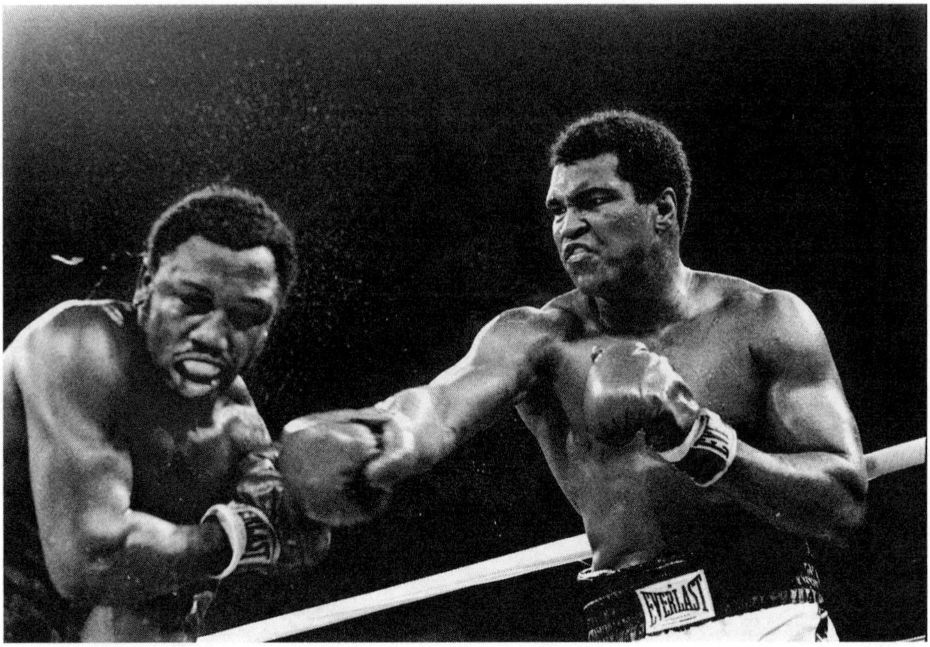

FIG. 24. Spray flies from head of challenger Joe Frazier as champion Muhammad Ali connects with a right in the 9th round of "The Thrilla in Manila," October 1, 1975. Ali won on a 14th round TKO. The third Ali-Frazier bout was consumed by the personal animosity between the two men and Ali's brazen extramarital affairs. (AP Photo/Mitsunori Chigita).

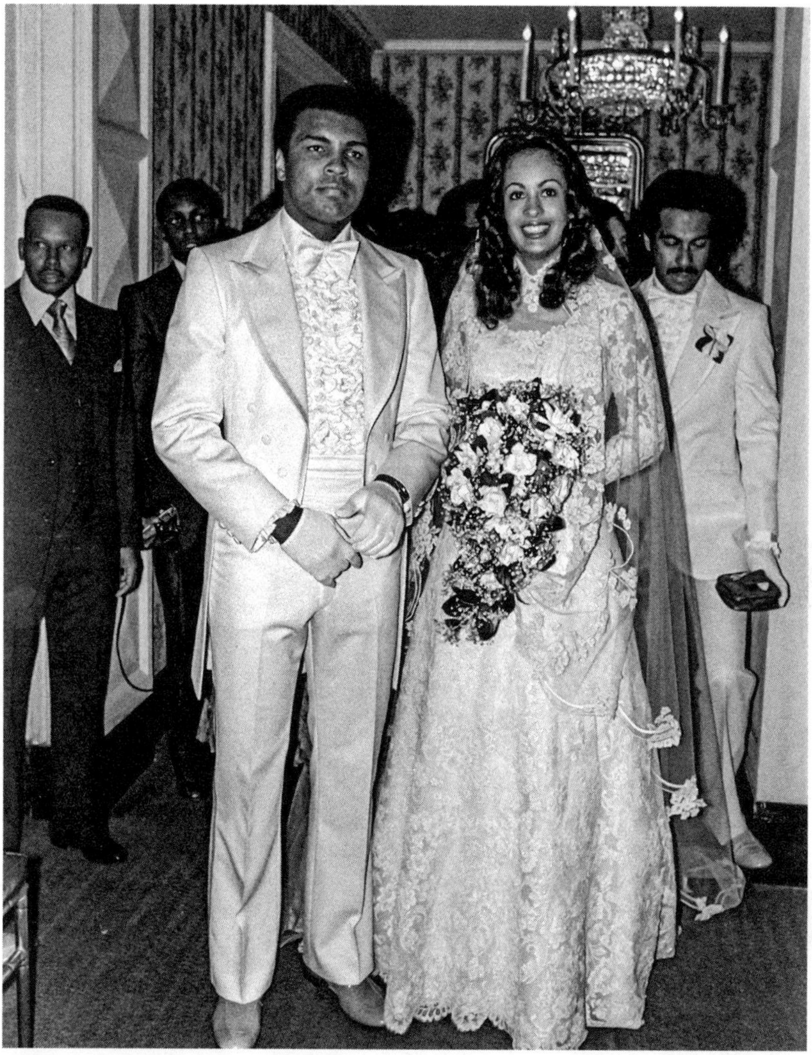

FIG. 25. Heavyweight champion Ali and his bride, Veronica Porche, June 19, 1977, following their wedding in Los Angeles. It was Ali's third marriage. His relationship with Porche went back to Zaire and along with his endless womanizing contributed to the end of his marriage to Belinda Boyd (Khalila). (AP Photo/stf).

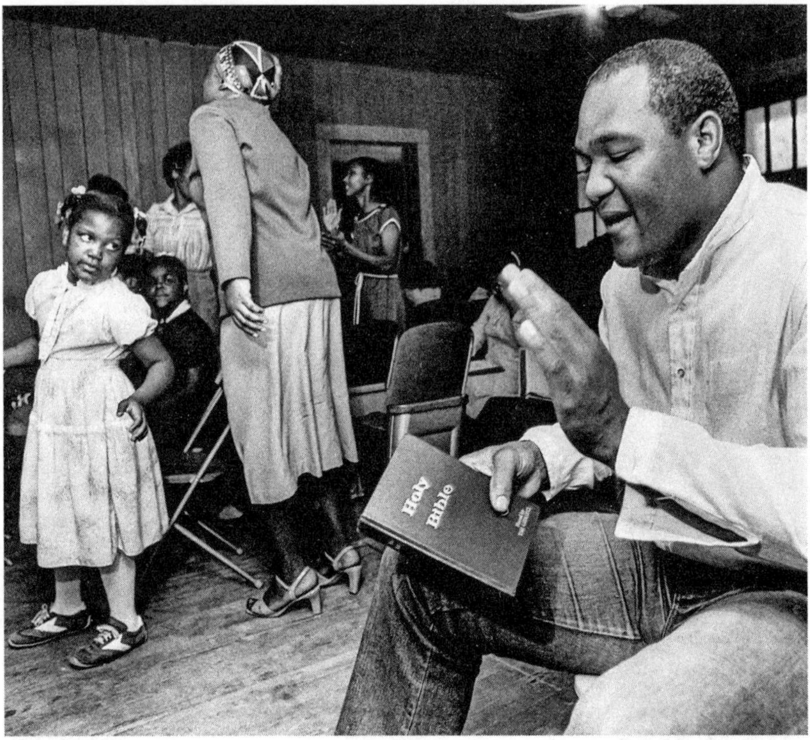

FIG. 26. After losing to Jimmy Young in Puerto Rico in 1977, Foreman was born again, quit boxing, and became an evangelical preacher in Houston, where he started his own church and his George Foreman Youth Center. Here he holds his Bible during a prayer meeting July 9, 1981. (AP Photo/Ed Kolenovsky).

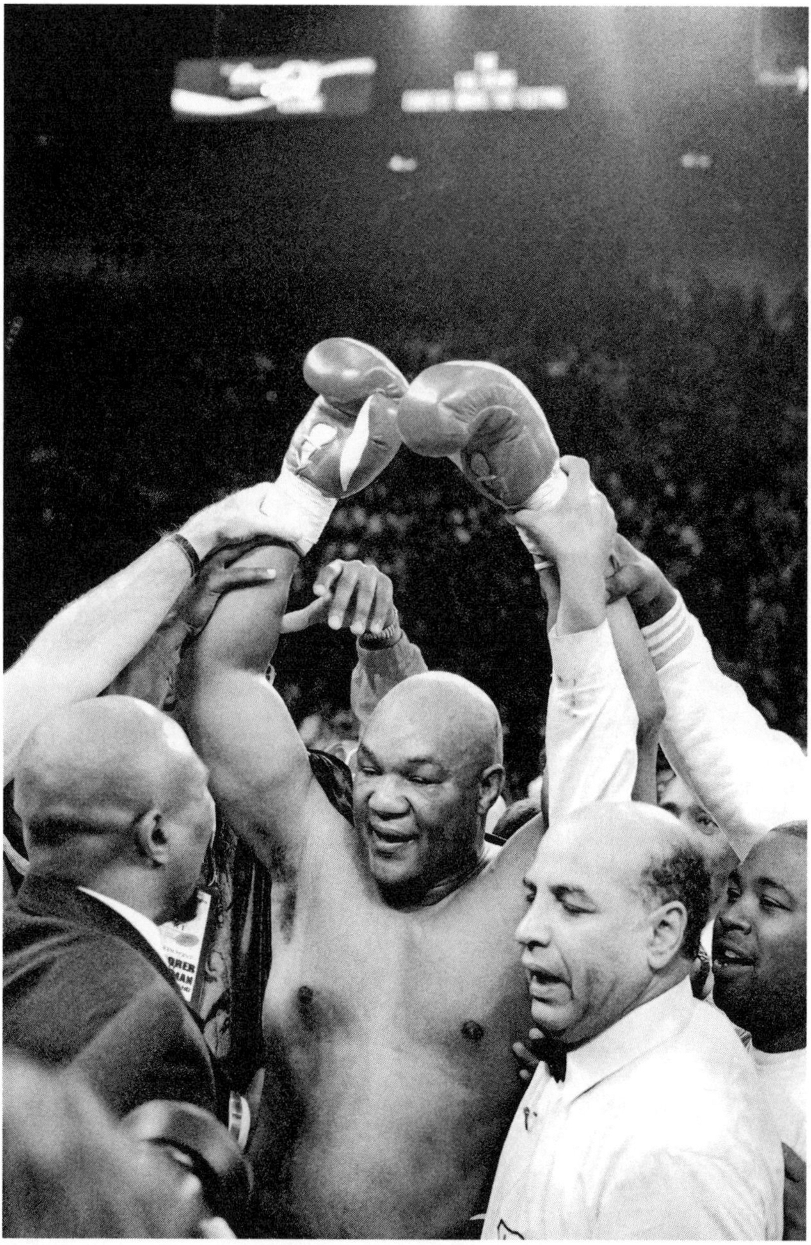

FIG. 27. In one of the sport's greatest reversals, ten years after leaving boxing, Foreman returned to the ring. On November 5, 1994, he reclaimed the title by knocking out Michael Moorer in the 10th round in Las Vegas. The paunchy, 45 year-old, became the oldest man to win the heavyweight crown. (AP Photo/ Lennox Mclendon).

FIG. 28. Former heavyweight champion George Foreman poses during a promotional event for his Lean-Mean-Grilling Machine in Tokyo, April 10, 2007. Starting in the '90s, Foreman's personality transformation brought on by his religious conversion from sullen black man to smiling, self-deprecating everyman made him an excellent, race-neutral crossover pitchman for products as diverse as Meineke Mufflers, McDonalds, KFC and The Grill. (AP Photo/Kin Cheung).

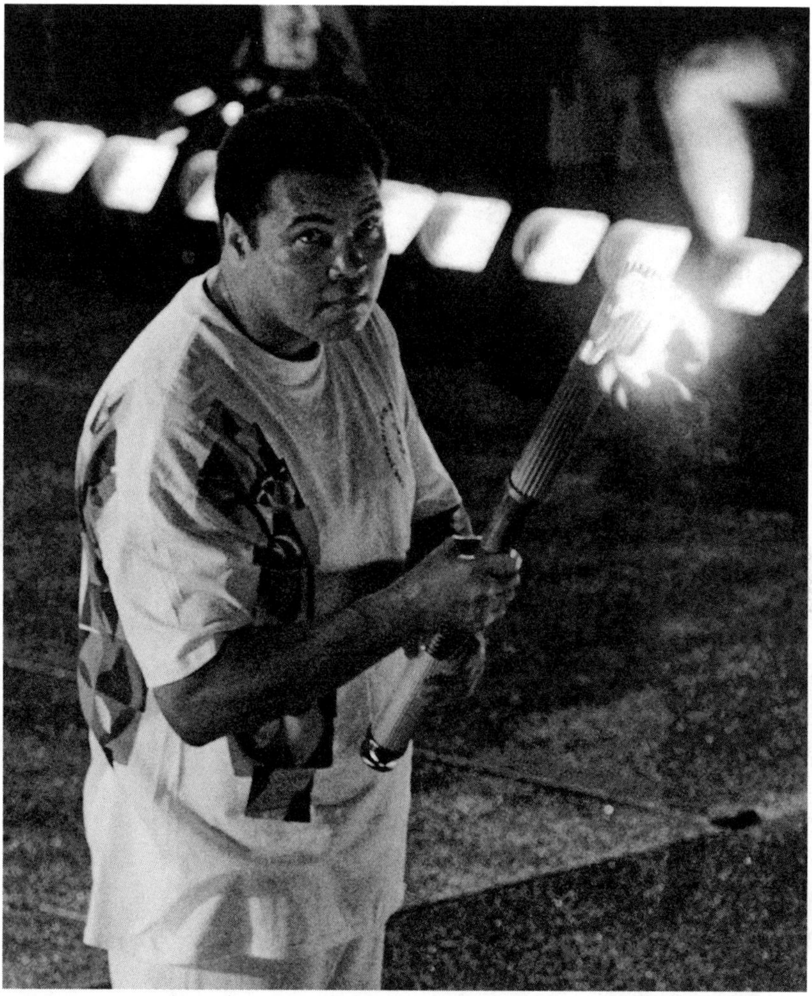

FIG. 29. Diagnosed in 1984 with a form of Parkinson's, Ali's image dimmed. Engineered in part by his 4th wife, Lonnie, Ali was invited to light the cauldron at the opening of the Atlanta Olympics July 19, 1996. With shaky hands, shuffling feet, and subdued voice the ex-champ was no longer the agile fighter of his youth or the outspoken critic of racist America. He became a symbol of persistence against adversity and physical disability. Soon his endorsements increased. (AP Photo/Doug Mills)

FIG. 30. Together again. George Foreman looks on as Will Smith hugs Ali after the two former champions appeared on stage after *When We Were Kings* (1996) was awarded Best Documentary Film, March 24, 1997. (AP Photo/Susan Sterner).

7

VIOLENT CORONATION IN ZAIRE

The King was back at home in Africa to reclaim his crown and that is what he did today.

DREW "BUNDINI" BROWN, *SALONGO*, 31 OCTOBER 1974

The effigy of George Foreman as the Superman of the ring was shattered among the rubble of the destroyed statues of Livingston and Stanley, representing white domination, down in the distant Congo.

DAN DANIEL, *THE RING*, JANUARY 1975

"The plot couldn't be better," noted Dave Anderson in the *New York Times*. "In perhaps the most dramatic scenario in boxing history, Ali had regained the heavyweight title at the age of 32 by outpunching a 25-year-old slugger who had recorded 24 consecutive knockouts in a previously unbeaten career," and he accomplished this in the former Belgian Congo much to the astonishment of millions of fans watching in theaters around the globe, and the many who followed the fight over the radio or on the front pages of their morning newspapers. In the heart of Africa he had returned from exile to his former exalted state. As his corner man Bundini Brown declared, "The King was back at home in Africa to reclaim his crown and that is what he did today." He proved, according to most accounts, "he is a gladiator. He just might be 'the greatest,' as he always proclaimed."[1]

Reclaiming the crown provided a sense of personal redemption after Ali's years in exile, but even more than a personal vindication, the triumph of an underdog over such a powerful opponent cemented Ali's place as a sports superstar, an American legend, and a global icon, especially across Africa and the Islamic world. Indeed, many fans agreed with Foreman that the fight had turned into a morality play, with Ali as good and Foreman as evil. Why was this so? As 1974 was coming to a close, many Americans were doubtful about the strength of the American dream. United States participation in the Vietnam War had finally ended, and although the South Vietnamese government momentarily remained in power, it looked like the war would be the first major loss in American history. At home the threat of impeachment of President Nixon over the Watergate affair forced his resignation. Americans doubted they could trust a government that abused its powers, attacked its citizens, and could not prevent either a humiliating defeat abroad or a recession and runaway inflation at home caused by the oil embargo. The government seemed a pitiful and often immoral giant not worthy of the nation's trust.[2]

Americans were awakening to the realization that the full weight of the federal government had been used against the two major political movements of the day: the black freedom and antiwar movements. In that environment the most that one could hope for was to survive these catastrophes. As Foreman had come to stand for the strength and power of the establishment and the flag-waving "silent majority," his loss to Ali provided a momentary redemption for the rebellious values of the 1960s. In an era when successful black and white radical activists were at the mercy of the rising wave of conservatism, the victory by the underdog vindicated those who, like Ali, had challenged white supremacy at home and abroad, and those who had fought to end what they saw as an immoral imperial war against a much weaker foe. So too many saw in Ali's victory a vindication of the values of the generational revolt against authority. That the victory occurred in Africa between a global black hero and a black man considered a tool of white colonialists also served to confirm Ali's role as a champion of global black liberation. Ali's victory gave many hope that their "underdog" quest for freedom from the establishment and colonial rule was still possible and morally justified.

So much of the meaning of the bout was bound up with the unexpected victory of the underdog over such an overpowering force as George Foreman, and the rope-a-dope tactics by which the victory was achieved. Ali's triumph appeared greater because it was so unexpected. As the older and weaker opponent, according to Ronald Kisner, *Jet*'s sports editor, Ali found himself "to be a Daniel in the lion's den, a man without a prayer." In lauding Ali as *Sports Illustrated*'s "Sportsman of the Year" for 1974, George Plimpton put it well. For many sports writers "he may be the most astonishing athlete of our time. Charismatic. Talented. Outspoken. Possibly of tragic stature. Unpredictable—both in the ring and out." One never knows what sort of fight he will deliver, noted Plimpton. "The only sure bet is that you're going to be surprised. Even his opponents can never be sure what he's going to do."[3]

Plimpton and other observers were not alone in their surprise, especially given how many people were frightened that Foreman might seriously injure Ali. Dick Schaap, covering the fight for *Sport* magazine, was one of those "afraid that Foreman might inflict some terrible damage upon Ali, might scramble his mind, or worse, mess up his pretty face." As the fight progressed it took him and "millions of others" through a full range of emotions. Early on Schaap feared that Foreman's formidable punches were wreaking havoc as he battered a seemingly helpless Ali along the ropes. Gradually, however, he like millions of others realized that Ali was not just a stationary target being pummeled but was in fact defending himself well and tiring out his opponent. By the seventh round the idea that Foreman could hurt Ali "seemed ridiculous." Schaap's only feeling then was curiosity over whether Ali could knock him out. When he sent Foreman toppling to the canvas, there was only one emotion left: "Elation, total ecstatic elation, a sudden realization that the worst does not have to happen, that logic can be beaten, that the defeat of logic can be one of the sweetest feelings in the world. Of course he's the greatest." The picture accompanying Schaap's article shows the iconic image of Foreman twirling to the canvas with Ali looking on in wonder. The caption: "After Ali had performed his wizardry, after he had sapped Foreman's strength, all that remained was George's fall."[4]

The emotional experience of the match, as described by Schaap, certainly contributed to the evaluation of the bout as a great title fight and a superhuman accomplishment by the recrowned heavyweight champion. Whether one rooted for Foreman or Ali, the range of emotions that the fight evoked had everyone on the edge of their seats and made the ending all the greater for Ali and all the worse for Foreman. It was the knockout, following the emotional ups and downs of the bout—and especially the fear during the early rounds that Ali could not survive and would be severely battered and knocked out—that capped the fight and provided fans with a sense of triumph.

The blows that toppled Foreman at the end of the eighth round came so quickly but paradoxically seemingly in slow motion that no one watching could dispute Ali's accomplishment. Indeed, everyone had a chance to see and vicariously experience the powerful sequence of punches that ensured Foreman's defeat and Ali's miracle. The image of Ali staring in wonder at his own handiwork as his huge opponent pirouetted to the canvas in an almost-languid collapse became the iconic picture of the fight that was repeated endlessly in newspaper articles and television clips in countries around the globe. The knockout was so dramatic that the outcome seemed foreordained. The pictures of the knockout deepened the impression of Foreman's defeat as more than a simple loss in a well-fought fight. Ali's dramatic and overwhelming victory and the way he achieved it sealed his legend and went a long way to convincing the boxing establishment of his greatness. The expected apocalypse that was to be Ali's defeat did not happen.[5]

If Ali's triumph surprised the world, George Foreman's shocking and humiliating loss forced him to come to terms with physical defeat for the first time in his life as a professional boxer and one of the few times in his entire life. Needless to say, it was a devastating experience for him and his many fans. From being called invincible, he had gone to being derided as *The Ring*'s Dan Daniel put it, "the most stupid defender of the title in the history of the heavyweight class." As Foreman made his way back to his dressing room, the groggy, weary, and dispirited former champion found it difficult to comprehend how he could have lost. After all, he was a 3 to 1 favorite going into the fight, and never before in his professional experience had he suffered a loss. In fact, he had never even been knocked off his feet. Losing seemed incomprehensible.[6]

Ever since his teens he had relied on his size and his power to intimidate his opponents and define who he was. Now, however, everything had changed. "For a twenty-five-year-old who had the world kneeling at his feet, losing stinks. I felt empty, totally empty," he later recalled. The day after the fight was no better. Following a sleepless night, Foreman faced the first day without the heavyweight crown moping on the couch in his suite, dark glasses hiding his swollen eyes. His older friend and adviser, Mr. Moore (no relation to Archie Moore), a man who had seen him through marital difficulties and other problematic episodes in his young life, snatched the glasses off his face, and told him: "You be proud of that. You let the photographers take your picture like that. And you smile. You're not putting on any dark glasses."[7]

Still, it was hard to put a happy face on the defeat. Ali summed up the feelings about the fight that both men shared. As he put it, the rope-a-dope was a great strategy, "and when I fought Foreman, he was the dope." The previously unbeaten Foreman, noted the *Ghanaian Times*, "was reduced to shambling ruin by Ali's dazzling artistry and relentless psychological warfare," and the belief that he was one of the deadliest punchers in the business was shattered. Former champion Jack Dempsey expressed disgust at the defeated champion's amateurish performance, and the sporting press in general noted that Ali's masterful and intelligent performance had exposed the myth of George Foreman. In *The Ring*, Dan Daniel took note of this fact: "The effigy of George Foreman as the Superman of the ring was shattered among the rubble of the destroyed statues of Livingston and Stanley, representing white domination, down in the distant Congo." Even more depressing, his miserable performance, concluded Daniel, precluded a rematch. In its coverage of the fight, the *Ghanaian Times* summed up much of the African view. "Foreman was made to look ridiculous by Ali's skill and some spectators were laughing at the champion's discomfort by the seventh round." In a kinder assessment, Daniel concluded that it was apparent that "it will be sometime before Foreman recovers from the mental and physical setback he suffered at Zaire."[8]

Indeed, Foreman and his camp struggled to come to terms with such an overwhelming and humiliating loss. For such a powerful aggressor, defeat came at a moment, the mid-1970s, when the American people were also forced to wrestle with the humiliating loss of the all-powerful American military after more than ten long years of war in Vietnam—a war that no one but the Viet Cong and the North Vietnamese believed the United States could lose. Parallel to the large numbers of Americans deeply disturbed by the futile demonstration of its power, Foreman shared elements of this culture of defeat by leveling unfocused anger toward the man who had beaten him. In interview after interview, the ex-champion revealed that immediately after the bout he developed a powerful and all-consuming hatred toward his triumphant opponent. As Foreman recalled in his spiritual autobiography, "I *hated* Muhammad Ali . . . I would have loved nothing more than to kill him in the ring." Another equally powerful response was to deny that he had been defeated at all. Like the powerful US military and the national victory culture that it represented, Foreman charged that he had not lost his title in the ring or on the battlefield. Rather, both were defeated behind the scenes by enemies who used trickery and subterfuge. In his mind Foreman had not been defeated in a clear-cut manly battle; rather, he was stabbed in the back by everyone, including his friends and allies.[9]

At a brief press conference at Charles de Gaulle Airport on November 2 during his stopover in Paris, Foreman at first declared: "Ali won the fight. There are no doubts." Shortly thereafter, however, he contradicted himself and set off a controversy over the outcome of the fight. Claiming that he deserved a rematch because of too many irregularities, the disappointed former champion charged: "There's the counting of the referee. He counted me out too quickly. There's also the story about the ropes; some journalists have reported that they were really taut [*sic*] to favor Ali who wasn't ignorant of it. My adversary was very often sitting in them like on a chair." Along with the charge of a quick count by the referee, loose ropes, and poisoned water, as we saw in the previous chapter, Foreman's underlying complaint was that the leaders of his team—especially Dick Sadler—had not paid attention to the condition of the ring and thereby did not adequately look after their warrior in the heat of battle. As the disappointed young man saw it, it was his leaders, not the fighter himself, who were responsible for poor executive decisions that then hindered their charge on the field of battle.[10]

Indeed, it appeared that it was his relationship with his own corner that upset Foreman the most. At times he admitted that he fought a stupid fight, but he quickly turned his anger and his humiliation against his own team, especially trainer Dick Sadler. Why, for example, did his handlers fail to check out the ring in advance of the fight as had Angelo Dundee? Why did they continue to urge him to keep on the attack long after the tactic was no longer working? Even more important, what was wrong with the water they gave him to drink in his corner? In his autobiography, the embittered former champion claimed that someone in his corner had doctored the water he sipped just before the bout started. "'Rope-a-dope' the fight got nicknamed," Foreman wrote, when he told a reporter he believed his water "may have been mickeyed. What else, I asked, could account for that medicinal taste and my terrible tiredness? What else, I asked, could account for how sick and sore I felt for a month afterward?" Later he heard that Sugar Ray Robinson, watching the fight at a New York theater, remarked that Foreman seemed drugged. In fact, Foreman recollected Sadler once talking about a fixed fight with which he had been involved. Had this happened here? In the recent past, moreover, Foreman had had a falling out with Sadler after his manager managed to sell more parts of his fighter to investors than existed, leaving the champion in the position of not owning any part of himself. This had resulted in a break in their relationship for a while that had been patched up for the Rumble in the Jungle. After Zaire, Foreman concluded that Sadler had betrayed him and could no longer be trusted. Like many Americans coming to terms with the defeat in Vietnam, Foreman often treated his loss as "a stab in the back" by those close to him. "I felt like the protective shield over me was gone," declared the defeated warrior. "There was a complete lack of concern about my well-being." One thing is certain: the loss convinced him that Sadler had to go.[11]

For Foreman, as for many of his fellow Americans, the post-Vietnam 1970s proved a difficult and disturbing period. Losing a war for the first time in its history or losing by way of knockout for the first time led to a questioning of individual and national identity rooted in winning and power. No wonder national political figures depressed by military defeat looked for ways to transform defeat into victory. As Foreman put it, "I was robbed of the victory and I was furious." Dan Daniel's prediction that it would take years for Foreman to get over his defeat proved amazingly accurate. It certainly took him a long time—sixteen months—before he returned to the ring, a testament to how severely his self-confidence had been shaken to the core. More immediately, rather than return to the United States where he would be bombarded with embarrassing questions about the fight, he stayed on in Paris at Mr. Moore's behest and sought consolation in the arms of an old girlfriend. Yet he was too troubled to enjoy her attentions. After several days of abuse she left Paris an emotional wreck. No better off himself, Foreman, accompanied by Mr. Moore, left too. Instead of going home to Houston or Livermore, California, however, the two men detoured to Los Angeles, where the depressed fighter picked up another girlfriend for a getaway escape to Hawaii. Once again, his mind was still too wrapped up in the magnitude of his defeat to enjoy himself. During fitful nights, he would awaken with a start in a cold sweat, tormented by memories of the fight. "If only I hadn't dropped my hands; if only I hadn't walked into those punches; if only I'd left Zaire and been treated by a doctor; if only I'd called off the fight; if only the ropes." After his girlfriend abandoned the sinking ship, Mr. Moore stayed on, worried that George looked "depressed enough to do something stupid to myself." Moore also put up with George's rage, helping him to vent the anger that needed an external outlet or it would turn inward and completely destroy the distraught former champion.[12]

When the two men returned to Foreman's Houston birthplace, they did so in a brand new Rolls-Royce. The ex-champion hoped that if he drove up in a big, expensive car people in his old Fifth Ward neighborhood would not immediately remind him of his defeat. One friend brought him down immediately, however, by asking, sarcastically if his car was a Toyota. He definitely did not want to hear that several relatives had rooted for Ali. His cousin Willie Carpenter, moreover, who had served as his equipment manager for many years, accused him of taking a dive in Zaire. Foreman was dumbfounded that a family member could even think that of him. Equally disturbing, celebrities whom he had met as champion turned their backs on him. Bob Hope, for example, had featured Foreman on his television show and had promised to help him become an actor after his fighting days were over. Yet when Hope never contacted him again after the loss, Foreman was devastated to realize that the Hollywood star liked him only when he held the title. When the two men met several months later on the *Tonight Show*, Hope acted as if they were meeting for the first time.[13]

Clearly, "losing had knocked me off my axis." Without the title, he felt, "I was nothing. As champ, I'd imagined people considered me the ultimate man." Foreman still had a dozen cars, three houses, a ranch, and tons of money. Yet having lost his title, life was empty. "I envisioned people making fun of me behind my back. Those miserable thoughts tortured my mind for the next two and a half years." Depressed, even entertaining thoughts of suicide, he decided to rebuild from the inside, "to become the man who hadn't yet hit the canvas in Zaire three months before. The only way to do that was to win back the championship." This time he vowed to die rather than lose. In search of an elusive rematch with Muhammad Ali, however, he first had to demonstrate to himself and the rest of the sporting world that he was still a powerful warrior rather than a pathetic shell of his former self.[14]

While George Foreman struggled with the nightmare of defeat, African Americans and many younger whites greeted Muhammad Ali's victory as far more than a sporting achievement. Rather, it served as the vindication of a black folk hero who symbolized black pride and black liberation and mirrored their own struggles against the overwhelming power of white supremacy in America. In a match pitting two models of blackness against each other, noted black poet and intellectual Quincy Troupe, Ali had, in winning, "spiritually and symbolically represented millions upon millions of people who, also in the face of heavy odds and during crucial times throughout the world's history, had said, 'No,' and in the end had the remarkable staying power not only to survive, but to emerge from the struggle with a glorious and significant victory." As a result, Ali's knockout of Foreman "was greeted by jubilation all over the world. People danced in the streets, went to bars and got merrily drunk, interrupted shows with screams of joy, ran down the streets shouting, 'Ali, bombayed, bombayed!'" In contrast to Foreman's patriotism, "African Americans recognize in Ali our own struggle for dignity, beauty and survival in a hostile America. He has been a mirror image of our own collective struggle for freedom and dignity in this racist-to-the-bone, hypocritical country." As a result, noted Troupe, "When he won, we all won, much in the same way that Joe Louis won for all of us during the Thirties and Forties."[15]

For many African Americans, the way Ali won was just as important as the victory itself. In a morality play rooted in black folklore, the far weaker combatant succeeded in defeating a much more powerful opponent who threatened to annihilate him and making him look "like a man who had drunk one too many at four in the morning than a champion fighting to retain one of the world's most precious gems." As the decided underdog, Ali relied on improvisation and superior ring intelligence to lay a trap for his foe. Like the smaller animals of black folk tales, Ali used his wits to survive while Foreman slavishly followed the instructions of his corner. "The surprise is that I did not dance," Ali declared. "For weeks I kept hollering, 'Be ready to dance,' but I didn't dance. That was the surprise. That was the trick." Various observers highlighted Ali's improvisational ability and compared him to animal tricksters. George Plimpton, we have seen, compared him to a "sly mouse" tricking "a big cartoon wolf," just as *New York Times* columnist Dave Anderson, noted that "a bee battered a lion," with, as Ali had predicted, "brains." Wit and style beat, as *Time* described Foreman, "a human battering ram" who stalked his opponents "like a robot with gloves." As Ali told the press, "Don't ever match no bull against a master boxer. The bull is stronger but the matador is smarter."[16]

Similarly, Ali's victory was not just the victory of an underdog, it was the victory of a garrulous and verbally adroit figure rooted deeply in vernacular black culture over a largely silent and withdrawn champion. In fact, Ali's verbal skills were a key part of the rope-a-dope strategy. While the referee was busy giving both fighters their instructions, for example, Ali spent his time taunting the champion. He continued this tactic at crucial points throughout the bout, goading Foreman to anger by declaring that the champ's powerful blows were ineffective. The angrier Foreman became, the less he was able to think straight and the more he kept trying to land the one knockout punch. Even before the match Ali indulged in verbal joking and bragging. He claimed he had wrestled an alligator, was faster than a light switch, and cut his opponents like a razor. Usually, however, Foreman chose not to respond, and Ali found himself squaring off in rhyming battles not against the champ but against the champ's verbally agile trainer and confidant, Archie Moore. Of course, this only highlighted that Foreman was lacking in the verbal department. As Troupe declared, Ali "has always been a great talker, and the Black community has always loved a great talker." Troupe traced this cultural style to "an African oral tradition" that could be seen in the preacher, the blues singer, the corner rapper, the dozens player, the joker, and the pimp. Not only did Ali come out of this tradition; he was "the first prize fighter to use this form so effectively to publicize himself and endear himself to a receptive Black community."[17]

The Ali-Foreman matchup also highlighted the fact that the new champion had set a precedent as one of "the few boxing champions to utter sounds beyond the customary monosyllabic words." Whereas many conservative blacks and whites were disappointed that their silent symbol of patriotism was so badly beaten, Ali had become a folk hero of mythic proportions who felt no compunctions about speaking out on issues outside the boxing arena. Whether referring to the Nation of Islam, the Vietnam War, Christianity, or the deep-seated white supremacy of America, he defied the powerful forces, represented by Foreman, which wanted to quiet him forever. Like Foreman and the white silent majority, the government, the military, and the boxing establishment all failed to shut up "the Louisville Lip."[18]

Ali's triumph over an establishment symbol transformed him into a full-fledged black folk hero beloved by all sorts of African Americans, but especially antiwar black and white youth who had defied the authority of the American power structure and actually won a major victory after being derided, as was Ali, as un-American traitors for their opposition to the Vietnam

War and American racism. As one of the few major black dissidents still standing, Ali's victory made him a symbol of those other black heroes who had defied the white establishment and its representatives but who had been killed in the struggle, like Martin Luther King, Malcolm X, Medgar Evers, and numerous Black Panthers, or who were living in exile, like Stokely Carmichael. As a trickster and a rebel in the tradition of other hard men who had defied white racism, Ali reigned as a full-fledged opposition hero, the baddest of them all. He was the man who had beaten "the man." Maybe it was just coincidence, but there was at least a subtle irony in the juxtaposition in South Africa's *Pretoria News* of the iconic picture of Ali watching Foreman pirouette to the canvas under the headline "Magnificent Ali Is the Greatest—Again," next to a headline that read "Nixon Critical."[19]

The successful triumph over such an imposing enemy struck a deep chord among black people everywhere. First and foremost was the Nation of Islam. In his comments after the fight, Ali credited his surprising performance to Allah, who "has power over all things." Indeed, Ali noted that without the power of Allah behind him, he would not have achieved the eighth-round knockout. With that as proof, the new champion urged his listeners to follow his example, read *Muhammad Speaks*, and attend the local mosques to improve their lives. Nation of Islam officials could not be happier. Since he had declared himself a Muslim in 1964, the Nation had used the champion as a powerful representative of their philosophy of black pride, self-help, and a conservative form of black nationalism. His physical perfection and his many victories transformed the boxer into a warrior for the Nation; his picture dotted the pages of *Muhammad Speaks*. In addition, the NOI had relied on his financial contributions to the organization. Despite the split with Elijah Muhammad in 1969 over his return to boxing, which meant he was not a full member at the time of the fight, Ali's message had even greater appeal to fans as he promised that his next fight would be on behalf of building a black hospital in Chicago under the Muslim's auspices. He hoped that his victory would serve to regularize his status. When he finally retired, he planned to use his global celebrity as champion to serve his faith and his people as a minister for Islam worldwide.[20]

Not only did Ali's intentions raise Islam's profile at home; they also increased Arab support for the challenger abroad. Two days before the fight, an Arab-African solidarity meeting, sponsored by the Arab League, opened in Kinshasa, thus swelling the number of Muslims present in the city who supported the underdog. One visiting Islamic missionary announced that thousands of Muslims were praying for an Ali victory. When Dick Sadler learned of this, he reached into African American folklore to retort, "Prayers are good for prayer meetings but they don't do much for bear meetings." Readers of Egypt's *Al Ahram* got the word but did not dismiss the sentiment. "By believing in God, justice, and himself," the newspaper noted, Muhammad Ali was able to regain the heavyweight throne.[21]

Having reclaimed his crown, Ali used it as a platform to spread his religious and racial goals around the globe. In a *Playboy* interview shortly after the fight, he not only laid out the Nation of Islam's philosophy of black separation and a coming apocalypse that would chastise America for its racism; he also declared his pessimism about race relations in the United States. "America don't *have* no future!" he declared. "America's going to be destroyed! Allah's going to divinely chastise America! Violence, crime, earthquakes—there's gonna be all *kinds* of trouble" as payback for "all its lynchings and killings of slaves and what it's done to black people. America's day is over—and if it doesn't do justice to the black man and separate, it's gonna *burn*!"[22]

As an international spectacle, the fight dramatized in the cultural realm the importance of global black power that by the early 1970s had surpassed the integrationist thrust of the civil rights movement. After returning to the United States, for example, Ali promoted a Pan-African philosophy as he praised Zaire and other independent black African states as a counter to American white supremacy. As he told *Playboy*, at first he was skeptical about the fight being in Zaire, a country "supposed to be so undeveloped." Being in Zaire, he said, "opened my eyes." Here were "black people running their own country. I saw a black president of a humble black people who have a modern country. There are good roads throughout Zaire and Kinshasa has a nice downtown section that reminds you of a city in the States." From the black pilots to the black stewardesses, hotel owners, and teachers, "it was like any other society except it was all black." In contrast to what he saw in Africa, "black people in America will never be free so long as they're on the white man's land." Freedom would occur only when black people had their own nation in North America. Black people, asserted the new champion, were "*tired* of being slaves and never having nothing. We're *tired* of being servants and waiting till we die and go to heaven before we get anything." Unlike Zaire, he asserted, "we're a whole nation of slaves still in bondage to white people."[23]

Despite continued skepticism about the specifics of the Nation of Islam's philosophy, black people expressed their pride in Ali as a black folk hero in a variety of ways. At DC's Capitol Arena, nearly all of the seventeen thousand black fans rooted for Ali, because, noted a doctor in attendance, "he was black man enough to stand on his own two feet and suffer the consequences." When he won, everyone "walked out filled with pride and brotherliness and black self-love." The experience was similar at a theater on Chicago's South Side, where at first the size and strength of Foreman made Stokely Carmichael, briefly back in the United States on political business, extremely nervous. But then the Africans began their "Ali, bomaye" chant, which was picked up by the men and women in the audience, and Carmichael "felt a wave of new confidence." When the knockout came, it was greeted by "absolute pandemonium." Likewise, the audience in a Harlem movie house chanted in an "almost primeval way" for Ali after he survived the second round, that fatal round by the end of which Foreman previously had destroyed his opponents. When in the eighth round, "the people's champion" reclaimed his title by flooring the official champion, "the crowd stood, right arms raised high, fists clenched." Some in the crowd were clearly "stunned by the swiftness of the ending. 'Ali! Ali! Ali!' they screamed." According to the newspaper account, these were not the super-fly types in elegant attire who stood out at the Ali-Frazier rematch, but rather they were "plain, ordinary folks" who lined up as early as 6 p.m. in front of Loew's Victoria Theater at West 125th Street and Seventh Avenue in support of "the brash, cocky, spirited Ali." An audience of postal clerks, keypunch operators, social workers, and other regular folk were surprised and delighted by the outcome. "I was for Ali, but I thought Foreman had a very good chance," declared Ralph Davis, age thirty-four. "I didn't expect this," he added just as the crowd was booing the defeated Foreman as he left the ring. Others were equally ecstatic. "I told you, he's beautiful, I just love him! . . . He's the people's champion." Many in the crowd seemed unable to believe that Ali had regained the title he had been "stripped of" in 1967. "I'm totally surprised," declared a postal clerk. "I did not want to see him get hurt. I cried when Joe Frazier beat him up" in 1971. Meanwhile, Gregory O'Bryant expressed the common appreciation that Ali used "scientific methods" against "wild, super aggressive punches."[24]

Letters to the editor and articles in the domestic black press further expressed an overwhelming appreciation for the larger social and cultural implications of Ali's victory. In *Jet* Ronald Kisner praised Ali's determination: "Something bigger than life was approaching . . . it was no exaggeration. No broken jaws, man's laws, knockdowns, layoffs or delays could stop Ali from reaching his destiny." This was a man determined to overcome all physical and political obstacles and he had triumphed. For John Carlisle III, of Westbury, New York, Ali's victory carried personal identification and important political weight. "I am so proud that Muhammad Ali won the world heavyweight championship," he wrote to *Jet*. "For more than three years, he was exiled from the ring for his refusal to serve in the armed forces." Even more, Carlisle gave him credit for paying "a special thanks to the Black nation by having the fight in Zaire." Beverly Blackman, from Long Island City, New York, agreed that "Brother Muhammad Ali" was not only "the greatest" but also had contributed to her happiness and that of "millions of other brothers and sisters the world over. You have made everything crystal clear to anyone who has ever doubted you." Seku S. Wattara, of Baltimore, saw the victory as a matter of racial pride. "He really is a Brother that the Black race can be proud of," the letter writer concluded. "Anyone who doubts that he is the greatest of all time should climb into the ring with him."[25]

African Americans celebrated Ali's victory as a matter of racial solidarity, a pattern not seen since Joe Louis's heyday in the 1930s and 1940s. Even though his opponent was black, Ali's triumph was viewed as a victory over the injustices of the white world. As president of Morehouse College, Hugh M. Gloster, told Ali in front of four thousand students: "As much as you are admired by boxing fans in general, you are admired even more by the members of your own race. You are our main man." Taking back his title that "'they' had taken from him" because of his religion and his refusal to be drafted, made him an overarching symbol of racial pride in an era when black pride was at its apex. As the *Chicago Defender* put it, "Now the self-appointed Messiah of blacks everywhere, to Harlem, to South Africa, to the slums of the cities of all the world, he preaches pride in being black, pride in the determination to overcome, to meet the white man's world on its own terms, and to defeat it." He amuses many, frightens some with his tirades: "There are blacks who greet him with laughter and glee as he excoriates the white world, but there are also blacks who take his vitriolic, militant speeches as a green light to overthrow the white man's establishment."[26]

Ali's antiestablishment stance was highlighted when he returned to Louisville, Kentucky, on November 8 for Muhammad Ali Day. At a central plaza, seven thousand people, mostly black, but many whites too, gathered to honor a "black folk hero and the most famous defender of the faith of Islam." Although a boxer, he stood before the crowd "like a Black Prince," with his face unscarred and, "as men's faces can be, . . . something approaching beautiful." A triumphant living symbol that black was beautiful, Ali received greetings from "those who genuinely loved him," as well as, finally, "some of the bigshots who shied away from him in the old days when he was considered a traitor and a bum for refusing to enter military service and for changing his name from Cassius Clay to Muhammad Ali." As he walked through the crowd, people nearly trampled one another to touch him. "It was," wrote Charles Sanders in *Ebony*, "an outpouring of black love upon a man for whom black people have gained profound respect—for refusing to knuckle under despite the cruelest pressures; for standing up for what he believed even though it cost him, in dollars and otherwise, far more than most men are willing to lose, and for refusing to give up and for trying hard enough and often enough to eventually triumph."[27]

Many black intellectuals hailed Ali's triumph as a victory for 1960s black and white radicalism. In a special issue of *Black World*, scholars, poets, and artists hailed Ali as a "Creative Black Man," celebrated his "Spiritual Victory," and placed him in the tradition of black folk heroes in the United States. While Samuel F. Yette noted that whites often controlled black images, narrowing them to comic or tragic tropes, other contributors emphasized that Ali was "a creative person," a cultural hero who symbolized the cultural explosion of the sixties and black vernacular culture with his verbal agility, poetry, bragging, humor, and toasting. Like artists or musicians, according to playwright Clay Goss, he used his imagination to become champion, and "he captured *our* imagination, in the process turning his struggle into our struggle and in turn our struggle into his own." As a celebrity, Ali transformed the platform he created of the ring into an image of himself "that reflected many of the positive aspects of all Black men who are engaged in the struggle for freedom and human dignity." Who else but Ali, Goss asked, was capable of believing he could knock out the invincible Foreman?[28]

Defeating Foreman in Zaire represented the culmination of Ali's heroism as a radical opposition figure, and for many commentators, it went beyond the black community. What surprised Quincy Troupe, for instance, was that young whites heartily agreed. Unlike the celebrations after victories by Joe Louis in the 1930s and 1940s, where primarily black people made their happiness public, "this time it was different. People of every nationality, color, religious persuasion celebrated the victory of Ali," and with satellites and modern mass communications, this triumphant joy was felt all over the world. Young whites seemed "genuinely moved by Ali's great victory, seemed to have wanted it to happen as badly as Third World people." Indeed, in depressing 1974, with all the scandals, the riots against busing, and Watergate, "Ali's victory was a spiritual victory" for all in a "completely demoralized and spiritually bankrupt nation." Where many Americans had lost faith in the democratic political system and where energies for radical change were ebbing in the face of the traumatic shocks that buffeted the land, "Ali's victory was like a beautiful and soothing balm that washed over all of us" and renewed faith that positive change was possible. In a large sense, Ali's victory vindicated those protestors "silenced by murder and jail sentences, or shouted down" as "irresponsible and radical—'un-American.'"[29]

Indeed, both black and white young people rooted for Ali as a symbol of the generational and cultural revolt of the 1960s, a figure who gloried in self-expression in and out of the ring. Grown older by 1974, they still felt the lingering remains of a war that had consumed their lives, their prospects, and their outlook. In a time during the sixties when revolutionary change seemed possible, many young whites and blacks had forged interracial alliances and made heroes of black—and some white—cultural figures who appeared to be breaking racial and cultural boundaries. As Troupe noted, it was not just Ali, but musicians like Bob Dylan, Jimi Hendrix, John Coltrane, Miles Davis, Pharoah Sanders, Smokey Robinson, Curtis Mayfield, and James Brown who "influenced an entire generation with their revolutionary approach to music and their lifestyles." The way Ali fought the match elevated the confrontation with Foreman into a larger conflict over the values of the 1960s. In his younger days, Ali had challenged boxing orthodoxy with his dancing, the way he held his hands low, and his poetic predictions as much as he defied political and racial orthodoxy. In Zaire, however, Ali surprised everyone by not dancing and by defying authority and perceived wisdom. When asked whose idea it was to go to the ropes and not dance as he had been predicting for months, "Me," Ali replied. "I don't have no trainers. They just work for me. I had to beat George at his own game."[30]

At the heart of the battle between the two phenomenal black heavyweight fighters lay the agonizing weight of the just-concluded Vietnam War. The political currents that continued to divide the nation found their champions in the Rumble in the Jungle. Foreman came to represent the US position in Vietnam. As he put it immediately after the bout, in contrast to Ali's position: "I'm an American. I love my country. If I was ever in a position, I would fight for it with all my might." Conversely, it was Ali's response to the draft, rooted in his Islamic religion that ultimately cost him his title. David's surprising victory over Goliath served to vindicate boxing fans and the general public—white and black—who had opposed the war with such vehemence. With US participation in the Vietnam War drawing to an ignominious close, it was much easier to accept Ali's opposition to the war as based on conviction and the government's attempts to punish him as an abuse of power. The victory, moreover, demonstrated that it was possible to survive the persecutions of the government and the majority of the population and actually triumph. For many, Ali's triumph over great odds to achieve his goals could be taken for the ultimate uphill struggle against the war itself.[31]

Defeating the patriotic Foreman only confirmed Ali's status as a hero for white and black opponents of the Vietnam War. Events during New York City's own Muhammad Ali Day in early November made this clear. At a celebration at the largely African American Boys' High School in Brooklyn's Ocean Hill-Brownsville neighborhood, ten-year-old Shirley Sykes delighted the champion with a poem she had written for the occasion, a poem that emphasized Ali's racial views and his opposition to the war. "The trouble began when he refused to fight," began the poem, "The Vietnamese who happened to be non-white." When the war was over, the verse emphasized, "they let him fight / And he tried to win with all his might / Now here's the latest: / Muhammad IS the greatest." Later that day at the official ceremony at city hall that included many more white fans, Ali had Shirley Sykes repeat her poem. The war, in other words, was a racial war waged against a nonwhite people by a white American government, and Ali and those who opposed the war were justified in their opposition.[32]

Equally important, the bout not only featured standard-bearers for opposing positions on the war; in a number of ways it symbolically reenacted America's frustrating experience in that long and fruitless conflict. As a symbol of American power, Foreman relied on his overwhelming size and strength, rather than finesse, in the match, and he relished his ability to knock out opponents early and in convincing fashion. This led to overconfidence in his own power and underestimation of the enemy's strength. In addition, the champion followed the lead of his corner to a fault and at crucial moments in the battle proved unable to change his tactics as the situation demanded. Instead, he kept throwing bombs that time and again failed to subdue a weaker and more resourceful enemy. In the end he exhausted his energy, lost his confidence and will, and was defeated because of his own failings rather than as a result of the strength of his clever foe.

As the avowed opponent of the Vietnam War, Ali managed to transform Zaire into his home field and stun his powerful foe to achieve an upset victory. Much like the Viet Cong and its North Vietnamese allies, Ali surprised the world—not only by winning but by winning so convincingly that the whole idea of victory culture was placed in doubt. Using an impenetrable defense, the challenger unleashed just enough sneaky offense to weaken Foreman's resolve. Even as Foreman continued to throw the heavier punches and win the early rounds, Ali, as Foreman himself acknowledged, "owned their hearts and minds more completely with every punch he absorbed." At the same time, Foreman proved incapable of winning the support of the Zaïrois people. His aloofness and distance was a clear indication that he was "miserable about being in Zaire, and in Africa," noted Suruba Ibumando Wechsler, a Zaïroise woman who kept up with the event via local radio and newspapers. By contrast, she declared, Ali "seemed to be having the time of his life, here in the very heart of Africa. He mingled with everyone, young and old, rich and poor, black and white."[33]

As a spectacle that captured the attention of the entire globe, moreover, the fight publicized the 1960s narrative linking domestic racial oppression and white imperialism to a global constituency. The celebration in Louisville highlighted the victory as one over white supremacy at home as well as abroad. Indeed, describing the events in Louisville that day, Charles Sanders noted that Ali, who surely knew how symbolic it would be "(and what a slap in the face it would be to those American 'patriots' who took away his title), arranged to triumph in Africa and in a country where white men once took away some other things—they once chopped off the fingers and whole hands of black men" who failed to provide King Leopold of Belgium their quota of rubber, minerals, and precious metals. Indeed, Ali represented an international uprising of defiant blackness. "How many millions of black people and Third World people there must have been," mused Sanders, "who saw Ali, on TV, or there in the ring, in Africa, facing George Foreman, also a black man, but who, for reasons bordering on the metaphysical or on religion or something sent to Ali alone their good wishes by Western Union of the Black Mind!" That he represented a worldwide challenge to white supremacy was made clear when the new champion brought "proof" to his Louisville admirers of "what Africans have accomplished since gaining independence from colonial powers." His Nation of Islam belief that blacks could achieve greatness without help from whites was reinforced when he introduced the young pilot who flew him from Kinshasa to Paris aboard President Mobutu's DC-10 jet plane, a symbol of modern civilization. At a luncheon linked to his official day, Ali reminded Louisville's mayor that "you white folks still think Africans live in trees. Well, this man here ain't no tom-tom beater, he's a highly-skilled pilot who can fly a jumbo jet as good as any white man!"[34]

On a different level, Nigerian Olu Akaraogun took the occasion of Ali's defeat of Foreman to assess "the meaning of Muhammad Ali for the Black World." In one of the many contemporary discussions of Ali's importance, Akaraogun noted that Ali's victory was a victory over American racism at home—and abroad. The greatness lay in identifying "with the exploited and downtrodden masses in Africa and wherever else." As a supporter of global Black Power, Ali "embodies and at the same time shares the aspiration and hopes of Black people everywhere." The fact that he had reclaimed the title "thwarted the efforts of the American power structure to cheat and deprive him of his legitimate claim to the world crown." As a black man, moreover, "Ali had the revolutionary consciousness to realize that he had no business shooting down fellow 'coloured' people in Vietnam." If anybody should be shot, "it had to be the white supremacist who had exploited and enslaved Africans and Asians for centuries." White America's taking away his title was typical of American justice, a claim which resonated with millions of African Americans in the United States. According to Akaraogun, Ali's greatness lay not only in reaching the top and becoming materially successful like other black champions, but in his realization that it was "his duty to identify with the exploited and downtrodden Black masses in Africa and wherever else they are in the world."[35]

In turn, the African setting for the Super Fight of the Century encouraged most black Africans to view Ali's victory as a symbolic reenactment of their own liberation from Western colonial control. Nowhere was this more apparent than in Zaire. In the days leading up to the fight, most citizens of Zaire, government officials, sports figures, and fans maintained a diplomatic neutrality befitting their host position, but in reality they were overwhelmingly pro-Ali. "I was especially surprised by the enthusiasm of the spectators before, during and after the fight. Those I had asked their opinion before the fight were all for the two boxers," noted journalist Mario Gherarducci: "'May the best man win!' was what most said. But, at the moment of truth, everyone was for Ali."[36]

While the stadium roared with the chant of "Ali, bomaye," whenever Ali threw a punch, afterward those who remained in their seats or took to the surrounding streets, reenacted the fight with an enthusiasm as if they themselves were the victors. Even at six in the morning, the swampy streets were filled "with ecstatic youngsters chanting 'Ali, Ali, Ali." They squared off against each other, doing the Ali shuffle, "sometimes knee deep in waters cascading down the narrow streets, and even falling down and pretending to be the flattened Foreman." As Thomas A. Johnson reported in the *New York Times*, those who attended the fight happily stayed up all night watching the fight and celebrating. In the morning others listened to their stories of the bout at bus stations, markets, streets, and backyards. They recounted "in this modern, urban capital, the beginnings of the legends that are to grow out of Muhammad Ali's upset victory over George Foreman here in styles similar to tribal criers, story tellers and historians of their ancient past." Hours after the fight the city remained alive with the thrill of the big event and Ali's surprise victory.[37]

Ali proved the clear favorite because the Zaïroises identified their still-young liberation from Belgian colonial rule with the new titleholder. His victory became a vicarious reenactment of their colonial rebellion against their former European oppressors and a sign that the independent black and Islamic states were equal to those in the west. The people of Zaire supported

Ali despite the odds because they knew him, explained Malonga Suka, an unemployed nineteen-year-old man. "They have heard the name and savored the reputation for ten years," and they really had no knowledge of George Foreman. As the young Zaïrois said: "This is a great day for Zaire and for black people. Zaire is the winner here today."[38]

Ali's many comments about the sophisticated modernism of Zaire fit well with President Mobutu's attempt to define the new nation as a civilized country entirely different than the conceptions of the Belgian Congo promoted by the former Belgian rulers and many other Western countries. Just pulling off such a colossal gamble as staging such a massive international event in the face of widespread doubt and constant criticism caused many Zaïrois officials and ordinary citizens to proclaim that the big winner of the Super Fight of the Century was "Zaire itself." Despite the many difficulties, as evidenced by the problems of the Zaire 74 music festival, the staging of such a prestigious event as this title fight with "two sons of Africa" not only demonstrated the greatness of the country to its people but, even more important, "showed the world that what had once been the fratricidal former Belgian Congo was now a leader of modern Africa with the funds, skills and eagerness to gamble for all the world's attention." Just as the odds were stacked against Ali in his last shot at the title, so too were the odds against a developing black African nation such as Zaire pulling it off without a hitch. Not only did the match come off ;the fight itself and Ali's dramatic victory put the nation on the map, promoted its image at home and abroad, and helped legitimate Mobutu's Popular Movement for the Revolution party for a long time to come.[39]

Once Ali won, Zaïrois officials and ordinary citizens too could finally abandon their official neutrality and express their relief and joy that Ali had carried the day. For local analysts, the incredible atmosphere surrounding the fight was about more than the Zaïrois love of sport. For Moaka Toko, writing in *Elima*, "it's about national pride" in organizing such a grand and complex international sporting event. Given the neocolonial doubts about Zaire staging such an important match, Suruba Ibumando Wechsler recalled that not only was the entire country's attention fixed on the fight, even in her provincial town of Kongolo in far eastern Zaire, people talked about little else in the months before the bout. Kongolo, like the rest of the nation, "was solidly in the corner of our great hero, Muhammad Ali. After all, Ali was a black man, a descendant of Africans, while Foreman, we all knew, was white." Despite learning that Foreman was indeed blacker than Ali, she noted that the Zaïrois called him *mondele*, or "white man," and associated him with the Belgian colonialists. When Ali pulled off his great upset, "the whole nation felt they had won something much more important than a boxing match, it felt as if we had somehow been liberated once again from the Belgians and all those who had colonized and humiliated Africa." In effect, the fight demonstrated to the world the organizational skills, discipline, and hospitality that were the foundations of Mobutu's philosophy.[40]

Zaire was not the only African nation that reveled proudly in Ali's victory. After all, throughout black Africa the Reuters news service noted that he was billed as "the people's choice," because he was a "symbol of independence and freedom from White domination for millions of Blacks in the United States and elsewhere in the world." There was no doubt who four thousand fans favored at Nairobi's Kenyatta's Conference Center: "The entire crowd rooted for Ali and roared excitedly with every blow." When the knockout came in the eighth round, the audience jumped for joy. In Abidjan, the capital of Ivory Coast, groups of fans expressed their joy by driving around the main avenues of the city and honking their horns in celebration. After listening to the fight over radio, hundreds of fans in Accra, Ghana, "went mad with joy." One fanatical Ali supporter ran bare chested through the city, waving his white shirt in victory, while many fans were "seen openly hugging and congratulating each other in appreciation of the resounding victory of their idol."[41]

President Senghor of Senegal, one of the major architects of Negritude as a Pan-African ideology, recognized Ali's victory as a celebration of African independence. Immediately after the bout he sent a congratulatory message to Ali, "the great militant of Black civilization." Senegal's *Daily Sun* added that, "in Senegal, Ali's victory is considered like that of Africa, as the triumph of the oppressed." One proof of this veneration of Ali as a symbol of black African liberation occurred as Norman Mailer was flying home soon after the fight. His airplane landed at Yoff Airport in Dakar at one in the morning for what was intended as a brief stop, but it was prevented from taking off for several hours because thousands of local Senegalese had received word via a radio bulletin that the new champion might be on board. Surrounding the plane, they demanded that Ali come out to greet them. So insistent were they that they had to see—and believed they had a right to see—their newly crowned heavyweight champion that they refused to allow the airplane to take off until a delegation had come aboard to observe for themselves that Ali was not among them. Needless to say they found no Ali and were exceedingly disappointed. Finally, however, they let the plane take off.[42]

In his assessment of the fight in Dakar's *Le Soleil,* Mass Diack emphasized how important the outcome was for Africans in general. Reporting from Kinshasa, Diack declared that everyone wished for an Ali victory because "Ali is an African." Yet even more important, Ali's triumph took on greater significance because it was a victory "for all the rebels," and "especially a defeat for all that large part of the American public who would have certainly taken pleasure in seeing Foreman demolish Clay." At bottom, this fight "stands for the one that American conservatives and liberal democrats have been engaged in already for many years," he said. Having said no to the Vietnam War and refusing to act as an oppressor, Ali became a villain to much of America while Foreman remained white America's hero because he opposed the 1968 Olympic protesters with his flag-waving gesture: "And that fierce hatred vowed by these two parts of America for each other was expressed this morning in Kinshasa in all of its plainness by two brothers of the same race who had chosen to fight for different causes." More than a personal rehabilitation, the article concluded: "It's a victory of all the oppressed in the Third World that we should sing about this morning. Instinctively, the whole of Africa had united itself behind Mohammed Ali who today had become the beloved one on our continent. We all recognized him as our defender."[43]

On a different level, officials of other recently liberated African states were also delighted by Ali's victory. They, too, were proud that another black African nation had successfully organized such a super fight in Africa. Colonel Hassine Hamouda of Tunisia, for example, attended the fight as the official delegate of the World Boxing Council. He maintained that Foreman did not box well enough to win, but he was pleased to announce in his report to the council that Zaire's organization of such a global spectacle was a sign of African progress. As Zaire's *Elima* crowed: "It's not just Zaire alone that is honored by the complete success of the organization of the fight of the century. It's also the Continent that benefits from Zaire's defiance of those who have always underestimated the organizational capacity of Africans."[44]

Underneath pictures of Ali knocking out Foreman and Mobutu introducing the two fighters to the nation, an article in *Elima* detailed the official responses of African nations to the "Rumble in the Jungle." Colonel Yhombi Opango of the neighboring People's Republic of Congo wired a telegram immediately after the match to express his pride in Zaire's handling of the bout. Me Kamanda we Kamanda, the general secretary of administration of the Organization of African Unity, in the name of the secretary of the Organization of African Unity, sent words of congratulation to President Mobutu: "Our appreciation, our satisfaction, our great admiration for the impeccable organization on African soil of the greatest fight of all time between the world's two best boxers, Muhammad Ali and George Foreman. The grandeur of this historic sporting event resides in the demonstrated capacity of Africa to perfectly organize this event in an under-developed country." Even more, the OAU praised the "magisterial demonstration of what the African man can do, what the peoples and the governments of Africa which are peaceful, free and independent are capable of." All of Africa has taken heart from this defense of African dignity and "African unity, consciousness and determination." If that were not enough, the general secretary of the Supreme Council for Sports in Africa, M. Jean-Claude Nganga, praised Mobutu and added, "This success is a legitimate satisfaction for all Blacks around the world."[45]

Muhammad Ali's decisive upset victory over George Foreman in 1974 transformed him into one of the few oppositional heroes of popular culture to have survived the dominant world's attempts to eliminate, discourage, or defeat them. At home in the United States and across the globe, Ali's victory exerted a measure of revenge for those black liberationists who had been killed, silenced, and betrayed. Even more notably, he was an opposition hero who not only survived into the more conservative 1970s but triumphed. In *Bonnie and Clyde*, *Chinatown*, *The Parallax View*, *Butch Cassidy and the Sundance Kid*, *The Wild Bunch*, *Pat Garrett and Billy the Kid*, *The Harder They Come*, and *Easy Rider*, to cite only a few prominent films of the era, the rebellious or questioning heroes usually meet death or destruction at the hands of a corrupt society. Although their efforts are doomed, the rebellious heroes achieve a kind of nobility in their futile opposition to mainstream society. Despite their nobility, however, they do not survive. If they do, they are severely compromised and helpless in the face of overwhelming and corrupt official power. In addition, starting with *Dirty Harry* and continuing through *Death Wish*, a slew of right-wing heroes took their revenge on black and white rebels who were characterized as criminals and social vermin who needed to be eliminated. By contrast, Ali stood out as a rebel against American society who after a long struggle and despite the attempts by the authorities to punish him, triumphs rather than succumbs to overwhelming power or merely survives. At the apex of his fame, Ali represented the thoroughgoing antiestablishment hero, the man who challenged the system and won.[46]

Immediately upon his return from Zaire, Ali found himself awash in adulation. Previous enemies extolled his virtues. The *Ring* named him Fighter of the Year, which reversed the magazine's refusal to award him that honor in 1967 on the grounds that he was a bad example for American youth. In addition, the Boxing Writers Association named him Fighter of the Year, he was awarded the Hickcock Belt as the outstanding athlete for 1974, and *Sports Illustrated* honored him as Sportsman of the Year. Equally important, a Harris poll confirmed that the public considered Ali one of the greatest heavyweights of all time. Of 1,271 fans, 81 percent rated him as one of the greatest heavyweight champions of all time and 25% said he was the greatest of them all. When broken down by race, 56 percent of blacks rated him "the best ever," and 37 percent as "one of the best." Among whites, however, only 19 percent considered him the best, and 61 percent dubbed him one of the best. Despite the disparity, both groups overwhelmingly designated the new champion as one of the all-time greats. "There are certain heroes of sports who transcend games and contests they participate in," noted sports columnist Maury Allen. "They become folk heroes, figures of such enormity they cross standard barriers." Of the six athletes who achieved this status since the 1930s, Allen argued, "Muhammad Ali does it best of all. It is time to recognize Ali for what he is; the greatest athlete of his time and maybe all time and one of the most important and brave men of all American time." It was time, Allen declared, "to end the bitterness and forget the past."[47]

This reversal of fortune was best exemplified by the string of Muhammad Ali Days that greeted him upon his return to the United States. Louisville mayor Harvey I. Sloane proclaimed November 8, 1974, to be Muhammad Ali Day and renamed Armory Place, a downtown street, Muhammad Ali Place, "so that everyone will know that the world's greatest athlete is from Louisville." Such a public honor had eluded him since his Olympic gold medal in 1960 because officials in Louisville and elsewhere considered him "a traitor and a bum for refusing to enter military service and changing his name from Cassius Clay to Muhammad Ali." For the most part, white politicians were now eager to appear alongside the champion, despite their past opposition to his beliefs.[48]

An equally notable change of heart could be discerned in Chicago's mayor Richard J. Daley, who honored the champion with the city's Medal of Merit on its own Muhammad Ali Day. In 1966, however, the mayor, along with Governor Otto Kerner, heeded the outrage of veterans groups and politicians of all stripes to cancel his title fight with Ernie Terrell, in order to punish the champion for his unpatriotic stance toward the Vietnam War. With the war behind them, the Black Muslims a seemingly quiescent presence in his city (as compared with the Black Panthers), the diminution of violent civic upheavals, and Ali's intention to raise money for a black hospital and shopping center in the city, the mayor was more than willing to stand beside a black folk hero and bask in his reflected glory. Through it all, however, Ali asserted quite openly that he was going to keep standing up for his Nation of Islam beliefs. As he told *Jet*'s Ronald E. Kisner and other reporters in Chicago, "Now that I've had my little say physically, I can say what I want to say," including "When I'm in Africa I'm at home. . . . That's my little world over there."[49]

Perhaps the greatest sign of an altered landscape for the returning hero was the invitation extended by President Gerald Ford to the White House for a presidential reception on December 10, 1974. Given Ali's refusal to comply with the draft and serve in Vietnam, neither President Lyndon Johnson nor President Richard Nixon would have anything to do with him, let alone invite him to the White House. President Ford, however, extended his invitation after the United States had withdrawn from Vietnam yet still remained torn apart by the war, the Watergate scandal, the impeachment and resignation of President Nixon, and a deepening recession. As a sports fan and as president, Ford claimed that he wanted to recognize Ali as the best in his field: "But beyond that, when I took office, we as a nation were pretty much torn apart." In that environment, Ford wanted to help heal these deep divisions: "Having Muhammad Ali come to the Oval Office was part of our overall effort. I felt it was important to reach out and indicate individually as well as collectively that we could have honest differences without bitterness." Meeting with the controversial new champion was "part of my overall effort to heal the wounds of racial division, Vietnam and Watergate." Like many others who now stood up to honor a man long attacked for his religious, racial, and political positions, the president was forced to admit that Ali "was a man of principle." While the tide had turned in Ali's favor, however, there remained large pockets of opposition to him as a Black Muslim and as a draft evader, hot topics through the rest of the 1970s. *Jet* magazine reported that three thousand letters were sent to the White House in protest against his reception there, but it was unclear whether it was because Ali was a Muslim or because of his opposition to Vietnam.[50]

Although gratified by his newfound acceptance, Ali continued to promote the principles of the Nation of Islam. Indeed, in reclaiming the heavyweight crown he believed he now had a bigger platform for his religious and racial beliefs. Claiming to represent God, he promised to "take this title and use it to help my people in all that I can. We have prostitution problems, dope problems, gang fighting, killing. The world heavyweight champion can be pretty influential." In fact, the champion often declared that he could not retire, as much as he might like to, because he had so much more work to do in helping to build the black nation. In this atmosphere, the champion had little interest in fighting Foreman again anytime soon. On the contrary, Ali sought a series of easy bouts to allow him to stay in shape by boxing on a regular basis, earn significant amounts of money, and enjoy his newfound status as an American hero.[51]

8

ON TOP AND NOWHERE

Either you're on top, or you're nowhere.

GEORGE FOREMAN

While Muhammad Ali basked in the spotlight after Zaire, George Foreman fled from public scrutiny into a private hell that threatened to lead to suicide. In a world that venerated success and disdained losers, Foreman knew that "either you're on top, or you're nowhere." In the midst of his despair he found no one he could turn to and no one he could trust. As a result of his ring success, he still enjoyed riches and fame, money and women, but nothing seemed to fill the hole in his soul. Having lost his identity, he blamed his manager-trainer Dick Sadler, referee Zack Clayton, and most of all Ali, whom he hated with a passion for taking his title and destroying his manhood. After sixteen months of despair, however, he vowed to recover his identity as a man by beating the man who had taken it away from him under false pretenses. Back on the comeback trail in search of a rematch, he was determined to show that he was still the toughest man alive. Once he got Ali back in the ring, Foreman was convinced that he would demonstrate that his loss was just a fluke and that he was a winner after all.[1]

As Foreman continued to wrestle with losing, Ali discovered that winning was a lot more complicated than he had imagined. Despite being honored by mayors and presidents, he soon realized that staying alive as the champion would prove increasingly difficult. Over the course of the late 1970s, he was often on the defensive to keep his title and his reputation intact against a hungry crop of heavyweight contenders, the ravages of time, and diminishing physical skills. Increasingly his victories seemed less triumphant and clear cut, and more tentative and ambiguous. In fact, even before beating Foreman, Ali heard calls for his retirement by boxing fans and boxing professionals fearful that he would be seriously hurt in the ring. For Ali's fans, "Stayin' Alive" was a fervent hope that their aging champion could continue to survive in a world of limits and looming defeat.[2]

Ali himself had fed the idea of retirement when he declared before the Rumble in the Jungle that he would exit the ring whether he won or lost. In fact, the new champion reversed himself after his victory, declaring that he could not retire, as much as he might like to, because he had so much more work to do in helping to build an independent black nation. In addition, as champion, the lucrative offers he received to keep fighting were too much to ignore. As Zaire demonstrated, he would continue as a rebellious hero, but the monetary rewards of his fights threatened to overshadow his principles and remove him far from his fan base. In other words, would success spoil Muhammad Ali in an era of narcissism and self-indulgence? And while he grew tired of the training necessary to remain at the top of his game, fighting kept him in the limelight, and the public acclaim was too much for him to give up. Besides, he was still the best fighter around, and he found the actual fighting gave him a joy that could be found nowhere else. Increasingly, this hero of the 1960s put his flaws on display.[3]

Both Ali's positive impulses and his flaws were evident in his first title defense against little-heralded challenger Chuck Wepner, dubbed "the Bayonne Bleeder" for his propensity to cut easily. Scheduled for March 24, 1975, the fight was to be an easy one to allow the champ to stay in shape by boxing on a regular basis. Promoted by Don King, whose star had risen as a result of his prominence in Zaire, the Wepner fight was to be the first where Ali gave away the profits after expenses. As reported in *Jet*, Ali announced at a press conference that from this fight on "all the profits will be given away." This impulse arose from the guilt he experienced over having amassed a fortune without doing much to help poor black people. Driving through Gary, Indiana, in his Rolls-Royce, "I saw this little girl with hardly any clothes on standing at a bus stop with her mother," Ali explained. "It was zero degrees, and she had no shoes." He gave her mother $100: "I've spent $100 on some dinners. All of a sudden I felt so guilty. I've never felt like this in 14 years of fighting." The experience moved him to donate money from the Wepner fight to poor African Americans in Atlanta, Philadelphia, Louisville, Gary, or elsewhere through various black organizations such as the NAACP, the United Negro College Fund, and the Nation of Islam. This proposal led black sports columnist and frequent Ali critic A. S. "Doc" Young, to call this "the best idea Muhammad Ali has ever had, the best proposal he has ever presented to the public. If he follows through on his declaration, he will make the most important individual financial contribution to Black causes in the history of sport."[4]

This grand stance burnished his image as a black folk hero, but the Wepner fight, like much else during the second half of the 1970s, laid a little tarnish on that image. Part of the problem was that instead of offering Foreman a rematch, Ali decided instead on a series of easy fights that would offer a respite from years of constant training and self-discipline. As for a rematch with Foreman, he asserted that his decisive victory proved that Foreman was no longer a worthy contender. In contrast, he may have surmised that he had been lucky against Foreman the first time around and that the ex-champion would not be so easily fooled again. With little to fear from Wepner, Ali did not train very hard—a practice repeated numerous times in his second reign as champion—and he was decidedly unimpressive.

For the fight that inspired Sylvester Stallone's *Rocky* (1976), Wepner came in as a 10–1 underdog. Despite being given no chance, he "was a man with a fair right hand and a yard of sheer unmitigated guts." With Wepner "trying every minute of every round until his will no longer could carry his body," the fight lasted until 2:41 of the fifteenth round when "he went to the canvas as much from the exhaustion of futile effort and wild swinging as from the series of lefts and rights that he received from a savage two-fisted attack mounted by the champion." Ali started off dancing on his toes, but this proved ineffective. Midway through he stood flat-footed, facing a challenger who kept coming in regardless of Ali's jab and the powerful blows he landed to his face. In the ninth, Ali was caught by a long Wepner right and down he went for a mandatory eight count. Later the champion claimed he tripped on his own foot, but the referee ruled it a knockdown. Still, by the twelfth it was clear that Ali would win: "The only question in anyone's mind was whether the courageous Wepner, willing to take any amount of punishment for his chance at the heavyweight title and all its rewards, could go the distance." He came close, but a flurry of rights and lefts ended his attempt and sent him to the hospital to have the cuts over his eyes sewn up. While he was clearly outclassed against Ali, the challenger proved that "he was no bum."[5]

For Ali, however, the fight raised a number of disturbing themes. In his first defense he was "still the best heavyweight around," noted *The Ring*, and with the exception perhaps of Joe Frazier, he stood head and shoulders above the rest of the pack. Yet his fights were uneven. He showed signs of age, he was often out of shape, he no longer dazzled, and perhaps most disturbing, he got hit a whole lot more than he ever did in the past. He still showed flashes of "blinding speed" in his combinations, "but these instances are separated by periods of standing flat-footed taking all an opponent can offer in the guise of wearing his adversary down." In sum, declared *The Ring*, "Ali is not the finely oiled fighting machine with the grace of a ballet dancer and the attack of a cobra that he once was. There are times in which his roar is a meow." Already the magazine predicted a sad end, with Ali running through the mass of contenders, including Joe Bugner, Ron Lyle, Ken Norton, Foreman and then Frazier, "until that evening when he is drained of too much of his greatness and the sands of time drag him away from his crown."[6]

Although the first defense of his title was not impressive, Ali was now acknowledged by *The Ring* and other boxing publications as the key to boxing's success. All in all, he dominated 1975 with a total of four title defenses, climaxing with perhaps the greatest fight of his career—against Joe Frazier in Manila. Although the *Ring* considered 1974 the year of the biggest heavyweight championship fight of all time because of the world interest and financial return generated by Ali-Foreman, it was clear that Ali made 1975 "a bigger one for future boxing historians than 1974 by appearing twice in the United States and twice in other countries in defense of his crown." After finishing off Wepner in March, the champion looked mediocre and absorbed a good deal of punishment against hard-punching Ron Lyle in Las Vegas on May 16. It took a knockout in the eleventh to win. Sponsored by the government, Ali met Joe Bugner in Malaysia in July in a dull fifteen-round fight. Instead of a knockout, the champion "had to be satisfied to punch the clock in workmanlike fashion." The fight was forgettable, but the setting was glamorous. Fighting in a Muslim nation, Ali continued to promote himself as the representative of worldwide Islam and a Third World figure of liberation.[7]

The pattern was set for the rest of Ali's career. He was "staying in shape while running around the world and the US attempting to make friends and be a super salesman for himself and for boxing." He generously donated to various causes and was a fighting champion not seen since Joe Louis took on all comers. What was different was the frequency of his defenses abroad that drew on his fame as a Third World hero and were heavily financed by governmental leaders who sought to burnish their stature through their association with Ali. Promoted jointly by Don King, the government of the Philippines, and Bob Arum, Ali underscored his role as a global hero by fighting former champion Joe Frazier in Quezon City outside Manila in the Philippines on October 1, 1975, at 10 a.m. In this case President Ferdinand Marcos was willing to guarantee a $3 million payday for Ali and $2.5 million for Frazier to distract a restless population from martial law, an ongoing communist rebellion, and a growing dissatisfaction among Muslims with the government. As in Zaire, the first heavyweight title fight in the Philippines would promote international investment and showcase a stable society under the president's "wise" leadership. In fact, Ali met with various Muslim groups to emphasize the Marcos regime's desire for Muslim-Christian amity. The two men had fought twice before, and there was bad blood between them. This, plus the international setting, laid the groundwork for one of the greatest fights in heavyweight history, and some would argue, the greatest of Ali's career. As *The Ring* put it, "the Thrilla in Manila" actually lived up to its name, surpassing in excitement their previous two bouts and in Nat Loubet's opinion, "Ali's meeting with George Foreman a year earlier."[8]

Given Ali's mediocre performances since Zaire, few expected much from a third meeting between these two men. For Joe Frazier, the fight represented his last chance at the title; few gave him a shot. In perhaps his greatest fight, he beat Ali in their first battle but then was destroyed by Foreman in 1973. Then Ali beat him on points in February 1974, which qualified Ali for his match with Foreman. Frazier fought only twice over the next year and a half, knocking out Jerry Quarry and Jimmy Ellis, which Dick Schaap called meaningless victories. With the Vietnam War over, the third match had none of the overarching domestic religious-political narrative that had surrounded their first fight back in 1971. Indeed, Schaap noted, "The first heavyweight championship fight in the history of the Philippines was going to be a joke, an Ali super-promotion, a great hype. But it would not be a great fight." The joke was Ali's crude taunting of the proud, working-class Frazier with a rubber gorilla that he pulled out on every occasion and announced, "It's gonna be a chilla and a thrilla, and a killa when I get the gorilla in Manila."[9]

Rather than a political or religious battle, this was a grudge match. "We have a score to settle, 'My Man' and I," Frazier declared. "I apologize! I apologize for not being as flashy as Clay. All I can do is fight! Fight and live my life like a man! His time has come. He is finished." Throughout the buildup, Ali ridiculed Frazier's talents and his chances, but even more he depicted him as an ugly animal. During a workout at Deer Lake, Ali yelled to the crowd, "Joe Frazier should give his face to the Wildlife Fund! He so ugly, blind men go the other way!" If that was not enough, he added, "He not only looks bad! You can smell him in another country!" Holding his nose, he asked, "What will the people in Manila think? We can't have a gorilla for a champ. They're gonna think, lookin' at him, that all black brothers are animals. Ignorant. Stupid. Ugly. If he's champ again, other nations will laugh at us." These hateful words made Frazier's blood boil. "Whatever you do, whatever happens," he demanded of trainer-manager Eddie Futch: "Don't stop the fight! We got nowhere to go after this. I'm gonna eat this half-breed's heart right out of his chest." As a champion of black pride, Ali's remarks appeared to have stepped over the line into racial caricature, depicting Frazier as a less than human gorilla who was too black physically and not black enough politically. While this was part of Ali's attempt to get under his opponent's skin, it made Frazier a man willing to die to achieve vengeance.[10]

Despite low expectations, the fight turned out far better than anyone could have foreseen, "an incredible demonstration of skill and courage on the part of both men." Ali started quickly, dominating the first couple of rounds as if he wanted to fulfill his prophecy of an early knockout. Standing flat-footed, he unleashed a series of powerful jabs and combinations that repeatedly landed on the onrushing Frazier's jaw. Like their first fight, however, Frazier came on in the middle rounds, gluing himself to Ali's chest, giving the champion little room to get off, and landing his own vicious left hooks to the body. Ali employed the rope-a-dope, crouching in the corner, letting Frazier punch away, but to no avail. According to Nat Loubet, "Frazier had too much smoke and fire," and he hurt the champion with hard body shots. In one of Frazier's biggest rounds, the sixth, he landed two left hooks to Ali's head that bounced him back on the ropes. Going into the seventh, Loubet judged Frazier ahead and the fresher of the two. "They told me you were all washed up," Ali grunted at one point. "They told you wrong," responded the challenger. Frazier was bobbing and weaving, taking Ali's best punches as if they were nothing. He smashed his way in close and "appeared to be on the verge of becoming the third man to regain the heavyweight title."[11]

After ten rounds Ali seemed to be fading, the fight even. He sat on his stool, body sore, head down. He told his corner that he was so exhausted that he might not be able to go on much longer. In the eleventh it looked to be true. Once more Frazier trapped him in the corner, pounding his body and head with wicked shots that should have toppled the champ. At the end of the round *Sports Illustrated*'s Mark Kram had Frazier ahead 6-4-1. Could this be a reprise of their "Fight of the Century?" Not this time. In the twelfth round, Ali some-how caught a second wind, "a tired fighter came to life, went up on his toes, reached down into his reserve of stamina." Standing in the center of the ring, Ali used long right hand leads to keep Frazier away. The challenger, game as always, could not get off his left hook. Massive bumps emerged around his eyes. At the end of the round, Frazier told his corner, "I can't pick up his right." Still, the match remained very close. The last three rounds would decide the outcome.[12]

Midway through the thirteenth round Ali ripped a right hand into Joe's face as he was coming in and sent his mouthpiece sailing out of the ring. The punch stopped Frazier in his tracks and threw him back several steps. He was stunned, unable to bob and weave, flat-footed with little movement, "a style made to order for Ali." As Kram described it, this was the most savage round of the forty-one that the two men fought. With Frazier a sitting duck, Ali unleashed combinations that pounded Joe's face into a pulp, bloodied his mouth, and opened a cut under his right eye. Nine straight right hands smashed Frazier's left eye, thirty or so in the round. The skin was puffed up under the right eye and below and above his left eye. Unable to see where the punches were coming from, Frazier was fighting blind and taking a beating. One after another solid right and left landed square in his face. At the end of the fourteenth round, an extremely worried Eddie Futch examined Frazier's grotesquely swollen eye and, over Frazier's bitter opposition, called an end to what looked like unmitigated slaughter. Ali was the winner by TKO in the fourteenth round.[13]

For boxing fans and commentators, the Thrilla in Manila proved Ali's greatness for once and for all, and enhanced Frazier's reputation as well. According to *The Ring* the third battle between the two bitter antagonists "was the best heavyweight championship fight in the history of the game. Certainly it was one of the most exciting battles in heavyweight annals." Usually these "fights of the century" were overhyped affairs that did nothing but disappoint. "The Thriller of Manila [*sic*]," however, "presented the acme of action, the winner in absolute doubt until, in the thirteenth round, Joe got careless and left an opening which Ali did not ignore."[14]

With his greatness as a fighter assured, by the fall of 1975 Muhammad Ali stood at a critical juncture, as did American culture. As exemplified by his third bout against Joe Frazier, the religious and political themes of his bouts were beginning to wane. Unlike the Rumble in the Jungle, which carried anticolonial, anti-Vietnam, and black nationalist ideas, the Thrilla in Manila highlighted more traditional themes of boxing: money, personal pride, and personal animosity, but in Ali's case, with a continuing overlay of Muslim disdain for "ignorant," unenlightened blacks like Frazier. More to the point, both men earned millions in fights supported and bankrolled by dictators around the globe. As a global hero because of his politics, Ali's international bouts allowed him to trade on his nonwhite status without having to put much effort into emphasizing the point. After this bout with Frazier, politics and religion faded farther into the background. Ali was fighting for personal pride, millions in cash, and ostensibly to help black people through investments in shopping centers and businesses that rarely materialized. At the same time, the Frazier fight allowed Ali to articulate his black nationalist views for the last time in a *Playboy* interview conducted while he was preparing for Frazier but that hit newsstands in November 1975, shortly after the match. Significantly, his views were totally divorced from the fight itself and from his future bouts too.[15]

Over the course of the following few years, Ali's rhetoric softened as befitted his greater acceptance by the larger American society, exemplified best perhaps by his several invitations to the White House by President Ford. Equally important, the Nation of Islam changed direction after the death of its leader, Elijah Muhammad, on February 25, 1975, and the passing of the torch to his son Wallace Muhammad. With Ali's support, Wallace moved the Nation away from a black nationalist theology based on color. The transformation into a movement aligned more with traditional Islam meant that membership was not restricted solely to African Americans. Indeed, whites could join. These changes split the Nation, with Louis Farrakhan and Jeremiah Shabazz continuing to lead a branch based on Elijah Muhammad's original ideas. As a member of the board overseeing the transformation, Ali declared, "I've changed what I believe, and what I believe in now is true Islam." Ali's split with the Nation was critical to his becoming "a lasting American hero," according to Michael Ezra, "because it allowed him to renounce earlier statements about whites, politics, and interracial relations." As the champion told the *New York Times*: "I don't hate whites. That was history, but it's coming to an end. We're in a new phase, a resurrection." Elijah Muhammad, Ali said, preached independence, pride, and self-discipline. "He stressed the bad things the white man did to us so we could get free and strong." Now, however, "his son Wallace is showing us there are good and bad regardless of color, that the devil is in the mind and heart, not the skin. We Muslims hate injustice and evil, but we don't have time to hate white people. White people wouldn't be here if God didn't mean them to be." According to Shirley Norman in *Sepia*, Ali even relaxed his views on interracial marriage, although he remained personally against it. "Now I say," she quotes him, "if two people love each other and find unity and peace with one another, then it's their business—and color don't mean nothing." It was not color that makes people good or bad: "After all who's a better example than me that races can all get along with each other?"[16]

Ali's changing religious views made him less radical and hence more acceptable to whites, but his sexual behavior diminished his standing among black and white women. In an era of outspoken feminism, the views articulated by Ali and the Black Muslims underscored patriarchal values coming under sustained attack and demonstrated the splintering of various radical movements. Despite Ali's image as "sexy a specimen of manhood as can be imagined," noted Shirley Norman in *Sepia*, "there are also liberated females, both black and white, who scorn 'the greatest' as the epitome of a 'sexist male chauvinist pig,' as the Women's Lib crowd terms the kind of man who believes as Ali in the superiority of the male animal." Part of the Nation of Islam's appeal lay in its support for black male dominance and female subservience in a society that undercut the black man's ability to support his family effectively or provide for the safety and security of black women and children. With the heavyweight champion as its representative, the Nation of Islam offered a potent model of black masculinity. Based on the Koran, Ali told Norman that males should be "in charge of women, because Allah hath made the one of them to excel the other." According to the laws of nature, a woman must "always look up to her man. And if she don't have a man, then she better find one to look up to . . . or she's no kind of woman."[17]

The *Playboy* interviewer asked the champion why the Muslims were so restrictive toward women. Ali's reply was revealing: "Because they should be. Women are sex symbols." Although he admitted to being a sex symbol himself, Ali noted that men "don't walk around with their chests out. Anyway, I'd rather see a man with his breasts showing than a woman. Why should she walk around with half her titties out? There gotta be restrictions that way." Muslim women had to wear demure clothing, avoid makeup, and keep their hair covered in public. The religion also prohibited premarital sexual experimentation. It was clear that men made the rules: "In the Islamic world, the man's the boss and the woman stays in the background. She don't *want* to call the shots." While women's liberation movements argued that women should control their own lives, Ali declared that, unlike Christian women, "Muslim women don't think like that. See the reason we so powerful is that we don't let the white man control *our* women. They obey *us*." As to careers for Muslim women, Ali noted that many had careers but not in white men's downtown offices where they had been "used" by white men. Against that threat, "we protect our women, 'cause women are the field that produces our nation. And if you can't protect your women, you can't protect your nation." If white men attempted to sexually violate black women, they should be killed.[18]

Starting in the Philippines, the public learned that the image of Ali's perfect Muslim marriage was undermined by his private sexual behavior. As *Life* reporter Dave Wolf put it, the prefight story surrounding the Manila match was not war or religion; it was "Ali's women," a subject hitherto unreported by the press. Despite his marriage to Belinda (who had taken the Muslim name Khalilah), who was his second wife and the mother of his children, Ali had had a voracious sexual appetite for many years. Indeed, the morning of his upset loss via a broken jaw to Ken Norton in March 1973, publicist Harold Conrad found him in bed with two women. This was not unusual. Lloyd Wells, a member of the champion's entourage, was charged with recruiting women for Ali. One camp aide even boasted to Shirley Norman that the champ could bed four women in an hour. On the surface, however, his marriage was a sterling example of a Muslim family in which the man led his wife and family while she bowed to his male superiority. When the champion introduced his stunning young paramour Veronica Porche to Ferdinand Marcos as his wife, however, Ali's personal life, his sexual habits, and the nature of his family life went public. Absent a religious or political narrative, Peter Bonventre covered the incident in a four-page *Newsweek* spread entitled "The Ali Mystique," which detailed his history of sexual high jinks. Ali took the unprecedented step of calling a press conference to defend his marital infidelity and male sexual privilege. All men, he argued, including male reporters, required girlfriends to satisfy their sexual needs. "I won't worry about who you sleep with, if you don't worry about who sleeps with me," *Jet* reported him saying. As long as the affair remained private, Belinda could ignore it. Now, however, the cat was out of the bag, and the story spread quickly. When Belinda read the story, she immediately flew to Manila, went directly to the Hilton Hotel, and proceeded to attack Ali and wreck his suite. Then she flew home. The marriage was all but over.[19]

As the story circulated in the press, Ali's heroic image underwent a slow but subtle shift toward a hero with feet of clay. Along with discussions of his ring prowess, his personal problems and his sexual proclivities drew attention. *Jet* sports editor Ronald Kisner framed the issue in a cover story that asked, "Has Success Spoiled Ali?" With his reclaimed title and his great wealth, Ali personified success. Despite his wealth, however, "Ali has fashioned an image of a man who remained uncorrupted and was spiritually tough as he was physically powerful." The Veronica Porche affair had begun to sour that image and made his loyalists question whether success had gone to his head. Chicagoan Len Badillo, for example, declared, "When a man gets a lot of money, I guess he thinks he can do anything," including introducing the young "bombshell" as his wife. An unhappy Belinda, fighting valiantly to save the marriage clearly drew the public's sympathy as she acknowledged Ali's history of sexual dalliances. While she wanted to save her marriage, "If he don't want me then I'll leave. I will always be in love with him. As far as I'm concerned, nothing can come between us. I don't care how many Veronicas come up, I'm not going to leave." His statements made him seem heartless and selfish, self-indulgent and narcissistic, especially when he announced on the *Dinah Shore Show* that Belinda should be happy since he had bought her houses, furs, jewels, and a Rolls-Royce, and he "should be able to tell her what to do." For her part, Belinda did not "feel lucky being married to him. I married Muhammad Ali when he wasn't as famous as he is now. I liked him as a person. The kind of person who takes care of the family." But he was a Jekyll and Hyde with a split personality. One is Cassius Clay the sensualist and carouser; the other is the religious Muhammad Ali. Referring to his statements that black women must be protected from white men, she intimated that he was a hypocrite with separate rules for husband and wife. He liked the ruling image, the provider image, but he also wanted to be able to indulge his desires. Ultimately, she had married him during his exile, during "his worst times," when they had little money. Now she hoped that the marriage could be saved.[20]

Their failing marriage continued as a subject of public discussion. The reaction in *Jet* was mixed, but the discussion focused on Ali's personal behavior, less on his public role. Sixteen-year-old Cynthia Lane, of New York City, for instance, warned Ali not to "mess up." If he let anything break up his beautiful family, she declared: "Of all the things he's done for Black people, I'm sorry. But he hasn't just lost a fan, but a young girl who really cares." Ali had his defenders, to be sure, but the spotlight remained on his personal relationships with Belinda and Veronica. Ajamo Yero Upton, of Washington, DC, declared that success had not spoiled Ali. As a public figure he was sure to make mistakes, "but as Blacks we can't begin to treat him as the white race does." A true black, he had worked everything out with Belinda: "This Manila deal is another way the white media has of trying to make Ali look bad in the eyes of Blacks." For Upton, Ali "is and always will be the Black man's champion." Many others continued to respect Ali, but they also praised Belinda as a real woman trying to hold her family together despite all the gossip. As Laura West, of Rockford, Illinois, put it, "Our Black men need strong women like her, she is truly a great lady and a beautiful person." Betty Washington, of Sparta, Illinois, agreed but was more critical of Ali: "If Muhammad Ali cannot see how blessed he is to have her as his wife and mother of his children, then he is not the greatest, he is a loser!" After one bad early marriage to Sonji Roi, a cocktail waitress, that ended in divorce, he should have been appreciative of a good wife, said Washington. "He needs to mature." Debra Jackson, of Baltimore, touched on the underlying issue: "His ego has finally dragged him down. He is degrading his beautiful image and embarrassing his lovely wife, Khalilah."[21]

While Ali continued to receive respect and accolades for his public activities, his private life made him seem more and more a hollow symbol of a politically active era. His heroic edge was being chipped away as he aged and pursued a more narcissistic life with Veronica after his divorce from Khalilah. As the steadfast wife and mother, Khalilah earned respect for her refusal to discuss Veronica or the child she and Ali were expecting. Although she professed her love for Ali, by the end of 1976 after nine years of marriage, she sought a divorce from a man who no longer followed the precepts of Allah despite all his protestations to the contrary. Although Ali remained a member of the World Community of Islam in the West, he put his life in Veronica's hands. The couple announced their marriage for Father's Day, June 1977, which *Jet* called a good thing since she was expecting their second child. The elaborate wedding took six months to plan and featured minimal Islamic touches at the

Beverly Wilshire hotel's Le Grande Trianon ballroom in Beverly Hills before 250 guests. The bride wore a wedding gown from I. Magnin, estimated to cost $4,000, and the Ali brothers wore white tails. After a five-minute civil ceremony, with few Muslims present, Ali and his "regally elegant" bride led off the dancing with a waltz. Here was a champion rich and in love, living out a fantasy in his new Los Angeles home. After years of rigorous training and self-discipline required by his boxing career and a much-stricter Muslim regimen, Ali now seemed to live a life of luxury and ease dictated by his riches.[22]

At the same time, the champ still devoted time and energy to political and religious causes. As the co-chair of the Hurricane Carter Trust Fund, for example, he joined a rally to free the unjustly convicted former middleweight boxer. He pledged $100,000 to help "save the NAACP," and he continued to donate money to the Muslims. In addition, the champion was still loved and admired for the political role he played in igniting the sports revolution, bringing boxing to its international apogee, and earning great riches for himself and other boxers. Increasingly, however, fans called for Ali to retire. A figure of a receding rebellious past, Ali's fights carried much less political or religious purpose and revolved around the champion's desire for money to pay his $2 million divorce settlement, his continuing contributions to the Muslims and other causes, and the expenses that came with his luxurious life style and his huge entourage. Parallel to the declining rebellious impulses in American culture, Ali appeared to be an older and tired symbol of a different era trying to survive and stay alive in the new age. For many boxing fans, especially white ones, he was the privileged holder of the title, often the beneficiary of biased judging in his favor, against younger and hungrier foes.[23]

Perhaps the first sign that Ali was past his prime occurred immediately after the Frazier match. In "A Letter to Ali and Joe," for example, boxing fan Hugh John Furlong called for Ali—and Frazier—to retire. Thanking them for their courage, artistry, and toughness, he believed "the time has come for you both to call a halt." After Manila "there lurks the danger now that to return to the well would be once too often and in doing so would allow someone of inferior class and courage the boast that he ruined either of your careers." That certainly was the case with Ali. After Manila each fight seemed harder, each foe stronger, while Ali's skills appeared to erode in bout after bout. He remained the best and continued to beat the best, but more and more fans had to wonder whether he would survive and win and whether in fact he had won increasingly close decisions. According to trainer Angelo Dundee the wear and tear on his body were apparent. No longer invincible, Ali seemed a mere mortal whose every bout seemed in doubt.[24]

In 1976 he kept fighting. Even bouts against weaker foes earned him $1 million or more. After unheralded Jean-Peter Coopman, for instance, he met legitimate contender Jimmy Young in April 1976, followed by a weak Richard Dunn in Munich, and then a farce with Japanese wrestler Antonio Inoki in Tokyo that had fans wondering why Ali was squandering his talents. The Young match was supposed to be another breather; Ali hardly trained. At 230 pounds he turned in one of his worst fights. Although he won a unanimous fifteen-round decision, many irate fans believed that Young actually won and that biased judges allowed Ali to survive with his title intact. Charles Swedberg, of Odessa, Texas, for instance, called the unanimous decision "a farce" in *The Ring*. At the end of the fight "Young seemed aware and alive and Ali, dead, beat, without spirit and flabby." Indeed, Ali's offense "looked like a kitten playing with a marshmallow." All in all, "the fight looked rigged." Henry M. DiCarb Jr., of Massillon, Ohio, called it "the worst decision . . . in heavyweight history." Never was "a man robbed more blatantly," by "the so-called 'greatest,'" who was "humiliated by a 15-1 underdog." He called for an investigation.[25]

Although the champion survived against Young to the relief of his fans, his knockout of Richard Dunn was the last of his career. When he fought Ken Norton for the third time for $6 million, the outcome was again disputed. For *The Ring*'s Nat Loubet, the September 1976 bout was a lackluster affair whose fifteen-round decision divided fans. Norton was the aggressor, ahead going into the thirteenth round. Only a big fifteenth round saved the victory for Ali. Ali's punches lacked power, his clowning appeared pitiful, and the rope-a-dope left him inactive: "As Ali grows older it is noticeable that his legs are no longer what they were, and that his once vaunted combinations are slower and not so sure of the mark." The only memorable matter was that viewers "were equally divided as to who won." Usually close fights go to the champ but a visibly upset Norton was sure he had won. "If you saw Ali's face at the end," Norton said later, "he knew I beat him. He didn't hit me hard the whole fight." When the result was announced, "I was bitter, very bitter" toward the judges. Again Ali managed to survive, but his skills had declined severely.[26]

Ali's busy personal life, his divorce, and his starring in and promotion of a movie of his life, *The Greatest*, diverted him from serious training. But given his poor performances, the film contains "more than a touch of nostalgia" in its footage of his rise, his exile, and his comeback against Foreman. Compared to past glory days, the present question was whether he could survive and retire undefeated. That likelihood seemed increasingly remote. Seven and a half months later, Ali took on unknown Spaniard Alfredo Evangelista. Ali's sloppy performance led *The Ring*'s Nat Loubet to demand that Ali retire. "The once magnificent fighting machine" that made him one of the greatest, "is but a shell of its former greatness." After clowning through the early rounds, he was too exhausted to do much. At times the fans booed him. He looked better against Earnie Shavers later that year on September 29, 1977, but it took a strong fifteenth round to get the decision, which Shavers disputed. Once again, though, Ali was lucky to survive. Baseball commissioner A. B. Giamatti did not think Ali beat Shavers "any more than many think he beat Ken Norton in September of 1976, or beat Jimmy Young in the spring of 1976." In the past he took pride in not being hit. In his later years, he took pride in getting hit but not hurt. His speed gone, he lay on the ropes absorbing punishment but managing to survive—often barely. His steep decline caused concern in those around him. After Shavers, Madison Square Garden promoter Teddy Brenner refused to host his future fights and his "fight doctor," Ferdie Pacheco, quit when he saw lab reports indicating severe damage to Ali's kidneys and his overall physical condition.[27]

It was all but over. In what was to be another easy fight, Ali met light heavyweight Olympic gold medalist Leon Spinks in early 1978. With only seven professional victories, Spinks was sure to lose. No one told Leon. The young and hungry ex-marine wore down a fighter who looked tired and old at thirty-five, winning a unanimous fifteen round decision. In September 1978 in front of a record indoor crowd of 63,532 at the New Orleans Superdome and the second largest television audience in history, a better-trained Ali beat Spinks to become the only heavyweight champion to hold the title three different times. Although Ali won, it was another dull fight that highlighted how little he had left as well as how much damage drinking and drugging had done to an out-of-condition Spinks. Ali triumphed once again, but it felt like he had barely survived. His fans realized he could go no farther.[28]

If there was any doubt that the 1960s were definitely over, broadcaster Howard Cosell, in "the greatest broadcast of my life," quoted icon Bob Dylan's "Forever Young," a nostalgic ode to fading youth as Ali exited the ring in New Orleans. Soon after Ali retired. According to novelist Ishmael Reed, nostalgia for a bygone era seemed to be the underlying reason that so many people supported Ali's last hurrah. According to Reed, Ali's victory was another sign of "sixtomania now sweeping the country," a reminder "of the turbulent decade, of Muslims, Malcolm X, Rap Brown, the Great Society, LBJ, Vietnam, General Hershey, dashikis, afros, Black Power, MLK, RFK. He represented the New Black of the 1960s . . . glamorous, sophisticated, intelligent, international, and militant." Still, as Reed surveyed the crowd, he realized that while the celebrities rooted for Ali, "the busboys were for Spinks." Ali had become part of the establishment, a star who moved in totally different circles. In their eyes, Leon was "the people's champ," one of them, drinking in New Orleans dives, acting wild, being arrested for a traffic violation. Leon was one of those the "establishment has told to get lost," part of "the underclass" left behind as better-off African Americans enjoyed new opportunities in a racially transformed world.[29]

Ali's career may have sputtered out, but he remained a beloved but nostalgic icon for a radical era rapidly receding into the past. In contrast, Foreman's defeat in Zaire was met with scorn by boxing fans, and he faded as a relevant pugilistic standard bearer for the Job Corps and the silent majority. The decline of both Ali and Foreman as viable heroes during the latter years of the 1970s suggests just how unstable and ambivalent American culture was at time when the nation was at a crossroads. While most boxing fans focused on Ali's declining skill as a way to measure the relevance of the rebellious past, underneath the radar during the late 1970s Foreman and American culture were still obsessed with the psychic damage of defeat—in the ring and in Vietnam. Foreman's eventual comeback demonstrated that American culture and society were on the verge of profound transformations that no one could have predicted.

Foreman continued to find it extremely difficult to come to terms with losing in a society that venerated winners and shunned losers. For almost two years he was mired in confusion as he sought to reclaim his identity as a winner and as a man. Yet his confusion did not derive from the loss alone. Indeed, just like Ali, troubles in his personal life threatened to overwhelm him. Just weeks before the Rumble in the Jungle, Foreman had a son born to him and his woman friend Pamela Clay, although the two had already broken up. Despite his desire for a son, Foreman denied that the boy was his because he distrusted women as gold diggers who only wanted the money and luxurious life attached to a heavyweight champion. This led to a court case that prompted *Jet* to say that the ex-champion had lately been fighting more outside the ring than in it. Clay claimed nothing for herself, but she asked for $3,000 a month in child support, $30,000 for attorney fees, and $5,000 in court costs. The previous June, Clay had brought a $5 million assault and battery suit against Foreman, but that was dropped. The blood tests ordered by Foreman's lawyer proved the child was his. Now he had two children, and he looked for girlfriends willing to babysit them. That was not the life young women thought association with a rich champion would gain them, and Foreman kept pursuing and discarding one woman after another. None of them brought him the peace of mind he sought.[30]

Even more confusing, soon after he returned from Zaire, Foreman learned that the man he thought was his father was not his biological father after all.

One day his sister Gloria told him that J. D. Foreman was not his father. This revelation quickly produced a torment familiar from his childhood when his brothers and sisters would infuriate him by making fun of him and treating him as somehow different from the rest of the Foreman family. His new knowledge was one more unsettling disturbance to his whole identity.[31]

Angry and confused, his identity hanging by a thread, Foreman knew he needed help, but where could he turn? Only crazy people went to therapists, he reasoned, and certainly tough fighters didn't. Meanwhile, his mother and other close relatives were poor, ignorant people whose advice he considered worthless. Normally a boxer would turn to his manager or trainer, but having decided that Sadler was part of the problem, Foreman had only himself to rely on. As a result, he decided to rebuild himself into the man who had not been knocked out in Zaire. To do that he would have to win back his title, but that would prove difficult. As the newly crowned champion, Ali had little incentive to risk his title against someone who would be harder to bamboozle a second time with a rope-a-dope. In this situation, Foreman believed that he would have to force Ali to give him a rematch. To do that he would have to prove to boxing fans that his loss was just a fluke and that he was still the toughest boxer alive. The fans would then demand that a reluctant Ali had to put his title on the line against George.[32]

To exorcise the ghosts of Zaire and his humiliating loss of manhood, Foreman set out to publicize how tough he was still, much as the prisoners of war were transformed from symbols of defeat into icons of victory, and much as foreign policy makers under President Gerald Ford in the Mayaguez incident in Kampuchea were eager to prove that the United States was willing to use its military might abroad after the debacle of Vietnam. These tendencies culminated in the right wing's desire to overcome "the Vietnam Syndrome" wherever possible. Having just lost in humiliating fashion to Soviet-backed forces in Vietnam and Kampuchea, the Ford administration set out to demonstrate its resolve and stand up to the Russians by launching a CIA-led war in Angola with the help of President Mobutu of Zaire. Similarly, after the loss to Ali, Foreman became even more obsessed with establishing his tough-guy reputation. He had always kept big animals on his ranch, but now he sought publicity for being a guy tougher than the toughest animals. By having a lion and a tiger as pets, he would demonstrate how mean he was. Other boxers were quick to notice: "'Man, that George Foreman is crazy! He walks around his ranch with a lion and a tiger. George isn't afraid of anyone or anything! Don't mess with George Foreman.'" Comments like these were music to his ears.[33]

Foreman's obsession with publicizing his masculinity led to a cover story in late 1974 in *People* magazine, a new venture in celebrity journalism at that time. The idea was to "'prove' that I was the world's strongest man," by seeming to hold a cow aloft by himself so that people "will realize that I must have been robbed in Africa in that fight against Ali." On his ranch in Marshall, Texas, Foreman stationed five guys at the head of the seven hundred pound animal and five at the tail. When the photo was cropped, it would appear that he alone was holding up the huge animal. Unfortunately, one of the men slipped and then all of the others let go. Foreman was left with the cow wrapped around his shoulders, proving in fact how strong he actually was. When the photo appeared, his friends and enemies in the boxing world were astonished that he could hold a cow in the air by himself. He hoped they got his point: "Something must have been really wrong with George when he fought Ali in Africa. I mean, the man can carry a cow! Surely he was strong enough to have beaten Muhammad Ali."[34]

While Foreman and his publicist Bill Caplan staged the photo as a way to convince the public, it seems apparent that the strategy was aimed equally at bolstering the ex-champion's own self-confidence in his shaken identity. It took him six months after Zaire to get back into the ring at all. When he started boxing again, on April 26, 1975, however, it was for a hokey exhibition against five opponents in one night, each of these bouts to go three rounds. "It was a crazy thing to do, but to tell you the truth, I was a bit unhinged during that period of my life." Although Foreman was skeptical, promoter Henry Winston convinced him that fighting five men was a way to prove his toughness. Beating five guys would convince the world that the loss to Ali was a fluke.[35]

Once promoter Don King entered the picture based on his ability to nail down a suitable arena and attract a national television network, the promotion turned into a three-ring circus. Five fighters agreed to appear at Toronto's Maple Leaf Gardens, among them Alonzo Johnson, Jerry Judge, Terry Daniels, Charlie Polite, and Boone Kirkman. All five were eager to increase their name recognition and boost themselves into the big money by beating a former champion on national television. On the surface Foreman appeared content with his performance. He knocked out Johnson, Judge, and Daniels, and battered Polite and Kirkman. However, King hired both Muhammad Ali and Howard Cosell to do the commentary for ABC Television. Instead of Foreman being able to demonstrate his strength and prove he deserved another shot, he set himself up to further humiliation at the hands of his tormentor and his sidekick at ringside. As he recalled, throughout the bout Cosell kept repeating that the match was a "travesty," a "disgrace," and a "discredit" to a great sport. Indeed, some of the fighters were so upset with the judging that a near riot erupted in the ring, with some of the corner men getting into it with each other. Jerry Judge pushed Foreman after their bout, Foreman then punched Judge, and the two men wrestled each other to the canvas until their trainers pulled them apart. Terry Daniels also showed no respect for the ex-champion. After the decision went against him, he and Foreman ended up throwing punches at each other. Then Foreman shoved one of Daniels's corner men, who was also punched by one of Foreman's seconds. Ali, meanwhile, piled on by heckling Foreman from his ringside seat. Although George felt he proved that he had the stamina to go at least twelve rounds, he and the public could not ignore the verbal battle between him and Ali. That turned Ali's fans against Foreman and reduced the exhibition to the level of professional wrestling. Chanting "Ali, Ali," the crowd booed the star of the show, and some even threw garbage into the ring. To show he was not bothered, Foreman flexed his muscles like a muscleman, which made him seem sour and surly.[36]

Instead of boosting Foreman's stock, the exhibition extravaganza turned into a further humiliation. *Jet* magazine found his behavior in the ring ludicrous. According to the magazine, he hopped like a bunny and danced like an elephant on a string. Plus, few took his foes seriously, and his angry verbal exchanges with Ali convinced *Jet* that he was no longer "Mr. Nice." When a woman friend told him that he had become "a mad man, a bad man," he realized that the rest of the world must have seen him as "Jack the Ripper. I guess the camera doesn't lie. It had captured me perfectly: George Foreman, the man you love to hate. I was shattered." While some boxing fans thought Foreman might have a shot at the title again once Ali retired, his actions after Zaire increasingly alienated the public. John T. Hale, of Buffalo, New York, attended what he called "the Foreman Circus" in Toronto and found it "a disgrace." In his opinion, *Ring* magazine should have hollered against the whole thing: "It was a badly managed show and Foreman ran through the five like a tyro." He predicted, "It will take George a long time to get over the effects of the injuries he suffered in the public mind." This was on top of what Joric Kellogg, of New York, called "all of those pitiful excuses after losing." If he was so tough, why did he not quit stalling and get back into the ring for a real fight?[37]

After the fiasco in Toronto, Foreman began to take real steps toward a rematch against Ali when he fought hard-hitting Ron Lyle, a ranked contender, at Caesars Palace in Las Vegas on January 24, 1976, fifteen months after the disaster in Kinshasa. Like Foreman, Lyle had suffered a major setback against Ali in May 1975. Whoever lost this match would probably fall out of contention. To get him in shape, Foreman hired a new trainer, the veteran Gil Clancy, who had him fight a tune-up with Jody Ballard, against whom he exhibited a viciousness that was really intended to punish Ali, the family members and friends who had betrayed him after the defeat, every teacher who had dismissed him, and every kid who had called him a bad name. One more tune-up, this time against Eddie Brooks, and he and Lyle were set to lay it on the line in what turned out to be a no-holds brawl.[38]

After a feeling-out period in which both men exchanged jabs during round one, Lyle unloaded an overhand right to Foreman's jaw, which stunned him but left him still standing as the bell rang. Lyle came out for round two looking to finish the job. Using his jab, though, Foreman held him off until he smashed Lyle with a left upper cut and then a combination that sent Lyle to the ropes, where Foreman continued to punch away. An accidental early bell saved Lyle from a knockdown. In the third round the two men punched away at each other with little concern for defense. Then came the fourth round. Lyle hit George with a powerful right and a flurry of hooks. Foreman went down in a heap. It looked like his worst nightmare all over again. Unlike Zaire, this time he could not blame his water, loose ropes, or anything else. He jumped up quickly, but Lyle immediately floored him again. As he sat on the canvas, Zaire flashed through his mind once more. In Africa he had not fought back when he was knocked down, but this time he got up determined to win or die in the ring. As Lyle came in for the finish, Foreman knocked him down, and when he got up, Foreman knocked him down again. The carnage continued through round five, when Foreman's punching power overwhelmed Lyle and knocked him out. Foreman felt restored by the conviction that he could get off the mat and fight to the death. Redeemed as a man again in his own eyes, he was once again Big Bad George with the sportswriters. Next stop, Ali?[39]

Not so fast. After his grueling fourteen-round brawl with Frazier, Ali preferred easier prey. Various promoters insisted that Foreman fight Joe Frazier instead. Aware of how dangerous Frazier still was, despite losing to Ali in Manila several months earlier, Foreman was reluctant. Everyone in boxing knew that Ali might retire, so getting to him soon was imperative. However, George and his trainer Gil Clancy were hopeful that if Foreman beat Frazier convincingly, Ali would put off retirement because of public demand and because he would not want boxing fans to think that he was afraid of a renewed Foreman. For Frazier, the June 1976 bout was his last hurrah. Having lost to Ali the previous fall, Frazier had little left. Once again, though, Foreman was the villain. Most fans at New York's Nassau Coliseum rooted for Frazier, who entered the ring with his head shaved and booed Foreman. However, "Smokin' Joe's" fire was soon extinguished. In the fifth round Foreman had him on the ropes and caught him with a punch that opened a cut over his eye and sent his mouthpiece and a number of teeth flying into the seats. Another hard shot and a flurry of punches and Frazier hit the canvas. He got up at four but took the mandatory eight count. Another Foreman combination and Joe was down again. He got off the deck, glassy eyed, bleeding from his nose and his right eye, completely defenseless. His manager signaled to the referee, and at 2:26 of the fifth round the referee stopped the fight. The end, noted *The Ring*'s John Ort, was "a sorry picture of a once great champion, bleeding and hurt, in the ring which once brought him wealth and glory." As Foreman stood over him, glaring, the crowd booed. With a 42–1 record, however, Foreman had demonstrated that he deserved a rematch with Ali.[40]

On the surface, the victory "leaves George Foreman as 'King of the Mountain' again," noted John Ort, "or maybe it only looks like it." Despite a convincing win and clear signs that he was back, Foreman had to battle the hostility of fans. Against Frazier, Norton, and Ali, "the heroes of our time," he looked like a "heavy" not a "hero," a bad guy. This was demonstrated versus Frazier when the crowd booed him and cheered for Joe. But "what," wondered Ort, "turned the cheers that he received in the 1968 Olympics in Mexico City to boos today?" He had no explanation, other than the fact that "everyone wants somebody to hate in boxing. George fills the bill, a big strong guy, who represents the 'bully on the block.'" Although he was a former patriotic hero, Foreman's anger and surliness since winning the title had turned him into a bully. He was not only a loser who had disappointed his fans by failing so badly against Ali, he was a bad loser. No longer seemingly a humble nice guy, Foreman now appeared to be someone whose pleasant demeanor had tricked fans into seeing him as something he was not. The only thing he could do was keep fighting and winning in the hope that the boxing federations or the fans would force Ali to give him the return match.[41]

To force Ali to fight him, Foreman agreed to Don King's idea that he fight three showcase bouts on ABC television during 1976 and 1977. After knocking out unbeaten Dino Dennis in four rounds, the number one contender did the same against Pedro Agosto in January 1977. Foreman was set for the third match two months later against Jimmy Young in San Juan, Puerto Rico. Young had proved himself one tough customer. In his recent fight against Ali, he had outboxed and outsmarted the aging champion, although he lost the bout in a disputed decision. As a result, both Young and Foreman saw the fight as an unofficial elimination bout, with the winner getting a rematch against Ali for the heavyweight crown. In fact, the WBA was planning to strip Ali of his title if he refused to meet Foreman should he beat Young. Despite universal predictions that the powerful ex-champion would easily knock out his opponent, Young himself asserted that he would win via knockout in what would be his "shining hour." His quick hands and feet, along with his six-foot-two height would allow Young to stay away from the still-robotic Foreman, tire him out, and then dispatch him in the later rounds, just as Ali had done. The bout proved the turning point of Foreman's life.[42]

On March 17, 1977 Foreman and Young, a 3-1 underdog, squared off on a steamy night in San Juan's Roberto Clemente Stadium for the right to face the increasingly vulnerable Ali. As in Zaire, the match did not go Foreman's way. The fight started slowly, with Foreman pursuing Young but not cutting off the ring against his fast-moving opponent. Each round he survived, the more confident Young became. According to John Ort, for the first six rounds "George did little more than hold, grab, and wrestle in his efforts to corner Young." Foreman ascribed his slow start to what promoter Don King had told him a few days before the match. Knocking guys out too quickly, King advised, was hurting the ability of the television networks to run commercials and make a profit off his fights. If he wanted a big payday for the rematch with Ali, he should avoid an early knockout. In response, Foreman toyed with Young, jabbing him into the ropes. When he hurt Young in the third round, he claimed to have backed off because it was too early. Young's confidence only grew the longer he lasted. In the seventh, Foreman landed a big left hook to Young's forehead, followed by a hard right, buckling his knees. Instead of launching the knockout blow, Foreman hesitated, wondering if King would be satisfied with a seven-round bout. George's brief hesitation gave Young the chance to move out of danger. Although Foreman pursued him for the next two minutes of the round, Young escaped. At the bell, Young lifted his hands in victory while the crowd chanted his name.[43]

Having expended so much energy trying for the knockout in the seventh, Foreman was drained. By contrast, Young felt he had escaped disaster and was now emboldened. He fought more aggressively, while in the eighth and ninth Foreman appeared very tired. An energized Young came back "like gang busters, moving in and out, landing short rights to the head and body of George." In the tenth Foreman again tried but failed to land the shot that would turn the tide. Instead, "he punched himself out and let Young come back toward the end of the frame." According to *The Ring*, Young won the last two rounds. In the twelfth, Foreman needed a knockout to win. He chased Young, attempting a desperate right uppercut. Young countered with a wild shot that caught Foreman as he was coming forward and dropped him to one knee. In a frenzy, Foreman rose at the count of one and went after Young hoping for a knockout. At the bell, he believed he had won, but deep down he knew that the judges had already given it to Young. Indeed, the decision was unanimous for Jimmy, who was now on top of the world. Foreman declared that, "I took at least eight of the 12 rounds, but lost anyway because the judges went with the crowd," who cheered Young and booed Foreman throughout the match. George claimed he understood because he was no hero. In his dressing room, George hit rock bottom.[44]

For the second time in his career, Foreman left the ring as the loser. Everything he had been working toward, revenging himself against Ali, becoming a winner again, exorcising the humiliation of Zaire, restoring his tough masculine identity went down the tubes. In his agony and despair, he experienced a profound but frightening transformative experience: a "born-again" religious conversion that would lead to his retirement from the ring. As sports columnist Jerry Izenberg noted, based on a two-hour phone call at 1:30 in the morning from the former champion, Foreman underwent "an incredible emotional and physical odyssey." Whatever happened in the dressing room, "it changed the course of George Foreman's life in one sweeping, agonizing trauma which still inspires amazement in his voice when he tries to verbalize the incredible impact on him."[45]

This is a story that Foreman has told repeatedly as he sought to spread the good news of salvation through Jesus and answer questions from a skeptical sporting world. While there have been many other conversions from the secular to the religious realm in African American history (Henry Armstrong, Little Richard, Al Green, and numerous others), Foreman's conversion came at a time when the renewal of evangelical Protestantism was on the rise in American life in general. Having survived the perilous era of Vietnam and Watergate, many Americans turned to evangelical Christianity for solace and meaning. At the same time, African Americans were no longer flocking to a splintered Nation of Islam as Ali had done in the early 1960s. As black energies shifted toward practical politics, there was also a growing movement toward self-reform removed from the lures and temptations of modern America. Seeking an identity beyond winning and losing, Foreman stood at the tip of a vast iceberg that counseled black and white Americans to remove themselves from the stresses and strains of the material world.

As he related to Izenberg: "I was in the dressing room after the fight and I was weak. I started to talk and I began to realize that every sentence I spoke . . . had the word 'death' in it. Then it was like every three words and then it was every word . . . 'death . . . death . . . death." Foreman amplified the experience in his two autobiographies. The dressing room was so hot, he recalled, that he started to panic. "Maybe it was the heat that made my thought come in such a rush." He reminded himself that despite losing a fight, he was still all right. He could retire, do television and films, comment on boxing. He told himself: *"You're still the world-famous George Foreman. You can always find something to do."* He had money and houses, he reminded himself: *"You can retire and die."* Over and over death intruded into his thoughts. *"You believe in God,"* he heard. *"Why are you afraid to die?"* Was that the voice of God? he wondered. If so, he tried to make a deal with the Almighty: *"I'm George Foreman . . . I can still box. I can give money to charities."* But the voice thundered in response: *"I don't want your money. I want YOU."*[46]

At that point, Foreman believed he was in fact dying. "The invincibility I'd always felt had been an illusion," he said. His knees buckled and he entered a deep dark void. He was totally alone, filled with panic, hopelessness, sorrow, and isolation. In that realm of death and nothingness, everything that had formed Foreman's identity melted away to nothing—money, cars, houses, clothes, women. All the things of the American dream that he thought would satisfy him, all the riches that being champion conveyed, all the outer markings of success that he craved, all the winning that had brought him no peace—feeling that he truly was dying, he cried out: "I don't care if this *is* death. I still believe there's a God."[47]

At that instant, he felt a gigantic hand reach out and lift him out of that terrifying place. He found himself back in his dressing room lying on the floor, surrounded by his frightened handlers and corner men who lifted him back onto the table. For the first time in his life he felt at peace. To everyone's astonishment, he cried out: "I'm George Foreman! I just lost that boxing match. I don't care where You're taking me—I lost the fight, and I'm who I want to be. I don't want to be anyone else!" When Dr. Keith West attempted to move his head, George had the sensation of blood flowing from thorns in his head. Everyone in the dressing room looked at him as if he had lost his mind. In frustration he sat up on the table and yelled at the top of his lungs, "JESUS CHRIST IS COMING ALIVE IN ME!" Spilling out of his mouth came snatches of the Bible, and instead of his lifelong anger, there came the language of love. He jumped in the shower, and continued to shout, "HALLELUJAH, I'VE BEEN BORN AGAIN!" He was so filled with peace and love that, stark naked, he tried to get out of the dressing room to spread the word. All assembled thought he had gone crazy and tried to stop him. "As for me," he recalled, "I had never felt that wonderful in all my life! This born-again experience was everything I ever wanted." It was joy and euphoria. For the first time in his life, he felt at peace. He was a new man. The old George was gone; a new George emerged.[48]

His hatred and anger toward Ali and those who had betrayed him in Zaire and thereafter slowly ebbed away. Before his born-again experience he had hated Ali with a passion. It was an anger that knew no bounds. After losing his crown to him in Zaire, "I would have loved nothing more than to kill him in the boxing ring." Foreman also wanted to kill everyone who had undermined him, such as his friend Leroy Jackson and most of all Dick Sadler, whom he blamed for poisoning him in Zaire and preventing him from winning in the most crucial match of his life. Now, filled with love, he began to forgive everyone, Ali included, and he let his identity as "big bad George" fade away. In one of many late-night phone calls, he even spoke to Ali about his love for the man who had defeated him and who Foreman unsuccessfully tried to convert to Christianity.[49]

Foreman's experience was not unique in the late 1970s. A strong impulse in the culture of the era was the survival of the apocalypse—of disaster, war, floods, fire. Unlike Ali, who triumphed and retained his heroic image, even as it faded into nostalgia, Foreman survived losing and the descent of his life into near madness by turning to evangelical religion. By retiring from boxing and withdrawing into street preaching, he slowly took on a much more humble role in the cultural firmament. At first, of course, he thought he could continue to fight again, "because maybe I could treat the whole thing like it was a dream. But I couldn't," he said. Instead, he soon began giving his testimony to various churches, including Dr. Robert Schuller's Church of the Garden Grove.[50]

Having been given a choice of how to live his life, Foreman believed he could not fight again. He had been a fighter and a sinner, he related: "And now, without fighting, without fame, without fuss, I'm a happy man." Starting with himself, he learned to accept his losses. Rather than treat defeat as the equivalent of spiritual death, Foreman began to see his defeats as an indication that he must change himself. As a result, he sought a simpler, more disciplined, and conservative mode of existence. This included giving up fornication, excessive consumption, and hanging out with the wrong crowd. While Ali's womanizing was revealed to the public, Foreman followed a different path. Losing turned out to be the key to victory. As he had reformed himself, he sought to help others reform as well. He became a street preacher, a man who belonged to no organized religion but converted sinners one by one on the streets of Houston and spoke to congregations wherever he was invited. Acutely aware of the poverty around him, Foreman ignored government programs as a solution, but he worked on a personal basis to help people who had suffered economic, racial, romantic, and other forms of loss to overcome their own personal defeats. His evangelical street pitch made it clear that he too was familiar with loss. "I'm George Foreman, ex-heavyweight champion of the world," he declared on a Houston street after leaflets with his picture as an Olympian waving his small American flag circulated, "and I'm here to tell you about Jesus Christ." His mission was to forge a personal transformation in the lives of individuals one person at a time and as someone who had suffered great loss he felt he had the background and the experience to help others. Eventually he headed his own small congregation, the Church of the Lord Jesus Christ, and soon he was involved in creating a gym for underprivileged youth in a Houston ghetto, working individually there, too, to keep them on a righteous and law-abiding path. It appeared that he had put boxing behind him.[51]

For ten years—until 1987—he fulfilled his promise never to fight again. But then everything changed once more for Foreman, as it did for Ali, too. During the 1980s both men were out of the ring. While Ali still enjoyed a public presence all over the world and remained perhaps the best-known individual across the globe, another divorce, the onset of Parkinson's disease, the collapse of his fortune, and several embarrassing scandals dimmed his heroic image. Foreman, meanwhile, stayed away from boxing and led a happier life as a preacher. In 1987, though, he returned to the sport to raise money for his youth gym and soon embarked on a comeback. For both Foreman and Ali, as well as for two other principals in the Rumble in the Jungle—Don King and Mobutu Sese Seko—the 1990s would bring another surprising turn.

9

WHEN WE WERE KINGS

> So while a guy like Jesse Jackson will be out there preaching in a spiritual vein and a guy like Martin Luther King showed us the mountaintop and took us to the promised land, I'm trying to take you to the bank.
>
> DON KING, *BLACK COLLEGIAN*, 1981

In 1996 Muhammad Ali and George Foreman stepped back into the ring once
again in the Academy Award–winning documentary *When We Were Kings*. For many Americans the film account of the Rumble in the Jungle was a revelation in its depiction of the two old warriors at the peak of their prowess in Africa, along with two other major figures who had made the epic international prizefight possible: promoter Don King and President Mobutu Sese Seko of Zaire. As the documentary looked back twenty years, filmgoers entered a world as exotic as the African setting of the fight. For younger viewers, Ali was not merely an ailing, nostalgic figure—a ghost from the past—he was once again a vital political force from a time when sports carried overt political weight and Ali served as an outspoken exemplar of the black freedom movement. With the primary focus of the film firmly fixed on Ali's quest to reclaim his title and achieve personal redemption, Foreman once again came off as merely the foil for Ali's ambitions, the victim of the rope-a-dope, and the spectacular loser who had performed his brief function and now could shuffle back into history as a character deserving to be forgotten. Despite his being a heavyweight champion of the world at the time of the documentary's release, Foreman's accomplishments and his comeback since 1987 received nary a mention.[1]

What is surprising, however, is how much had changed in the twenty-two years since the actual fight. In 1996 it appeared that a gigantic reversal of fortune had occurred in the lives of the two men. The fifty-four-year-old Ali may still have been revered by the public, but he was a nostalgic reminder of a heroic past, something of a pathetic public figure suffering from Parkinson's disease and a reputation tarnished by bad business decisions and marital disappointment. Increasingly removed from the public eye, the once-voluble champion trembled noticeably and could hardly speak above a whisper as a result of his illness. In addition, by the late 1980s and 1990s, the rebellious black spirit of the 1960s had waned, as had the antiwar movement and, along with it, Ali's reputation. In fact, as Michael Ezra has documented, *When We Were Kings* was one of many conscious attempts to resurrect Ali from the historical graveyard by rehabilitating his reputation.

While Ali seemed a shadow of his former physical and political self in the mid-1990s, George Foreman had surprised everyone by successfully returning to the ring in 1987 after a ten-year layoff. In 1994, almost twenty years to the day of his disastrous loss in Zaire, he won the heavyweight crown once again at the age of forty-five, the oldest man ever to accomplish that feat. Equally surprising, while the once outspoken Ali could barely speak, the previously sullen and withdrawn Foreman spoke endlessly about God, grills, mufflers, McDonald's, and his color-blind allegiance to the American dream. Witty and self-assured, Foreman was born once again, as if he had assumed the mantle of Ali's verbosity. Older, smarter, patient, and humorous, he had seemingly exchanged personalities with his old foe. To Budd Schulberg, who had covered the Rumble in the Jungle, Foreman's reversal of fortune seemed the stuff of movies. When he fought for the title in 1991, in what turned out to be a losing effort against Evander Holyfield, Foreman appeared to Schulberg to have been transformed into a black Rocky or a black Lazarus, not the man Schulberg had seen as a gold medal Uncle Tom back in 1968. Now a humble preacher who exorcised the painful ghosts of Zaire, Foreman stood as an ordinary everyman hero, someone with whom all could identify.[2]

By the 1990s, the once triumphant Ali was on a downward spiral. It started with his last few years in the ring, when he barely survived against often inferior opponents. Then came his ill-advised mission to Africa to garner support for the American-led boycott of the 1980 Olympic Games in Moscow. Since he first won the title and announced his allegiance to the Nation of Islam, Ali claimed that boxing was of secondary importance; his primary concern was his religion and his access to world leaders. As he prepared for the Foreman battle, Ali repeatedly declared that once he retired he would serve Islam as a preacher and use his fame to bring about world peace. In 1979, retired from the ring, he got his chance. This time, however, it was at the behest of the Carter administration, which chose him as its representative to convince independent black African nations to boycott the upcoming Moscow Olympic Games to protest the Soviet invasion of Afghanistan. Relying on his enormous prestige in Africa, Ali flew across the globe only to be met with criticism and disillusion. Most African leaders expressed outrage that the United States sent an athlete—even one as celebrated as Ali—rather than a diplomat to discuss matters of such political significance. In addition, they pointed out to the former champion that he did not fully understand the issues and that the Carter administration was using his fame and his race in an attempt to manipulate them. When the Supreme Council for Sport in Africa had promoted a boycott of the 1976 Montreal Olympics in protest against the New Zealand rugby team's visit to South Africa, the United States had refused to join the black African effort. The Soviet Union, however, had supported the boycott and various other black anticolonial efforts. As a result, many African states refused to align themselves with the United States in this renewed Cold War flare-up. Ali's mission proved a humiliating failure. A grand diplomatic career seemed out of the question.[3]

Bored and humiliated, Ali decided to return to the ring in a match promoted by Don King at Las Vegas's Caesars Palace in 1980. Although he came in lithe and trim, the former champion was no match for reigning heavyweight champion Larry Holmes. Despite Ali's boasts, Holmes's strong left jab and overhand right were too powerful for Ali. The rope-a-dope tactic that had served him well against Foreman in Zaire proved of little avail. Unable to mount any offense, he spent most of the bout in the corner or on the ropes as the younger and stronger Holmes treated him as a human punching bag. By the tenth round Holmes was in tears as he destroyed his idol. Herbert Muhammad had seen enough and signaled Angelo Dundee to throw in the towel. It was clear to fans everywhere that Ali was a shell of his former self, but he tried one more time, against Trevor Berbick in 1981, only to meet the same fate. He had long claimed that unlike other black heavyweight champions, with Joe Louis especially in mind, he would leave the ring victorious. It was not to be.

Even worse, in 1984 at the age of forty-two, the symbol of fluid, graceful movement in the ring was diagnosed with a form of Parkinson's disease. There had been signs of physical deterioration since the late 1970s, but Ali and his handlers ignored the problem. Ferdie Pacheco, for example, noticed that he was receiving injections for various ailments and concluded that Ali was suffering from malfunctioning kidneys. When no one took his warnings seriously, Pacheco quit after the Shavers bout, worrying that the problems would only get worse. Around the same time Hank Schwartz and Jerry Izenberg, among many others, began to notice that Ali was slurring his words. Because of his age in 1980 (thirty-eight) and concern for his health, he was required by the Nevada State Boxing Commission to undergo a complete physical at the Mayo Clinic before it would issue him a license to box against Holmes. Although he appeared to pass with flying colors, there was a disturbing indication that there was a hole in the membrane covering his brain. By 1984 the signs of trouble were too much to ignore. Slurring of words, sluggishness, feelings of weaknesses, stiffness, and the inability to perform normal household tasks finally sent Ali to a neurologist, who diagnosed him with Parkinson's syndrome. While Ali continued to deny it, the physicians concluded that over the course of his boxing career he had suffered repeated brain trauma.[4]

Prescribed a course of L-DOPA, the former champion experienced a relief from his symptoms, and he appeared generally cheerful as he rejected signs of pity on the faces of his many fans. Still, the disease continued to ravage his body until the trembling, slurring of speech, stiffness of movement, the stolid facial appearance, and an inability to speak very loudly were noticeable to all. At the same time, his personal life deteriorated. His philandering proved too much for Veronica, and his third marriage ended in divorce. Along with the financial burden that the divorce entailed, the failure of his marriage added to a sense of depression and failure.[5]

Ali had always claimed he would not end up like Joe Louis, broke and sick, an object of pity rather than pride, but it looked more and more as if he was following Joe down that well-worn path. This was especially true of his finances, which by the late 1980s were in a perilous state. With his boxing career over, the periodic infusions of millions of dollars stopped abruptly. Little was coming in, but a lot continued to flow out. He had three wives to support and six legitimate children, as well as several he sired outside of marriage. In addition, for years he had given huge donations to the Nation of Islam, and he continued that practice with the branch he supported after the split. Along with that, he gave generously to a wide variety of political and race organizations, among them the United Negro College Fund, the NAACP, and campaigns for black hospitals and other similar ventures. The champion also continued to be the main support of his family, including his brother Rahman and his parents, Cassius Clay Sr. and Odessa Clay, who had separated and maintained separate households. Equally draining, he maintained a huge entourage of friends, family, and hangers-on who looked to him for financial support. Then, of course, were the women, who continued to come and go, usually with some financial sweetener attached. Like Joe Louis, he was very generous to anyone with a sob story.

One would think that a champion of his stature would attract huge endorsement contracts for a variety of prestigious products. Despite being one of the most recognized people on the planet, however, the face and fist of

Ali adorned only Roach Motel boxes during the late 1970s and early 1980s. Ali still conjured up images of black rebellion and black pride and was thus seen as too reminiscent of the 1960s to attract white consumers. Plus, Ali had little interest in business. In 1978, Robert Abboud, the chief executive officer of First National Bank of Chicago, volunteered to set up a group of financial counselors to help Ali gain control of his money and guide him toward secure and lucrative investments, including commercial endorsements. After some initial success, the financial advisers quit in frustration. The people around Ali undercut the committee's advice as they instead promoted competing deals and schemes from which they sought to benefit. Moreover, the advisers were hamstrung by deals Ali had already made. They would suggest lucrative endorsements with athletic shoe and clothing companies, for example, only to discover that Ali had signed a half-baked contract with a fly-by-night competitor that just wasted his money. The situation worsened after Ali moved to Los Angeles and then fought Holmes. Frustrated that the former champion was undercutting their efforts, his advisers eventually gave up. Ali's finances continued their downward spiral.[6]

Equally disturbing, the retired champion's name was tarnished when it was used by Harold Smith to embezzle $21.5 million from Wells Fargo Bank. Later in the decade an Ali business partner, Richard Hirschfeld, used his ability to imitate the champ's voice over the phone for his own political and economic projects, thereby dragging Ali's reputation through the mud. When he moved to Los Angeles in 1980, moreover, Ali bought the most expensive mansion ever purchased by a heavyweight champion and lived a seemingly out-of-touch luxurious life with Veronica and his children in Fremont Place, an elite black enclave in the city, far removed from the many black fans who had so idolized him and made him "the people's champion." When he and Veronica divorced in 1986, the ever-generous Ali invalidated their prenuptial agreement to give her the mansion, half his trust fund, and millions in alimony and child support.[7]

Other events further dented the champ's reputation. In 1984, he, like former heavyweight champions Floyd Patterson and Joe Frazier, endorsed Ronald Reagan for president after Jesse Jackson withdrew from the battle to become the candidate of the Democratic Party. Ali's motivation remains unclear. His opposition to the Vietnam War was rooted in his religious identity as a member of the Nation of Islam, which opposed wars that were not religiously sanctioned by Allah. Moreover, the Nation's denunciation of alcohol and drugs and the promotion of patriarchy and personal self-discipline could push him toward conservative political positions as the world altered around him. Reagan's support for school prayer might offer some explanation, since Ali himself continued to see himself as a promoter of religion in an increasingly secular world. A more cynical interpretation involves Ali's relationship with President Jimmy Carter. After President Ford invited Ali to the White House following his victory in Zaire, Ali announced, in response to a reporter's question, that if he voted it would probably be for Ford. However, at Don King's behest, Ali refused to endorse the president and cost Ford critical black votes in Ohio. Courted by Carter, Ali was again invited to the White House, but even more was offered the important diplomatic role in the administration's effort to garner the support of African nations for a boycott of the Moscow Olympic Games of 1980. Because Ali was embarrassed in that effort, four years later he may have been susceptible to more conservative appeals. Liberal opinion might ignore the endorsement of Reagan by other former champions, but Ali's actions engendered disappointment that a former figure of dissent had moved so far to the right, much like the nation itself. The collective sigh of regret and the general head shaking by black liberals like Andrew Young and Julian Bond and his former antiwar white followers did nothing to preserve Ali's reputation.[8]

While Ali entered the 1990s something of a forgotten man, his old nemesis George Foreman, a truly forgotten man, was on the verge of the most remarkable comeback of his career, becoming not only the world heavyweight champion but also a full-fledged crossover star. To some extent, the chain of events that occurred in Zaire now came full circle. After his born-again experience in 1977, Foreman stayed away from boxing and shunned the limelight for ten years. Having fought in the ring fueled by anger and hatred, he came to consider boxing incompatible with Christianity's ethic of love. How could he hit another man with anger and malice, he wondered, especially if that person had done nothing to him? Remarried and content, the father of many children, he ministered to his flock and helped troubled youth at what became the George Foreman Youth Center. The youth center was his way of helping young people stay out of trouble and out of jail by developing individual skills of self-discipline that would benefit them in their future lives, just as the Job Corps had done for him.

By 1987, however, Foreman discovered that trying to keep the youth center alive was draining his savings, which he would need for the education of his many children. He began speaking in churches and other venues to raise money, but he quickly tired of what seemed like begging. Applying for government grants, moreover, was time wasting, and he was far more comfortable with working to save individuals one by one than chasing ever-diminishing amounts of government money for youth programs. Rather than begging, he realized that he could raise more money by returning to the ring. Unlike Ali and other former champions who made the mistake of coming back against a current champion and losing badly, Foreman was determined to start over again from the bottom and gradually work his way into contention and, equally important, shape. After ten years away from boxing, his weight had ballooned to more than three hundred pounds, and getting in shape would take some time.

When he first announced his return to the ring, most observers were incredulous and treated him and his quest as a joke. Not only was it ridiculous that a grossly overweight thirty-eight-year-old wanted to reenter the ring to fight for the heavyweight title, but his quest also underscored how the heavyweight field had hit bottom, splintered as it was by champions recognized by numerous competing sanctioning bodies. Champions came and went, and no one could remember who they were. Only in this environment could a comic figure like Foreman even dream of a championship fight. As one sports reporter put it: "But, my friends, it is now official. Professional boxing is now a monumental joke, an iota away from wrestling, which at least makes no pretense about being anything other than a mockery for money."[9]

Ironically, however, instead of avoiding a hostile press and sulking in isolation as he would have done in the past, Foreman showed off a totally different personality that eventually won the press and the public to his side. When he was called fat he made jokes about his eating habits. Called slow, he remarked that he was as fast as it took him to get to the refrigerator. After years of preaching, he had developed a sense of humor and a confidence in himself in public that he had never displayed during and immediately after his championship years. Indeed, many commentators acknowledged that while Ali was relatively silent, Foreman was now the garrulous and verbose one. The difference was that while Ali had used his wit against his opponents or his ringside straight man, Howard Cosell, Foreman turned the joke on himself, thereby anticipating and neutralizing criticism and taking his own celebrity image down a peg. In a very real sense, he was humbling himself before the public but in a humorous way that invited boxing fans to identify with him rather than root against him. Everyone who encountered Foreman remarked on the fact that he seemed to be a totally different person from the dope who was roped by Ali in Zaire: "Eighteen years later, Foreman has rope-a-doped us all." For four years he'd let the world make fun of him—his age, his belly, and his comeback: "Not only has he allowed it, he has encouraged it and contributed to it. You had a Foreman fat joke? He had one funnier."[10]

As he fought his way into contention and turned the criticism of his age and condition against himself, Foreman also transformed his image for a new era in

American culture. As Budd Schulberg remarked, Foreman's improbable quest turned him into a black Rocky, who like the character created and portrayed by Sylvester Stallone, pursued a million-to-one shot against external forces that gave him no chance. Unlike the flashy and arrogant Ali-like champion who possessed superhuman skills, Foreman-Rocky sought redemption in the eyes of a hostile public and in himself. Starting in the late 1970s and continuing throughout the Reagan years, political and cultural observers bemoaned the absence of "true" American heroes—usually white and male—who could stand for old-fashioned values of individual success, straight masculinity, and patriotism. There had been oppositional figures like the Ali of the late 1960s or mid-1970s, but no "true" hero all Americans could look up to. As Foreman pursued the title, he attracted a wide swath of fans who turned out for his bouts. Contrary to what promoters expected, his fights began to sell out. He not only still carried the memory of his patriotic image going back to the 1968 Olympics—now suitable to a more patriotic era—he also had become an ordinary American fighting against the skepticism of society, the ravages of time, and his own personal limitations to keep hope alive. Fans flocked to him, Foreman believed, because they were middle aged and hoped that he could recapture some glory for them. Rooting for this past champion gave them a second chance to see history: "They'd grown up and had kids, and wanted their kids to love America. So they appreciated me for what I'd done. At least, that's what I was thinking as the cheers increased." A key element in his new identity was his refusal to discuss race or promote himself as a black hero. Instead, he connected with ordinary white and black Americans as one who would succeed on his abilities as an individual rather than the member of any particular group.[11]

His moment back in the spotlight first came again in 1991, when after three and a half years of fighting himself into shape, he secured a title fight against Evander Holyfield in Las Vegas. Foreman faced the usual criticism—he was too fat, too slow, and at age forty-two, too old. But he also attracted a good deal of respect as a man transformed by his religious awakening into a clean, honest, hardworking, blue-collar guy who had overcome his losses in the past and deserved a chance to show what he could do. Like the country, he had experienced defeat and humiliation, but he had endured. Foreman's comeback was part and parcel of renewed national pride and patriotism. To everyone's surprise, he gave Holyfield a real fight. Although he lost the decision, he established himself as a worthy contender for the title and redeemed himself in the eyes of the boxing world. And true to his image, the next day he was back in Houston for Sunday-morning services at his church.[12]

His newfound celebrity as an American everyman traveled far beyond the ring. In fact, his facility with the press and the media, and his "friendly" color-blind image, attracted major corporations eager for a crossover star who could appeal to blue- and white-collar customers regardless of color. Like O. J. Simpson, who sold cars for Hertz, and more spectacularly, Michael Jordan, who served as the face of Nike, Foreman became a pitchman for Meineke Mufflers, McDonald's, and in 1996 the George Foreman Lean Mean Fat-Reducing Grilling Machine. He also became a respected boxing commentator for HBO. By the end of the 1990s, Foreman had earned millions through his endorsements of commercial products. Moreover, like O. J. Simpson or Michael Jordan, he never made any hint of race or politics. Although Foreman never went so far as to say, as Simpson did, "I'm not black, I'm OJ," he had little interest in political or racial statements. His ultimate triumph was thus as a hero who showed that ordinary Americans—black and white—could achieve success as individuals within the confines of the capitalist system if only they held onto their dreams. By the 1990s he was part of a larger trend among black athletes to downplay race and racial solidarity as they reaped the rewards as individuals who were now included in American life and the American economy.[13]

Foreman's improbable comeback reached its apogee on November 5, 1994, against Michael Moorer at the MGM Grand in Las Vegas. Despite a seventeen-month layoff after a disappointing loss to Tommy Morrison for the vacant World Boxing Organization title, the forty-five-year-old Foreman managed to become the oldest man to fight for and win the heavyweight crown. As he told trainer Angelo Dundee, who also had come full circle since Zaire to work in his corner, for twenty years Foreman had been haunted by the ghosts of Zaire. In his attempt to exorcise those ghosts, he came into the ring wearing the faded boxing trunks with World Heavyweight Champion printed on them that he had worn the night he was humiliated by Ali. As the match progressed, however, the left-handed Moorer held all the cards, moving away from Foreman's power while stinging the slower challenger with right hand jabs at will, followed by powerful left hands. Bloodied and behind on the judge's cards going into the tenth round, Foreman had to knock out the champion to have any chance of victory. To do that, he had to wait for Moorer to stand in front of him so George could hit him with a powerful right. Despite warnings from his corner to keep circling away from Foreman's right, the overconfident Moorer went for a knockout standing right in front of George. That was all Foreman needed. While old and slow, he still had his power, and it was that power that knocked out Moorer. Twenty years after Zaire, Foreman was heavyweight champion of the world once again.

By winning the title, Foreman achieved "the impossible dream" and exorcised the ghosts of Zaire. Once a monster superhuman, now he was an overweight, funny teddy bear who made whites feel comfortable. Unlike ex-champ Mike Tyson, moreover, who went to prison as a convicted rapist, the very symbol of an angry, out-of-control superpredator who was the face of trapped angry ghetto youth, the new champion was a born-again preacher, a humble giant, and a million-dollar pitchman for a wide range of American products. Foreman made a fortune in ads and endorsements. Starting in 1995, he earned 40 percent of the profits of each Foreman grill sold, or $4.5 million a month. In 1999 Salton Inc. bought out the use of his name for $127.5 million in cash and another $10 million in stock. Overall, Foreman earned more from his endorsements than he ever made in the ring. In fact, when he lost his last fight and the title to Shannon Briggs in November 1997, he used his brief postfight interview with ring commentator Larry Merchant to promote the grill. Eventually, the popular kitchen device went on to sell eighty million units and Foreman became one of the wealthiest athletes in the world. In the 1990s, according to the Foreman perspective, for "good" African Americans, as well as for white America, all things were possible if one believed in oneself and the beneficence of American society. And it was with that message that Foreman went on to become a "success" preacher over the next ten years, advising listeners to his lectures and readers of his advice books that to be a "knockout entrepreneur," all one needed to do was believe in oneself, never give up, not recognize any obstacles, and believe in God. If one followed those rules, nothing could stop you—even racism, about which he had nothing to say—because in America success was available to all.[14]

George Foreman was not the only one rehabilitated by the 1990s. For Muhammad Ali the process began slowly. In 1986 he married Lonnie Williams, an intelligent and supportive young woman concerned about his physical, financial, and spiritual health. Over the following several years she worked hard to shrink his entourage and reclaim his cultural authority. She and Ali hired Thomas Hauser to oversee a vast oral history account of his career, *Muhammad Ali: His Life and Times* which came out in 1991 and served as a counterweight to his autobiography, *The Greatest*. The book sought to revive Ali's legend as an antiwar and antiracist hero, and along the way criticized his ties to the Nation of Islam and diminished his antiwhite sentiments.

The culmination occurred at the 1996 Olympic Games in Atlanta. Ali opened the games by lighting the Olympic flame. Broadcast by NBC television, the surprise appearance by Ali galvanized the stadium and the viewing audience at home. Visibly trembling with the effects of Parkinson's, the champion returned to the national and international stage once again as a popular hero. Announcer Bob Costas acknowledged Ali's debility in his commentary but emphasized that he was "still a great, great presence. Still exuding nobility and stature, and the response he evokes is part affection, part excitement, but especially respect." In turning him into an all-American hero, Olympic officials and NBC had to counter the lingering memory of Ali as an unpatriotic oppositional figure, his years as a crusader for the antiwhite Nation of Islam, and his opposition to the Vietnam War. In fact, the broadcast transformed him into a more generalized figure of inspiration. A key to this new gloss occurred at the half time of the US Dream Team's gold-medal basketball match against Yugoslavia, when IOC president Juan Antonio Samaranch gave Ali a replica of the gold medal he had claimed to have thrown away in protest against the racist treatment he had received in a segregated Louisville restaurant and a confrontation with white supremacist bikers shortly after winning his gold medal at the 1960 Rome Olympics. Detailed as a key event in becoming a radical Black Muslim in *The Greatest*, the backstory now was declared untrue. Rather than a protest symbol, the medal had instead been lost. Forgiven by the nation, Ali saw his role as "Mankind coming together. Martin Luther King's home. Muslims see me with the torch."[15]

Visibly struggling to hold the torch steady, Ali stood as a heroic symbol of inspiration and persistence against all obstacles. Despite some initial reluctance, he agreed to serve as the face of the Michael J. Fox Foundation's campaign against Parkinson's. Similar to Foreman's championship victory, he showed that not even a devastating disease could stop him. In that sense, Ali became a generalized symbol of moral transcendence and possibility rather than a crusader for a particular religion or politics. His Muslim past was diminished and his critique of racism was now generalized as criticism of all forms of religious and racial discrimination; he became an icon of persistence. Yet he was not just a figure of moral inspiration; he was finally a safe figure available for commercial exploitation. His danger lessened, advertising contracts began to roll in until his death: Gucci, Movado, Adidas, and countless more. By the time the Muhammad Ali Freedom Center was inaugurated in 2005, the family was able to attract the major corporate backing of Ford, General Electric, and Yum Brands. There was also a partnership with the United Nations for a venture that said nothing substantial about his religious and political past and a good deal about his role as a fighter for global peace and tolerance, civil rights, and equality. The center's mission statement said it all: "To promote respect, hope, and understanding, and to inspire adults and children everywhere to be as great as they can be." Based on the ads, the Olympics, and the Freedom Center, Ali was once again the Greatest, but few could comprehend why he had ever been so controversial.[16]

Aside from the two major protagonists in the Rumble in the Jungle, *When We Were Kings* reminded the public of the crucial roles in that colossal sporting event played by two other black men, promoter Don King and President Mobutu Sese Seko of Zaire. Along with Ali, both King and Mobutu turned out to be the big winners of the fight. Officially, King was a vice president of Video Techniques in 1974. Over time, King mentioned Video Techniques and Hank Schwartz less and less and Don King Productions more and more. In the public's mind, King was the only man who could have put together an international championship bout of this magnitude. Almost as much as Ali, he represented the aspirations and potential achievements of black America as central players on the American and world stage.[17]

The public role he played at the Rumble in the Jungle and his association with Ali propelled King to the forefront of the boxing world. Along the way he shouldered his partner Schwartz into a secondary role in the Ali-Bugner fight in Malaysia. By the time of Ali's Thrilla in Manila against Joe Frazier, according to a disgruntled Schwartz, King "had effectively hijacked the event and established himself as the promoter of the event." Their partnership was essentially over, forcing Schwartz to rebuild Video Techniques to concentrate once again on the satellite communications end of the business.[18]

King's growing reputation for underhandedness did not go unnoticed. After Manila, Ali's manager Herbert Muhammad stepped back from too close an association with King because he did not think the promoter could be trusted. For the third Ken Norton bout in 1976, in fact, Herbert had King's old enemy Bob Arum handle the promotion. To a degree he was right. By the time of Ali's disastrous comeback against Larry Holmes, King was the promoter but he skimmed off $1 million from Ali's promised $8 million prize; Ali was forced to sue him in court. Through the promise of huge paydays for heavyweight championship fights, however, King was able to control the heavyweight division. Banking on black pride and racial solidarity, as he had with Ali and Foreman, as well as promises of great wealth and fame, King used his control of heavyweight champion Larry Holmes to become the kingpin of boxing. He remained so through the next century. Holmes eventually sued King for skimming from his purses, as did many other black heavyweights who came under his charge.

As the best-known promoter in boxing, King illustrated the rising prominence of African Americans in many areas of American life while at the same time demonstrating the harsh reality of the prejudiced "free" market to which minorities were forced to adapt. The emergence of closed-circuit television, satellite communications, and the eagerness of foreign and domestic millionaires to invest in international matches worked to transform boxing into a worldwide business. With his ability to negotiate with foreign governments and black boxers as he chased capital wherever it existed, King could promise black heavyweights that he would protect them from rapacious white promoters and bring them huge paydays in bouts around the globe. In the process, King became a millionaire who liked to remind people of his success. "I will never apologize for possessing wealth," King noted. "I have nothing to apologize for. I have earned every penny of it." As a former hustler he achieved that wealth by understanding the dog-eat-dog nature of the boxing business and by skating along the edges of illegality. Throughout his career, he found himself in and out of court for a series of crimes. Although he was never convicted, several aides were not so lucky.[19]

Perhaps the most notorious case was the United States Boxing Championships Tournament in 1977. Cosponsored by ABC and *The Ring* magazine, which validated the credentials of the contestants and originated the idea, the tournament was intended to create bouts for American fighters up and down the weight divisions to bring American boxers back into the prominence they had lost in the lesser divisions to fighters from other countries. As a sign of the tournament's high profile, Howard Cosell and then heavyweight contender George Foreman were hired as broadcasters. With his genius for grasping the cultural moment, King publicized the tournaments as a boost to American patriotism and a free gift to armed forces personnel "as thanks to them for protecting us around the world." The US boxing team at the 1976 Montreal Olympics won a record number of gold medals, led by the clean-cut Sugar Ray Leonard, Howard Davis, and the two brothers Michael and Leon Spinks. Building on the nationalist fervor that boxing witnessed as a result of these victories and as an antidote to losing the war, King publicized the tournament as an opportunity to foster a whole new crop of Rocky Balboas who otherwise would never get a chance to shine and succeed.[20]

That King had his finger on the nation's desire for patriotic heroes is hard to deny. In pursuit of the widest possible audience, he secured the cooperation of ABC and the US Navy. A memo to King from the navy pledged support for the tournament in exchange for King's helping the armed forces attract black recruits. In a post-Vietnam era when the draft no longer existed and recruitment had dropped considerably, the Defense Department signed on to this unprecedented program, agreeing to hold the elimination bouts at air force and navy bases and aboard a US Navy aircraft carrier. This delighted American service personnel but also ABC, which would save on expenses and achieve a respectable, patriotic setting far removed from the grimy clubs associated with boxing's seamy past. As one Defense Department official put it, boxing was popular, and "King *is* boxing." While King denied that any deal was made, he emphasized his willingness to recruit for the armed services. "To be able to serve your country is what a man is all about," and the military was great "for blacks to learn how to use their skills."[21]

Had the tournament run its course it might have been remembered as a great American sporting spectacle and a precedent for future endeavors to boost American boxing. Unfortunately, after several rounds, rumors emerged of gross irregularities, and ABC had to appoint a special investigator to look into the matter. According to Edward Kiersh, "The Watergate of boxing" had begun. Managers of fighters not invited to participate charged that they were excluded because they failed to agree to kick back a portion of their prize money or because they did not agree to have King's partners manage their fighters should they win. In addition, several fighters claimed that they lost their bouts because they refused to knuckle under to King's control. Heavyweight Scott LeDoux and his manager charged that two of King's advisers, Al Braverman and Paddy Flood, controlled most of the fighters in the tournament and influenced who would win. To take part, LeDoux claimed he had to pay a booking fee between 10 percent and 15 percent, as did other fighters. Finally, investigators charged that *The Ring* failed to adequately vet the rankings of several boxers. Its own reputation at stake, ABC canceled the rest of the tournament, several King associates were fired, and both *Ring* associate editor John Ort and James Farley, the tournament's commissioner, had to step down. While King's reputation was tarnished, he escaped prison.[22]

Because of his promotion of six Ali bouts and control over Larry Holmes, however, King managed to rebuild his reputation through hard work, big paydays, growing connections to the WBC, which had control of Mexican and Latin American fighters, and his tireless work ethic. Through it all there remained an odor of corruption and illegality, however. King's response was that he was a black man from the ghetto who was a target for the boxing establishment that could not accept a black man in such a prominent position. At the same time, he argued that he did not do anything differently than other major boxing kingpins, whether Frankie Carbo or Mike Jacobs. In addition, King maintained that having his son manage fighters that King promoted—a clear conflict of interest—was no different from the way the Lou Duva family or the Dundees operated. However, what was also true is that he was charged by black boxers with cheating and mistreating them, and this story recurred from Ali through Earnie Shavers, Larry Holmes, Tim Witherspoon, and Mike

Tyson. As Larry Holmes put it, "Don King looks black, lives white, and thinks green."[23]

King was probably correct in his assertion that he did not do anything different from other boxing promoters. Still, he was and is a figure of black sporting business success, and in that he is a pioneer, as he would tell anyone who would listen. Up from the ghetto, a former numbers king, a former murderer, a former prisoner, he managed to succeed in a hostile white world—but in an era when his talents of nurturing black pride in boxers made it all possible and when he had white mentors who needed his skills to relate to black fighters. This is indeed remarkable, but it was clear that King quickly adapted to the capitalist system that boxing so often symbolized. A giant success with a vast farm in Ohio, offices atop Rockefeller Center, and worldwide influence, he represented the conclusion of the era by the 1990s. As he told one interviewer: "Martin Luther wanted to take us to the promised land. Jesse Jackson wanted to take us to church. I want to take us to the bank." For all the talk of black pride and solidarity, King was a symbol of success in a dog-eat-dog realm where only the top dogs survived.[24]

In *When We Were Kings*, as in real life, President Mobutu Sese Seko of Zaire was the distant presence who loomed over the Rumble in the Jungle. With his leopard-skin hat, glasses, and distinctive walking stick, his portrait graced Mai 20 Stadium as the powerful figure most responsible for delivering this gift to his people and the world. In the immediate aftermath of the bout it appeared that he had established himself as a strong leader and a symbol of African grandeur. With his authenticity policy and his move toward nationalization of foreign-owned businesses, he seemed to have successfully navigated a third way between communism and capitalism. At the same time, it looked like he had managed to take control over the identity of his African nation for the first time. In an era of Black Power and Pan-African hopes, for a brief moment he attracted a portion of the American black community with his nationalist rhetoric. Whatever they might have thought privately, both Ali and Foreman—and members of their entourages—paid homage to the beneficence of this strong, independent African leader.

Only the *Nation* magazine initially dissented from this glowing picture of a leader who symbolized African grandeur and Third World independence versus neocolonialism. In his postmortem of the fight, Stephen Weissman pointed out that the secretive Risnelia corporation was in fact owned and controlled by Mobutu. The offshore company was a shell entity designed to transfer money from the Zaire national treasury to Mobutu. As a result, Risnelia paid for the fight out of public funds, but banked the profits for the private benefit of Mobutu. Profits were not the major issue initially, however. For the regime, the goal was attracting foreign investment with an image of stable political and economic leadership. Over time, however, the balance shifted as Mobutu increasingly skimmed millions of the public's money. Yet in the growing era of global capitalism, the fight's promoters proved willing to overlook this financial abuse because they themselves engaged in similar practices. Chartering their own companies in Panama was a way to avoid American taxes and public scrutiny and facilitate their economic involvement around the world. In the modern world of boxing, capital moved freely, if often secretly, from the constraints of any particular nation. With its reliance on offshore shell companies to hide profits and avoid taxes, boxing helped pioneer the emergence of unregulated global capitalism.[25]

By the late 1970s, Zaire's image as a symbol of African greatness and enemy of neocolonialism was shattered. While the afterglow of the fight still lingered in the world's imagination, the economy of Zaire plunged into chaos. The policy of nationalization known as Zairianization turned over the foreign control of agriculture and commerce, especially by Belgians, to local control in 1973. The result was a scramble for wealth among Mobutu's supporters and a division of the spoils to major ethnic groups. Expatriates fled and businesses failed. At about the same time, the nation suffered from the steep rise in the price of oil after the oil embargo by the Organization of Petroleum-Exporting Countries, and the simultaneous drop in the price of copper. In the subsequent turmoil of inflation and depression, the economy never recovered. Mobutu abandoned authenticity and he was forced more heavily than before to rely on brutality to remain in power as he and his allies became even more corrupt. Zaire came to be known as a kleptocracy. By the 1980s and 1990s, public investment in infrastructure had collapsed and nothing seemed to be working—telephones, roads, electricity.[26]

Mobutu's delicate balancing act of Africa, the West, and the Third World also unraveled after the Rumble in the Jungle. He had forged an in-between identity that relied on an increasing anticolonial image as well as an alliance with the United States. After losing so badly in Vietnam, President Ford and his national security adviser Henry Kissinger saw Angola as the place for a muscular response to the Soviet Union and communism. Prompted by the United States to invade Angola in November 1975, to preserve the Portuguese colonial regime in alliance with South Africa, Mobutu lost his gloss as an independent leader and reconfirmed his status as a puppet of the Central Intelligence Agency. Increasingly, through two wars occasioned by the invasion of former Katanganese province secessionists living in Angola, he received the backing of the United States against communism and chaos in Africa. Supported by the United States, though sometimes with distaste, Mobutu's authority and brutality went unchecked.[27]

While the Ali-Foreman fight highlighted a new image for Zaire, in the end the collapse of the economy and the rise of authoritarianism in the country failed to change the West's perception of the former Congo as the heart of darkness. In fact, during the run-up to the bout, American and other Western writers and reporters were increasingly baffled by the regime's censorship policies, the inexplicable bureaucratic delays, and the role of the military in walling off Foreman from the press. One of the major images taken away from the country was that during the delay forced by Foreman's cut, both fighters were prisoners of the government. Similarly, images of backwardness and exoticism still reigned among sportswriters at least, and perhaps among fight fans in general. After all, the title match has continued to be known as "The Rumble in the Jungle," which the Zairian government detested. George Plimpton spent an inordinate amount of time investigating the role of witch doctors in the fight's outcome; Henry Schwartz celebrated the fight's successful conclusion by traveling to the interior to dance with the Watusi warriors, followed by a special dinner that featured the hands of a gorilla as the main course. In the 1990s, *When We Were Kings* added to the imagery by treating the African drumming that filled the stadium before, during, and after the fight, as well as Miriam Makeba's darting, snakelike performance at Zaire 74 as major leitmotifs of the event. In an Africa as primitive as this, according to the movie, the strong hand of a Mobutu was required.[28]

By the 1990s, the Congo once again had become the symbol for all that was wrong with Africa. Zaire looked like a failed state as rebellions grew, internal wars over territory increased, and Mobutu seemed brutal and out of touch. Finally, in 1996, as Ali and Foreman were enjoying their renewed fame, Mobutu was forced to flee. Riddled with cancer, he died in 1997, his illness serving as a symbol for the *corps politique* of the land he had ruled since 1965. It was easy to blame Mobutu as a symbol of modern Africa, and less easy for Western powers to accept complicity for supporting such a dictator in return for access to Zaire's vast mineral riches and assistance against communist rebels in Africa. Similarly, it was difficult to accept colonial and imperialist responsibility for insisting that such a vast territory made up of more than two hundred ethnic groups could form one national entity. The lines on the map created by Henry Stanley never fit the realities on the ground. Tragically the citizens of Zaire paid for the sins of the West as well as for the authoritarian policies of Mobutu.

In the end, *When We Were Kings* offered a nostalgic look back into the past when great black figures walked the land. That it was primarily nostalgia was created by the shift in the public images of Ali and Foreman. By the 1990s Ali was in the midst of transformation into a religious saint whose humanism knew no bounds and hence was suitable for lionizing and commercializing. Foreman's religious conversion transformed him into a friendly giant, an ordinary American hero who, like Ali, was depicted as a model of success. Gone was racism and poverty, present was the idea that if one believed and persisted—against obstacles of poverty or Parkinson's—one could succeed. In this subdued political atmosphere, Don King stood out as the representative of the system's willingness to accept new voices and new peoples on an equal basis—much like Zaire was able to compete with New York for the bout—but also with the understanding that this was a rapacious form of equality in a world dominated by the market. In their ability to navigate the dog-eat-dog nature of this neoliberal and neocolonial world, both Don King and Mobutu symbolized that only the strong survived and the weak would have to look out for themselves. Still, while Foreman seemed the perfect embodiment of a market society open to all, there radiated out from his friendly visage the idea of Christian love that could be utilized to overcome society's artificial barriers between people. As for Ali, although his image, too, had softened and his rebellious edge had been transmuted into a soft and fuzzy portrait of rectitude, principle, and brotherhood, there would always remain the image of the fighter who was willing to challenge the world's most powerful government in the name of religious duty and racial protest. Faded, to be sure, but not forgotten, Ali, with his use of sports as a platform to challenge American policy, would find new life as an inspiration to black athletes such as Colin Kaepernick and LeBron James, who decades after Ali have unleashed a wave of protests against police brutality and the murder of African Americans.

Despite the fate of the individual participants, the Rumble in the Jungle stood as a spectacular event balanced between two worlds. By bringing black champions to the heart of Africa, the fight emphasized the entrance of new players in the world's cultural and political firmament. Ali, Foreman, King, and Mobutu were all signs of the growing power and presence of African Americans, African American culture, and the Third World. At the same time, new technologies such as the communications satellite, the computer, and the jet plane meant that different cultural figures—especially sports and musical celebrities—would play a much greater role than particular nations in the creation of world culture. Modern technology and communications also meant that huge sporting and musical events could be held anywhere on the globe—hence Zaire, Malaysia, and the Philippines. However, to put these superevents together required vast amount of capital, made possible by deals with various dictators and secretive offshore banks and corporations. In this way, the new global sporting world was a harbinger of the world we live in today—towering figures of sport from minority backgrounds operating in a world dominated by market values. The stars reap the benefits, and lesser lights, like so many poor African Americans and Africans, are left far behind.[29]

NOTES

INTRODUCTION

1 Norman Mailer, *The Fight* (1975; London: Penguin Books, 1991); George Plimpton, *Shadow Box: An Amateur in the Ring* (Boston: Little, Brown, 1977); Budd Schulberg, "Journey to Zaire," *Newsday*, October 1974, reprinted in *Sparring with Hemingway* (Chicago: Ivan R. Dee, 1995), 169–81; *When We Were Kings*, produced and directed by Leon Gast (DAS Films, David Sonenberg Productions, Polygram Filmed Entertainment, 1997), DVD, 89 mins.

2 Michael Ezra, *Muhammad Ali: The Making of an American Icon* (Philadelphia: Temple University Press, 2009), 154–55. Other accounts of the bout that emphasize Ali's personal redemption are Muhammad Ali, with Richard Durham, *The Greatest, My Own Story* (1975; New York: Ballantine Books, 1977); *The Greatest*, produced by John Marshall, directed by Tom Gries and Monte Hellman (Columbia Pictures, 1977), 101 mins.; *Ali*, produced and directed by Michael Mann (Columbia Pictures, 2001), 157 mins.

3 For Ali as a 1960s hero, see Mike Marqusee, *Redemption Song: Muhammad Ali and the Spirit of the Sixties* (London: Verso, 1999); and Budd Schulberg, *Loser and Still Champion: Muhammad Ali* (Garden City, NJ: Doubleday, 1972). See also Leigh Monteville, *Sting Like a Bee: Muhammad Ali vs. the USA, 1966–1971* (New York: Random House, 2017); and David Remnick, *King of the World: Muhammad Ali and the Rise of an American Hero* (New York: Random House, 1998). For the first comprehensive biography of Ali, see Jonathan Eig, *Ali: A Life* (New York: Houghton, Mifflin, Harcourt, 2017). For the general athletic revolt expressed in the 1968 Olympics, see Amy Bass, *Not the Triumph but the Struggle: The 1968 Olympics and the Making of the Black Athlete* (Minneapolis: University of Minnesota Press, 2002); Harry Edwards, *The Revolt of the Black Athlete* (New York: Free Press, 1969); Douglas Hartmann, *Race, Culture and the Revolt of the Black Athlete: The 1968 Olympic Protests and Their Aftermath* (Chicago: University of Chicago Press, 2003); and Othello Harris, "Muhammad Ali and the Revolt of the Black Athlete," in *Muhammad Ali, The People's Champ*, ed. Elliott Gorn (Urbana: University of Illinois Press, 1995), 54–69. For breadwinner liberalism, see Robert O. Self, *All in the Family: The Realignment of American Democracy since the 1960s* (New York: Hill and Wang, 2012), 17–46.

4 William L. Van Deburg, *Black Camelot: African-American Culture Heroes in Their*

Times, 1960–1980 (Chicago: University of Chicago Press, 1997). For the debate about the meaning of black manhood, see various letters to the editor in *Jet* during the late 1960s and 1970s.

5 For an overview of the boycott movement against South Africa, see Douglas Booth, "Hitting Apartheid for Six? The Politics of the South African Sports Boycott," *Journal of Contemporary History* 38, no. 3 (2003): 477–93.

6 Penny Von Eschen, *Satchmo Blows Up the World: Jazz Ambassadors Play the Cold War* (Cambridge, MA: Harvard University Press, 2006) analyzes the role of jazz musicians in American policy during the Cold War; Damion L. Thomas, *Globetrotting, African American Athletes and Cold War Politics* (Urbana: University of Illinois Press, 2012), examines the role of sports in the Cold War and has the most detail on State Department–sponsored tours.

7 Richard Hoffer, *Bouts of Mania: Ali, Frazier, and Foreman and an America on the Ropes* (Boston: Da Capo Press, 2014) provides a useful narrative of the global boxing phenomenon of the 1970s.

8 Dave Anderson, "Chant of the Holy War: Ali, Bomaye," *New York Times*, 28 October 1974, n.p., in Ali Vertical File, Schomburg Center for Research in Black Culture, New York City. The flowering of and the debate about Black Power and black nationalism, both of which played a crucial role in the match, continued its important role into the 1970s. See William L. Van Deburg, *New Day in Babylon: The Black Power Movement and American Culture, 1965–1975* (Chicago: University of Chicago Press, 1992); and Peniel Joseph, *Wait 'Til the Midnight Hour: A Narrative History of Black Power in America* (New York: Henry Holt and Co., 2006).

9 Theresa Runstedtler *Jack Johnson, Rebel Sojourner: Boxing in the Shadow of the Global Color Line* (Berkeley: University of California Press, 2012). See also Gail Bederman, *Manliness and Civilization: A Cultural History of Gender and Race in the United States* (Chicago: University of Chicago Press, 1995); Randy Roberts, *Papa Jack, Jack Johnson and the Era of the White Hopes* (New York: Macmillan, 1983). For more on the white masculine ideal, see John F. Kasson, *Houdini, Tarzan, and the Perfect Man: The White Male Body and the Challenge of Modernity in America* (New York: Hill and Wang, 2001).

10 Lewis A. Erenberg, *The Greatest Fight of Our Generation: Louis vs. Schmeling* (New York: Oxford University Press, 2005). Brian Bunk, "Harry Wills and the Image of the Black Boxer from Jack Johnson to Joe Louis," *Journal of Sport History* 39, no. 1 (Spring 2012), 63–80, argues that black heavyweight Harry Wills prefigured Louis's respectability strategy to campaign for a title match with Jack Dempsey during the 1920s.

11 On the 1970s as a transformational era, see Thomas Borstelmann, *The 1970s: A New Global History from Civil Rights to Economic Inequality* (Princeton, NJ: Princeton University Press, 2012). Invaluable on the shift since the 1970s as manifested in athletics is Walter LaFeber, *Michael Jordan and the New Global Capitalism* (1999; New York: W. W. Norton, 2002). Gene Collier, "Mr. Jordan, You're No Muhammad Ali," *Pittsburgh Post-Gazette*, 20 January 1999, n.p., as quoted in LaFeber, *Michael Jordan*, 188. For other important analyses of the 1970s, see Peter Carroll, *It Seemed Like Nothing Happened: The Tragedy and Promise of American Life during the 1970s* (New York: Holt, Rinehart & Winston, 1982); Bruce Schulman, *The Seventies: The Great Shift in American Culture, Society, and Politics* (2001; New York: Da Capo Press, 2002); Beth Bailey and David Farber,

eds., *America in the Seventies* (Lawrence: University Press of Kansas, 2004). For more recent works, see Self, *All in the Family*; and Jefferson Cowie, *Stayin' Alive: The 1970s and the Last Days of the Working Class* (New York: New Press, 2010).

12 William Graebner, "America's Poseidon Adventure: A Nation in Existential Despair," in Bailey and Farber, *America in the Seventies*, 157–80.

13 "Foreman Owes It All to Ali," BBC Europe, http://news.bbc.co.uk/sport2/hi/boxing/3957807.stm#top, 29 October 2004.

CHAPTER 1

1 On breadwinner liberalism and military manhood, see Robert O. Self, *All in the Family: The Realignment of American Democracy since the 1960s* (New York: Hill and Wang, 2012), 17–24.

2 Tracy E. K'Meyer, *Civil Rights in the Gateway to the South: Louisville, Kentucky, 1945–1980* (Lexington: University of Kentucky Press, 2009); and author interview with historian John Cumbler, 25 October 2016.

3 Jack Olsen, "Growing Up Scared in Louisville," *Sports Illustrated*, 18 April 1966, 95–99.

4 Olsen, "Growing Up Scared," 97–98. For Martin and the bike, see Houston Horn, "Who Made Me Is Me!" *Sports Illustrated*, 25 September 1961, 40.

5 For Fred Stoner, see Michael Ezra, *Muhammad Ali: The Making of an Icon* (Philadelphia: Temple University Press, 2009), 17–18.

6 Nat Fleischer, "Fleischer Talked Harmonica Boy Clay out of Jeopardy at Olympic Games in Rome," *The Ring*, August 1967, 6–7, 34, discusses how his fraternization threatened to disrupt his training for the final round. Horn, "Who Made Me Is Me!" *Sports Illustrated*, 42.

7 Horn, "Who Made Me Is Me!" 42; Thomas Hauser, *Muhammad Ali: His Life and Times* (New York: Simon and Schuster, 1992), 28. For Joe Louis and sacrifice, see Lewis A. Erenberg, *The Greatest Fight of Our Generation: Louis vs. Schmeling* (New York: Oxford University Press, 2005), 166–98.

8 Muhammad Ali, with Richard Durham, *The Greatest, My Own Story* (New York: Ballantine Books, 1975), 24, 55–80, 61 (on "mud huts"); "Huge Civic Welcome Awes Olympic Champion," *Louisville Defender*, 15 September 1960, 1, 2, 16; Clarence Matthews, "Ambassador Clay" *Louisville Defender*, 1 September 1960, 13.

9 Ezra, *Muhammad Ali*, 12–17.

10 For boxing investigations and its criminal links, see Steven Riess, "Only the Ring Was Square: Frankie Carbo and the Underworld Control of American Boxing," *International Journal of the History of Sport* 5 (May 1988): 29–52; Jeffrey T. Sammons, *Beyond the Ring: The Role of Boxing in American Society* (Urbana: University of Illinois Press, 1990), 130–83. For Liston's mob ties, see Robert Steen, *Sonny Boy: The Life and Strife of Sonny Liston* (London: Kingswood Press, 1993); and Nick Tosches, *The Devil and Sonny Liston* (Boston: Little, Brown, 2000).

11 Ezra, *Muhammad Ali*, 20–26. Details of the contract are in Angelo Dundee, with Bert Randolph Sugar, *My View from the Corner: A Life in Boxing* (New York: McGraw-Hill, 2008), 59.

12 LeRoy Neiman, "Real Clay Is Sincere, Determined," *The Ring*, January 1967, 35.

13 For new fighting style and generational drama, see Budd Schulberg, *Loser and Still Champion: Muhammad Ali* (Garden City, NJ: Doubleday, 1972), 33–36. On

masculinity and homosexuality, see Self, *All in the Family*, 75–100; James Gilbert, *Men in the Middle: Searching for Masculinity in the 1950s* (Chicago: University of Chicago Press, 2005); and Barbara Ehrenreich, *Hearts of Men: American Dreams and the Flight from Commitment* (New York: Anchor Books, 1983).

14 Ali and Dundee quoted in Hauser, *Muhammad Ali*, 39. Ali, *The Greatest*, 146–47. For predictions and press, see Houston Horn, "Fast Talk and a Slow Fight," *Sports Illustrated*, 31 July 1961, 44; "Elusive Prophet," *Jet*, 7 February 1963, 7. For Clay as celebrity, see Dundee, *My View*, 68, 76 (on boasting and predicting). Andrew Joseph Hale, "How Voice Operates in Popular Culture through the Performance Persona of Muhammad Ali" (MA thesis, San Jose State University, CA, 1994), has an excellent analysis of Ali's verbal style as the key to his public persona.

15 Ezra, *Muhammad Ali*, 32–33, discusses Gorgeous George's influence.

16 Angelo Dundee, quoted in Jack Olsen, "All Alone with the Future," *Sports Illustrated*, 9 May 1966, 35–36. Ali, quoted in Horn, "Who Made Me Is Me!" 41–42.

17 Dundee, quoted in Olsen, "All Alone," 53. Ring vets cited in "How Boxing Experts Rank Clay," *Sports Illustrated*, 9 May 1966, 53.

18 For Ali as a 1960s symbol, see Mike Marqusee, *Redemption Song: Muhammad Ali and the Spirit of the Sixties* (London: Verso, 1999); Jeffrey T. Sammons, "Rebel with a Cause: Muhammad Ali as Sixties Protest Symbol," in *Muhammad Ali: The People's Champ*, ed. Elliott Gorn (Urbana: University of Illinois Press, 1995), 160–64; Schulberg, *Loser and Still Champion*, 33–36; *Requiem for a Heavyweight*, produced by David Susskind, directed by Ralph Nelson (Columbia Pictures, 1962). Cassius Senior is from Horn, "Who Made Me Is Me!", 40. Clay, quoted on Louis, "'I Don't Want Louis's Tax Problems,' Says Clay," *Jet*, 24 November 1960, 54.

19 For generational revolt, see Dundee, *My View*, 61.

20 "Clay Pours in Gloves, Fulfills 4th Round Boast," *Jet*, 29 November 1962, 54 (for "Youth versus Age and Experience"). For Clay's prediction and Moore's appearance, see Dundee, *My View*, 73. Ezra, *Muhammad Ali*, 40–53, calls the Moore fight a seminal text and Clay a good-natured bad boy through 1963.

21 On JFK, the NAACP, and liberal views of the two fighters, see Alan H. Levy, *Floyd Patterson: A Boxer and a Gentleman* (Jefferson, NC: McFarland & Co., 2008), 140–59. Clay's role in the revival of boxing is from Dan Daniel, "Who Will Be New Pilot of Expansion Era for Heavies?" *The Ring*, July 1967, 8–9, 11–13, 33, quote at 8. See also Dundee, *My View*, 78–79.

22 "Liston-Patterson Match Duplicates; Clay Next?" *Jet*, 8 August 1963, 60, for Liston's invincibility. Dundee, *My View*, 91 (for "old man"). Cake and poem are in "Clay Has His Say about Way He Spends His Day," *Jet*, 6 February 1964, 58–59.

23 Dundee, *My View*, 92–96. *Jet*'s take is from Bobbie Barbee, "Cassius Clay Follows Prediction," *Jet*, 12 March 1964, 57.

24 For the best account of the Liston bout, see David Remnick, *King of the World: Muhammad Ali and the Rise of an American Hero* (New York: Random House, 1998), 183–204.

25 "165 Million Europeans Watch Fight," *New York Times*, 26 February 1964, sec. 3, 2; and "Fight Facts," *Chicago Tribune*, 25 February 1964, sec. 3, 3.

26 For Clay's press conference, see Bobbie Barbee, "Cassius Clay Follows Prediction," *Jet*, 12 March 1964, 56–57. See also Barbee, "Will Link with Malcolm X Hurt Cassius Clay's Boxing Career?" *Jet*, 26 March 1964, 50–57.

27 Jack Olsen, "Learning Elijah's Advanced Lessons in Hate," *Sports Illustrated*, 2 May 1966, 37–43; Ali, *The Greatest*, 23–25; Randy Roberts and Johnny Smith,

Blood Brothers: The Fatal Friendship between Muhammad Ali and Malcolm X (New York: Basic Books, 2016), xx–xxiv.

28 Ali, *The Greatest*, 24, 55–80.

29 Gerald Early, "Muhammad Ali as Third World Hero," *Ideas from the National Humanities Center* 9, no. 1 (2002): 6. For more on Ali's racial views and quotes about blackness, see Olsen, "Learning Elijah's Advanced Lessons," 38.

30 "Clay Has His Say about How He Spends His Day," 58–59. For similar sentiments, see "'What's So Bad about Black Muslims?' Clay Asks," *Jet*, 24 October 1963, 57; and Bobbie E. Barbee, "Will Link with Malcolm X Hurt Cassius Clay's Boxing Career?" *Jet*, 26 March 1964, 50–57.

31 Ali quoted in Olsen, "Learning Elijah's Advanced Lessons," 43; Barbee, "Will Link with Malcolm X Hurt?" 51.

32 On name controversy, see Robert Lipsyte, "The Champion Looks Down at His Title," *New York Times*, 24 March 1964, 4; first Cannon quote from Hauser, *Muhammad Ali*, 102; second Cannon quote from Jimmy Cannon, column, *NY Journal American*, 26 January 1965; Greene quote from Hauser, *Muhammad Ali*, 104; "I Don't Steal," *Amsterdam News*, 28 March 1964, 28.

33 Charles P. Howard Sr., "Muhammad Ali (Cassius Clay) Serious Young Man in Ghana," *Baltimore Afro-American*, 6 June 1964, 20, in Ali Vertical File, Schomburg Center for Research in Black Culture, New York; and "Alas, Poor Cassius!" *Ebony*, July 1965, 144, Ali Vertical File, Schomburg Center.

34 "Alas, Poor Cassius!" *Ebony*, July 1965, 144, Ali Vertical File, Schomburg Center.

35 Malcolm X, with Alex Haley, *Autobiography of Malcolm X* (New York: Grove Press, 1964), 306–8. David K. Wiggins, "Victory for Allah," in *Muhammad Ali: The People's Champ*, ed. Elliott Gorn (Urbana: University of Illinois Press, 1995), 94–95. "I'm champion of the whole world" quote from Marqusee, *Redemption Song*, 82–83, 102–23 (Black Atlantic). "My people's background" quote from Barbee, "Will Link with Malcolm X Hurt," 56. For Ali's role in the conflict between Malcolm X and Elijah Muhammad, see Manning Marable, *Malcolm X: A Life of Reinvention* (New York: Viking Press, 2011); and Roberts and Smith, *Blood Brothers*.

36 Early, "Muhammad Ali as Third World Hero," *Ideas* 9, no. 1 (2002): 6. For an example of his bragging going over well in Ghana, see "Report Clay Revives 'Lip,'" *Jet*, 4 June 1964, 54–55.

37 Howard, "Muhammad Ali (Cassius) Serious Young Man in Ghana," *Baltimore Afro-American*, 6 June 1964 (first quote); "Muhammad Ali in Africa," *Sports Illustrated*, 1 June 1964, 20 (second quote). Ali quote about meeting Nkrumah is cited in Early, "Muhammad Ali as Third World Hero," 13, probably from *Evening News*, 20 May 1964.

38 "M. Ali (Clay) Says Imperialism Defaces Your Country's Image," *Republic* (Cairo), 5 June 1964, 9; and "Muhammad Ali's Personality," *Republic* (Cairo), 7 June 1964, 9.

39 Traveling companion from Hauser, *Muhammad Ali*, 12. For more on the trip, see Marqusee, *Redemption Song*, 124–29. Thomas R. Hietala, in "Ali and the Age of Bare-Knuckle Politics," in *Muhammad Ali: The People's Champ*, ed. Elliott Gorn (Urbana: University of Illinois Press, 1995), 133, draws similar conclusions.

40 For Fleischer's view, see "Champ Ali Named *Ring*'s Fighter of Month," *Jet*, 1 July 1965, 53.

41 Floyd Patterson, "I Want to Destroy Clay," *Sports Illustrated*, 19 October 1964,

42–61; Floyd Patterson, "Cassius Clay Must Be Beaten," *Sports Illustrated*, 11 October 1965, 79–98; and Muhammad Ali, *Playboy* interview, 1965, cited in Dundee, *My View*, 115–16, 116 (for importance of name).

42 A good description of the match is in Hauser, *Muhammad Ali*, 139–42.

43 For the role of Main Bout, see Michael Ezra, *Muhammad Ali: The Making of an Icon* (Philadelphia: Temple University Press, 2009), 93–118. Ali's announcement in H. J. McFall, "Cassius Clay Tells Plan to Form a Negro Company," *Louisville Defender*, 13 January 1966, 1. For more details, see "Jim Brown, Muhammad Ali Plan Ring Organization," *Jet*, 27 January 1966, 57; and Dan Daniel, "Army? Terrell? Where Is Clay Headed?" *The Ring*, March 1966, 7–8, 63.

44 On the draft, see Jeffrey T. Sammons, *Beyond the Ring: The Role of Boxing in American Society* (Urbana: University of Illinois Press, 1990), 200–217; Suzanne Freedman, Clay v. United States: *Muhammad Ali Objects to War* (Springfield, NJ: Enslow Publishers, 1997). Mendel Rivers quoted in "Rivers May Seek Change in Draft," *New York Times*, 26 August 1966, 3; Ali quoted in Robert Boyle, "Champ in the Jug?" *Sports Illustrated*, 10 April 1967, 30. The role of the Justice Department and the FBI, which it oversaw, raises suspicions of a conspiracy to negate Ali's dangerous influence by drafting or jailing him. For the FBI's COINTELPRO program designed to disrupt black organizations and undermine black organizations, see Roberts and Smith, *Blood Brothers*, 162, 171. Self, *All in the Family*, 52–56, argues that expanding the draft pool to include formerly unqualified black, Chicano, and poor white men was part of the War on Poverty's attempt to use the military to provide them with the proper discipline and employment skills for them to assume their roles as breadwinners. This policy led to higher casualty rates for these populations.

45 Ali quoted by Robert Lipsyte in Hauser, *Muhammad Al*, 144–45; Red Smith, *New York Herald Tribune*, 23 February 1966.

46 Tunney is quoted in Ali, *The Greatest*, 163. For Ali's depiction of his critics, see Tex Maule, "Showdown with a Punching Bag," *Sports Illustrated*, 28 March 1966, 36.

47 On Ali's global support and "colored immigrants," see Nat Fleischer, "Nat Fleischer Speaks Out!!!" *The Ring*, August 1966, 5. For the "silent majority," see Rick Pearlstein, *Nixonland: The Rise of a President and the Fracturing of America* (New York: Scribner, 2008).

48 For Johnson, see Al Buck, "Clay-Johnson Parallels Warn Cassius Beware," *The Ring*, June 1966, 12. Ali religion quote and Fleischer on military are in Fleischer, "Nat Fleischer Speaks Out!!!" 5. "Freak" in Dan Daniel, "Clay Tops List with Many Claims to Top Rating among Oddities," *The Ring*, August 1966, 31–32. On flag, see Dan Daniel, "Mildenberger May be Next Opponent for Clay," *The Ring*, August 1966, 10–11, 38.

49 Louis and Daniel quoted in Dan Daniel, "Ring Champion Should Be Set for Army If Called—Louis," *The Ring*, June 1966, 17. Robert Earl, "The Case for Muhammad," letter to editor, *The Ring*, October 1966, 32; Frank Allerdice, "He Wants to Forget Clay," letter to editor, *The Ring*, September 1967, 28. For "Growing American Boy," see Dan Daniel, "Ring Readers Back Bypass of Clay for 1966 Citation," *The Ring*, April 1967, 28. For more black GI opinion, see "What GI's Think about Ali's Draft Dispute," *Jet*, 15 June 1967, 44–46. Lewis Erenberg, *The Greatest Fight of Our Generation: Louis vs. Schmeling* (New York: Oxford University Press, 2005), 166–98, and Lauren Sklaroff, *Black Culture and the New Deal: The Quest for Civil Rights in the Roosevelt Era* (Chapel Hill: University of North

Carolina Press, 2009), 123–57, discuss the role of the NAACP in Louis's army service.

50 "Martyr" and "laws of Allah," are from Tex Maule, "Champ in the Jug?" *Sports Illustrated*, 10 April 1967, 30; "Warrior" in Tex Maule, "Showdown with a Punching Bag," *ibid*, 28 March 1966, 36.

51 Editorial, "Muhammad Ali—The Measure of a Man," *Freedomways*, Spring 1967, 101–2. For the new definition of black manhood, see Self, *All in the Family*, 53–54.

52 King sermon quoted in Ezra, *Muhammad Ali*, 124. Jackie Robinson, "In Defense of Clay," *Pittsburgh Courier*, 18 March 1967, in *The Muhammad Ali Reader*, ed. Gerald Early (Hopewell, NJ: Ecco Press, 1998), 72. For growing respect for Ali as a civil rights leader, see Mike Marqusee, *Redemption Song: Muhammad Ali and the Spirit of the Sixties* (London: Verso, 1999), 167–75, 196–205.

53 Bill Russell with Tex Maule, "I Am Not Worried about Ali," *Sports Illustrated*, 19 June 1967, 18–21.

54 Ali's Louisville speech quoted in Marqusee, *Redemption Song*, 213–14. At the Congress of Racial Equality's annual convention in 1967, attended by Ali and representatives of the SNCC and the Black Panthers, President Floyd McKissick presented the champion with the CORE award "for being the greatest heavyweight champion of all time and bringing honor, glory and truth to millions by his willingness not to fight against other nonwhite people in the immoral and unjust war in Vietnam." See Bill Nunn, "Change of Pace," *Pittsburgh Courier*, 13 May 1967, 14. For the growing view of internal colonialism, see Self, *All in the Family*, 54.

CHAPTER 2

1 Gilbert Rogin, "George Has the Rhyme, Pappy the Reason," *Sports Illustrated*, 7 October 1968, 74.

2 Harry Edwards, *The Revolt of the Black Athlete* (New York: Free Press, 1969).

3 George Foreman and Joel Engel, *By George: The Autobiography of George Foreman* (1995; New York: Simon and Schuster, 2000), 4–5. Mother's background in George Foreman, with Ken Abraham, *God in My Corner: A Spiritual Memoir* (Nashville, TN: Thomas Nelson, 2007), 5.

4 On the neighborhood, see Vic Ziegel, "From the Bottom to the Top," *New York Post*, 27 January 1973, n.p., Foreman Vertical File, Schomburg Center for Research in Black Culture; Foreman, *God in My Corner*, 4–5 for hunger.

5 Foreman, *By George*, 8–9.

6 Dime anecdote in Tim Tyler, "George Foreman: The Great White Hope," *Sport*, July 1973, 80.

7 Bob Waters, "The George Foreman Transformation," *Newsday*, 29 March 1978, back page, George Foreman Vertical File, Schomburg Center.

8 "Vicious" teenager from Foreman, *God in My Corner*, 7–8. "I was a delinquent," Ziegel, "From the Bottom to the Top," *New York Post*, 27 January 1973. "You had to learn to fight," from "Total Failure: How George Foreman's Losses Showed Him the Way," National Public Radio, 24 May 2017. Foreman, *By George*, 16–21, for all other quotes.

9 Richard Hoffer, *Something in the Air: The Story of American Passion and Defiance in the 1968 Mexico City Olympics* (New York: Free Press, 2009), 1–5.

10 Job Corps ad in Hoffer, *Something in the Air*, 115; Tyler, "Great White Hope," 81–82; Ziegel, "From the Bottom to the Top," *New York Post*, 27 January 1973, n.p., says Foreman saw the ad in the local pool hall.

11 Robert O. Self, *All in the Family: The Realignment of American Democracy Since the 1960s* (New York: Macmillan, 2012), 17–46.

12 Idyllic Grants Pass in Foreman, *By George*, 25–26. Teaching and building in Tyler, "Great White Hope," 82.

13 Foreman, *God in My Corner*, 10.

14 Kibble, in Foreman, *By George*, 29–31.

15 Broadus quote about size, martial arts, and "fearless" from Tyler, "Great White Hope," 82–83; Broadus quoted about counselor and being responsible for Foreman in Ziegel, "From the Bottom to the Top."

16 Briggs in Nat Loubet, "Foreman, 19, Aspires to Success as Pro Champ," *The Ring*, February 1969, 12. Broadus quote and tennis shoes in Ziegel, "From the Bottom to the Top." Broadus on basics and "right from wrong" in Twombly, "Champ," *New York Times Magazine*, 24 March 1974, n.p., Foreman Vertical File, Schomburg.

17 Amateur record in Loubet, "Foreman, 19," 12; Broadus quote in Tyler, "Great White Hope," 83. "I was somebody," quoted in Twombly, "Champ," *New York Times Magazine*, 24 March 1974, n.p., Foreman Vertical File, Schomburg.

18 On "poster boy," "humanitarian," and Broadus offer, see Foreman, *By George*, 42–44. Drugs in Tim Tyler, "George Foreman: The Great White Hope," *Sport*, July 1973, 83.

19 Broadus quoted in Ziegel, "From the Bottom to the Top." On Broadus's role and boxing as "my best opportunity," see Foreman, *By George*, 46–47. Medal quote from Tyler, "Great White Hope," 83.

20 On Olympic qualification bouts, see Loubet, "Foreman, 19," 36. Broadus quoted in Hoffer, *Something in the Air*, 121.

21 For cocoon, see Foreman, *By George*, 55–56. I owe my understanding of the massacre to Eric Zolov, *Refried Elvis: The Rise of the Mexican Counterculture* (Berkeley: University of California Press, 1999), 120–31; and Zach McKiernan, "The 1968 Mexico City Olympics and the American Press," undergraduate student seminar paper, Loyola University Chicago, in author's possession.

22 Edwards, *Revolt of the Black Athlete*, 89–90, xxvii–xxviii.

23 Edwards, *Revolt of the Black Athlete*, xxvii–xxviii. See also Randy Roberts, "The Black Rebellion in American Sports," in *Winning Is the Only Thing, Sports in America since 1945* (Baltimore: Johns Hopkins University Press, 1989), 163–87.

24 For the politics of sport and the 1968 Olympics, see Damion L. Thomas, *Globetrotting, African American Athletes and Cold War Politics* (Urbana: University of Illinois Press, 2012). Smith quoted in Edwards, *Revolt of the Black Athlete*, 104. For more on the gesture, see Amy Bass, *Not the Triumph but the Struggle: The 1968 Olympics and the Making of the Black Athlete* (Minneapolis: University of Minnesota Press, 2002); Douglas Hartmann, *Race, Culture, and the Revolt of the Black Athlete: The 1968 Olympic Protests and Their Aftermath* (Chicago: University of Chicago Press, 2003); Kevin Witherspoon, *Before the Eyes of the World: Mexico and the 1968 Olympic Games* (DeKalb: Northern Illinois University Press, 2008); Tommie Smith, with David Steele, *Silent Gesture: The Autobiography of Tommie Smith* (Philadelphia: Temple University Press, 2007).

25 Ali quoted in "Boycott Comments Divided," *San Jose Mercury News*, 25 November 1967, 68. For "hobo" and college guys, see Foreman, *By George*, 54–58; and Dave Zerin, *What's My Name, Fool? Sports and Resistance in the United States* (Chicago: Haymarket Books, 2005), 94–96.

26 For Gault's background, see Hoffer, *Something in the Air*, 201. Gault quoted in *New York Times*, 23 October, 1968; Hartmann, *Race, Culture and the Revolt*, 298n89; and Rogin, "George Has the Rhyme," *Sports Illustrated*, 7 October 1968, 74.

27 Smith quoted in Edwards, *Revolt of the Black Athlete*, 104.

28 For the aftermath of the protest, see Smith, *Silent Gesture*, 179–93.

29 On Foreman's Olympic boxing matches, see Tyler, "Great White Hope," *Sport*, July 1973, 83; Dan Daniel, "Is George Foreman the Next Champ?" *The Ring*, July 1971, 39; Foreman, *By George*, 58–59.

30 For Foreman's anger after the expulsion, see Foreman, *By George*, 56–57.

31 Girsch's flag quote in George Girsch, "Foreman a Gentle Giant," *The Ring*, May 1973, 42. Foreman quoted in *By George*, 59.

32 For flag kissing before final bout, see Loubet, "Foreman, 19," 11. "This mark of confidence" and following quote are from *The Ring*, July 1971, cover story, 7. Marc Leepson, *Flag, an American Biography* (New York: St. Martin's Press, 205), 227–36, 240–44, details the bitter symbolic battles over the American flag during the Vietnam War.

33 Ali quoted in Mark Kram, *Ghosts of Manila* (New York: HarperCollins, 2001), 162–63. For three flags, see Zerin, *What's My Name, Fool?*, 94–96. "Fighting Corpsman," in Rogin, "George Has the Rhyme," *Sports Illustrated*, 7 October 1968, 74.

34 Quote by Nixon's rep in Foreman, *By George*, 53, 60 (Nixon speech).

35 For Humphrey's speech and the interest of both campaigns, see R. W. Apple Jr., "Olympic Boxing Champion Is Used as Symbol by Both Major Candidates," *New York Times*, 3 November 1968, 84. For Foreman's choice of Humphrey, the celebrities, and meeting with LBJ, see Foreman, *By George*, 60–61. The picture of Foreman, flag, and Humphrey is from, *Jet*, 21 November 1968, 31.

36 Job Corps award from Loubet, "Foreman, 19," 10.

37 "Pressure Mounting for George Foreman," *Chicago Defender*, 15 November 1968, 34. Reagan quote in Vic Ziegel, "From the Bottom to the Top."

38 Hartmann, *Race, Culture, and the Revolt*, 159–60; *Sports Illustrated*, 28 October 1968, 160, 27; "10 Biggest Sports Stories of the Year," *Chicago Tribune*, 29 December 1968, sec. B, 4.

39 Flag in Larry Borstein, "The Olympic Story, Foreman and Harris Champs," *The Ring*, January 1969, 20. More flags in Jersey Jones, "Frazier-Foreman Predicted," *The Ring*, November 1970, 30; Dan Daniel, "Here Comes Foreman," *The Ring*, November 1970, 6; Wells Twombly, "Champ," *New York Times Magazine*, 24 March 1974, n.p., "Foreman" Vertical Fire, Schomburg Center; Lombardi, in Foreman, *By George*, 61, 64 (Oakland parade).

40 Panthers, salesgirl, and friend in Foreman, *By George*, 61–62. Reverend Martin quoted in Ziegel, "From the Bottom to the Top."

41 "Outcast," in Foreman, *By George*, 62. Uncle Toms in Tyler, "George Foreman: The Great White Hope," *Sport*, July 1973, 83. Robinson quoted in Amy Bass, *Not the Triumph*, 285.

42 For his choices, see Foreman, *By George*, 64–65. For more details, see Foreman, *God in My Corner*, 13–14; Loubet, "Foreman, 19," 11.

43 Sadler quoted in Tyler, "George Foreman," *Sport*, July 1973, 83–84. Dan Daniel, "Here Comes Foreman," *The Ring*, November 1970, 7, expressed the doubts of Foreman's readiness.

44 Muller quoted in Tyler, "George Foreman," *Sport*, July 1973, 83–84.

45 On training with Liston, see Foreman, *God in My Corner*, 14; Foreman, *By George*, 65–69, 72–79 (for sex), 72 ("boxing was my wife," and Frazier and Brown).

46 For "whirlwind," see Ziegel, "From the Bottom to the Top." Futch's dismay is in Ronald K. Fried, *Corner Men: Great Boxing Trainers* (New York: Four Walls Eight Windows, 1991), 335–36. Upset and description of bout in Nat Loubet, "Foreman's Kayo of Frazier One of Top Feats in Boxing History," *The Ring*, April 1973, 6–9.

47 Arthur Mercante, "Second Knockdown Was Turning Point Says Ref Mercante," *The Ring*, May 1973, 7, 36. For Frazier's take on the fight, see Joe Frazier, with Phil Berger, *Smokin' Joe* (New York: Macmillan, 1996), 130–35.

48 "LBJ's Death, Foreman's Title Win Called Ironic," *Jet*, 8 February 1973, 59.

49 George Girsch, "Foreman a Gentle Giant," *The Ring*, May 1973, 8. For flag and no Black Power, see Larry Borstein, "The Olympic Story, Foreman and Harris Champs," *The Ring*, January 1969, 20; Shirley Norman, "With Foreman, It's U.S.A. All the Way," *The Ring*, October 1973, 6, 34.

50 Tyler, George Foreman, *Sport*, July 1973, 79–80, 86; Twombly, "Champ," n.p.

51 Tyler, "George Foreman," *Sport*, July 1973, 79–80, 86. Twombly, in "Champ," describes Foreman's meeting with the students.

CHAPTER 3

1 Elombe Brath, "Ali-Foreman Fight Shaping Up as Battle of Armageddon," *New York Amsterdam News*, 26 September 1974, sec. A, 1.

2 Public opinion shift is discussed in Michael Ezra, *Muhammad Ali: The Making of an Icon* (Philadelphia: Temple University Press, 2009), 149–50.

3 Ali quoted in Mark Kram, *Ghosts of Manila: The Fateful Blood Feud between Muhammad Ali and Joe Frazier* (New York: HarperCollins, 2001), 102, 99–104 (for more on the Quarry bout); "Ali Does It: Stages 8-Round Bout in Atlanta," *Jet*, 17 September 1970, 56.

4 The list is from "Mrs. Ali Misses Who's Who Celebrity Guests," *Jet*, 12 November 1970, 14. For Nixon persecution of black militants equated with Ali's sentence, see John H. Britton, "Black Militants Face Showdown in Struggle to Avoid Prison," *Jet*, 16 January 1969, 14–20.

5 Ronald Kisner, "Ali Quells Quarry on Maddox 'Day of Mourning' Before Capacity Crowd," *Jet*, 12 November 1970, 51–56.

6 Kisner, "Ali Quells Quarry.'" For the bomb threat, see "Ali's Spouse Flees Bomb Threats," *Jet*, 12 November 1970, 14. Abernathy quoted in "Purse for Bout above Estimate," *New York Times*, 28 October 1970, 37, as in Ezra, *Muhammad Ali*, 150. Ali quoted in "The Black Scholar Interviews Muhammad Ali," June 1970, reprinted in Gerald Early, ed., *The Muhammad Ali Reader* (Hopewell, NJ: Ecco Press, 1998), 89. For Mrs. King, see Robert Lipsyte, "'I Don't Have to Be What You Want Me to Be,' Says Muhammad Ali," *New York Times Magazine*, 7 March 1971, reprinted in *Muhammad Ali Reader*, 97.

7 Cordell S. Thompson, "Muhammad Ali's Purse Put at $600,000; Looks to Frazier," *Jet*, 24 December 1970, 52–54; Ezra, *Muhammad Ali*, 150–151.

8 "Disgrace" and "Russia," in "Frazier Calls Muhammad Ali 'Loud Mouth'," *Milwaukee Star*, 21 June 1969, 16. For "fists," "Rizzo," and "Tom," see Lacy J. Banks, "Can Anybody Beat This Man?" *Jet*, 18 February 1971, 52–56.

9 Budd Schulberg, *Loser and Still Champion: Muhammad Ali* (Garden City, NJ: Doubleday, 1972), 106–7, 128. Gumbel quoted in Thomas Hauser, *Muhammad Ali: His Life and Times* (New York: Simon and Schuster, 1991), 223–24.

10 For a description of the Ali-Frazier match, see Kram, *Ghosts of Manila*, 141–47. "And This One, Too," letter to editor, *The Ring*, July 1971, 32; Franklin Crandall, "How about This?" *The Ring*, July 1971, 32.

11 Gumbel in Hauser, *Muhammad Ali*, 224–25. Ali on Gaddafi and the Islamic world in Ali, *The Greatest*, 249–51. For black nationalist quotes, see Ambalavaner Sivanandan, "On the Passing of the King," April 1971, reprinted in *A Different Hunger: Writings on the Black Resistance* (London: Pluto Press, 1982), 69. For an example of his resentment, see Joe Frazier, "Cassius Who?" *Ebony*, May 1972, 68–76.

12 For the Supreme Court decision, see Suzanne Freedman, Clay v. United States: *Muhammad Ali Objects to War* (Springfield, NJ: Enslow Publishers, 1997), 65–78. See also Samuel Regalado, "*Clay aka Ali v. United States*, 1971: Muhammad Ali, Precedent, and the Burger Court," *Journal of Sport History* 34, no. 2 (Summer 2007): 169–82. For Frazier's bitterness, see Joe Frazier, with Phil Berger, *Smokin' Joe: The Autobiography* (New York: Macmillan, 1996), 95–99, 130.

13 For his attitude as champion, "surly and angry," see George Foreman and Joel Engel, *By George: The Autobiography of George Foreman* (New York: Simon and Schuster, 1995), 85–101.

14 Foreman quoted in Foreman, *By George*, 94. Koyama quoted in Leonard Gardner, "Stopover in Caracas," *Esquire*, October 1974, 304. Koizumi's account of the Roman fight is in Joe Y. Koizumi, "Foreman's Two-Minute Kayo of Roman Brings Fruitless Hassle," *The Ring*, November 1973, 6–7.

15 Clark and Foreman on his anger in Wells Twombly, "Champ," *New York Times Magazine*, 24 March 1974, n.p., Foreman Vertical File, Schomburg Center.

16 For Foreman's meanness, see Gardner, "Stopover in Caracas," 185–86. Foreman describes bout in Foreman, *By George*, 100–101. For a comparison of Norton and Foreman, see Dan Levin, "His Fight Plan Is a Planter's Punch," *Sports Illustrated*, 25 March 1974, 34–36. For more on the bout, see Tex Maule, "Buenas Noches, Señor," *Sports Illustrated*, 8 April 1974, 21–23.

17 Ali quotes in Gardner, "Stopover in Caracas," 306. Foreman's response is in Foreman, *By George*, 101.

18 King quoted in "George Foreman vs. Muhammad Ali," *Sportsworld*, September 1974, 11.

19 Thomas Borstelmann, *The 1970s: A New Global History from Civil Rights to Economic Inequality* (Princeton, NJ: Princeton University Press, 2012). For more on the rise of Third World boxing, see Jeffrey T. Sammons, *Beyond the Ring: The Role of Boxing in American Society* (Urbana: University of Illinois Press, 1990), 221.

20 Muhammad Ali, with Richard Durham, *The Greatest, My Own Story* (New York: Ballantine, 1976), viii. See Danyel Tobias Reiche, "Why Developing Countries Are Just Spectators in the 'Gold War': The Case of Lebanon at the Olympic Games," *Third World Quarterly* (2016): 1–16, http://dx.coi.org/10.1080/0143659

7.2016.11774; and Jiyeon Kang, Jae-On Kim, and Yan Wang, "Salvaging National Pride: The 2010 Taekwondo Controversy and Taiwan's Quest for Global Recognition," *International Review for the Sociology of Sport* 50, no. 1 (2015): 98–114, for the desire to use sports to boost a state's stature.

21 Ezra, *Muhammad Ali*, 154–155. For the international nature of the promotion, see "The Cash," *Sportsworld*, September 1974, 10. For governmental ability to sponsor global matches, see "Playboy Interview: Don King," *Playboy*, May 1988, 65.

22 "As Nat Loubet Sees It," *The Ring*, August 1974, 5; Borstelmann, *The 1970s*, 139 (for early satellites); Schwartz, *From the Corners*, xv, 5.

23 Hank Schwartz, *From the Corners of the Ring to the Corners of the Earth: The Adventure behind the Champions* (Valley Stream, NY: CIVCOM, 2009–2010), 120. Eric Porter, "Affirming and Disaffirming Actions: Remaking Race in the 1970s," *America in the Seventies*, ed. Beth Bailey and David Farber (Lawrence: University Press of Kansas, 2004), 50–74, notes that in the early 1970s race became a positive asset for blacks.

24 Schwartz, *From the Corners*, 21–80; David Berman, "Foreman-Ali Promoters Predict Record Viewing of Closed Circuit TV," *The Ring*, September 1974, 19–34.

25 Schwartz, *From the Corner*, 62, 91–102.

26 Schwartz, *From the Corners*, 11–17.

27 King atom bomb quote in "The Amazing Saga of the New King of Boxing," *Sepia*, October 1975, 26. "Where the power lies" quoted in "The Promoters," *Black Enterprise*, July 1976, 22. See also Mark Kram, "The Fight's Lone Arranger," *Sports Illustrated*, 2 September 1974, 32. For a positive view of King, see Sammons, *Beyond the Ring*, 219–25.

28 Howard B. Woods, "Big Fight Black Blast," *Chicago Defender*, 14 September 1974, 8. Shabazz quoted in Hauser, *Muhammad Ali*, 260.

29 Mark Ribowsky, "Killer to King," *Sepia*, October 1975, 31–32.

30 Jack Newfield, *The Life and Crimes of Don King: The Shame of Boxing in America* (London: Virgin, 1996; reprint, Sag Harbor, NY: Harbor Electronic Publishers, 2003), 13–26; Kram, "The Fight's Lone Arranger," 30–34.

31 Milton Viorst, "Deal of the Century: The Ali-Foreman Fight," *New York Magazine*, 5 August 1974, n.p., Don King Vertical File, Schomburg Center, on King's use of jail. Ribowsky, "Killer to King," 32 for "toothpick." For "a number," see Edward Kiersh, "The Man Who Would Be King Takes a Fall," pt. 1, *Crawdaddy*, 4 August 1977, 37. For more on King, see "Interview: Don King," *Playboy*, May 1988, 51–68.

32 All quotes from James Borders, "The King of Pugilistica," *Black Collegian*, February–March 1981, 55–56.

33 Newfield, *Life and Crimes*, 30–42.

34 Newfield, *Life and Crimes*, 43, 52–53. Elbaum quoted in Hauser, *Muhammad Ali*, 262–63. Dan Daniel laments the decline of New York's control of boxing in "New York Boxing in Jeopardy as Greatest Title Fight in History Set in Africa," *The Ring*, September 1974, 6–7, 59.

35 Schwartz, *From the Corners*, 103. King quoted in Viorst, "Deal of the Century," *New York Magazine*, 5 August, 1974, n.p., Don King Vertical File, Schomburg Center; and Thomas Hauser, *The Black Lights* (New York: McGraw-Hill, 1986), 75.

36 For international promotion, see "The Cash," *Sportsworld*, September 1974, 10; Kram, "The Fight's Lone Arranger," 32.

37 For the Caracas bout, and King's and Schwartz's quotes, see Schwartz, *From the*

Corners, 123–26. For information on Panama's late twentieth-century role in offshore capitalism, see Alan Rusbridger, "Panama: The Hidden Trillions," *New York Review of Books*, 27 October 2016, 33–35.

38 For Arum as antiblack and the appeal to black pride, see Newfield, *Life and Crimes*, 57–59. Use of Elijah Muhammad's words in Ribowsky, "Killer to King," *Sepia*, October 1975, 32. After a one-year suspension by Elijah Muhammad, Ali was accepted back into the fold in an arrangement that put off his becoming a minister until he left boxing.

39 For King's appeal to George, see Ribowsky, "Killer to King," 32. "I told Foreman" from Don King, "Foreman OK'd Fight in Frisco Parking Lot," *The Ring*, October 1974, 66; "Until you beat Muhammad Ali," in Ali, *The Greatest*, 456.

40 Foreman's dissatisfaction in Jack Welsh, "For Foreman, Zaire Is Already Money in the Bank," *Boxing Illustrated*, July 1974, 9, and Schwartz, *From the Corners*, 211–12.

41 For details, see Alan Hubbard, "Ali's African Sunset," *Sportsworld*, September 1974, 10; Newfield, *Life and Crimes*, 62–64; Schwartz, *From the Corners*, 160–173; author's interview with Bill Caplan, Foreman's publicist, 3 November 2017.

42 Newfield, *Life and Crimes*, 64–67; Weymar quoted by Schwartz, *From the Corners*, 75.

43 King quoted in Kram, "The Fight's Lone Arranger," 34. Percentages and David Frost's participation and 75 percent of revenue are from Alan Hubbard, "Ali's African Sunset," *Sportsworld*, September 1974, 10. See also Milton Viorst, "Deal of the Century: The Ali-Foreman Fight," *New York Magazine*, 5 August 1974, n.p., Ali Vertical File, Schomburg Center.

44 Jack Welsh, "1 Billion People Will See It on Giant Screens," *Boxing Illustrated Special Commemorative Issue*, [September or October] 1974, 40, Special Collections, Notre Dame University. Estimated profits from Hubbard, "Ali's African Sunset," 10. Similar estimates in Michael Thompson-Noel, "Ali Fight Likely to Gross $18m," *Financial Times of London*, 30 October 1974. King quoted in Welsh, "For Foreman Ali, Zaire," 11.

45 For airplane and globalization, see Borstelmann, *The 1970s*, 172–73. Mobutu's DC-10 in Jim Mann, "Zaire—Country of Curious Changes," *Chicago Tribune*, 26 August 1974, C3. For Schwartz and King's jet lag, see Schwartz, *From the Corners*, 161, 184; for Hercules, see 186.

46 Alan Hubbard, "The Country," *Sportsworld*, September 1974, 11–12.

47 Aloys Kabanda, *Ali/Foreman: Le combat du siècle a Kinshasa 29–30 October 1974* [Ali/Foreman: The fight of the century] (Sherbrooke, QC: Naaman, 1977), 27–31, for the conversation in Abu Dhabi. "Violent Coronation in Kinshasa," *Time*, 23 September 1974, 101, confirms that the two met, but has it in February 1974 in Kuwait. For sport as American monopoly, see Sammons, *Beyond the Ring*, 221.

48 "Gladiators" from "$10 Million Bet," *New York Times*, 27 October 1974, 227. Mandungu Bula quoted in Stan Hochman, "Two Attitudes Clash in Fight Promotion," *New York Times*, 29 July 1974, n.p., Ali-Foreman Vertical File, Schomburg Center. For the theme of exile and return as narrative of Ali's autobiography, see Gerald Early, "Some Preposterous Propositions from the Heroic Life of Muhammad Ali: A Reading of *The Greatest: My Own Story*," in *Muhammad Ali: The People's Champ*, ed. Elliott Gorn (Urbana: University of Illinois Press, 1995), 83–84.

49 Mann, "Zaire," C3. For Mandunga Bula on stability, see "Fight to Benefit African Nation," *Chicago Defender*, 20 July 1974, 20.

50 Michela Wrong, *In the Footsteps of Mr. Kurtz: Living on the Brink of Disaster in Mobutu's Congo* (New York: Perennial, HarperCollins, 2001), 70–74.

51 Wrong, *In the Footsteps*, 74–84. For more on the CIA, see Sean Kelly, *America's Tyrant: The CIA and Mobutu of Zaire* (Washington, DC: American University Press, 1993). This is the optimistic "boom period" described in the novel by V. S. Naipul, *A Bend in the River* (1979; New York: Vintage International Books, 1989), 85–182.

52 Mobutu quoted in Wrong, *In the Footsteps*, 91, 94.

53 Kevin C. Dunn, *Imagining the Congo: The International Relations of Identity* (New York: Palgrave Macmillan, 2003), 22–23, 26–28 (for background on Stanley, Leopold, and images of the Congo). For brutality and genocide, see Adam Hochschild, *King Leopold's Ghost: A Story of Greed, Terror and Heroism in Colonial Africa* (Boston: Houghton Mifflin, 1998). Stanley and primitive Africa is from Marianna Torgovnick, *Gone Primitive: Savage Intellects, Modern Lives* (Chicago: University of Chicago Press, 1990), 9–34. Henry Morton Stanley, *The Congo and the Founding of Its Free State* (New York: Harper and Brothers, 1885), 1:59–60, as in Dunn, *Imagining the Congo*, 26–28. Critical is Patrick Brantlinger, "Victorians and Africans: The Genealogy of the Myth of the Dark Continent," in *"Race," Writing and Difference*, ed. Henry Louis Gates Jr. (Chicago: University of Chicago Press, 1986), 185–222.

54 For the earlier images of Africa, see Gail Bederman, *Manliness and Civilization: A Cultural History of Gender and Race in the United States* (Chicago: University of Chicago Press, 1995), 170–232; Theodore Roosevelt, *African Game Trails: An Account of the Western Wanderings of an American Hunter Naturalist* (New York: Charles Scribner's Sons, 1910); Edgar Rice Burroughs, *Tarzan of the Apes* (1912; New York: Ballantine, 1983). Dunn, *Imagining the Congo*, 61–103, explores the colonial books and films.

55 For aspects of authenticity, see Ghislain Kabwit, "Zaire: The Roots of the Continuing Crisis," *Journal of Modern African Studies* 17, no. 3 (September 1979): 381–407; Kenneth Lee Adelman, "The Recourse to Authenticity and Negritude in Zaire," *Journal of Modern African Studies* 13, no. 1 (March 1975): 135. Wrong, *In the Footsteps*, 95.

56 For more on dress, see Kabwit, "Zaire," 390; Adelman, "Recourse to Authenticity," 135. As the embodiment of the nation, see also Kabwit, "Zaire," 387–91.

57 Dunn, *Imagining the Congo*, 116–24.

58 Stephen R. Weissman, "Fisticuffs for Mobutu," *The Nation*, 30 November 1974, 559; Adelman, "Recourse to Authenticity," 136–37; Dunn, *Imagining the Congo*, 125–26; Zaire reaction to fight in Wrong, *In the Footsteps*, 95.

59 Mann, "Zaire," C3; Henry S. Hayward, "Zaire, Land of Foreman and Ali," *Christian Science Monitor*, 25 October 1974, n. p., Ali-Foreman Vertical File, Schomburg Center.

60 Mandungu Bula quoted in Stan Hochman, "Two Attitudes Clash in Fight Promotion," *New York Times*, 29 July 1974, n.p., Ali Vertical File, Schomburg Center.

61 King in Gardner, "Stopover in Caracas," 310; "new life" in Alan Hubbard, "The Country," *Sportsworld*, September 1974, 11.

62 For Schwartz and Rainbow Room, see Schwartz, *From the Corners*, 221–22. Griffin Booker, "Black Pride at Stake in Big Fight in Zaire," *New York Amsterdam News*, 27 July, 1974, A1–A3, in Ali Vertical File, Schomburg Center.

63 For billboards, see, "$10 Million Bet," *New York Times*, 27 October 1974, 227.

64 King in Hubbard, "The Country," 11.

65 Schwartz in Newfield, *Life and Crimes*, 69–70; and Schwartz, *From the Corners*, 217.

66 On the symbolic import of the stadium, see Mavomo Nzuzi Zola, "Enfin un Nouveau Stade du 20-Mai!" [Finally a new 20th of May stadium!], *Salongo*, 23 September 1974, 8. Schwartz in Newfield, *Life and Crimes*, 69–70. For more on infrastructure work, see Thomas A. Johnson, "Zaire Prepares with Pride for Foreman-Ali Fight," *New York Times*, 2 July 1974, 44; and Kimpoza Mayala, "Le Stade du 20-Mai Fait Peau Neuve" [The 20th of May stadium has a new look], *Elima*, 16 August 1974, 12.

67 Solomons in, Hubbard, "The Country," 11, 12 (Edwards' doubts).

68 Schwartz, *From the Corners*, 239–40.

69 Schwartz, *From the Corners*, 240; and Angelo Dundee, with Bert Randolph Sugar, *My View from the Corner, A Life in Boxing* (New York: McGraw Hill, 2008), 174, including Pacheco quote. Ali as an African and Foreman's face a mask are in "Fighters Show Signs of Plans," *Chicago Defender*, 24 October 1974, 41.

70 Dundee, *My View*, 174. Schwartz, *Four Corners*, 245–46.

71 Dundee, *My View*, 174–75; "less than" and "these people hate dogs," in Rick Talley, "A Stitch in Time Would've Helped," *Chicago Tribune*, 21 September 1974, C3; author's interview with Caplan, 3 November 2017.

72 American Embassy to Secretary of State, Doc. No. 1974KINSHA07909, Film No. D740260-0080, 17 September 1974, Electronic Telegrams 1/1/1974–12/31/1974, Central Policy Files, Records Group (RG) 59, 7/1/1973–12/31/1976, US National Archives. "Foreman was bleeding" and "promoters," are in Dundee, *My View*, 176–77.

73 Dundee, *My View from the Corner*, 177, quotes Ali's plea; American Embassy to Secretary of State, Doc. No. 1974KINSHA07909, Film No. D740260-0080, 17 September 1974.

74 American Embassy to Secretary of State, Doc. No. 1974KINSHA07909, Film No. D740260-0080, 17 September 1974.

75 American Embassy to Secretary of State, 18 September 1974, Doc. No. 1974KIN-SHA07959, Film No. D740261-1191, Electronic Telegrams, RG 59, US National Archives. Bula's quotes appeared in "How Zaire Displayed Footwork," *New York Times*," 14 November 1974, 63, 66. For Schwartz's role, see his *From the Corners*, 250–52. The flap with the press and the vagueness of the date are in "How Zaire Displayed Footwork," 66.

CHAPTER 4

1 Stewart Levine in interview with author, 1 June 2017; his discussion of the Jewish New Year is quoted in *Soul Power*, produced by David Sonenberg and Leon Gast, directed by Jeffrey Levy-Hite (Sony Picture Classics, 2010), special commentary, 93 mins.; and in Rob Woollard "Zaire 74 Legendary Music Festival," *The Telegraph*, http://www.telegraph.co.uk/expat/expatnews/72221001/Zaire-74'legen dary-African-music. On the cut, see Ronald E. Kisner, "Zaire Show Goes on Despite Delay of Fight," *Jet*, 3 October 1974, 8–10.

2 Jack Newfield, *The Life and Crimes of Don King: The Shame of Boxing in America*

(London: Virgin, 1996; reprint, Sag Harbor, NY: Harbor Electronic Publishers, 2003), 70, 78–80.

3 For the African musicians at the festival, see *Zaire 74: The African Artists*, produced by Hugh Masekela and Stewart Levine (Chisa Records, 2017), 2 CDs.

4 Lukundu Sampu quoted in T. M. W. "Special Festival," *Elima*, 30 September 1974, 13. For Ali on Zaire 74, see Budd Schulberg, "Journey to Zaire," originally in *Newsday*, October 1974, reprinted in *Sparring with Hemingway* (Chicago: Ivan R. Dee, 1995), 172.

5 Levine quoted in Woollard, "Zaire 74 Legendary Music Festival." This was confirmed in Levine's interview with author, 1 June 2017. Lloyd Price quoted in *Soul Power*. Etta James and David Ritz, *Rage to Survive* (New York: Villard Books, 1995), 216. For interest in the black arts, see Larry Neal, "Any Day Now: Black Art and Black Liberation," *Ebony*, February 1969, 54–58, 62.

6 Quotes from Hugh Masekela and D. Michael Cheers, *Still Grazing: The Musical Journey of Hugh Masekela* (New York: Crown Publishers, 2004), 274–77; "Twelfth year of exile," from *Zaire 74: The African Artists*; Levine, interview, 1 June 2017.

7 For Bell, see Michael Kelly, "Wattstax: Part I," *Waxpoetics* 11 (2005): 54. Domenico Ferri, "Funk My Soul: The Assassination of Martin Luther King Jr. and the Birth of Funk Culture" (PhD diss., Loyola University Chicago, 2013), 162. See also Rob Bowman, *Soulsville, U.S.A.: The Story of Stax Records* (New York: Schirmer Trade Books, 1998), 267–71; and Pat Thomas, *Listen, Whitey! The Sights and Sounds of Black Power 1965–1975* (Seattle: Fantagraphics Books, 2012), 143–47. Shaw and radio stations in Bowman, *Soulsville*, 268.

8 Levine, interview; Masekela, *Still Grazing*, 154–74.

9 Masekela, *Still Grazing*, 4–79; big bands, 9, 59–60, 69–70.

10 Masekela, *Still Grazing*, for Apollo; 130–54, 164 for Belafonte, Makeba, and roots of hybrid jazz.

11 For Belafonte's role in generating world music and promoting music as a form of protest and resistance, see Judith E. Smith, *Becoming Belafonte, Black Artist, Public Radical* (Austin: University of Texas Press, 2014).

12 Levine quoted in Woollard, "Zaire 74 Legendary Music Festival." Masekela, *Still Grazing*, 278–80. Fela's inability to leave Nigeria is discussed by Levine in the special commentary of *Soul Power*.

13 Price quoted in Thomas A. Johnson, "Music Fete in Zaire Has Poor Box Office But Makes a Big Hit," *New York Times*, 25 September 1974, 10; Masekela, *Still Grazing*, 280–84. For more on Gast, see Russ Slater, "It Was Our Thing, a Latin Thing: An Interview with Leon Gast," 24 November 2011, http://www.soundsandcolours.com/subjects/film/it-was-our-thing-our-latin-thing-an-interview-with-leon-gast/. On Monk and McManus, see special commentary in *Soul Power*.

14 Levine, interview; Masekela, *Still Grazing*, 283–86.

15 For "mood was electric," and all-night parties, see Masekela, *Still Grazing*, 283–84; Fred Wesley Jr., *Hit Me, Fred: Recollections of a Side Man* (Durham, NC: Duke University Press, 2002); Johnson, "Music Fete in Zaire," 10, says that thirty-two groups appeared, but then says that seventeen were from Zaire and fourteen from abroad. Levine quoted in Woollard, "Zaire 74 Legendary Music Festival." For lack of tourists, high prices, and disappointing attendance, see David B. Ottaway's "Zaire's Cultural Festival Draws Blacks of Three Continents," *Washington Post*, 22 September 1974, A13, and "Zaire Festival, a Comedy of Errors," *Washington Post*, 25 September 1974, D1, D8.

16 Paul Gilroy, *The Black Atlantic: Modernity and Double Consciousness* (Cambridge, MA: Harvard University Press, 1993); and George Lipsitz, *Dangerous Crossroads, Popular Music, Postmodernism and the Poetics of Place* (New York: Verso, 1994).

17 For "home," see "Good to My Ear," *Time*, 1 February 1960, n.p., Makeba Vertical File, Schomburg Center for Research in Black Culture. Miriam Makeba, with Jim Hall, *Makeba: My Story* (New York: New American Library, 1987), 1, 15, 17–18, 22, 44–51; 58–62, 65 (for early musical experiences).

18 For Rogosin, see Milton Bracker, "Xhosa Songstress," *New York Times Magazine*, 28 February 1960, n.p., Makeba file, Schomburg Center; Dave Hepburn, "African Girl Overnight Sensation," *Sepia*, June 1960, 14, 16; and Makeba, *Makeba*, 66–67, 73–74.

19 Makeba, *Makeba*, 96–104. For more on her quick rise, see Bracker, "Xhosa Songstress." For the quote about Belafonte, see Hepburn, "African Girl Overnight Sensation," 16. See also "Makeba . . . A Pure Diamond from South African Mines," *Pittsburgh Courier*, 9 June 1962, 21. For Belafonte's account, see Harry Belafonte, with Michael Shnayerson, *My Song: A Memoir* (New York: Alfred A. Knopf, 2011).

20 For her return to Africa, see "Miriam Makeba: Back to Africa," *Sepia*, April 1963, 39; the quotes are from Makeba, *Makeba*, 109–10.

21 She also testified against apartheid at the United Nations. See Kathleen Teltsch, "Miriam Makeba, at UN, Scores South African Race 'Nightmare,'" *New York Times*, 17 July 1963, n.p., Makeba Vertical File, Schomburg Center; Makeba, *Makeba*, 113–19, 127–28, 219; and Richard Cabrera, "The Miriam Makeba Story," *Sepia*, July 1968, 62–65. See also Jerry Tallmer, "Singing Envoy,'" *New York Post*, 30 July 1963, n.p., Makeba File, Schomburg Center.

22 Makeba, *Makeba*, 154–66, for her marriage to Carmichael and its consequences. See also Cabrera, "The Miriam Makeba Story, *Sepia*, July 1968, 65. "Angrily militant" is from "Miriam Makeba Says She Is Being Boycotted," *New York Post*, 10 December 1968, n.p., Makeba File, Schomburg Center.

23 Her hair style and traditional dress can be seen in *Soul Power*. For more, see Makeba, *Makeba*, 90, 135, 182.

24 "Most respected," "we're all the same," and 1971 Africa tour from M. Cordell Thompson, "James Brown Goes through Some New Changes," *Jet*, 30 December 1971, 59. The documentary *Soul Power* shows James Brown on the last night playing to a full house. In fact, he headlined the first night at 3:55 a.m. with only a few thousand people in attendance. For the actual lineup, see "Special Festival," *Elima*, 23 September 1974, 16, which says James Brown headlined the first night, while the Fania All-Stars were also on the bill. The latter would be brought back on Monday night. Ottaway, "Zaire Festival, D-1, D-8, attended the concerts and reported that Brown headlined the first night to a small audience, while Miriam Makeba and B. B. King suffered the same fate on the second night. Budd Schulberg, "Journey to Zaire," in *Sparring with Hemingway*, 179, reported the same thing. The lineup also confirmed by American Embassy to Secretary of State, R 250945Z Sep 74, Doc. No. 1974KINSHA08159, Film No. D740270-0272, National Archives.

25 For Brown as representative of 1960s and 1970s militant black rage and manhood, see Rickey Vincent, *Funk: The Music, the People and the Rhythm of the One* (New York: St. Martin's Press, 1996), 7–8; Thompson, "James Brown Goes through Some New Changes," 55–56. For Watkins's take on black entertainment, see Mel Watkins, *On the Real Side: Laughing, Lying, and Signifying* (New York:

Simon and Schuster, 1994). Marc Eliot, introduction to James Brown, *I Feel Good: A Memoir of a Life of Soul* (New York: New American Library, 2005), 7. For contemporary articles covering different phases of Brown's career, see *The James Brown Reader: 50 Years of Writing about The Godfather of Soul*, ed. Nelson George and Alan Leeds (New York: Plume, 2008).

26 Eliot in Brown, *I Feel Good*, 8–12.

27 For Brown's biography, see James Brown and Bruce Tucker, *James Brown: The Godfather of Soul* (1986; rpt., New York: Thunder's Mouth, 1990); Cynthia Rose, *Living in America: The Soul Saga of James Brown* (London: Serpent's Tail, 1990); and Brown, *I Feel Good*, Brown quoted at 59, 66–67; Eliot "Cry of Liberation," 13-15. On soul and funk, see Markus Schmidt, "The One, James Brown's Rap," *Waxpoetics* 21 (February-March 2007): 41. See also Anne Danielson, *Presence and Pleasure: The Funk Grooves of James Brown and Parliament* (Middletown, CT: Wesleyan University Press, 2006).

28 William L. Van Deburg, *Black Camelot: African-American Culture Heroes in Their Times, 1960–1980* (Chicago: University of Chicago Press), 231. For his discussion of the "one," see Brown, *I Feel Good*, 71–72. Ferri, *Funk My Soul*, argues that the shift to the one and much of funk itself came as a response to King's assassination.

29 Brown, *I Feel Good*, 72–75, 80–81.

30 Brown, *I Feel Good*, 85–88; John H. Johnson, "The Unity of Blackness: The Secret of Success," *Ebony*, November 1975, 132.

31 For more on this theme, see Kelly A. O'Connor, "Male Fashion" (PhD diss., Loyola University Chicago, 2013), 69–70.

32 Brown, *I Feel Good*, 145–47.

33 Brown, *I Feel Good*, 154–69 for 1968, his political activities, and the fate of "Say It Loud."

34 On the new band, see Wesley, *Hit Me, Fred*, 133–34. On male sexual assertiveness, see Ferri, *Funk My Soul*, 38–39, 42–44, Vincent quoted at 56. M. Cordell Thompson, "Brown Vows to Support PUSH," *Jet*, 6 December 1973, 94; Tony Bolden, *The Funk Era and Beyond: New Perspectives on Black Popular Culture* (Hampshire, UK: Palgrave Macmillan, 2008), 52.

35 Celia Cruz, with Ana Cristina Reymundo, *Celia: My Life*, trans. José Lucas Badue (New York: Rayo, 2004), 140–41. Pacheco and the All-Stars were covered extensively by the Zaire newspapers. See Tumba Mukamba Wamunda, "Special Festival," *Elima*, 23 September 1974, 16; and "Un coup d'envoi sensationnel" [A sensational kickoff], *Salongo*, 23 September 1974, 9. The documentary *Soul Power* says the All-Stars performed the second and third nights. An earlier documentary, *Celia Cruz and the Fania All-Stars Live in Zaire 74*, directed by Leon Gast, produced by David Sonenberg (Gravity Limited, 1989), says they performed the first and third nights, which accords with Zaire press accounts.

36 Christopher Small, *Music of the Common Tongue: Survival and Celebration in Afro-American Music* (London: Calder; New York: Riverrun Press, 1987), 426–45, discusses the common threads of black music in the Americas and reasons for the differences. See also Sam Floyd, *The Power of Black Music: Interpreting Its History from Africa to the United States* (New York: Oxford University Press, 1995); John Storm Roberts, *Black Music of Two Worlds: African, Caribbean, Latin and African American Traditions*, 2nd ed. (New York: Schirmer Books, 1998).

37 *Celia Cruz and the Fania All-Stars Live in Zaire 74*. Unfortunately, the documentary mixes the repertoire of both nights, leaving the viewer to guess which songs were performed on which night.

38 Frances R. Aparicio, *Listening to Salsa: Gender, Latin Popular Musics, and Puerto Rican Cultures* (Middletown, CT: Wesleyan University Press, 1998), 66–82; César Miguel Rondón, *The Book of Salsa: A Chronicle of Urban Music from the Caribbean to New York City*, trans. Frances R. Aparicio, with Jackie White (1980; Chapel Hill: University of North Carolina Press, 2008), 1–34, 37–40.

39 Rondón, *Book of Salsa*, 1–40; Lipsitz, *Dangerous Crossroads*, 79–83. For more on the hybridization of the music, see Robert Baron, "Syncretism and Ideology: NY Salsa Musicians," *Western Folklore* 36, no. 3 (1977): 209–25. Colón quoted in Leonardo Padura Fuentes, "Willie Colón Interview," in *Faces of Salsa: A Spoken History of the Music* (Washington, DC: Smithsonian Books, 2003), 29–30; "Johnny Pacheco interview," *Faces of Salsa*, 59.

40 *Nuestra Cosa* (*Our Latin Thing*), directed by Leon Gast, produced by Jerry Masucci (Vampi Soul DVD, 1972), documents the All-Stars jamming at New York's Cheetah Club in 1971 and the neighborhoods from which the music sprang. Alfredo Lopez, "It Don't Mean a Thing If It Ain't Got That Clave," *Village Voice*, 7 November 1977, 49. For the political connections, see Felix M. Padilla, "Salsa: Puerto Rican and Latino Music," *Journal of Popular Culture* 24 (Summer 1990): 92–94.

41 Padilla, "Salsa," 94.

42 Pacheco quoted in "Johnny Pacheco interview," in Padura, *Faces of Salsa*, 57–58. The intense competition among record companies allowed musicians to experiment and get their product sold. This is a key point for Padilla, "Salsa," 91. For Fania's role, see Lopez, "It Don't Mean a Thing," 49; and Rondón, *Book of Salsa*, 37–51. For an earlier portrait of barrio life and the racial dilemmas of Puerto Ricans in New York, see Piri Thomas, *Down These Mean Streets* (New York: New American Library, 1967); Lipsitz, *Dangerous Crossroads*, 3–20.

43 Cruz, *Celia*, 130–38. For a brief sketches of her career, see Jon Pareles, "Celia Cruz, Petite Powerhouse of Latin Music Dies at 77," *New York Times*, 17 July 2003, 89; and Thomas Zaleski, "Celia Cruz," *The Guardian*, 17 July 2003, http://www.theguardian.com/news/2003/jul/18/guardianobituaries.arts. See also Juan Moreno Velázquez, liner notes to *Celia & Johnny* (1974; Fania Records CD, 2006).

44 The list of Zaire bands is from Gary Stewart, *Rumba on the River: A History of the Popular Music of the Two Congos* (London: Calder; New York: Riverrun Press, 1987), 206–18; "Festival in Zaïre," *Salongo*, 26 September 1974, 8; "Festival spécial," *Elima*, 23 September 1974, 16; Robin Denselow, liner notes to *Zaire 74: The African Artists* (Chisa Records, 2017).

45 Christopher Small, *Music of the Common Tongue*, 426–45. See also Graeme Ewens, *Africa O-Ye! A Celebration of African Music* (New York: Da Capo, 1992), 26–38. Stewart, *Rumba on the River*, 15–46, charts the development of Congo rumba.

46 Stewart, *Rumba on the River*, 76–79; Jesse Samba Wheeler, "Rumba Lingala as Colonial Resistance," *Image [&] Narrative, Online Magazine of the Visual Narrative*, March 2005, http://www.imageandnarrative.be/inarchive/worldmusica/jessesambawheeler.htm.

47 Wheeler, "Rumba Lingala."

48 Stewart, *Rumba on the River*, 83–100.

49 Stewart, *Rumba on the River*, 210–17.

50 Franco's life, music, and status as a folk hero is covered in Graeme Ewens, *Congo Colossus: The Life and Legacy of Franco and OK Jazz* (Norfolk, England: Buku Press, 1994); Ewens, *Africa O-Ye!*, 132–37; Stewart, *Rumba on the River*, 52–73; Ken Braun, liner notes to *FRANCOphonic, Africa's Greatest: A Retrospective*, vol. 1, *1953–1980* (Sterns Music, 2008).

51 Stewart, *Rumba on the River*, 170–74.

52 Braun, liner notes to *FRANCOphonic*, 30–32; Stewart, *Rumba on the River*, 194–205.

53 "Festival in Zaïre," 8.

54 For how the cut affected tourism, see Al Harvin, "For Tourists in Zaire, There's Still a Music Festival," *New York Times*, 18 September 1974, 48. Masekela, *Still Grazing*, 284-86. Price's woes are from Newfield, *Life and Crimes of Don King*, 81. For the house arrest and wrangling over the rights and the profits, see also Levine, interview with author, 1 June 2017.

55 Vincent, *Funk*, 185; Brown, *I Feel Good*, 179–88. For more on Brown and disco, see Steve Bloom, untitled clipping, *Soho Weekly News*, 28 June 1979, 13-16, James Brown Vertical File, Schomburg Center.

CHAPTER 5

1 One hundred thousand in crowd from "Foreman et Ali au Stade du 20-Mai" [Foreman and Ali at the Mai 20 Stadium], *Elima*, 24 September 1974, 7. For the stadium's symbolic importance, see "Enfin, un nouveau stade du 20-Mai" [Finally a new Mai 20 stadium], *Salongo*, 23 September 1974, 8; "Discours du Citoyen Tshimpupu Kaninda" [Speech of Citizen Tshimpumpu Kaninda], *Salongo*, 23 September 1974.

2 George Foreman and Joel Engel, *By George* (New York: Simon and Schuster, 1995), 108.

3 Bingham quoted in Hauser, *Muhammad Ali: His Life and Times* (New York, Simon and Schuster, 1991), 270–71. For Ali honed to a fine edge, sparring partner, and waiting Foreman out, see Budd Schulberg, "Journey to Zaire," October 1974, in *Sparring with Hemingway* (Chicago: Ivan R. Dee, 1995), 175.

4 Schulberg, "Journey to Zaire," in *Sparring with Hemingway*, 176; Angelo Dundee with Bert Randolph Sugar, *My View from the Corner: A Life in Boxing* (New York: McGraw-Hill, 2008), 179–80; "Mission Impossible compound" from Rick Talley, "'A Stitch in Time' Would've Helped," *Chicago Tribune*, 21 September 1974, C3.

5 Foreman, *By George*, 107. Caplan quoted in Talley, "'Stitch in Time."

6 Quotes about the boxing crowd are from George Plimpton, "They'll Be Swinging in the Rain," *Sports Illustrated*, 30 September 1974, 37, 38. The press journey is from Jerry Izenberg, *Through My Eyes: A Sports Writer's 58-Year Journey* (Haworth, NJ: St. Johann Press, 2009), 129–31. See also Dick Schaap, "The Road to Zaire," *Sport*, December 1974, 6–7.

7 Schwartz, *From the Corners of the Ring to the Corners of the Earth* (Valley Stream, NY: CIVCOM INC., 2009–2010), 249–54.

8 Rainy season quote from Plimpton, "They'll Be Swinging," 38.

9 Schaap, "Road to Zaire," 8; Norman O. Unger, "Champ Bleeds on Fight Plans," *Chicago Defender*, 17 September 1974, 1; Anthony Blackwell, "Ali Plotting

Action," *Chicago Defender*, 24 September 1974, 24; Rick Talley, "'Stitch in Time,'" *Chicago Tribune*, 21 September 1974, C3. After the fight was over, Dan Daniel suggested that the cut may have been a ruse to help a then-overweight Foreman with more time to get in shape. Others may have had similar thoughts before the bout occurred. See Dan Daniel, "Ring Detective Explains Zaire Cut Eye Ploy, the Foreman Need for Delay," *The Ring*, February 1975, 8–9.

10 American Embassy to Secretary of State, Doc. No. 1974KINSHA07959, Film No. D740261-1191, 18 September 1974, Electronic Telegrams 1/1/1974–12/31/1974, Central Policy Files, RG 59, 7/1/1973–12/31/1976, National Archives, for "boredom and isolation." Dundee, *My View from the Corner*, 178, discusses the pendulum shift and how the delay affected Foreman. Daniel, "Ring Detective," 8–9. "Razor" poem in Clive Gammon, "Cut 'n Run versus the Big Gun," *Sports Illustrated*, 28 October 1974, 39. Ali's romance with Veronica Porche is discussed in Bill Caplan's interview with author, 3 November 2017; and Jonathan Eig, *Ali: A Life* (New York: Houghton Mifflin Harcourt, 2017), 388–89.

11 Ping-pong from Bill Caplan interview, 3 November 2017.

12 "Super Puncher," from Jack Welsh, "Foreman vs. Ali," *Boxing Illustrated*, June 1974, 8; George Girsch, "Foreman All-Time Kayo King among Heavy Champions," *The Ring*, January 1974, 10–11, 31.

13 "When I get a get a guy hurt," in Jack Welsh, "Foreman vs. Ali," 8. "When a man," in Dan Shocket, "George Foreman Insists: 'I'll Knock Ali Out Early!'" *World Boxing*, November 1974, 34–36. Sadler quoted in, "It Took Only Five Minutes," *International Boxing*, August 1974, 37. Dan Shocket, "Why George Foreman Will Whip Muhammad Ali," *International Boxing*," August 1974, 39, 54.

14 Jerry Quarry, "Foreman Will Kayo Ali!" *World Boxing*, September 1974, 28–31.

15 "Archie Moore: When Foreman Connects, Goodby Jaw," *Sports Illustrated*, 28 October 1974, 34.

16 "Archie Moore: When Foreman Connects." "If this fight had been held three years ago" and related quotes are from Robert Markus, "Likes Ali in Big Fight . . . but . . . ," *Chicago Tribune*, 29 October 1974, C3; Randy Neuman, "Ali-Foreman Fight in Africa: Public Relations vs. Pugilism," *New York Times*, 18 August 1974, 178.

17 Thomas Hauser, *Muhammad Ali: His Life and Times* (New York: Simon and Schuster, 1992), 266 (for "mummy"); Norman Mailer, *The Fight* (Boston: Little, Brown, 1975), 68 (for "big Black man").

18 Jack Welsh, "For Foreman Ali, Zaire Is Already Money in the Bank," *Boxing Illustrated*, July 1974, 13.

19 "Emotional iceberg" is from Don Majeski, "So It All Boils Down to This," *Boxing Illustrated*, [August or September] 1974, 68; "As Nat Loubet Sees It," *The Ring*, July 1973, 5.

20 Schwartz, *From the Corners of the Ring*, 277–80.

21 "No run-of the-mill" from Randy Neuman, "Ali-Foreman Fight in Africa," 178. Donn Bridgy, "This Epic Confrontation," letter to editor, *World Boxing*, November 1974, 14. See also William Fauntleroy, "Differing Opinion," letter to editor, *World Boxing*, November 1974, 14–15, for Ali righting the miscarriage of justice occasioned by the stripping of his title over Vietnam.

22 Steve Heger, "The Realistic View?" letter to editor, *World Boxing*, November 1974, 14.

23 "Nixon," quoted in Schulberg, *Sparring with Hemingway*, 172.

24 Wells Twombly, "Champ," *New York Times Magazine*, 24 March 1974, n.p., George Foreman Vertical File, Schomburg Center; Elombe Brath, "Ali-Foreman Fight Shaping Up as Battle of Armageddon," *New York Amsterdam News*, 26 September 1974, A1–A2.

25 "Guileless good guy" and "prose or doggerel," from "Violent Coronation in Kinshasa," *Time*, 23 September 1974, 100–101; Dan Shocket, "I'll Knock Ali Out Early," 36.

26 Time, "Violent Coronation," 102.

27 "Irked Foreman Rips Ali's Suit at Dinner," *New York Times*, 23 June 1974, 203.

28 Clancy quoted in Izenberg, "Does Ali Have a Chance against Foreman?" *Sport*, September 1974, 24. "Holy war" in Dave Anderson, "Chant of the Holy War: Ali, Bomaye," *New York Times*, 28 October 1974, "Ali" Vertical File, Schomburg Center for Research in Black Culture, and in "Ali's Ready for Foreman," *New York Amsterdam News*, 7 September 1974, 23. Pride in black Africa from Howard Bingham tape collection, cited in Hauser, *Muhammad Ali*, 265. In a telephone interview on 6 July 2016, Jerry Izenberg said two things beat Foreman: Africa and his boxing stupidity.

29 Hauser, *Muhammad Ali*, 265 (for "savages"); Foreman, *By George*, 107–8 (for "goof," "eyes following," and "Palookaville").

30 Kalonji Kabasele Mobayayi, "Muhammad Ali: Je suis le boxeur le plus scientifique, le plus rapide et le plus beau de tous les temps" [Muhammad Ali: "I am the most scientific boxer, the fastest and the greatest of all time], *Elima*, 29 October 1974, 15; "Portrait: Ali," *Salongo*, 30 October, 1974, 11. "Portrait: Foreman," *Salongo*, 30 October 1974, 10.

31 "Joe Frazier in Accra," *Ghanaian Times*, 29 October 1974, 1. See also "Amarteifio Heavily Tipped to Handle Fight," *Ghanaian Times*, 29 October 1974, 11.

32 Gammon, "Cut 'n Run," 32–34, 39.

33 Anderson, "Chant of the Holy War."

34 Schwartz, *Four Corners*, 282–86.

35 Schwartz, *Four Corners*, 286. The fighters' clothes and the cane story in Anderson, "Chant of the Holy War." See also Malonga Bouka, "Foreman: Je suis le plus fort et je garderai mon title" [Foreman: I am the strongest and I will keep my title], *Elima*, 28 October, 1, 16.

36 Foreman's remarks are from "Foreman, Ali Surprise Watchers," *Chicago Defender*, 28 October 1974, 24. For Foreman's psychological advantage, "sleek and menacing," and Ali's voice, see Alan Hubbard, "Sore Throat Zips Lip," *Pretoria News*, 28 October, 36. Black Power salute and quiet dignity from "Foreman Steals the Show," *Ghanaian Times*, 28 October 1974, 22. "Victory lap" from "12,000 Excited Fans See Aly-Foreman [*sic*] Weigh-in Ceremony," *Egyptian Gazette*, 28 October 1974, 4.

37 Thomas A. Johnson, "Mobutu Gives a Garden Party," *New York Times*, 29 October 1974, 45. See also "Le président-fondateur souhaite bonne chance aux deux boxeurs" [The president-founder wishes both fighters good luck], *Elima*, 30 October, 1, 8.

38 Johnson, "Mobutu Gives," 45; "President-Founder Wishes," 1, 8.

39 Johnson, "Mobutu Gives," 47. From Our Correspondent, "You Can't Listen to the Big Fight," *Pretoria News*, 29 October 1974, 3.

40 Dundee, *My View from the Corner*, 181–82. Goodman quoted in Hauser, *Muhammad Ali*, 272–73.

41 Welsh, "For Foreman Ali," 9.

CHAPTER 6

1 Jack Welsh, "The Ultimate in a Confrontation of Men," [September or October] 1974, *Boxing Illustrated*, special edition, editorial page, Special Collections, Notre Dame University.

2 "Universal Spectacle" from Elombe Brath, "Ali-Foreman Fight Shaping Up as Battle of Armageddon," *New York Amsterdam News*, 26 September 1974, A-1. "Fighter's Heaven" and Ali quote of one last goal discussed in Randy Gordon, "The Muhammad Ali Story," *World Boxing*, August 1974, 42–49, 64, 66. "Trainer Angelo Dundee: Ali by a Knockout in Nine or 10," *Sports Illustrated*, 28 October 1974, 34. Jerry Izenberg, interview with author, 6 July 2016.

3 Dave Anderson, "$10-Million Bet," *New York Times*, 27 October 1974, n.p. "Flamboyant mystique" from Dave Anderson, "Foreman 3–1 over Ali in Zaire Tonight," *New York Times*, 29 October 1974, 47.

4 For the fears of Wali Muhammad and Bernie Yuman, see Hauser, *Muhammad Ali*, 273, 274 (Elijah Muhammad's message). Mailer's account of who was in the dressing room and Ali's response is from Norman Mailer, *The Fight* (Boston: Little, Brown, 1975), 164–69.

5 For Bundini, the morose atmosphere, and Broadus, see "George Plimpton, "Breaking a Date for the Dance," *Sports Illustrated*, 11 November 1974, 25; and Mailer, *The Fight*, 166–71.

6 For cards and letters and *Chicago Tribune* headline, see Muhammad Ali, with Richard Durham, *The Greatest: My Own Story* (1975; New York: Ballantine Books, 1977), 481; Ferdie Pacheco, *Fight Doctor* (New York: Simon and Schuster, 1976), 128; Mailer, *The Fight*, 94.

7 George Foreman and Joel Engel, *By George: The Autobiography of George Foreman* (1995; New York: Simon & Schuster, 2000), 109. Sadler quoted in Plimpton, "Breaking a Date for the Dance," 24. For talking in ring and 4 a.m. fights, see Anderson, "Foreman 3–1 over Ali," 45. Moore's prayer was told to Norman Mailer by George Plimpton. See Mailer, *The Fight*, 175–76; Pacheco, *Fight Doctor*, 135, 137; Dundee, *My View from the Corner*, 183.

8 "Edge" from Ali, *The Greatest*, 491. For a description of crowd behavior, see Dundee, *My View from the Corner*, 184. Ali as hero and his fans, from Nat Loubet, "Ali Outfought, Outlasted and Outwitted Foreman in a Classic Upset," *The Ring*, January 1975, 7. Robe described in Plimpton, "Breaking a Date for the Dance," 24, and in Dave Anderson, "Ali Regains Title, Flooring Foreman," *New York Times*, 30 October 1974, 93; Pacheco, *Fight Doctor*, 138.

9 Mailer, *The Fight*, 176. Foreman's robe and Ali's taunting during the anthems is from Anderson, "Ali Regains Title," *New York Times*, 30 October 1974, 93. "Fighting Corpsman" comes from internet correspondence between author and Foreman, 5 January 2017. "No testing" and "the bigger," from Dundee, *My View from the Corner*, 184. I recollect the crowd gasping at the Armory in Albany, New York, where I saw the fight on 29 October.

10 Foreman, *By George*, 109–10. Gunfighters in Ali, *The Greatest*, 492, and insults at 492–93.

11 "Slugfest" from Loubet, "Ali Outfought, Outlasted," 8. For the fight description, see Foreman, *By George*, 110–11; *Muhammad Ali: The Greatest Collection* (Big Fights Inc., 1974; HBO, 2001), DVD; Plimpton, "Breaking a Date for the Dance," 22–28; Mailer, *The Fight*, 177–82.

12 Moore quoted in Hauser, *Muhammad Ali*, 275.

13 Plimpton, "Breaking a Date for the Dance," 23; Foreman, *By George*, 110–11.

14 Pacheco, *Fight Doctor*, 140; Dundee quoted in Hauser, *Muhammad Ali*, 276.

15 On Foreman's ability to cut off the ring and the rope-a-dope strategy, see "*Playboy* Interview: Muhammad Ali," *Playboy* (1975), Muhammad Ali Vertical File 1973–1978, Kaiser Incomplete, n.p., Schomburg Center for Research in Black Culture. See also Ali, *The Greatest*, 497. Michael Ezra, "How Muhammad Ali's Rope a Dope Myth Suckered America," *Deadspin*, 30 October 2014, https://deadspin.com/how-muhammad-alis-rope-a-dope-myth-suckered-america-1652932623, goes farther than any other analyst in challenging the rope-a-dope as a planned strategy. He also shows that by the end of the seventh round Ali was far ahead on the judges' cards: 4–2–1, 3–0–4, and 4–1–2. For those watching the fight in that overheated atmosphere, however, it did appear at first that Ali was getting pummeled and was on the verge of defeat.

16 *Muhammad Ali: The Greatest Collection* (DVD); "Muhammad on the Mountaintop," *Time*, 11 November 1974, 84–85; Plimpton, "Breaking a Date for the Dance," 26; Mailer, "*The Fight*," 185.

17 "Eked out" from Loubet, "Ali Outfought, Outlasted," 7; Pacheco in Hauser, *Muhammad Ali*, 274, and Shabazz at 274.

18 Foreman, *By George*, 111; *Muhammad Ali* (DVD); Ali quoted in Ali, *The Greatest*, 501–2.

19 Plimpton, "Breaking a Date for the Dance," 26; "Muhammad on the Mountaintop," 84–85; Foreman, *By George*, 111; Dundee, *My View from the Corner*, 186.

20 Taunts in Plimpton, "Breaking a Date for the Dance," 26; Dundee, *My View from the Corner*, 187, for both taunts and bombs and chants. Loubet, "Ali Outfought, Outlasted," 8 (for chants for Ali).

21 Foreman, *By George*, 111–13.

22 Dundee, *My View*, 187–88; Plimpton, "Breaking a Date for the Dance," 26.

23 Loubet, "Ali Outfought, Outlasted," 8. "How Clay Knocked Out Foreman—The Knockout King," *Al Ahram*, 31 October 1974, 1, 3–4. George's determination in Foreman, *By George*, 113. Elijah Muhammad's message in Plimpton, "Breaking a Date for the Dance," 26; Dundee, *My View from the Corner*, 188; Ali's thinking in Ali, *The Greatest*, 504.

24 For the last round, see *Muhammad Ali: The Greatest Collection* (DVD). Ali's taunt in Ali, *The Greatest*, 504. Last punches described by Dundee, *My View from the Corner*, 188. Foreman's recollection in Hauser, *Muhammad Ali*, 278, and Foreman, *By George*, 114.

25 Frost quoted in *Muhammad Ali: The Greatest Collection* (DVD); and Mailer, *The Fight*, 210.

26 Foreman on reporters and dressing room in Foreman, *By George*, 114–15. Plimpton's coverage of dressing room, in Plimpton, "Breaking a Date for the Dance," 26–27.

27 Plimpton, "Breaking a Date for the Dance," 28.

28 Foreman, *By George*, 114–17, for postfight recollections.

29 Ali's remarks are captured in *Muhammad Ali: The Greatest Collection* (DVD); and Dave Anderson, "Sports of the Times" column, *New York Times*, 31 October 1974, n.p., Ali-Foreman Vertical File, Schomburg Center.

30 Joe Louis quoted in "Words of the Week," *Jet*, 2 January 1975, 30. Anderson, "Sports of the Times"; reporter Jerry Izenberg quoted in Dundee, *My View from the Corner*, 18, confirmed in telephone interview, 6 July 2016.

31 Foreman, *By George*, 115, for rope-a-dope; for Ali calling him a dope, "supreme," and "lion," see "Playboy Interview: Muhammad Ali," *Playboy*, 1975, n.p., Ali Vertical File 1973–1978, Schomburg Center.

32 Foreman, *By George*, 115–16 for water, and 114 for quick count. For Ali calling him a sore loser, see "Playboy Interview: Muhammad Ali."

33 Dan Daniel, "Ring Detective Explains Zaire Cut Eye Ploy, the Foreman Need for Delay," *The Ring*, February 1975, 8–9.

34 "Referee Denies 'Count' Dispute, *Chicago Defender*, 4 November 1974, 30.

35 On being doped in Foreman, *By George*, 116, and on dehydration strategy, 109. On Foreman's poor condition, see Daniel, "Ring Detective," 8–9, 34. George Foreman email to author, 14 January 2017. For more on water and excuses for losing, see George Foreman interview with Michael May, "Total Failure: How George Foreman's Losses Showed Him the Light," NPR, 24 May 2017, https://www.npr.org/2017/05/24/528995768/total-failure-how-george-foremans-losses-showed-him-the-light.

36 Seeley Hagan, "Blesses Heaven for Muhammad," letter to editor, *The Ring*, February 1975, 28. Norton's remark in John Hall, "Ghost of Liston," *Los Angeles Times*, 31 October 1974, E3; Rick Talley, "Ali Knocks Out Foreman in 8th in Zaire," *Chicago Tribune*, 30 October 1974, E1.

37 Hall, "Ghost of Liston."

38 Anderson, "Sport of the Times."

39 George Plimpton, "Return of the Big Bopper," *Sports Illustrated*, 23 December 1974, 101, recounts Ali's thoughts.

40 Plimpton, "Breaking a Date for the Dance," 28; Hank Schwartz, *From the Corners of the Ring to the Corners of the Earth, The Adventure Behind the Champions* (Valley Stream, NY: CIVCOM Inc. Publishers, 2009–2010), 294–96.

41 Pacheco, *Fight Doctor*, 143.

CHAPTER 7

1 Quotes from Dave Anderson, "Sports of the Times," *New York Times*, 31 October 1974, n.p., Ali-Foreman Vertical File, Schomburg Center for Research in Black Culture. Brown quoted in Muboyayi Mubanga, "Bundini: "Foreman est fort mais peu intelligent" [Bundini: Foreman is strong but not very intelligent], *Salongo*, 31 October 1974, 11.

2 George Foreman and Joel Engel, *By George: The Autobiography of George Foreman* (1995; New York: Touchstone Books, 2000), 117.

3 Ronald E. Kisner, "Zaire Postscript: Ali Out Duels Foe for Crown," *Jet*, 14 November 1974, 52–54; George Plimpton, "Return of the Big Bopper," *Sports Illustrated*, 23 December 1974, 86.

4 Dick Schaap, "Death to Disbelievers," *Sport*, January 1975, 16–17.

5 For one example of the photos, see the pictures accompanying Rick Talley, "Ali Knocks Out Foreman in 8th in Zaire," *Chicago Tribune*, 30 October 1974, E1; Muboyayi Mubanga, "Ali vainqueur par K O et . . . aux points" [Ali winner by knockout . . . and by points!], *Salongo*, 31 October 1974, 11, discusses the legend.

6 Dan Daniel, "Foreman's KO by Ali Leaves Heavies without Titanic Punching Hero," *The Ring*, January 1975, 9–11. For the impact of the loss on Foreman, see Michael May's interview with him on "Total Failure: How George Foreman's

Losses Showed Him the Light," NPR, 24 May 2017, http://www.npr.org/2017/05/24/528995768/total-failure-how-george-foreman-losses-showed-him-the-light.

7 Foreman, *By George*, "funereal," 114; "losing stinks" and "what defined me as a man," at 117.

8 Ali quoted on "the dope," in "*Playboy* Interview: Muhammad Ali," *Playboy*, 1975, Ali Vertical File 1973–1978, Kaiser Incomplete, n.p., Schomburg Center. "Shambling ruin" and "shattered" are from "Ali: I'll Only Fight for $10 Million," *Ghanaian Times*, 31 October 1974, 1. "Ridiculous" quoted in "Eye Cut No Factor in Defeat," *Ghanaian Times*, 31 October 1974, 1; Dan Daniel, "Foreman's KO," 9–11.

9 Wolfgang Schivelbusch, *The Culture of Defeat: On National Trauma, Mourning, and Recovery*, trans. Jefferson Chase (2001; New York: Metropolitan Books, 2003). For the culture of defeat after Vietnam in the 1970s, see Rick Pearlstein, *The Invisible Bridge: The Fall of Nixon and the Rise of Reagan* (New York: Simon and Schuster, 2014). Hatred of Ali in George Foreman, with Ken Abraham, *God in My Corner: A Spiritual Memoir* (Nashville, TN: Thomas Nelson), 35–36.

10 "No doubts," "irregular fashion," and "counting by referee" quoted in Ntukani Nzuzu Musenda, "La contradiction de George Foreman" [George Foreman's contradictory comments], *Elima*, 8 November 1974, 15; Dan Daniel, "Ring Detective Explains Zaire Cut Eye Ploy, the Foreman Need for Delay," *The Ring*, February 1975, 8. For a rematch tied to irregularities, see "Foreman Asks for Big Fight Probe," *Daily Nation* (Nairobi), 4 November 1974, 22. Clayton quoted in "Referee Denies 'Count' Dispute," *Chicago Defender*, 4 November 1974, 30. See also "Foreman: 'I Beat the Count,'" *Ghanaian Times*, 1 November 1974, 10. For more on the controversy, see chapter 6.

11 Foreman, *By George*, 110, 115–16, discusses the water issue. For more on the effects of losing, see George Foreman, "George Foreman Speaks in Depth," *The Ring*, May 1976, 9–11, 37. For "protective shield" and the firing of Sadler, see Shirley Norman, "Exclusive Informal Interview with George Foreman," *The Ring*, May 1976, 12–13, 43.

12 "Robbed of victory" quoted in Foreman, *God in My Corner*, 16; Foreman, *By George*, 118–19.

13 Foreman, *By George*, 119–20.

14 Foreman, *By George*, 119 (for axis), 126 (ultimate man), 127 (rebuild). Tormented by loss of title, see Foreman, *God in My Corner*, 72.

15 Quincy Troupe, "The Spiritual Victory of Muhammad Ali World, *Black World*, January 1975, 34–44.

16 Ronald E. Kisner, "Zaire Postscript: Ali Out Duels Foe for Crown," *Jet*, 14 November 1974, 52–54. "Sly mouse" is from George Plimpton, "Breaking a Date for the Dance," *Sports Illustrated*, 11 November 1974, 23. Anderson, "Ali Regains Title, Flooring Foreman," *New York Times*, 30 October 1974, 93 (for "bee" and "brains"). For "human battering ram," see "Violent Coronation in Kinshasa," *Time*, 23 September 1974, 100. "Bull and matador" in "Muhammad on the Mountaintop," *Time*, 11 November 1974, 85.

17 Troupe, "Spiritual Victory," 43.

18 Troupe, "Spiritual Victory," 43.

19 For the two stories, see "Ali the Magnificent!" *Pretoria News*, 30 October 1974, 1. Ex-president Richard Nixon was severely ill with phlebitis. Other African newspapers had the same juxtaposition.

20 Ronald E. Kisner, "Zaire Postscript," 52–54. As reported in *New York Amsterdam News*, 25 May 1974, A-1, A-3, earlier in the year Ali told *Penthouse* that when he quit boxing, he would "go back to ministering the Muslim faith, spreading it throughout America." Bundini Brown in fact told Plimpton that Ali wanted the title back so he would eventually be reinstated in the Nation of Islam and use his title to gain converts to the religion. See George Plimpton, *Shadow Box* (New York: G. P. Putnam's Sons, 1977), 298–99. *Muhammad Speaks* continually covered Ali's doings in the regular feature, "From the Camp of the Champ," as in 14 May 1965, 21. See also "Champ's Strength Found in Islam," *Muhammad Speaks*, 16 September, 9.

21 For the Arab-African meeting, the Muslim missionary, and Sadler's quip, see Thomas Johnson, "Student First in Fight Line," *New York Times*, 30 October 1974, n.p., in Ali Vertical File, Schomburg Center. "How Clay Knocked Out Foreman—the Knockout King," *Al-Ahram*, 31 October 1974, 1. For the shift to black power, see Bruce J. Schulman, *The Seventies: The Great Shift in American Culture, Society, and Politics* (Cambridge, MA: Da Capo Press, 2002), 53–77.

22 Kisner, "Zaire Postscript," 52–54. For chastisement and apocalypse, see "Playboy Interview: Muhammad Ali."

23 "Playboy Interview." Ali returned to Zaire on 24 November 1974 at the invitation of President Mobutu to help celebrate the anniversary of the founding of the MPR (the Popular Movement of the Revolution), at which he praised Mobutu and Zaire as models to follow. See "Ali Retour au Zaïre" [Ali back in Zaire], *Elima*, 2 December 1974, 11.

24 Washington, DC, reaction in Charles Sanders, "Muhammad Ali Challenges Black Men," *Ebony*, January 1975, 121–26. For Chicago, Stokely Carmichael, with Ekwueme Michael Thelwell, *Ready for the Revolution: The Life and Struggles of Stokely Carmichael* (New York: Scribner, 2003), 710. For the reactions of fans in Harlem, see Sandy Satterwhite, "The People's Champ," unidentified periodical, n.p., Vertical File Boxing—Ali-Foreman, 3, 48, Schomburg Center. See also Les Matthews, illegible title, *New York Amsterdam News*, 2 November 1974, A-1, A-3, Vertical File—Boxing-Ali-Foreman, Schomburg Center.

25 Kisner, "Zaire Postscript," 53; Beverly Blackman, letter to editor, *Jet*, 21 November 1974, 4; Seku S. Wattara, letter to editor, *Jet*, 28 November 1974, 4.

26 "Ali Returns to Morehouse Where Comeback Started," *Jet*, 13 January 1975, 30; "Ali Followed His 'Destiny' to Victory," *Chicago Defender*, 16 November 1974, 19.

27 Charles Sanders, "Muhammad Ali Challenges Black Men," *Ebony*, January 1975, 121–26. See also "Ali Welcomed to Louisville Home," *Jet*, 28 November 1974, 54–55.

28 Samuel F. Yette, "Black Hero Dynamics and the White Media," *Black World*, January 1975, 22–28; Clay Goss, "Ali as Creative Black Man," *Black World*, January 1975, 30–33.

29 Troupe, "Spiritual Victory," 34–37.

30 Troupe, "Spiritual Victory," 41–43. Ali quoted in Anderson, "Sports of the Times"; Richard Pells, *War Babies: The Generation That Changed America* (N.p.: Cultural History Press, 2014) argues that Ali belonged to the generation born during World War II that emphasized self-expression and was preoccupied by questions of individual identity.

31 Foreman quoted in "Foreman's Face Gets Distorted," *Ghanaian Times*, 31 October 1974, 1. In the lottery system that replaced the draft, Foreman got a high enough

number that he would not have to serve in the military. Foreman email communication with author, 8 February 2017.

32 Vic Ziegel, "A Few Rounds with Muhammad," *New York Post*, 10 December 1975, n.p., Ali Vertical File 1973–78, Kaiser Inc., Schomburg Center. For Chicago's Muhammad Ali Day as opposed to Mayor Daley's opposition to Ali in 1966, see Ronald E. Kisner, "Ali Looks Ahead after Regaining His Title," *Jet*, 21 November 1974, cover story, 52–57.

33 "Hearts and minds," in Foreman, *By George*, 113. Foreman "miserable" and Ali having "time of his life" are from Suruba Ibumando Georgette Wechsler, *By the Grace of God: A True Story of Love, Family, War and Survival from the Congo* (Far Hills, NJ: New Horizon Press, 1999), 197–98.

34 Sanders, "Muhammad Ali Challenges Black Men," *Ebony*, January 1975, 121–26.

35 Olu Akaraogun, "The Meaning of Muhammad Ali for the Black World," *Indigo*, January 1975, 60–61, 63–64, Ali-Foreman Vertical File, Schomburg Center.

36 Gherarducci quoted in Mavomo Nzuzi Zola, "Connaisseurs, boxeurs et journalistes donnent leur point de veu" [Experts, boxers and journalists share their comments], *Salongo*, 2 November 1974, 9.

37 "Ali Returns to Morehouse," 30. "Ecstatic youth" in Alan Hubbard, "New Era Dawns for Ali in Zaire," *Pretoria News*, 31 October 1974, 38; Thomas A. Johnson, "Bout Lifts Morale of Zairians," *New York Times*, 31 October 1974, 55.

38 Malonga Suka quoted in Johnson, "Bout Lifts Morale," 58. Muboyayi Mubanga, "Foreman Battu" [Foreman knocked out], *Salongo*, 30 October 1974, 9–10, 13–16; Muboyayi Mubanga, "Foreman Battu" [Foreman knocked out in 8th round], *Salongo*, 31 October 1974, 9–10.

39 For countering Belgian and Western conceptions, see Kevin C. Dunn, *Imagining the Congo: The International Relations of Identity* (New York: Palgrave Macmillan, 2003), 105–6. Dunn also argues that the bout was a metaphor for Mobutu's rule. Both Ali and the president successfully figured out their opponents' weaknesses, used intelligence to divide and conquer them, and did so with perseverance and lightning speed. Johnson, "Bout Lifts Morale, 55, 58.

40 Moaka Toko, "Le défi du Zaïre et d'Afrique" [The challenge of Zaire and Africa], *Elima*, 31 October 1974, 1; Wechsler, *By the Grace of God*, 195–98. For showing world Mobutu's philosophy, see Bunzi dia Bilongo, "Ambiance extraordinaire autour d'un combat extraordinaire" [Extraordinary atmosphere around an extraordinary fight] *Salongo*, 31 October 1974, 12–13.

41 The Reuters quote is from "'I'll Dance It,' Says Ali," *The Standard* (Nairobi), 29 October 1974, 12. Nairobi audience reaction from "Several TV Owners Get a Free Show," *Daily Nation*, 31 October 1974, 22. Abidjan reaction in "Les réactions" [The reactions], *Le Soleil*, 31 October 1974, 8; "How Ghana Received His Triumph," *Ghanaian Times*, 31 October 1974, 15.

42 "Senghor's Message to Ali," *Ghanaian Times*, 1 November 1974, 10; Mailer, *The Fight*, 227–37. See also Ibrahima M'Bodj, "Ali n'etait pas a Yoff but . . ." [Ali wasn't in Yoff, but . . .], *Le Soleil*, 1 November 1974, 1, 5.

43 Mass Diack, "Une victoire des opprimés" [A victory for the oppressed], *Le Soleil*, 30 October 1974, 8.

44 Muboyayi Mubanga, "M. Hamouda: Foreman un boxeur indigne" [Mr. Hamouda: Foreman: An unworthy boxer] *Salongo*, 31 October 1974, 10; Toko, "Le défi du Zaïre," 1.

45 "Une nouvelle victoire du Mobutisme" [A new victory of Mobutism], *Elima*, 31

October 1974, 1. Nganga quoted in "Le combat Ali-Foreman est un succès populaire indéniable pour le Zaïre" [The Ali-Foreman fight is an undeniable popular success for Zaire], *Elima*, 2 November 1974, 1.

46 For a discussion of heroes in the popular culture of the 1970s, see William Graebner, "America's Poseidon Adventure: A Nation in Existential Despair," in *America in the Seventies*, ed. Beth Bailey and David Farber (Lawrence: University Press of Kansas, 2004), 157–80.

47 "Harris Poll Legitimizes Ali's Claim to Greatness," *Jet*, 12 June 1975, 45; Maury Allen, *New York Post*, 31 October 1974, n.p., as in Thomas Hauser, *Muhammad Ali: His Life and Times* (New York: Simon and Schuster, 1991), 280–81. See "Ali Named Fighter of the Year, *Jet*, 2 January 1975, 51, and "New York Beat," *Jet*, 6 February 1975, 58.

48 The best description of Muhammad Ali Day in Louisville is in Charles Sanders, "Muhammad Ali Challenges Black Men," *Ebony*, January 1975, 120–33. See also "Ali Welcomed to Louisville Home," *Jet*, 28 November 1974, 54–55.

49 Vic Ziegel, "A Few Rounds with Muhammad," *New York Post*, 10 December 1974, n.p., Schomburg Center," for Ali's Day in New York. See Ronald E. Kisner, "Ali Looks Ahead after Regaining His Title," *Jet*, 21 November 1974, cover story, 52–57, for Chicago.

50 Ford quoted in Hauser, *Muhammad Ali*, 281–82. For letters of protest, see Simeon Booker, "Ticker Tape U.S.A.," *Jet*, 30 January 1975, 11.

51 Kisner, "Ali Looks Ahead," 52–57.

CHAPTER 8

1 George Foreman and Joel Engel, *By George: The Autobiography of George Foreman* (1995; New York: Simon and Schuster, 2000), 115.

2 William Graebner, "America's Poseidon Adventure: A Nation in Existential Despair," *America in the Seventies*, ed. Beth Bailey and David Farber (Lawrence: University Press of Kansas), 157–80.

3 Ronald E. Kisner, "Ali Looks Ahead after Regaining His Title," *Jet*, 21 November 1974, cover story, 52–57.

4 Ronald E. Kisner, "Ali's Bold Plan to Use Fight Money to Aid Needy Blacks," *Jet*, 6 March 1975, 36–75, 55–59.

5 Nat Loubet, "Wepner's Gameness Dominant Factor as He Almost Goes Limit with Still Great Ali," *The Ring*, June 1975, 6–9, 50. For Wepner as the inspiration for *Rocky*, see Richard O'Connor, "From Chump to Champ," *Sport*, July 1977, 12, 16.

6 Loubet, "Wepner's Gameness Dominant," 7.

7 Nat Loubet, "Round-up 1975," *The Ring*, March 1976, 16. For the judges' scores, see Hauser, *Muhammad Ali*, 303.

8 For the political background to the fight, see Thomas Quinn, "When 'Malakas' Met the Greatest: Marcos' Philippines and the Thrilla in Manila," *Explorations: A Graduate Journal of South East Asian Studies* 9, no. 1 (2009): 79–86; Loubet, "Round-up 1975," 16. See also *Daily Bulletin* (Manila), 4 September–5 October 1975.

9 Dick Schaap, "The Manila Maulers," *Sport*, December 1975, 61–62.

10 For "score to settle," and "I apologize," see Joe Frazier, "I'll Make Ali Fight for

His Life," *The Ring*, December 1975, 8–9, 76. Ali's remarks and Frazier's reaction, see Mark Kram, *Ghosts of Manila: The Fateful Blood Feud between Ali and Joe Frazier* (New York: HarperCollins Perennial, 2002), 168–71. For analysis of this type of intrablack race baiting, see Michael Ezra, *Muhammad Ali: The Making of an Icon* (Philadelphia: Temple University Press), 157–58. For more on Frazier's being really burned about Ali's taunts, see Nat Loubet, "6 to 5, Pick 'Em, as Ali and Frazier Prepare for Third Meeting, in Manila," *The Ring*, December 1975, 10–11, 81.

11 Nat Loubet, "Ali's Victory over Frazier in 14, One of All Time Greats," *The Ring*, December 1975, 6–8. "Washed up" cited in Schaap, "Manila Maulers," 67.

12 Descriptions of the fight are in Loubet, "Ali's Victory over Frazier," *The Ring*, December 1975, 6–8, 35; Schaap, "Manila Maulers," 67; and Kram, *Ghosts of Manila*, 184–86.

13 For the thirteenth and fourteenth rounds, see Loubet, "Ali's Victory over Frazier," 6–8, 35; Schaap, "Manila Maulers," 67; and Kram, *Ghosts of Manila*, 186–187.

14 Nat Loubet, "Editorial, as I See It," *The Ring*, January 1976, 5. For fan appreciation, see Tom Pellin, "Letter to Editor," January 1976, 33; Harry Gibbons, "Letter to Editor," *The Ring*, January 1976, 33.

15 "*Playboy* Interview: Muhammad Ali," *Playboy*, November 1975, n.p., Ali Vertical File, Kaiser Inc., Schomburg Center.

16 Ezra, *Muhammad Ali*, 158; Hauser, *Muhammad Ali*, 294–95. Death of Elijah Muhammad and Ali as member of transition board and his urging Nation to follow Wallace is in Gregory Simms, "Nation Mourns Muslim Leader," *Jet*, 13 March 1975, 13–22, 52–57. For changes in membership policy, see Gregory Simms, "Muslims Drop 'Black' Label, Admit Whites," *Jet*, 3 July 1975, 22–25; Shirley Norman, "Muhammad Ali on Women, Sex and Marriage," *Sepia*, September 1975, n.p., Ali Vertical File, 1973-1978, Kaiser Inc., Schomburg Center.

17 Norman, "Muhammad Ali on Women, Sex and Marriage."

18 "*Playboy* Interview: Muhammad Ali." The need to respect black women was a staple of his message to black men. See an earlier version of his views in Charles Sanders, "Muhammad Ali Challenges Black Men," *Ebony*, January 1975, 128–32.

19 Wolf interview, in Hauser, *Muhammad Ali*, 320. For Conrad and the two women, see Kram, *Ghosts of Manila*, 151, 177 (Wells), 175 (Belinda). Four women is from Norman, "Muhammad Ali on Women, Sex and Marriage," *Sepia*, September 1975, n.p.; Pete Axthelm and Peter Bonventre, "The Ali Mystique," *Newsweek*, 29 September 1975, 58–61. The press conference is in Hauser, *Muhammad Ali*, 315–20. "Muhammad Ali Says Belinda Is the 'One and Only,'" *Jet*, 9 October 1975, 13. For more on Belinda and Manila, see Bob Waters, "Ali's Credibility Gap," *Newsday*, 2 November 1975, n.p., Ali Vertical File 1973-1978, Kaiser Incomplete, Schomburg Center. Jonathan Eig, *Ali: A Life* (New York: Houghton Mifflin Harcourt, 2017), 415–24, details Ali's blatant extramarital sex life. For Philippine coverage of the Veronica Porche incident, see Quezon D. Mangawang, "Ali and Frazier Swap Verbal Jabs in Palace," *Bulletin Today*, 19 September 1975, 1, 8, 10; Dingo Marcelo, "Ali Dismisses Belinda 'Stomp,'" *Manila Bulletin*, 28 September 1975, 1.

20 Ronald E. Kisner, "Has Success Spoiled Ali?" *Jet*, 16 October 1975, 54–58.

21 Cynthia Lane, "Don't Mess Up Ali," letter to editor, *Jet*, 23 October 1975, 4. See also Ronald E. Kisner, "Ali's Wife Talks about Marriage Strains," *Jet*, 30 October 1975, 21–25; Brenda Hicks, letter to editor, *Jet*, 6 November 1975, 4; Ajamo Yero

Upton, letter to editor, *Jet*, 6 November 1975, 4; Laura West, letter to editor, *Jet*, 13 November 1975, 4; Betty Washington, letter to editor, *Jet*, 13 November 1975, 4; Debra Jackson, letter to editor, *Jet*, 20 November 1975, 4.

22 "Muhammad Ali's Wife Talks about Life Without Him," *Jet*, 4 November 1976, 44–49. The new name for Ali and Wallace Muhammad's branch of Islam is in "Nation of Islam Changes Name to Fit New Image," *Jet*, 4 November 1976, 6. For the divorce, see Gregory Simms, "Marriage for Muhammad, Khalilah Ali Ends in Divorce, $$$$ and Respect," *Jet*, 20 January 1977, 12–16. For details of the June 1977 wedding to Veronica Porche, see Shawn D. Lewis, "Profile: Veronica Porsche before and after Event," *Jet*, 7 July 1977, 8–10; Gregory Simms, "Muhammad Ali Takes a Beautiful Bride," *Jet*, 7 July 1977, 12–18.

23 "Ali Goes to Trenton to Cop Plea for Hurricane," *Jet*, 6 November 1975, 48; "Muhammad Ali Makes Pledge of $100,000 to Aid NAACP," *Jet*, 22 1976, 16; "W. D. Muhammad Honored with Gala Dinner Party," *Jet*, 23 June 1977, 54–55.

24 Hugh John Furlong, letter to editor, *The Ring*, April 1976, 33; Angelo Dundee, with Bert Randolph Sugar, *My View from the Corner: A Life in Boxing*, foreword by Muhammad Ali (New York: McGraw Hill, 2008), 200–201.

25 Letters to editor from John M. O'Brien, Robert L. De Russo, Charles Swedberg, and Henry DiCarb Jr., *The Ring*, August 1976, 33.

26 Nat Loubet, "Ali-Norton #3: Lackluster Bout Controversial," *Ring*, September 1976, 6–9, 64. Norton quoted in Hauser, *Muhammad Ali*, 340.

27 Trudie Loubet, "'The Greatest' Recreates All the Excitement that Marked Muhammad Ali's Rise in Boxing," *The Ring*, August 1977, 34–35, 44; A. B. Giamatti, "Hyperbole's Child," originally in *Harper's Magazine* (December 1977), reprinted in *The Muhammad Ali Reader*, ed. Gerald Early (Hopewell, NJ: Ecco Press, 1998), 174. Demand for retirement is from Nat Loubet, "Editorial," *The Ring*, August 1977, 5. For the fight description, see John Ort, "Ali Beats Evangelista, but Loses to Father Time on Triple Championship Card," *The Ring*, August 1977, 12–13, 51. For the Shavers bout, see John Ort, "Ali Does It Again!" *The Ring*, December 1977, 8–10. For Brenner and Pacheco, see Hauser, *Muhammad Ali*, 344–45. Former light heavyweight champion José Torres saw Ali's sluggish performances as the result of boredom and so psychosomatic. See José Torres, "Ex-Fighter's Notes on the Champion," originally in *Black Sports* (February 1978), reprinted in Early, *Muhammad Ali Reader*, 175–82.

28 For the Spinks bouts, see Hauser, *Muhammad Ali*, 350–60.

29 Cosell quoted in Hauser, *Muhammad Ali*, 360. Ishmael Reed, "The Fourth Ali," in Early, *Muhammad Ali Reader*, 199–206, originally in Reed, *God Made Alaska for the Indians: Selected Essays* (New York: Garland, 1982).

30 "Fallen Champion Foreman Named in 'Vague' Suits of Marriage and Paternity," *Jet*, 9 January 1975, 46–47. See also *Jet*, June 12, 1975, 9.

31 George Foreman and Joel Engel, *By George: The Autobiography of George Foreman* (1995; New York: Touchstone, 2000), 120–23.

32 Foreman, *By George*, 127–28.

33 Sean Kelly, *America's Tyrant: The CIA and Mobutu of Zaire* (Washington, DC: American University Press, 1993), 206, 209–24; George Foreman, with Ken Abraham, *Knockout Entrepreneur* (Nashville, TN: Thomas Nelson, 2009), 113.

34 Foreman, *By George*, 128; Foreman, *Knockout Entrepreneur*, 114–15.

35 Foreman, *By George*, 128–29; Foreman, *Knockout Entrepreneur*, 115.

36 The description of the brawls after the bell comes from Ed McCoyd, *To Live and*

Dream: The Incredible Story of George Foreman* (New York: New Street Publishing, 1997), 49–50.

37 "Mr. Nice" is from "Foreman Blasts Foes: Fight Future Turns to Ali-Frazier," *Jet*, 15 May 1975, 49. "Jack the Ripper" is in Foreman, *By George*, 130. The "Foreman Circus" is in John T. Hale, letter to editor, *The Ring*, September 1975, 37. "Pitiful excuses" is from Joric Kellogg, letter to editor, *The Ring*, January 1976, 33.

38 Vicious punishment from Foreman, *By George*, 133.

39 McCoyd, *To Live and Dream*, 51–53; Foreman, *By George*, 133–35.

40 For the Frazier bout, see John Ort, "Foreman Drives Frazier into Retirement with KO in Five," *The Ring*, September 1976, 26–27, 46; and Kram, *Ghosts of Manila*, 203.

41 Ort, "Foreman Drives Frazier into Retirement," *The Ring*, September 1976, 26–27, 46.

42 Gordy Peterson, "Foreman Pounds Out Agosto in Four," *The Ring*, May 1977, 19, 56. Young's views are in Gregory Simms, "Young Predicts KO over Strong Foreman," *Jet*, 10 March 1977, 48–50.

43 Slow start, holding, and wrestling is in Ort, "The Experts Ask: What Now, George Foreman?" *The Ring*, June 1977, 10; Don King's advice and Foreman's view of the slow start and round seven is from Foreman, *By George*, 143–44.

44 Ort, "Experts Ask," *The Ring*, June 1977, 10–11, 42. "Hero" from Foreman, *By George*, 143.

45 Jerry Izenberg, "Foreman Tells His Story," *Staten Island (NY) Advance*, 23 December 1977, n.p., George Foreman Vertical File, Schomburg Center. See also Gregory Simms, "Foreman Quits for God and Mom: Heavyweights Sorry to See Him Go," *Jet*, 26 May 1977, 52–53: Bob Waters, "George Foreman's Transformation," *Newsday*, 29 March 1978, 95; Mike Marley, "George Foreman," *New York Post*, 6 April 1979, n.p., George Foreman Vertical File, Schomburg Center; George Vecsey, "Foreman Fights from Pulpit," *New York Times*, 17 November 1981, C13, C16. In a telephone interview with the author, 6 July 2016, Izenberg confirmed this information and Foreman's sincerity.

46 Izenberg, "Foreman Tells His Story"; Foreman, *God in My Corner*, 24–25.

47 Foreman, *God in My Corner*, 26–27.

48 Foreman, *God in My Corner*, 28–34.

49 Foreman, *God in My Corner*, 35–41.

50 Izenberg, "Foreman Tells His Story."

51 Jerry Izenberg, "George Foreman: God Gave Me a Choice," *Staten Island (NY) Advance*, 24 December 1977, n.p., George Foreman Vertical File, Schomburg Center. See also "Foreman Trades Ring for Pulpit," *Newsday*, 16 March 1980, n.p., George Foreman Vertical File, Schomburg. "Ex-heavyweight" from Jack Wilkinson, "Ex-Heavyweight Champ Foreman Socks It to 'Em from the Pulpit," *New Daily News*, 17 August 1980, n.p., George Foreman Vertical File, Schomburg.

CHAPTER 9

1 *When We Were Kings*, produced and directed by Leon Gast (DAS Films, David Sonenberg Productions, Polygram Filmed Entertainment, 1997), 89 mins.; Roger Ebert, "Review of *When We Were Kings*," http:/www.rogerebert.com/reviews/when-we-were-kings/1997.

2 Budd Schulberg, "The Second Coming of George Foreman," *Newsday*, April 1991, reprinted in *Sparring with Hemingway* (Chicago: Ivan R. Dee, 1995), 222–31.

3 For Ali's role in the 1980 boycott, see Nicholas Evan Sarantakes, *Dropping the Torch: Jimmy Carter, the Olympic Boycott, and the Cold War* (New York: Cambridge University Press, 2011), 115–18.

4 For the Mayo Clinic's report, see Thomas Hauser, *Muhammad Ali: His Life and Times* (New York: Simon and Schuster, 1991), 403–6, and Parkinson's diagnosis at 430–32.

5 Tim Shanahan, with Chuck Crisafulli, *Running with the Champ: My Forty-Year Friendship with Muhammad Ali* (New York: Simon and Schuster, 2016), 255.

6 Hauser, *Muhammad Ali*, 382–94.

7 Michael Ezra, *Muhammad Ali: The Making of an American Icon* (Philadelphia: Temple University Press, 2009), 162–63.

8 Shanahan, *Running with the Champ*, 255–57, argues that Ali was unsophisticated politically and that by 1984 he was endorsing a sitting president rather than a candidate.

9 John Gearan, "Boxing Now a Circus Act; Foreman, Though, Getting Last Laugh with Trip to Bank," *(Worcester, MA) Telegram and Gazette*, 11 November 1994, D2, http://flagship.luc.edu/login?url=http://search.proquest.com/docview/268568328?accountid=12163).

10 On the press, Foreman's new personality, and his media savvy, see Angelo Dundee, *My View from the Corner: A Life in Boxing* (New York: McGraw Hill, 2008), 280–85; and Dan Barreiro, "Foreman Deals in Fun, Not Logic," *Minneapolis Star-Tribune*, 19 April 1991, 01C, http://flagship.luc.edu/login?url=http://search.proquest.com/docview/418262501?accountid=12163.

11 William Graebner, "'The Man in the Water': The Politics of the American Hero, 1970–1985," *Historian* 75, no. 3 (Fall 2013): 517–43, discusses the search for the ordinary man as a hero. George Foreman and Joel Engel, *By George: The Autobiography of George Foreman* (1995; New York: Touchstone, 2000), 234.

12 For renewed national pride and patriotism during the 1980s and 1990s, see Christian G. Appy, *American Reckoning: The Vietnam War and Our National Identity* (New York: Penguin Books, 2016), 250–74.

13 For Foreman's crossover appeal as part of a larger trend, see Robert Lipsyte, "Star-Crossed Celebrities, Generations Later," *New York Times*, 30 December 1994, B12. For an analysis of Jordan, see Walter LaFeber, *Michael Jordan and the New Global Capitalism* (1999; New York: Norton, 2002).

14 Alice Weintraub, "George Foreman: Marketing Champ of the World," *Bloomberg News*, 19 December 2004, https://www.bloomberg.com/news/articles/2004-12-19/george-foreman-marketing-champ-of-the-world. For Foreman's views of success, see George Foreman, with Ken Abraham, *Knockout Entrepreneur* (Nashville, TN: Thomas Nelson, 2009).

15 For the gold-medal story, see Muhammad Ali and Richard Durham, *The Greatest: My Own Story* (1975; New York: Ballantine Books, 1976), 55–80. For the medal's symbolic return, see Ezra, *Muhammad Ali*, 175–80.

16 Ezra, *Muhammad Ali*, 186–90.

17 Hank Schwartz, *From the Corners of the Ring to the Corners of the Earth* (Valley Stream, NY: CIVCOM Publishers, 2009–2010), 319–27.

18 Schwartz, *From the Corners of the Ring*, 335.

19 Mark Ribowsky, "Killer to King: The Amazing Saga of the New King of Boxing," *Sepia*, October 1975, 26–27.

20 For more on the tournament, see John Ort, "U.S. Tourney Makes Spectacular Debut," *The Ring*, April 1977, 10–13, 45; Stu Berman, "Round Two: U.S. Boxing Championships," *The Ring*, May 1977, 20–21, 53; Gordon Peterson, "U.S. Boxing Tourney Tops in Action," *The Ring*, June 1977, 16–17, 51; Gordon Peterson, "U.S. Championship Tourney Approaches Climax," *The Ring*, July 1977, 12–14.

21 Edward Kiersh, "The Man Who Would Be King Takes a Fall," *Crawdaddy*, 4 August 1977, 34–40.

22 Kiersh, "Man Who Would Be King," 39–40. For more on the scandal, see Sam Toperoff, "Death of the Don King Tournament," *Sport*, August 1977, 26–40.

23 King's defense is in James Borders, "The King of Pugilistica," *Black Collegian*, February–March 1981, 54–55, and in "Playboy Interview: Don King," *Playboy*, May 1988, 51-68. Holmes quoted in Jack Newfield, *The Life and Crimes of Don King: The Shame of Boxing in America* (1995; New York: Sag Harbor Electronic Publishers, 2003), 147.

24 King quoted in Borders, "King of Pugilistica," 57.

25 Stephen R. Weissman, "Fisticuffs for Mobutu," *The Nation*, 30 November 1974, 558–59, uncovered Mobutu's connection to Risnelia through in an interview with its Swiss chairman, Raymond Nicolet. For a discussion of recent books on offshore companies, see Alan Rusbridger, "Panama: The Hidden Trillions," *New York Review of Books*, 27 October 2016, 33–35.

26 Keith B. Richburg, "Mobutu: A Rich Man in Poor Standing; As He Teeters in Zaire, Questions Mount over His Wealth," *Washington Post*, 3 October 1991, sec. A, A01, http://flagship.luc.edu/login?url=http://search.proquest.com/docview/307452094?accountid=12163.

27 See Sean Kelly, *America's Tyrant: The CIA and Mobutu of Zaire* (Washington, DC: American University Press, 1993), 213–40, for Kissinger and the CIA's use of Mobutu to prop up the Portuguese in Angola. For more on the later ties between Mobutu and the CIA, see Robert B. Edgerton, *The Troubled Heart of Africa* (New York: St. Martin's Press, 2002), 217–21.

28 Schwartz, *From the Corners of the Ring*, 299–301; George Plimpton *Shadow Box* (New York: G. P. Putnam's Sons, 1977), 314–17.

29 Thomas Borstelmann, *The 1970s: A New Global History from Civil Rights to Economic Inequality* (Princeton, NJ: Princeton University Press, 2012), discusses the two forces of the modern world: growing egalitarianism and the power of an overarching market society and its values.

INDEX